Death by Prison

Death by Prison

*The Emergence of Life without
Parole and Perpetual Confinement*

CHRISTOPHER SEEDS

University of California Press

University of California Press
Oakland, California

© 2022 by Christopher Seeds

Library of Congress Cataloging-in-Publication Data

Names: Seeds, Christopher, author.
Title: Death by prison : the emergence of life without parole and
    perpetual confinement / Christopher Seeds.
Description: Oakland, California : University of California Press, [2022] |
    Includes bibliographical references and index.
Identifiers: LCCN 2021056889 (print) | LCCN 2021056890 (ebook) |
    ISBN 9780520379978 (hardback) | ISBN 9780520379985 (paperback) |
    ISBN 9780520977020 (ebook)
Subjects: LCSH: Life imprisonment—United States—History. | BISAC:
    SOCIAL SCIENCE / Criminology | LAW / Criminal Procedure
Classification: LCC HV8711 .S44 2022 (print) | LCC HV8711 (ebook) |
    DDC 365/.60973—dc23/eng/20220127
LC record available at https://lccn.loc.gov/2021056889
LC ebook record available at https://lccn.loc.gov/2021056890

Manufactured in the United States of America

28 27 26 25 24 23 22
10 9 8 7 6 5 4 3 2 1

For Lindsay and Rhiannon

Contents

Introduction

Life imprisonment without the possibility of parole, a prison sentence precluding any reasonable opportunity of release during a person's natural life, began its rise in the United States in the mid-1970s. Since then the number of people sentenced to life without parole has increased dramatically, from a spattering in the early 1970s, to more than ten thousand in 1992, to in excess of fifty thousand in 2016 and upward.[1] Over the same time span, hundreds of laws were passed in the states and the federal system, extending life without parole sentences to a multitude of crimes and criminal statuses. The rapid growth of such a severe punishment is remarkable from a historical perspective. A century, even decades, ago, these developments would have been quite unexpected. As recently as the 1980s and 1990s, criminologists regarded what is referred to now as "LWOP" to be a fad, something that might be looked back on later, decades down the road and with a longer view, as a passing fashion: a punishment whose impact, they expected, would be muted by executive clemency.[2] But LWOP has long outlasted the distance of vogue. Life without parole sentencing is now firmly entrenched in American policymaking, judicial and prosecutorial decision-making, public discourse, and even the American vernacular.[3] So much so that the sanction was not long ago labeled "America's new death penalty" and its practice said to "define[] the logic" of contemporary American punishment.[4] Life without parole's embedding in US punishment—indeed, in US penality—is an emergent phenomenon of the late twentieth century.[5]

If one permits collapsing fifty-one different criminal legal systems into a single entity, it might be said that LWOP is something the United States does. Life imprisonment has escalated worldwide of late, but to

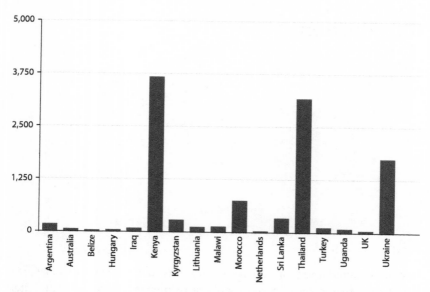

FIGURE 1.   Prisoners serving whole life sentences worldwide (excluding United States), 2016. *Source:* Dirk van Zyl Smit and Catherine Appleton, *Life Imprisonment: A Global Human Rights Analysis* (Cambridge, MA: Harvard University Press, 2019).

compare lifetime sentencing in the United States to elsewhere in the world, one has to completely change the scale (figures 1 and 2).[6] In contrast to Europe, where whole-life sentencing registers as a human rights concern and is scrutinized by international courts,[7] the United States Supreme Court has never adjudicated the constitutionality of life without parole per se, and recent concern over life without parole sentencing for juveniles markedly stops with the unique frailties of youth.[8] In contrast to nations in which perpetual imprisonment has been the subject of persistent and vigorous debate in political arenas and public forums,[9] in the United States life without parole is less a point of dispute than a middle ground on which sides otherwise at odds find bipartisan agreement—as an alternative to a death sentence, for example, or as a complement to low-level sentencing reform.[10] Further, people sentenced to life without parole—while classified among the condemned under many state laws and denied the medical care and programs available to prisoners with opportunities for release—only rarely if ever receive the constitutional protections afforded capital defendants, such as heightened due process, automatic proportionality review, and bifurcated individualized sentencing proceedings.[11] In the

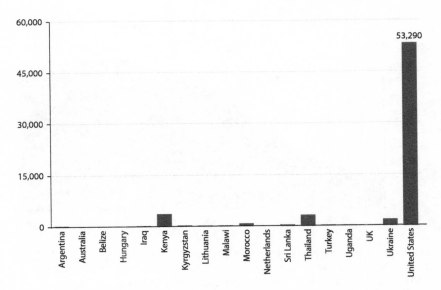

FIGURE 2. Prisoners serving whole life sentences worldwide (including United States), 2016. *Source:* Dirk van Zyl Smit and Catherine Appleton, *Life Imprisonment: A Global Human Rights Analysis* (Cambridge, MA: Harvard University Press, 2019).

contemporary United States, in sum, life without parole is a standard way of punishing people convicted of serious and violent crimes, as well as some who commit nonviolent crimes, and yet it takes place without the scrutiny one might expect for an extreme punishment. Life without parole in the United States is remarkable, in other words, not only for its cruelty but for the way in which it is exercised—that is, as a *matter of routine.*

Yet if life without parole is a standard element of contemporary American penal practice, even ingrained in the nation's cultural imagination, just how it came to be so has not been carefully articulated or explained. Knowledge of the processes that led to life without parole's emergence in the last quarter of the twentieth century, and of what fuels its continued expansion, remains general at best. To be sure, there are conventional wisdoms about LWOP's rise. For one, life without parole is often packaged within explanations of the late twentieth-century hardening of American punishment, among the laws and policies that produced mass incarceration.[12] The packaging is apt insofar as life without parole did spread amid a flow of tough-on-crime sentencing policy associated with the war on drugs, truth-in-sentencing initiatives, and three-strikes laws.[13] Many people now graying and dying in prisons across

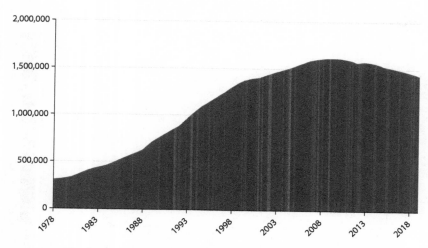

FIGURE 3.   Total prisoners in US state and federal prisons, 1978–2019.
Source: National Prisoner Statistics, [United States], 1978–2018 (ICPSR 37639);
and E. Ann Carson, *Prisoners in 2019* (Washington, DC: Bureau of Justice
Statistics, 2019).

the United States were placed there twenty to thirty years ago under what
at the time were relatively new state or federal life without parole sentencing laws. When sentencing policy hardened, particularly in the 1990s, life
without parole laws and populations multiplied (figures 3 and 4). From this
perspective, the punitive turn is a plausible basis for the proliferation of this
severe punishment.

Another common perspective credits LWOP's rise to modern death penalty politics and related abolition efforts. Support for life without parole
among members of the anti–death penalty movement and capital defense bar
inspired greater use of the sentence while simultaneously curbing left-wing
opposition.[14] In the process, life without parole made possible a sort of capital
net widening, expanding the range and number of people sentenced for capital crimes. Death sentences, after peaking in the United States in the mid- to
late 1990s, have fallen markedly since the millennium, yet the number of life
without parole sentences continues to grow (figures 4 and 5). Over the past
decade, US states have abolished the death penalty at a regular clip, and in
each instance life without parole has been inserted in its place. Estimates differ
on just how much credit LWOP deserves for the death penalty's decline, but
there is little question that the abolitionist strategy of touting it as an alternative to capital punishment has worked, at the level of policy and at the level of
litigation, to a significant degree.[15]

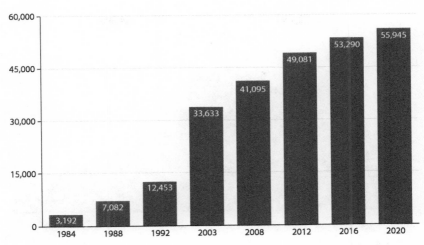

FIGURE 4. Prisoners serving LWOP in US state and federal prisons, 1984–2020. *Sources:* Donald Macdonald and Leonard Morgenbesser, *Life without Parole Statutes in the United States* (Albany: New York State Department of Correctional Services, Division of Program Planning Research and Evaluation, 1984); Emily Herrick, "Survey: Lifers, Part I," *Corrections Compendium* (April 1988): 10-11; Kathleen Maguire, Ann L. Pastore, and Timothy J. Flanagan, *Sourcebook of Criminal Justice Statistics* (Washington, DC: Bureau of Justice Statistics, 1992); Marc Mauer and Malcolm Young, *The Meaning of Life: Long Prison Sentences in Context* (Washington, DC: The Sentencing Project, 2004); Ashley Nellis and Ryan S. King, *No Exit: The Expanding Use of Life Sentences in America* (Washington, DC: The Sentencing Project, 2009); Ashley Nellis, *Life Goes On: The Historic Rise of Life Sentences in America* (Washington, DC: The Sentencing Project, 2013); Ashley Nellis, *Still Life: America's Increasing Use of Life and Long-Term Sentences* (Washington, DC: The Sentencing Project, 2017); and Ashley Nellis, *No End in Sight: America's Enduring Reliance on Life Imprisonment* (Washington, DC: The Sentencing Project, 2021).

Flanked by mass incarceration on one side and the modern death penalty on the other, one might see life without parole from a distance as a confluence of these two streams, with punitive sentencing trends and opposition to capital punishment funneling together to drive its growth. Given the recent decline in death sentences and the resonance between death-in-prison sentencing and populist calls to "lock 'em up and throw away the key," each of the narratives may have a compelling ring and an intuitive appeal. With death penalty politics on the one hand and the policies that generated mass incarceration on the other, we seem to have the life without parole explosion of the late twentieth century covered.

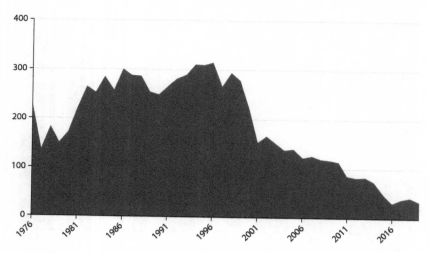

FIGURE 5. New death sentences in the United States, 1976–2019. *Source:* Death Penalty Information Center, 2020, https://deathpenaltyinfo.org/facts-and -research/dpic-reports/dpic-year-end-reports/the-death-penalty-in-2020-year -end-report.

There is, however, more to say. This book argues that the rise of life with-out parole in the last quarter of the twentieth century is not simply a matter of growth; it is also a phenomenon of change—in definition, in practice, and in meaning. As existing literature concentrates on LWOP's increased use in recent decades, change in the punishment itself has been underplayed, if not overlooked. LWOP is usually seen as a punishment that long existed and was simply revived. Yet for most of the twentieth century, as early chapters of this book emphasize, life without parole sentences carried with them a reasonable possibility of release. The way in which LWOP is practiced and commonly understood today—that is, as a perpetual prison term—is a result of processes that occurred over years and were produced by many lines of descent. Accordingly, when we focus on LWOP's expansion in tough-on-crime policy, which swelled in the mid-1990s, or point to LWOP's advance as a death penalty alternative, which occurred principally from the early 1990s onward, we are witnessing a variety of actors picking up and putting to use what was then a newfangled punishment, only just readily at hand.

This shift of frame—to see that life without parole is an old punishment with new practices and new meanings—is important because it reveals life without parole to be a penal form that, more than proliferating, has transformed. Shifting the frame is also important because, with such a transformation in mind, one can better recognize that the rise of life without parole relates to something broader: an increase in, or better, a routinization of, imprisonment until death. With LWOP as a pallbearer, the enterprise of imprisoning until death has become a standard and widely accepted way of dealing with people who are convicted of serious and violent crimes. This too is quite remarkable from a historical perspective. The following statement, made in the 1860s by sentencing reformers Enoch Wines and Theodore Dwight, may appear to a reader in the contemporary United States both curious and foreign: "It is always tacitly assumed that imprisonment must not be perpetual, but whether that assumption is founded on any reason supposed to arise out of the nature of things, or whether it only rests on the present state of public feeling, I know not."[16]

As the opening chapters of this book discuss, putting people in prison forever was once a practice and an idea that met with hesitance, if not resistance, in the penal field. Today, however, vast numbers of people in the United States are imprisoned until they die without any reasonable opportunity for review. Alongside life without parole are other forms of imprisonment until death: extremely long sentences that outlast life spans and parole-eligible sentences under which prisoners are consistently denied release.[17] Driven in part by the growth of *all* of these forms, the number of people imprisoned until death in US penal systems has dramatically increased, as has the number of elderly dying in US state and federal prisons.[18] So the phenomenon in question is not simply LWOP; it begins with LWOP but encompasses new ways of thinking about and practicing death in prison in many forms.

There is an affinity between mass imprisonment and death by prison, to be sure. But the latter is also distinct, as it concerns a specific disregard for the indignity of dying in confinement. This insight is important. It helps us understand, indeed it is essential for understanding, why, even as political will and public opinion unite in efforts to dismantle the infrastructure of mass incarceration, LWOP sentencing nevertheless continues to grow. Putting many people in prison is one thing; putting many people in prison until death is yet another. As this book sets out, the rise of perpetual confinement has corresponded with mass incarceration, but it has its own trajectory, its own specific conditions of possibility—and recognizing this matters when it comes to understanding why much of the hard-end penal philosophy and infrastructure of the late twentieth century remains, even as low-level reform and downsizing take place.[19]

Fewer than fifty years ago, imprisonment until death (i.e., perpetual confinement) was an exceptional outcome; today, it accounts for an increasing number of prison sentences in the United States. As life without parole has become perpetual confinement, perpetual confinement has become accepted as an ordinary thing to do; the contemporary transformation of LWOP is simultaneously the history of the rise of a penal system and a penality that uncritically accepts imprisonment until death. The question must be asked: *What accounts for the shifts in penal practices and the social imagination whereby the United States has become accustomed to imprisoning individuals until death, without reevaluation, and without any reasonable expectation of release?*

THE EMERGENCE OF LWOP

This book offers a critical inspection of contemporary American punishment by focusing on one of its singular features: the routine use of life imprisonment without the possibility of parole as a form of perpetual confinement. Drawing on extensive archival research, an original national survey of legislation authorizing life without parole, and a comprehensive review of primary and secondary historical source material on US punishment, the study spans US history with life sentencing from past to present but concentrates on a period of years from the early 1970s through the mid-1990s. This period precedes the prime era of mass incarceration policy and, as the book shows, it also predates the national death penalty abolition movement's full turn to LWOP as an alternative to capital punishment. Yet the period comprises formative years, during which the current sanction, practice, and concept of LWOP took shape.

The book's long historical perspective and detailed inspection of state-level and institutional-level processes break new ground in several ways important for making sense of life without parole sentencing. Taking a long historical view helps to reveal that a life without parole sentence now means something different than it once did: it is no longer a punishment, as it was for the first two-thirds of the twentieth century, from which release is reasonably possible. To mark this distinction throughout the book, I refer to the life without parole sentence as we know it today as "LWOP" and use the acronym only for that purpose. Historical perspective also helps show that with LWOP has come a new orientation toward perpetual confinement: the stance that imprisoning people until they die is generally appropriate for those who have committed violent and serious crimes was not entrenched in US penality in earlier decades, but it is today. Relatedly, the book articulates an affinity *as well as* a distinction between a tough-on-crime ethos and the practice of perpetual confinement. The distinction is significant because in contemporary US penal policy, even as states seek to cut back on mass incarceration's excesses by reducing prison time for low-level offenses, death-in-prison sentences are nevertheless increasingly used.

This study also has broader implications. For one, it holds importance for understanding processes of institutionalization and, more specifically, change and continuity in penal forms. As we will see, to appreciate the variety with which states use LWOP, one must look to proximate causes. But in addition, to grasp the unique attachment of the United States to LWOP one must also look beneath proximate causes to the frameworks of practice and understanding that serve as a background. The idea that much of what people do is organized and framed by background-level matters that they take for granted is now customary in the social sciences. The basic point—that much of what we do is habitual, and that habits and beliefs may not be questioned until the correspondence between experience and the "background" falls away or out of synch—has been understood and re-understood, stated and restated, for generations.[20] The point may seem rather abstract for a study about sentencing. Yet one of this book's arguments is that understanding how US society has come to accept life without parole as perpetual confinement, and perpetual confinement as routine, requires it. A lesson from the history of life without parole, for studies of law and punishment in particular, is to give attention to the background and to how ways of doing things and thinking about things, practices and understandings, are enabled and disabled. Beyond the greater empirical foundation this history provides, it highlights processes by which new ways of practice and of thinking arise from (and solidify in) their contexts.

A second theme is spun from the first. The processes of gradual institutional change that led to the routinization of perpetual confinement have ramifications for understanding LWOP's character as well as the character of punitive laws, policies, and practices more generally. In this investigation, punitiveness, now such a clear characteristic of acts and practices associated with LWOP, is not always a predominant trait. Rather, one often finds a lack of attention, an acceptance, a sidestepping of responsibility. In confronting the emergence of perpetual confinement in American punishment, one must confront not only punitiveness but disregard.

Disregard, a lack of attention or care, is no stranger to discussions of punishment or the prison and is central to analyses of racism and the intersections between race and punishment in the United States; indeed, the natural life sentence has been said to exemplify a disrespect for human dignity that defines American punishment.[21] But more than a way of describing an attitude or an aspect of a societal common sense underlying American punishment, and more than a general strategy of denial or ignorance,[22] disregard is present here as a feature of *practices* carried out by various state and public actors that together contribute to *processes* through which LWOP as perpetual confinement is institutionalized. In the chapters of this book, many different permutations of disregard appear, often operating in tandem with others, and generally accumulating over time: structural adjustments in penal laws and practices that removed opportunities for review of sentence with little direct acknowledgment or discussion; governors' decisions not to listen to accounts of rehabilitation, much less the day-to-day interests and needs of people serving life sentences; jurists in constitutional analyses of cruel and unusual punishment collapsing the differences between lifetime prison sentences and much shorter prison terms; anti–death penalty advocates saving for later their moral qualms about life without parole; and legislators leaving the costs of funding large-scale prison expansion and the challenges of confining a large geriatric population for decades down the road. As significant to LWOP's history as decisions to punish harshly are choices *not to consider*. As this book documents the circumstances in which new practices and understandings of perpetual confinement arose and solidified, it reveals how disregard itself is institutionalized in American punishment.

RESEARCHING PERPETUAL CONFINEMENT

This study's methodological approach responds to the state of a nascent but steadily developing research field. Research on life sentencing stands to gain from more rigorous attention to the subject's boundaries and from a richer core of historical insight. I approach the subject of life without parole, accordingly, with empirical attention to specific locations in the manner of penal state research, looking to strategic sites in states as well as institutions; my interpretive method and theoretical perspective are also informed by work employing a broad historical lens with an epistemological focus that is trained not only on actions and events but also on concepts.

The Life Sentencing Canon

Social science benefits from a tension between broad generalization and empirical detail: each captures aspects the other will miss, and "one kind of study provokes and facilitates the other."[23] To date, academic discussions of life without parole sentencing leave such a dialectic underdeveloped.

On the one hand, what is known about life sentencing in the United States still wants for *empirical depth*. A great deal of existing information about life without parole sentencing is derived from policy reports.[24] For some time, Dirk van Zyl Smit's book *Taking Life Imprisonment Seriously* (2002) stood as the lone historical account directed to life sentencing. A pioneering work providing an overview of centuries of life sentencing in Germany, the United Kingdom, and the United States, *Taking Life Imprisonment Seriously* offers a compelling but necessarily summary look at life without parole sentencing in the United States.[25] More recently, a number of excellent books have advanced knowledge of life sentencing. Van Zyl Smit and Appleton's *Life Imprisonment* (2019) offers a magisterial descriptive account of life sentencing law and practice internationally; Herbert's *Too Easy to Keep* (2018) and Leigey's *The Forgotten Men* (2015) provide close looks at the lived experience of life without parole; Mauer and Nellis's *The Meaning of Life* (2018) makes a compelling policy argument against life sentences; and Ogletree and Sarat's *Life without Parole* (2012), like Steiker and Steiker's *Courting Death* (2016), introduces foundational arguments from a legal perspective.[26] These monographs are complemented by significant scholarship in social science and in law, including a growing number of theoretical analyses of LWOP, and important accounts of LWOP's development authored or coauthored by individuals who served or are serving life sentences.[27] The historical statements in these works, however, are for the most part brief and offered as backdrop rather than as interpretive historical accounts.[28] For years, even the most nuanced discussions of late twentieth-century developments in life sentencing have relied on the same stable of historical information, a small store adopted from a handful of publications that provided pockets of information about particular laws in particular states at particular times—accounts that made no claim to be definitive or comprehensive.[29]

On the other hand, more general statements about life without parole tend to cast the net a bit short, in a couple of ways. First is a narrow *historical frame*. Life without parole is now a major presence in capital cases, and since the 1990s tough-on-crime laws have introduced life without parole en masse. Scholarship and commentary understandably tend to see life without parole through these frames—that is, to perceive it as it presently functions. Yet assuming that current arrangements explain an object's history runs the risk of reiterating contemporary circumstances as historical claims: conventional wisdom might well explain the present, in other words, but not so well the past.

A second constraint on thinking about life without parole is a narrow *framing of the object*. Life without parole tends to be treated as a singular punishment, one more severe than others, and thus to be analyzed independently from related penal practices, even those that may also ultimately result in death in prison, such as life *with* parole sentences or long terms of years outlasting life spans. This assumption has been challenged in law and policy as some litigants, analysts, and scholars inject "de facto life without parole" or "virtual life" sentences into the conversation, voicing similar concerns and seeking the same remedies as they would with respect to life without parole.[30] Studies of life sentencing worldwide have also helped to complicate the conversation in this way.[31] In US Supreme Court precedent to date, however, LWOP remains understood as a punishment that is uniquely severe. In the academy, too, studies dedicated specifically to LWOP, regardless of their strengths, tend to reinforce the notion of LWOP's singularity. This definitional recursivity obscures important patterns and developments.

Approaching the topic of life without parole sentencing, then, one finds a need for (1) empirically detailed accounts of the conditions and processes that have generated life without parole in specific locations and (2) a broader frame of reference—specifically one that would (a) observe the contemporary use of life without parole in a longer historical frame while (b) paying heed to how life without parole arises in context and intersects with neighboring penal policies of sentencing and release. We need local-level empirical investigation; we also need critical historical perspective. Accordingly, this book utilizes state- and institutional-level inspections, detailed accounts of local arrangements and struggles in the manner of contemporary historically oriented scholarship on punishment, to generate a deeper empirical foundation about lifetime sentencing; the book also employs a genealogical approach, informed as well by principles evinced in institutionalism and historical studies of science, to uncover the conditions and contingencies that made the rise of LWOP as perpetual confinement possible and the processes by which the concept of life without parole and practices and understandings of perpetual confinement transformed.

Empirical Depth and Focus on Proximate Causes

For decades, influential historical accounts in the sociology of punishment have been pitched at a macro level, privileging broad structural and political theories that analyze punishment on a national scale. As scholars note, however, studies of broad social, economic, political, and cultural forces work at a level of abstraction with a particular limitation when it comes to studying American criminal justice.[32] Because the administration of crime and punishment in the United States is governed primarily at the state level, broad-level studies are distanced from proximate causes: large-scale forces only influence law and policy once translated through state and local institutions by state and local actors.[33] Studies of particular states or institutions, therefore, provide a necessary complement to macro-level work: while they speak definitively only to happenings in a specific locale, they illuminate general knowledge and understanding of penal phenomena, draw attention to the contingencies and diverse conditions that produce variance across jurisdictions, and encourage thinking about penal change with greater complexity.

Scholarship shows, for example, how specific historical institutional and cultural backgrounds influence the environments in which penal change takes place: what actors see as puzzles, the arguments and justifications they mobilize, the solutions they propose.[34] It illustrates the manner and extent to which interest groups, from prosecutors, law enforcement, and corrections officers to victims' rights and feminist groups, alter penal policy.[35] It has helped elicit the role of state political structures and the synergy between local, state, and federal criminal justice policy and jurisprudence.[36] Complemented by a growing literature by historians on the policies that undergirded mass incarceration,[37] this work has helped bring into focus the penal "field": the "composition of actors, taken for granted assumptions and categories, and predominant orientations [that] channel [] trends in particular directions."[38]

The present book brings such a perspective to the study of life without parole, examining developments in law, policy, and practice at the state level as well as tracing contributions from different stations—key institutions in the penal field—including the US Supreme Court, state departments of corrections, and the national anti–death penalty movement.

As emphasized earlier, however, there is more to the phenomenon in question than increased use. To be sure, the rise of life without parole in the United States is a story of the expanding scope and prevalence of a punishment in law and policy, but as this book will show, it is *also* a story of how practices and conceptualizations of the life without parole sentence and keeping prisoners confined until death have changed. Fully analyzing this makeover demands a step back in historical scope and vigilant attention to how the object of study—the life without parole sentence—is defined and redefined by its surroundings.

Critical Historical Perspective and Focus on the Background

What we perceive as concrete entities in the social world are context-dependent arrangements changing at all times in conversation with their environment, if sometimes in ways that are hard to perceive or at a pace that is too slow to recognize. As such, elements of the social world—including those we often take for granted—are better seen as social constructions that are not inevitable and, likewise, not immutable. This kernel of wisdom underlies much contemporary social theory, and I bring it to bear in this book, drawing on related insights from several lines of thought: genealogies of knowledge (following the work of Michel Foucault), historical studies of science (particularly the tradition of historical epistemology), and studies of institutions (in a broad sense) focused on institutionalization and institutional change. All, despite their differences, prioritize close attention to the conditions that enable certain practices and the backgrounds that make certain concepts possible.

Taken in a broad sense, the social arrangements called "institutions" are regularized processes by which people "order relevant aspects of the world" as a means of orienting themselves for action.[39] Institutions in this sense are bundles of practices and understandings that observers may tend to see as fixed, but which are in fact ever-developing arrangements whose staying power is a function of the resonance that the practices and understandings have with existing behavioral, cognitive, and material norms.[40] Put generally, institutions are enabled and stabilized (or disabled and destabilized) insofar as practices and understandings make sense or are successful in social interactions.[41]

We can think of life without parole sentencing as an institution in this way: involving a series of practices that are carried out by actors across the penal field, from prosecution through trial, to corrections, to of course the people serving the punishment; involving a variety of beliefs about the punishment held by actors in the penal and legal fields as well as the general public; and involving various material aspects, such as statutes or legal decisions, that reflect beliefs and practices and also influence them. David Garland uses the term "complex" to refer to the network of elements that make up punishment: the "totality of discursive and nondiscursive practices through which [an object of study] is enacted, represented, and experienced."[42] Institutions, taken in a broad sense, share the scope and intricacy of what Garland refers to as a complex but also necessarily include a notion of stability achieved through corroboration with existing surroundings. Like processes elsewhere in society, changes in the field of punishment involve patterns of thought and behavior that are enabled and held together by existing social arrangements; penal change is as a general matter akin to other institutional change. Like the family, or the market, punishment is a social institution.[43]

At the crux of the idea of an institution involving a relatively stable connection between practices, understandings, and surrounding social arrangements is the principle that ways of doing and ways of thinking stick (or unravel) in a context. A second academic line valuable for its attention to context and to the processes by which practices and ways of thinking develop and change is the history and sociology of science. Of particular note is the tradition of historical epistemology, which concentrates on the environmental conditions in which scientists obtain ostensibly true statements and results.[44] Emphasizing how thought is constrained and tempered by the materials at hand and how ideas are rethought in different contexts, epistemologically oriented studies provide valuable models of how concepts arise from specific historical conditions or in specific "sites."[45] The development of a scientific theory, for example, is not simply a matter of a prior discovery being picked up and put to use in a new context; rather, the object of knowledge itself is altogether re-created and redefined by surrounding instruments, techniques, and thought styles. What is said generally about scientific knowledge applies to law and punishment as well: it involves "not merely a continuous revision of the contents and methods . . . it is a continuous revision of its object."[46] We might think of life without parole sentencing in this way, recognizing a distinction between LWOP as a contemporary object and life without parole as it was earlier in the twentieth century.

A broad approach to institutions, and a sensitivity to the background that enables certain practices and understandings to stick, also complement an overarching framework for historical study that Michel Foucault refers to as "genealogy" or, on occasion, as a "history of the present."[47] Genealogy, a critical, effective historical enterprise, has as its strength the ability to reveal underlying assumptions and trajectories of power and to expose the historical contingencies of disquieting practices that in the present moment one may take for granted.[48] In practice, genealogy begins with an act of framing—a diagnosis—of the present that sets the foundation for a rigorous examination of the historical conditions—the intersecting lines of "descent"—that make the social arrangement in question possible.[49] As central to genealogy as the notion of "descent" is the notion of "emergence," which implies an object in the making, a specific practice or concept coming into being.[50] This book employs the term "emergence" in this way, to refer to a moment in which the object of study takes shape, a product of many different lines intersecting, rather than arriving ready-made or simply appearing at a moment of origin.

In line with the approaches outlined previously, it bears emphasizing that this book is more interested in what enables than in what causes. The book's aim is a genealogical one. It seeks to achieve not a causal explanation, but an architecture of changes and the processes that led to them. In other words, the primary ambition is not to explain LWOP so much as show what *made it possible*. Relatedly, the book's ambition is not to describe the development of LWOP and perpetual confinement to equal extents across all jurisdictions, but to draw out major currents while showing them in certain circumstances in detail.

Assessing the value of genealogical inquiry for studies of penality, Garland put it well: "Using history as a means of critical engagement with the present," genealogy is "the uncovering of hidden conflicts and contexts as a means of re-valuing the value of contemporary phenomena."[51] Here, a diagnosis of the present leads to the following question, also set out earlier: What trajectories account for the shifts in penal practice and in the popular imagination by which the United States has become accustomed to the routine imposition of permanent incarceration? This book traces those lines, identifies those conditions of possibility, follows their processes, and shows the new or revised ways of doing and thinking about things. The objective in doing so is to "revalue the value" of perpetual confinement as a contemporary social practice.

ARGUMENT AND OUTLINE

Since the early 1970s, the United States has experienced an overhaul in how it punishes. Not so different from European states for much of the twentieth century—in terms of imprisonment rate, the extent of penal supervision, lengths of sentences, collateral consequences, and racial disparities across these measures—the United States is now an outlier on all fronts. Prevailing theories explain the expansive and punitive turn of American punishment in the late twentieth century with different emphases, by pointing to a rightward political shift, a discrediting of welfare, a backlash against civil rights, law and order politics, neoliberal economics, and increased mobility and suburbanization. With respect to crime and punishment, those broader developments were undergirded by class and race reorganization and promoted increased crime rates, greater public insecurity about crime, more hostile perspectives toward people who commit crimes, and a closer identification of the public with crime victims. As states addressed public insecurities once managed by social welfare programs with crime policy and penal policy, new political approaches arose in response.[52]

As the tumultuous social, economic, political, and cultural relations of the 1970s and 1980s operated through the field of punishment, this spurred several major upheavals in thinking and practice that singularly and significantly affected life sentencing.[53] The upheavals themselves are well known: (1) the death penalty, invalidated in 1972, resumed soon thereafter in a constitutionally regulated and narrowed form; (2) rehabilitation was challenged as a penal aim and its operational arrangements—indeterminate sentencing and parole release—were questioned, limited, and even removed in many states; and (3) governors cut back on the use of the clemency power that had traditionally been used to reduce the sentences of people convicted of the most serious crimes. States navigated the transformations in different ways depending on local history, culture, and institutional structure, and in the process many different vectors—not all overtly punitive—converged to produce and enable life without parole as we know it today.

LWOP arose where and when it did, in significant part, according to how the upheavals impacted existing state arrangements and how states responded. As states revised and narrowed the scope of capital punishment, previously death-eligible felonies were moved to noncapital categories, establishing foundations upon which LWOP would be built in coming years. Legislative discussions over how to resentence death row prisoners helped open a sphere of public and professional inquiry that gave newfound leverage to sentencing approaches such as mandatory minimums and truth-in-sentencing that would later become pillars of tough-on-crime policy. Concerns over inconsistency in judicial sentencing and administrative release, coupled with prison overcrowding and federal oversight, led states to experiment with fixed sentencing models and curtail parole. Doubts about the exercise of executive discretion placed scrutiny on commutation practices at the same time that governors were discovering that withholding clemency could be an effective way to gain political capital. Tough-on-crime laws punctuated the landscape, and the tendencies of such policy contributed to an emergent punitive ideology. Yet much of LWOP's development and growth was happening less directly, as frontline actors sought to solve local problems through the restructuring of penal codes, removal of parole, and retrenchment of executive practices by which people serving life sentences had once realized prison release—actions less about expanding LWOP than bent on ending other things.

These shifts in the terrain of US punishment in turn altered the way in which incarcerated people, courts, lawmakers, and eventually the public understood life without parole sentences. As it became increasingly unlikely that anyone sentenced to life without parole could expect release, people serving life and their advocates developed new litigation strategies and presented new constitutional claims. Eventually the US Supreme Court fielded several challenges to life sentences, and the resulting series of decisions—shaped by the upheavals concerning the death penalty, indeterminate sentencing, and clemency—solidified a new concept of life without parole: as a perpetual prison sentence and one, moreover, that was constitutionally permissible for a wide variety of crimes. From the 1990s onward, LWOP spread outward upon this groundwork. As actors from quite different positions (e.g., the anti–death penalty movement, prison administrators and staff, legislators, courts) encountered this stabilized concept of LWOP—as a distinct punishment *and* an ordinary one—they came to accept it as an aspect of American punishment.

In setting out the argument summarized here, this book offers some support for prevailing ideas about LWOP history but also challenges and reframes the conventional wisdom. With respect to LWOP's growth as an alternative to capital punishment, the book turns much of the received wisdom on its head, showing that LWOP grew significantly early on in noncapital quarters and that the national anti–death penalty movement later turned to LWOP only by relying on that development. With respect to the role of tough-on-crime politicking in LWOP history, the book reveals underlying changes in law and policy that were not primarily punitive, yet which set foundations that would later serve as resources in the punitive turn. The unique and complicated history of the United States with rehabilitation and indeterminate sentencing, pushed to the brink in the 1970s, is key to understanding the structural, discursive, and ideological shifts from which LWOP's new uses and meanings were forged between the 1970s and the early 1990s. Certainly death penalty abolition efforts and tough-on-crime politics remain in play, but they must be couched in a larger synergistic picture of crisis in American sentencing.

The major upheavals of the 1970s and 1980s in US punishment did not simply spur people to use LWOP more; they transformed life without parole sentencing as an institution, altering its material forms and its practices, laying foundations upon which the new meaning of life without parole made sense. Before LWOP could be picked up and used in the ordinary manner it is today—as a death penalty alternative, as a tough-on-crime hammer—there was a period in which practices changed and concepts developed and were validated, a period in which LWOP took shape.

As a way of conceptualizing the trajectory of the book's argument, it may be useful to visualize the twentieth-century history of life without parole in discrete periods.[54] In the first period prior to 1972, life without parole was generally thought of as a sentence offering a reasonable possibility of release through clemency. In the second period, between 1972 and (roughly) 1992, LWOP was developing in statutory law, in practice, and also as a concept, and the practices and understandings dominant in the earlier period were transformed in light of major upheavals in the penal and legal fields. A third period covers from the early 1990s onward, in which life without parole, now specifically recognizable as LWOP, is a distinct punishment allowing

> *Periods of Life without Parole*
>
> Period 1 (Prehistory): Before 1972
>> A life without parole sentence offers a reasonable possibility of release via executive review for clemency.
>
> Period 2 (Transformation): 1972–1991
>> Practices and understandings of life without parole are altered in the context of broad-scale national changes with respect to capital punishment, indeterminate sentencing, and commutation.
>
> Period 3 (LWOP): 1992 Onward
>> A life without parole sentence (commonly referred to as LWOP) offers no reasonable possibility of release.

no reasonable possibility of release. The book addresses all three, but ultimately focuses on the middle period, in which LWOP—as I refer to the manner in which life without parole sentencing is now practiced and understood—came about. The story is told through nine chapters in three parts.[55]

"Foundations," the first part, provides the historical setting. Perpetual punishments and life without parole sentences are not coextensive. This is so in two critical ways. First, while LWOP is a contemporary form of perpetual punishment, perpetual punishments have played a role in penal theories and practices for centuries. Second, life without parole is not, at least in name, a new punishment; sentences of life without parole have existed since the late nineteenth century (in effect, from the onset of parole), yet were not expected to lead to perpetual imprisonment, as LWOP is today. The first chapter draws on literature on American punishment to examine how perpetual imprisonment was conceptualized and practiced historically in criminal justice schemes. The second chapter offers an early history of life without parole, canvassing the ways in which life without parole sentences were used and thought of during the first two-thirds of the twentieth century. The third chapter returns to the present, setting up a juxtaposition between old and new. Focusing on the landscape of US sentencing in the 2000s, the chapter encounters LWOP as a common tool with a distinctly different meaning than before: as the finished product of a process that is the subject of this book. The chapter theorizes LWOP with the assistance of a well-known case and surveys how LWOP has developed in law across states and over time. Mapping the timing, scope, and prevalence of LWOP since the early 1970s highlights the need for research into how LWOP sentencing has been shaped according to the history, institutional composition, and culture of local penal fields.

"Eruptions," the second part, examines three major upheavals in the legal and penal fields and the processes by which LWOP emerged as states responded to those upheavals in the 1970s and 1980s into the early 1990s. Each chapter focuses on a different upheaval, using archival research to develop detailed state-level accounts. The fourth chapter engages with a monumental event of the late twentieth century in US punishment: the US Supreme Court's invalidation of the death penalty in *Furman v. Georgia* (1972). I show how, more than provoking an immediate rush to LWOP statutes, the short-lived abolition of capital punishment brought about underlying structural changes and contributed to discursive and ideological shifts in penal law and practice, setting a foundation for the growth of LWOP as perpetual confinement in subsequent years. The fifth chapter examines a second line by which LWOP emerged as an artifact of transition: as the United States's unique history with indeterminate sentencing and parole was dismantled, concerns over inconsistency in judicial sentencing and administrative release led states to experiment with fixed sentencing models and to cut back on parole. This dismantling removed the ground on which life sentences had long been defined, generating LWOP as a residual effect. The chapter also examines the relationship between LWOP and tough-on-crime legislation, showing how the rise of LWOP encouraged actors, in turn, to impose perpetual confinement in additional ways. The sixth chapter addresses a third major change that enabled LWOP: the retrenchment of executive clemency. The chapter focuses on Pennsylvania—a state in which all life sentences have been without parole since the 1940s—to explore the processes by which, as commutation practices were retrenched and restructured, life without parole became perpetual confinement.

"Adaptation and Solidification," the book's third part, explores how the prevailing contemporary meaning and practice of LWOP solidified as imprisonment until death. Expanding from state-level to national-level developments, each chapter examines a different institutional site. The seventh chapter looks at how the major upheavals in the legal and penal fields in turn influenced legal strategies, litigation practices, and eventually judicial decisions and constitutional law in pronouncements of the US Supreme Court. The eighth chapter examines the national anti–death penalty movement. In the history of life without parole, no interest group has been more important. Yet the movement's significance is often expressed as foundational. Reexamining the movement's role in LWOP history, the chapter recasts it from leader to follower, explaining how, over resistance and ambivalence, a majority of the movement eventually justified a turn to LWOP in the early 1990s by appealing to the existing buildup of LWOP from other quarters (including drug laws, habitual offense laws, and laws abolishing parole). The ninth chapter considers a third site of institutional realignment, the prison, examining how long-standing concerns over perpetual imprisonment, in terms of safety and resources, gave way as prison budgets bulged and prisons were built. A common theme across these chapters is that at sites where one might have expected resistance, one finds instead acceptance of LWOP and legitimization of perpetual confinement. In each case, influential actors with decision-making responsibilities, penal elites, performed a sort of "relabeling from above" that set LWOP in place as a punishment that was especially severe but no longer so objectionable.[56]

AGAINST DISREGARD

At the root of this study is a concern with people aging and dying over long periods of time in prison. The stories and voices of the incarcerated and formerly incarcerated are critical for understanding life imprisonment. On that note, however, it is important to underscore that this is not a book that focuses on the pains of lifetime imprisonment as experienced by tens of thousands of people today in the United States.[57] One must join the need for recognition of incarcerated people's stories and voices with the importance of telling the story of how this punishment came to be and how it assumed its place in contemporary society. This book focuses on the latter: the framework in which lived experiences of life imprisonment take place, that which makes them possible. In a sense, this book is uncovering the processes and the workings of an apparatus that is a means of silencing incarcerated people's voices—prisoner's voices.[58] It is about the complex processes by which very severe forms of punishment come into being and new ways of thinking about punishment come to be socially embedded—in this case, a way of thinking, with a grasp on the contemporary United States, in which imprisoning people until death is unremarkable and routine.

I have noted how this book's reframing of life without parole provides tools for recognizing an affinity with as well as a distinction between a tough-on-crime ethos and the practice of perpetual confinement. As the book provides an empirical and analytical foundation for understanding how the contemporary acceptance of such extremely severe punishment came to be, and with it new practices, new subjectivities, and new ways of thinking about death by prison, another feature of the US criminal legal system that must be addressed and analyzed is racial bias. Racial disparity in LWOP sentencing is higher than for US sentencing overall. Key, however, is to focus not simply on racial disparity in outcomes, but on *how* race factors in sentencing policy and decision-making and, specifically, in the practices that lead to perpetual prison sentences. Sociolegal and criminological scholarship recognizes multiple ways in which race plays a role in processes of conviction and sentencing, including express intentional discrimination, underlying attitudes and perceptions that link race with crime, coded political narratives, distorted media representations, and socioeconomic factors and structural criminal justice system arrangements that leave people of color more likely to face harsh punishment. Scholars emphasize that the disparate race effects reflected in sentencing numbers, for serious and violent crime in particular, are less a reflection of sentencing proceedings than of a circuit of bias that begins with social-environmental factors leading to crime and continues from policing to arrest and onward in a spread of decisions across the criminal justice system by a variety of actors; the "birdcage" is a compelling metaphor.[59] In these decisions, stereotypes linking race with crime play out in ways that are often less express and flagrant than deeply rooted and un- or understated.

This book provides historical evidence of these processes and how they contributed to the rise of LWOP. In doing so, the historical account offered here complements a policy argument sounded elsewhere: to meaningfully confront racial discrimination in the justice system, jurisdictions must curb sentencing at the hard end, including life without parole and other forms of perpetual confinement.[60] Perpetual confinement has had its greatest impact on people of color for a combination of reasons. Politicians and lawmakers have used high-profile crimes to reinforce associations between blackness and criminal activity and as a basis for enacting harsher sentencing laws as well as retrenching practices of parole and clemency. Legislators have enacted drug laws and habitual offense laws, with expected if not evident racially disproportionate impacts, authorizing life without parole for violent and sometimes nonviolent crimes.[61] But the matter is far broader: as the chapters of this book establish, a widespread series of decisions across the criminal legal process have left people who are African American, especially, but also people who are Latino, Native American, and poor Americans of all races and ethnicities, more likely to be eligible for perpetual prison terms. These are identifiable practices, but not all are so direct or intentional.

In revealing something important but hidden in contemporary experience, genealogy makes a statement about a general societal condition: it generalizes from the particular scenario under study, which is a strategic site for studying a phenomenon that itself is not so isolated. If we are to draw general societal messages from the inquiries herein, likewise lessons for sentencing policy, we should not stop with the harshness of this punishment, which in any event is already well known. The sociological relevance of LWOP, in other words, ought not be reduced to its punitive element. LWOP is rightly taken as exemplary of the cruel and exclusionary character of contemporary US punishment, but something else goes along with it. Imbued in the decisions and practices that generate and enable LWOP as perpetual confinement are a variety of forms of disregard: acceptance, acquiescence, ambivalence, a failure to care, a discarding of responsibility—all sorts of not doing and disposing.

At many steps in the recent history of life without parole sentencing one finds not only harsh punishment but a disregard for the impact of the decisions made about life sentencing. This book is about processes of the most extreme imprisonment, but it is simultaneously about processes of disregard as they pass over into neglect. The early role of perpetual confinement with the prison helps to reflect on this. From the first experiments with the prison in the United States through early uses of life without parole, perpetual confinement existed under conditions that were very harsh yet equally about removal, in both a physical and a psychological sense. The prison in early theorizing was a bleak house in an unknown space that could provoke fear simply by its secret location and foreboding lack of familiarity.[62] Those who entered its harsh conditions were threatened with and susceptible to lifetime confinement should they not find redemption; for those on the outside, the prison presented a distant horror by which they were simultaneously repelled and desensitized. From the 1970s to the 1990s, as actors in the penal field translated major upheavals in practice, life without parole often arose indirectly, a much less intentional operation than one might think; yet as the presence of LWOP as perpetual confinement became increasingly recognized, it was accepted by penal state elites and the public with relatively little alarm. In this more developed picture, the harshest of penal tools arises in complex ways, a product of ambivalence about disproportionate punishments based on race and the severe treatment of vulnerable populations, not only punitive intent. The punishment is extraordinarily severe; but seeing it only that way misses the aspect of "unconcern."[63] LWOP, in short, often came about indirectly, and America let it. And so it continues today: US society is not critical about when the punishment of LWOP is used, nor is US society attentive to the transformative changes that people go through in prison or the pains of aging that go along with and precede an in-prison death.

LWOP is a device that, in a multitude of ways, has come into being precisely to allow people not to worry, to put things off, to not reconsider. In this sense, LWOP is indeed the exemplar of contemporary punishment and policy that has produced mass incarceration. This is so not only because of its harshness, but because of its function of enabling members of the public and penal experts alike to forget and of allowing them to deflect the myriad responsibilities (social, moral, financial) that come with punishing.

PART I

Foundations

1. Perpetual Penal Confinement

Lengthy prison sentences are nothing new. Nor are sentences that might be expected to outlast an incarcerated person's life span. Minimum terms of twenty to twenty-five years have long been routine for first-degree murder in the United States. For centuries, natural life sentences have been authorized for seemingly irreparable criminals. Judges on occasion issue extremely long sentences even for nonhomicidal criminal conduct arising from a single incident. Parole and clemency, moreover, give state actors a prerogative to deny release indefinitely to life-term prisoners deemed particularly dangerous. Even in jurisdictions with penal systems strongly oriented toward treatment and rehabilitation, over the first three-quarters of the twentieth century such "ultimate penalties" were available in particular cases, and practices amounting to death in prison took place.[1] So the concept of treating certain "offenders" or "offender groups" as if they were infinitely excludable is not novel. Nor is the practice of using the prison as a virtual death chamber. What we know as LWOP marks one way in which people have faced the remainder of their natural lives in prison, but it is not the first or the only one. Incarceration until death has a history in penal thought and practice that is as old as the prison.

Yet if staying in prison for a lifetime has been an ever-present possibility for prisoners for centuries, actually confining people in this way was, throughout most of US history, a secondary outcome, an alternative for the exceptional case. Justifications for making such exceptions came in different forms: to make an example for purposes of general deterrence, as a preventive measure given an individual's established history of recidivism, because a person failed to reform or rehabilitate while incarcerated. More often than not, however, over the course of the nation's first two centuries imprisonment until death worked not as punishment's aim, but as a specter:

a dreaded possibility to motivate the behaviors and beliefs of prisoners and the public. One sees in the contemporary United States, then, a quite different way of thinking about and practicing imprisonment until death than what was characteristic historically: in the contemporary sentencing frameworks of most US states, a death-in-prison sentence is *not* reserved for the exceptional case.

With an eye to the present, this chapter establishes a foundation for understanding the routinization of LWOP and perpetual confinement in the United States by inspecting the history of life sentencing and other policies and practices by which incarcerated people faced the remainder of their natural lives in prison. The chapter draws from primary materials (including laws, legislative histories, judicial opinions, and news media) as well as a comprehensive review of secondary sources concerning the history of American penal policy and reform. My aim is not to present a precise historical account so much as to recognize the ways in which lifetime imprisonment has been placed in systems of punishment. Each example, ranging from the American colonies to the Progressive Era to habitual offense schemes to practices of convict leasing, encounters perpetual confinement as a product of its context, taking on particular forms and serving particular functions that reflect political strategies; penal aims; and underlying assumptions about crime, punishment, criminals, and prisoners.

Bringing together many disparate notes about life sentencing that have been posted in different projects and commentaries throughout the history of punishment in the United States, the chapter in effect reinterprets American penality through the lens of the life sentence. Lifetime sentencing has garnered relatively little attention in historical scholarship, but it has been an essential feature of American punishment. As we will see, incarceration until death has served as a conceptual anchor for some of the most influential theories in American punishment, a pillar of theories upon which the American penal system has been built. It has been a tool for overtly punitive programs, to be sure, but also for those seeking humane punishment and prioritizing redemption or rehabilitation.

As important as lifetime imprisonment was for prior penal theories and practices, however, its instrumental role in these schemes was exceptional and peripheral: exceptional because lifetime incarceration was not regularly applied as state punishment, and peripheral because when used it was called upon as a backup, along a secondary track, or as an unofficial practice. The prospect of never getting out of prison was a tool to encourage good behavior, a plan B should rehabilitation fail, a cruel and foreseeable consequence of the harsh and exploitative conditions of contracted penal labor. In this way, perpetual confinement was ancillary yet ever present, circumscribed yet hovering at the margins. The fact of being convicted of a crime reduced one's status, such that even if the formal sentence was not for life, there was a degree of risk that once imprisoned, one would never leave.

MODES OF PERPETUAL CONFINEMENT

Examining historical modes of incarceration until death involves a deliberate step with respect to how one conceives of prison sentences for life. It demands that one think of putting a person in prison "forever" as a particular *type* of punishment. As a manner of punishing, imprisonment until death bears some resemblance to long prison terms, but it is also distinct because it is defined by maintaining the prison sentence until a person dies. Putting a person in prison until they die also bears some resemblance to a death sentence, overlapping with capital punishment insofar as death is the end point, but it is distinct because a death sentence ends in execution at a set time and place, whereas the death process for a person sentenced to die in prison is a gradual one.[2] Although a prison sentence without release is similar to other severe punishments, then, it is also different: it is a long prison sentence unto death. One might refer to this type of punishment as a "virtual life" or "death in prison" sentence.[3] Generally, I use the term "perpetual confinement" to designate any combination of penal sanctions and practices that results in holding a person permanently in state custody.

I noted in the introduction the importance of thinking of perpetual confinement in this way. The matter of how to punish serious and violent crime is a universal puzzle for governments, in response to which states may turn to a variety of punishments that confine until death, and the manner and extent to which different states and nations, at different times, have used one form of perpetual confinement or another is rooted in local histories, structural arrangements, and cultural traditions.[4] Accordingly, when studying perpetual confinement, one should take care to analyze it as a type of punishment that operates within a context and pay attention to how its forms and functions vary with different political projects, economic arrangements, and social circumstances.

When using a current practice or idea as a touchstone for historical inquiry, there is an added concern. One must take care not to impose on the past an order of classification that did not then exist.[5] Certainly the risk exists with life without parole sentencing: one cannot uncritically interpret a statute authorizing "life without parole" in the first decades of the twentieth century as having the same meaning as a statute that authorizes "life without parole" in the first decades of the twenty-first. To avoid historiciz-ing a contemporary object, one must let the context, not preconceptions or "prenotions," define.[6] Turning to writings on crime and punishment, accordingly, one does best to look for perpetual confinement as it is grounded in practice and in systematic theories or commentaries. Working with fully developed theories that approach crime and punishment comprehensively allows one to witness perpetual confinement within a broader scheme, to see it in play with particular working ideologies and orienting ideas, under the conditions in which it was called upon to perform.[7]

In what follows, I draw from systematic statements on punishment at several important junctures in US penal history. Each treatise on penal reform evinces a dialogue between official and public meanings. As Charles Bright said with respect to the prison, just as a narrative exists between the prison and politics, there is also a narrative between the prison and the public sphere; the relation between the prison and society, in other words, demands a conversation and a justification for the prison that "fits."[8] My focus in the following descriptions is on how perpetual confinement is situ-ated in that dialogue. Just as the death penalty changes across different penal systems, and also the fine, so too does perpetual confinement.[9]

The Example

One of the most influential statements on perpetual confinement precedes the United States. Cesare Beccaria's *On Crimes and Punishments*, the clas-sic Enlightenment statement of penal reform, was widely influential dur-ing the founding period.[10] The treatise accords penal servitude in perpetuity an important if initially perplexing role. Beccaria, a political economist and cameralist, was concerned with optimal regulation of the state to further the monarch's peaceful and productive rule. Influenced by Enlightenment prin-ciples of economy, he valued utility. A benevolent state would promote the greatest happiness of its constituents by ensuring public safety and afford-able goods and services. Critical of loose arrangements in which criminal justice procedures and outcomes were largely directed by the discretion of prosecutors and judges, and in which corporal punishment, torture, and death were unnecessarily prevalent, Beccaria transposed an economic model for regulating commerce to the prevention and punishment of everyday crime.[11] He proposed a comprehensive, well-publicized penal code under which punishment would be swift, certain, and proportionate.

Beccaria also adhered to a humanist principle, aligned with social contract theory, by which all individuals, including those imprisoned, are worthy of respect and possess inalienable rights. The assumption that all individuals are rational, self-interested actors, who weigh costs and benefits in context, extends in Beccaria's work to the premise that each individual is also a potential criminal (given proper situational provocation). The public, as such, is susceptible to deterrence, and the person who commits a crime is not necessarily a social enemy. By this logic, Beccaria advocated "moderate and prolonged punishments" that would remain visible over time to spark recurrent reflection. "It is not the intenseness of the pain that has the greatest effect on the mind," he wrote, "but its continuance." Instead of flaming out in a single flamboyant spectacle, lasting public punishments provoked the "often repeated reflection that I myself shall be reduced to such a protracted and miserable condition if I commit similar misdeeds."[12] Deterrence was produced not only through public notice but by punishment available for routine observation.

Along these lines, Beccaria argued for replacing the death penalty with perpetual penal servitude. Although he opposed unnecessarily severe punishments, he accepted *public* penal servitude under certain circumstances as a productive display of hard labor. If capital punishment served the function of demonstrating state power by physically eliminating troublesome lawbreakers, by Beccaria's estimation perpetual servitude was no less harrowing but far more enduring. It spread the staged "tragedy" from a single moment across an indefinite duration, taking it from a single platform and dispersing it through space.[13] In a system aimed at prevention through publicity, certainty, and repetition, the endlessly repeated public ordeal held value as a lasting warning and a constant reminder: a lasting symbol of the rule of law that Beccaria found so central to political legitimacy.

At a glance, the grave cruelty of perpetual penal servitude—cruelty of which Beccaria was well aware—sits uneasily with his care for proportionality, his opposition to the death penalty and unnecessarily violent punishments, and his general respect for human dignity.[14] But on closer look, penal servitude's limited use in Beccaria's scheme is not so puzzling after all. Michel Foucault characterized Beccaria's scheme as "the punitive city," because punishment there was a conversation with society, comprised of signs disseminated through widespread and ongoing publicity.[15] One might think of perpetual servitude as a key to this "city," the conceptual anchor of a scheme in which punishment's primary function—directed more to the public than to the prisoner—was to prevent and deter. Punishment that was excessive, disproportionate, even barbaric for a particular case could be justified by its utility in providing a visible and repeated illustration. The dignity of a particular individual and evenhanded application of law could give way in certain circumstances to the public good served by making *an example*.[16]

The Retreat

Beccaria's influence in the United States is clear in Pennsylvania's criminal law reforms of 1786, which curtailed capital punishment and authorized the public punishment of wrongdoers. Chaining prisoners to wheelbarrows and forcing them to labor in clothes identifying them as convicts, however, was a short-lived experiment that prompted great criticism.[17] In concert with efforts elsewhere in the United States, Pennsylvania reformers soon turned to the prison as a technology for punishing crime.[18] The systematic thinking that laid the groundwork for those reforms against public punishment is attributable in significant part to physician and reformer Benjamin Rush.[19]

Like Beccaria's, Rush's views on punishment were linked to his views on government and forged in conversation with political activity. Yet the political context, the penal apparatus at hand, and the perspective on people who commit crimes undergirding his reform scheme could hardly have been more different. Rush's innovations were responses to and repositionings from Beccaria. Rush saw the prison as a practical necessity in the social environment of early democracy, which featured increasing population and urban density, expanding property rights, industrialization, and a newly developing and growing polity.[20] For Rush, democracy was a process of education and retraining in which the prison, no less than the school, was a privileged site for "transform[ing] the habits and mentalities of the citizenry."[21] Every prisoner was a potential citizen whose dignity rested in the capacity for penitence and redemption.

When Rush drew up plans for the first US prisons in the late eighteenth century, his vision was quite different from the way confinement had been used in the United States to date.[22] Confinement was problematic because it required consistent resources: a space in which to hold, a watchperson to guard, food and drink to serve the confined. Existing jails were small; capacity was limited, and consequently so was the use of incarceration. What Rush and other penal pioneers offered, therefore, was a departure; more than a two-room jail for short stays, the penitentiary would be a large building for terms of uncertain duration. In a significant passage, Rush refers to the prison interchangeably as "the house" or "the receptacle":

> Let a large house, of a construction agreeable to its design, be erected in a remote part of the state. Let the avenue to this house be rendered difficult and gloomy by mountains and morasses. Let its doors be of iron; and let the grating occasioned by opening and shutting them be

increased by an echo from a neighboring mountain that shall extend
and continue a found that shall deeply pierce the soul. . . . To increase
the horror of this abode of discipline and misery, let it be called by
some name that shall import its design. . . . If the receptacle for criminals which has been proposed is erected in a remote part of the state,
it will act with the same force upon the feelings of the human ears as
perpetual banishment.[23]

The three qualities that serve as guiding principles for Rush's prison
model all stand in contrast to Beccaria (as well as Dufriche de Valaze, to
whom Rush expressly contrasted his proposal). First, Rush valued the
prison as a deterrent, but not because of its public presence. Removal from
society to distant places and spaces was a useful source of fear. "The human
mind is disposed to exaggerate every thing that is removed at a distance
from it by time or place," Rush wrote (the correspondence with banishment was not lost on Rush, as though banishment could be accomplished
internally). Second, Rush sought to promote redemption and deterrence,
in prisoners and public, through a sense of the unknown: "Let the various kinds of punishment that are to be inflicted on crimes be defined and
fixed by law. But let no notice be taken in the law of the punishment that
awaits any particular crime. By these means we shall prevent the mind
from accustoming itself to the view of these punishments so as to destroy
their terror by habit."[24] Third, the duration of punishment would also be
unknown to the prisoner. "I conceive this secret to be of the utmost importance in reforming criminals and preventing crimes," Rush wrote. "The
imagination when agitated with uncertainty will seldom fail of connecting
the longest duration of punishment with the smallest crime."[25] Whereas
for Beccaria, the temporal value of a perpetual sentence was repetition, for
Rush it was indefiniteness. Prison conditions were dire, solitary confinement common, and the intentional opacity of imprisonment imposed a
heavy psychological burden. Discussions of life in early Pennsylvania prisons describe it as a soul death.[26] If Beccaria's vision was a "punitive city,"
Rush's was a dark cave, potentially a tomb.

Hope for release, however, was not absent. The person convicted of a
crime was for Rush a sinner who could be saved. Rush estimated humanity
would overcome brutal conditions through physical and spiritual labor.[27]
The threat of limitless time in the receptacle was ideally suited for inducing
internal reflection and reeducation. A prisoners' dignity as such was linked
to an austere faith to be discovered in the experience of imprisonment. For
those who failed, however, natural life imprisonment waited: "In confinement he may be reformed, and if this should prove impracticable, he may

be retained for a term of years, that will probably be coeval with his life."[28] All prison sentences, in Rush's scheme, were to be experienced as perpetual, even if only some would end that way.

The Island

Perpetual prison terms first appear in the penal codes of the colonies and early United States as a sentence of "natural life" for repeat offenses. Borrowed from English law, the natural life sentence mirrors another punishment used for those who broke the law and then broke it again: banishment. The idea of life in prison as an internal banishment surfaces throughout early US penal codes in repeat-offense statutes. Punishing recidivism, as such, is perhaps the classic role of perpetual confinement. Just as the prison substituted for transportation, natural life in prison could be seen as a domestic analog for exile abroad.

As old as the prison, the natural life sentence raises certain issues that have concerned prison administrators from the beginning. Holding apparently incorrigible criminals for long terms in a standard institution risked irreparably influencing or "prisonizing" those convicted of less serious crimes.[29] Reformers of different eras, accordingly, have proposed separate tracks of punishment or separate prisons.[30] A dramatic example of this way of thinking is the "perpetual workhouse" articulated by Daniel Raymond, a mid-nineteenth-century Maryland congressman and political economist who proposed it as part of a systematic plan for reform in response to a national survey on the penitentiary.[31]

Per Raymond, the character of human spirit was to accommodate hardship and persist. Raymond believed, therefore, that most people would not experience imprisonment as punishment for long: "If a man is sentenced to the Penitentiary for ten years, and after remaining there three months, becomes so accustomed to it as to enjoy an ordinary share of happiness, confinement for the remaining nine years and nine months is in reality without any effect whatever . . . and a mere mockery of punishment."[32] For Raymond, another "absurdity" was "to think to punish a man by compelling him to labor," which he saw as a cure for the human spirit.[33]

For imprisonment to be effective as punishment or reform, Raymond believed, it generally must operate for short durations (six months or less) under dire conditions. Accordingly, if a "first grade of criminals" could be dealt with by corporal punishment, and a "second grade" could be redeemed by short-term solitude and deprivation, there was a "third grade," those who commit the most serious and repeat offenses, for whom short terms would not suffice:

For the third grade of criminals, I would provide a perpetual workhouse, somewhat upon the plan of our present penitentiaries. I call it a perpetual workhouse because I would have none sentenced to it but for life. It is designed for incorrigible offenders, for whose reformation there is no hope, and whose characters render it dangerous to suffer them ever to be let loose again upon society. I would set them to work to prevent them from being a burden to the state, and as they are never again to be let loose upon society, it is of little importance what habits they form, nor can there be any objection to their enjoying as much happiness as is consistent with their safety. There can be no object in punishing them with idleness and solitude. . . . Indeed, all persons who have evinced that incorrigible depravity of heart, which renders them dangerous to society should be sentenced to this perpetual workhouse. To it I would sentence none but for life; since to confine them there for a term of years and then turn them upon society is to make them felons by a regular course of discipline.[34]

Raymond's point is important: if prison was to be effective, it would only be so temporarily; once a term exceeded six months, imprisonment was creating a danger, not addressing one. The prison was therefore appropriate for *either* short terms *or* life terms and nothing in between. The bifurcation between those banished to the island colony and those sent to a mainland prison highlights how different the character of confinement can be once individuals are simply written off. On the island that Raymond envisioned as a perpetual workhouse, the passing of time did not matter, nor did any institutional knowledge of what transpired.

Separate-track schemes such as Raymond's were few but not altogether absent in the early nineteenth century and foreshadow a perspective on criminality that would become influential at the century's end, eventually undergirding twentieth-century habitual- and sex-offense laws and practices.[35] As the emerging sciences of criminology, eugenics, and psychiatry converged on the criminal law, the notion of repeat offending changed. Where there once was "the offense and the penalty," by the late nineteenth century there was also the "criminal": a dangerous type whom criminology professed to understand and psychiatry vowed to reveal.[36] The recidivist was transformed from a person who committed the same offense multiple times (the repeat offender) to a criminal type (the habitual offender) predisposed to crime and a chronic threat to public safety.[37] Similarly, where once there were sex crimes now entered "sex offenders," a biological type of "degenerates, homicidal sex fiends, and perverts" suffering from maladies with vague and only ostensibly discoverable cures.[38]

Such concepts of social enemies, seen as posing risks to public health as much as to public safety, resonate with social Darwinism, eugenics, and other positivist and biosocial theories. As the prison was redefined as a place of treatment and rehabilitation, predetermined criminal types were rerouted to detention centers.[39] For most of US history, separate tracks for people preidentified as incorrigible were the most direct uses of perpetual confinement. Recidivist laws came in waves, often in response to moral panics, crystallized by entrepreneurs who shaped public concerns.[40] Many of those laws, however, were more symbolic than real: harsh on paper but rarely used and often nullified in practice.[41]

The Chance

Rush's vision of the receptacle motivated a number of penal projects (Eastern State Penitentiary, for example).[42] But his dream of opaque sentences for all prisoners did not catch on. Most often, judges imposed fixed terms that people were expected to serve in full. Life sentencing was used only for the most serious crimes and repeat offenses, and was rarely applied.[43] By the mid-nineteenth century, the prison was a nationally ingrained institution yet deemed a failure, and Rush's idea of the prison as reformatory had largely faded.[44] Skepticism toward the prison and related procedures such as fixed sentencing and executive clemency brewed. So when a renewed penal reform movement arose in the last quarter of the nineteenth century, it looked to a new technology: parole, a program for prison release. As reformer William Tallack said, emphasizing the prison's declining repute, "the main object of a prison is to be *empty*."[45]

This marks an early stage of what has become known as "penal welfare" or the "rehabilitative ideal," an approach to imprisonment focused on treatment and reform with an eye to release.[46] Life sentences were integral to this model. By the time of the 1870 National Congress on the Penitentiary in Cincinnati, the duration of imprisonment had been identified as one of the great puzzles of criminal justice. Fixed sentences, which were prevalent, tended to overpunish or underpunish. Prisoners might be released before they were "cured" or be "cured" but still detained, reformers urged, because the law arguably attempted the impossible.[47] "Justice is an abstraction, elusive as a sunbeam. . . . A criminal court is a trap to catch sunbeams. Neither the legislature nor the court can make use of a non-existing pair of scales with imaginary weights. . . . How long a time is uncertain and cannot ever be foretold in advance."[48] Further, courts in different jurisdictions, even judges in the same jurisdiction, applied fixed sentences differently for similar crimes, undercutting the equity and certainty of the law.[49] Clemency compounded the problem; a useful, even necessary, mechanism for regulating prison populations, as it could be used to alleviate overcrowding and manage prison morale, it was also a source of arbitrariness and graft. The "bitter and inescapable reality [of overcrowding] . . . made virtually indiscriminate pardoning a necessity," even as it was an "unwelcome remedy."[50] At the National Congress, penal reformers presented life sentencing data from a half dozen jurisdictions to back the argument that existing sentencing and release practices were arbitrary. In Ohio, for example, the average time served for life-sentenced prisoners was six years, seven months, and five days; in Wisconsin, it was six years—in both cases, shorter than many fixed terms.[51]

As a solution, reformers offered indeterminate sentencing, a system in which decisions were made during a prison term, not before; in which release was based on prison conduct, not mercy; and in which the decision makers were medical and administrative experts, not politicians or elected officials.[52] In this system, life sentences would be central. To fully consider the form and function of the life sentence in the context of indeterminate sentencing, it is useful to contrast the views of two reformers, Frederick Wines and Zebulon Brockway. Brockway's model, which was first practiced at Elmira prison in the 1870s and had spread to many states by the 1930s, set a minimum prison term after which parole was possible and a maximum term at which release was mandatory.[53] Wines by contrast reserved the label "indeterminate sentence" for a sanction with *no* minimum *or* maximum limit, in *all* cases a life sentence under which a prisoner possessed an opportunity for release, as soon as they proved rehabilitated but no sooner.[54] As Wines saw it, if not for the inherent human frailties of prison administrators and others positioned to make decisions about reform and release, there would be no need for any carceral sanction *other* than a life sentence.[55]

In Wines's ideal, the life sentence was precisely the opposite of a time sentence: clock and calendar were removed altogether and replaced with a goal-driven process of work.[56] Prisoners were shown, in other words, an opportunity to get out and were incentivized to earn it. This view of release as a product of labor, Progressive reformers expected, would justify prison sentences that were otherwise objectionably long.[57] It would also offer prisoners hope, which Wines captured in the notion of a "chance": "What the new criminology stands for is, in the first instance, discrimination between wrongdoers, and patient tolerance, under surveillance. . . . It cherishes no illusive expectation that the methods employed will accomplish the impossible: that all prisoners will yield to them. . . . But it insists that the convict is entitled to his chance—a chance which possibly he never before had."[58]

The opportunity to work toward rehabilitation, however, could be wasted and lost. As Wines stated, the "strength of the indeterminate sentence" was "its positive power to accomplish two distinct and desirable ends . . . to reform criminals who are susceptible of reformation and to relieve society perpetually of the presence of such as are irreclaimable."[59] Even Tallack, who considered perpetual confinement a slow death penalty, found it proper in "abnormal cases" for "intractable being[s]": "creature[s] with the speech and form of humanity but with . . . the malevolent passions of a demon."[60] As a London paper, *The Spectator*, put it, indeterminate sentencing was sure to work, "monsters and accidents excepted."[61]

In sum, given its open-ended character, the life sentence epitomized the Progressive reform strategy, providing prisoners an opportunity to change and leaving it to the expertise of a parole board to determine whether an individual was sufficiently rehabilitated. However, as reformers of that era and contemporary scholars alike emphasize, the indeterminate model was a two-sided affair with a "double soul."[62] For if a prisoner was deemed to have failed their chance—a decision potentially laden with stereotype and prejudice—social protection would outweigh rehabilitation and result in lifetime confinement.[63]

It is worth pausing to stress a point. It is essential to address perpetual confinement in context, which includes the theorists' political and social ambitions as well as their worldviews and underlying assumptions. Both Wines and Rush regarded prisoners as people in need of social rehabilitation if not cultural reorientation, and perpetual confinement served as a threat to motivate productive behavior. But connected with the idea of putting people away forever in these schemes is a notion that some people—because of their crimes, but more fundamentally because of their race, ethnicity, gender, class, or another demographic characteristic—are inferior, defective, and in need of training or treatment; if that training or treatment were not successful, lifetime imprisonment would, from the perspective of these theories, be acceptable and understandable. In short, while perpetual imprisonment is not the stated aim of the prison in theories such as those of Rush and Wines, its possibility is built into the rationale, inherent in the paternalism of the penal reformers.[64] The disposability of people imprisoned is inherent in the theories' foundational assumptions.[65]

The Lease System

The characteristic of entering prison and never coming out alive is shared by another paradigm in US punishment, one defined not just by the sentence itself but by the conditions under which the sentence is served: penal slavery.[66] Penal servitude until death has deep roots. In the Roman Empire, for example, citizens convicted of crimes could be stripped of their civic responsibilities and entitlements, sentenced to penal servitude, and rebranded as slaves at hard labor for the rest of their lives.[67] Centuries later in continental Europe, long terms at hard labor under conditions so severe that death was likely took the form of galley slavery, the *bagnes* (a stationary contract-labor site in navy yards under state control), and imprisonment with irons.[68] The pairing of status degradation with life-threatening labor finds an American analog in the legal rubric of civil death and the convict lease system, a legacy of Southern slave plantations and the Thirteenth Amendment to the United States Constitution.[69]

Civil death, first found in state codes of the late eighteenth century, removed the legal rights of people convicted of crimes, including property rights and the right to vindicate other rights in court.[70] Civil death was equivalent to losing legal personhood, leaving the prisoner a half person, with a double status as a human and regulated object.[71] This eroded status in turn enabled contractual penal labor practices that were often mortally threatening and that otherwise would have been legally untenable. When the Thirteenth Amendment abolished slavery, an exception allowed penal servitude for prisoners. The Thirteenth Amendment as such provides a "discursive link" between slavery and civil death in prison.[72]

For the economically minded penal operators of the nineteenth-century North and antebellum South, labor-based operations were self-sustaining enterprises in which social control and financial gain were on a par with crime control.[73] In the South, however, given the poverty of the states and the lack in most of a centralized bureaucracy, penal servitude took place not in prisons but at "outposts."[74] Convict leasing, penal farms, and chain gangs were seen as natural arrangements, reinstituting slavery by a different means.[75] Like slavery, convict leasing was an economy for profit, made possible by the subtraction of people's rights.[76]

Under the lease system, the court-imposed sentence—be it short or long, for a misdemeanor or a serious crime, upon a child or an adult—exposed the imprisoned person to conditions of confinement that could easily end in death before the end of their term.[77] Death under convict leasing was so foreseeable that commentators recognized it as a core component of the system. In a striking passage, George Washington Cable "runs down the table of deaths" from a Tennessee branch prison: "Found dead. Killed. Drowned. Not given. Blank. Blank. Blank. Killed. Blank. Shot. Killed. Blank. Blank. Killed. Killed. Blank. Blank. Blank. Killed. Blank. Blank."[78] In Georgia and South Carolina, he reported, a "large majority" of people leased had "for simple stealing, without breaking in or violence, been virtually condemned to be worked and misused to death . . . to 'work[] the customary loss of citizenship for life.'"[79] Death rates (and attempted escape rates) were also high in Texas and Alabama, but Arkansas, Mississippi, and Louisiana reflected "the system at its worst."[80] Given the severity of the conditions, the actual sentence hardly mattered.

The practice of penal slavery in the form of convict leasing shares with classic theories of the prison (Rush) and indeterminate sentencing (Wines) the character of a punishment that is not necessarily death in prison but is foreseeably so. In each, imprisonment is a form of social control that leaves the possibility of dying while incarcerated always on the table. In a portentous observation, Cable saw in actors carrying out convict leasing less an aim to harm than the "unadmirable spirit of enterprise"; he interpreted the unconcerned public reception of convict leasing as "little more than a listless oblivion, that may be reprehensible, but is not intentional, unless they are to be judged by the acts of their elected legislators."[81] Perpetual confinement carries with it a theme of forgetting the imprisoned, leaving them to the discretion of the institution, even in programs that seek to civilize and redeem.

Yet historically, the place of perpetual confinement was circumscribed; even in the deliberate and broad exclusionary penal model set forth by Raymond, a clear distinction existed between ordinary lawbreakers who would receive corporal punishment or short prison terms and the extraordinary lawbreakers whom the state could, on a separate track, imprison until death. Why was perpetual confinement designated a peripheral, exceptional role? Some answers are evident in the preceding vignettes: states had limited resources; people feared prisoners serving long terms would influence those serving shorter terms; capital punishment was an option for the most serious crimes and statement cases; and, insofar as a redemptive or treatment paradigm prevailed, lifetime incarceration was necessarily a reserve outcome even as the mode of punishing depended on it.

By contrast, in the sentencing frameworks that prevail in most US states today, perpetual confinement, with LWOP as its bellwether, is not reserved for the special case or separate track, and it is an official not an unofficial practice. Most US jurisdictions have adopted fixed sentencing schemes (including determinate sentencing, mandatory minimum sentencing, and truth-in-sentencing provisions) that authorize long and often mandatory prison terms. In this environment, beyond reflecting cruelty and exclusion, LWOP represents a system in which incarcerating until death is a standard sentence, a routine practice. A long historical perspective on perpetual confinement helps show the contemporary practice of lifetime punishment for what it is: a remarkably different approach than what existed prior to the 1970s. As such, this chapter provides a diagnosis with which to approach LWOP as an object of study: instead of simply asking how LWOP came to be used so much, one must ask how perpetual confinement became so ordinary.

2. Precursor and Prototype

The preceding chapter presented a historical inquiry into prior modes of perpetual penal confinement, different ways of thinking about and carrying out imprisonment for the entire life of a person. This chapter presents an inquiry concerning the historical practice and meaning of life without parole sentences in particular. If, as I argue, LWOP—as the life without parole sentence is known colloquially today—holds a particular meaning that helps define it as a uniquely contemporary punishment, life without parole as it existed for the first seven decades of the twentieth century evinced a prior form. This chapter describes that prior form and the state of it leading up to a precipice: a moment in time in the early 1970s on the cusp of several major upheavals in the penal field that would drastically alter American punishment and life sentencing.

One of the principal messages of this chapter is that life without parole has not always meant no release from prison. For much of the twentieth century through the 1960s, executive clemency served as a mechanism of prison release, one that in many states was applied with regularity. Via clemency, usually in the form of commutation, life sentences without parole could result in release after roughly seven to fifteen years. This should not be taken to mean that life sentences did not ever result in long stays or end as death in prison, but the prevailing bundle of laws and practices carried with it a concept of life sentences, with and without parole, according to which neither was interminable. Put another way, for most of the twentieth century a life sentence *without* parole was not so different from a life sentence *with* parole. And in the early 1970s, at the precipice of major upheavals in the penal field, both were waning: the average actual time served on life terms, with parole and without, was increasingly shorter.

LWOP'S PRECURSOR

Scholars of knowledge, particularly scientific knowledge, debate how best to refer to an object that precedes the current one. The present object might have the same name, even the same material, as a past object; nevertheless something has changed. "Precursor," referring to a substance from which another substance is formed through a reaction, is one term scientists use to refer to an earlier form that, while related, is nevertheless distinctly different in logic or concept. Used too casually, the term can be reduced simply to a difference in formal properties, but looking to formal properties alone tends to overlook the conditions in which concepts are formed. Context—the questions asked, the problems at hand, the instruments used, the prevailing style of thought—is fundamental to understanding what the object is.[1]

We might think of the difference between life without parole as it existed up until the late twentieth century and life without parole as it is practiced and understood now in something of the same way. Provided the foregoing caution is taken—and a form is analyzed as the product of particular sociohistorical conditions, arising from a particular way of seeing things—the term "precursor" is an apt way of distinguishing the practice and meaning of life without parole during the first two-thirds of the twentieth century from the punishment bearing the same name that emerged in the last quarter of that century and continues today. To fully appreciate the emergence of LWOP in the late twentieth century, we need to know something of that history and how sentences of life without parole were thought of and practiced earlier in the United States. That is, we need to know something about LWOP's precursor.

Early Forms

In the early United States, the life sentence entered as a legacy of British law. In early precolonial codes, such as that drawn up by William Penn or the penal code of the Massachusetts Bay Colony, one finds references to "natural life" or "perpetual imprisonment" as punishment for political crimes or for second offenses of serious crimes.[2] In eighteenth- and nineteenth-century statute books, one continues to find references to "life" or "natural life" sentences, primarily for repeat serious or violent offenses. As discussed in the preceding chapter, life sentences had a theoretical value that outpaced their actual use (Benjamin Rush, for example, conceived of life sentences as the ideal prison sentence, their indeterminacy essential to push people to redemption), in part because states lacked the resources to hold prisoners for substantial amounts of time. And when life sentences were in fact used, the limited data available suggest they were applied unevenly and that time served before release varied within and across jurisdictions.[3]

The previous chapter notes too how, at a pivotal juncture in US punishment in the last quarter of the nineteenth century, reformers proposed a system under which the precise end of a prison term would not be forecast at the time of sentencing. For the indeterminate sentencing system, which cast the prison as a site of treatment and rehabilitation, the life with parole sentence served as a vital instrument. US states adopted indeterminate sentencing and parole to varying extents, and a "congruity of philosophy and practice across the country remained in place until the 1970s."[4] The sentence of life imprisonment *without* the possibility of parole takes its name from the same era. It was a sentence that offered no right to administrative review for release, a life sentence over which the parole board had no authority.

For most of the twentieth century, laws authorizing life without parole generally came in one of two forms: (1) criminal statutes formally authorizing life without parole for certain crimes and (2) provisions in parole codes limiting the application of parole in certain circumstances, usually for life sentences or death sentences. Generally speaking, the former were rare and rarely enforced. Again, there were pragmatic reasons for this, insofar as states lacked the resources to build prisons that could hold people for long terms of years, much less lifetimes. In addition, for much of the twentieth century, lifetime sanctions withholding parole were in tension with the prevailing mode of thinking about punishment in the United States, which held that the prison should be an opportunity for reform, reevaluation, and ultimately release. This underscores a characteristic of penal laws explicitly authorizing natural life or life without parole in the nineteenth century and for much of the twentieth century: they were rather extraordinary statutes punishing extraordinary crimes or extraordinary patterns of criminal activity.[5]

Authorization for life without parole sentences was more commonly situated in parole codes. Such laws, invoking a historical relation between punishment and the executive branch, were a vestige of clemency arrangements that preceded the indeterminate system. Some state laws precluded the parole board from considering release for life-sentenced prisoners convicted of particular crimes, usually murder; in other states, laws precluded parole for all life sentences.[6] In states that did not adopt parole, all life sentences were in effect life without parole sentences, and release from prison depended upon the decision of a governor or executive body to commute the sentence. From this perspective, the key difference between life with parole and life without parole was a structural one.

Parole and Clemency: A Division of Labor

In theory, parole and clemency are different. Clemency in its purest form depends entirely on the will and subjective perspective of the executive actor; parole in its ideal form is an objective determination, informed by scientific expertise.[7] Clemency and parole nevertheless have shared a similar function historically. While often maligned as a mere exercise of mercy, throughout the nineteenth century and for much of the twentieth century executive clemency was "a key mechanism to manage the prison population, correct miscarriages of justice, restore the rights of former offenders, and make far-reaching public statements about the criminal justice system."[8] One can describe the relationship between parole and clemency for much of the twentieth century as a division of labor.

During the twentieth century many states transferred the duties of clemency to parole.[9] Efforts were made across American jurisdictions, moreover, to formalize and bureaucratize the clemency process, for instance by attaching a board of pardons.[10] Pardons boards began around the same time as administrative law and grew with it, inherently sharing concerns over unreviewable discretion; simultaneously, practices that were "in tension" with a bureaucratic rationality, such as clemency, "[fell] out of favor."[11] Nevertheless, states that discontinued or limited parole in the early twentieth century did so with the understanding that clemency would provide for and manage release.[12] South Dakota had one of the oldest such rules, prohibiting parole for all life-sentenced prisoners from 1913.[13] Pennsylvania, formalizing its parole system in 1941, expressly left out life sentences and death sentences, placing lifers on a separate track in which release would be determined by clemency.[14] Louisiana had a long-standing and well-known rule under which prison administrators would recommend for commutation prisoners who had served ten years and six months of their sentence with good conduct.[15]

Today many tend to assume that life without parole is a de facto death-in-prison sentence and, as such, that it is a punishment that will result in a longer time served than life *with* parole. But that is not necessarily the case, and it was not the case for the first two-thirds of the twentieth century.[16] Review for release from prison was something people sentenced to life without parole might bank on, and release itself was, if contingent, still a legitimate possibility. Up through the 1960s and 1970s, people convicted of crimes in Louisiana accepted plea deals to life sentences without parole based on the assurance that they would be reviewed for release after ten years and six months.[17] The average time served on a life without parole sentence in Pennsylvania between the 1940s and the early 1970s was between fifteen and twenty years.[18] In Michigan, the time served on life sentences with and without parole was similar until the mid-1960s.[19] To be sure, prosecutors seeking life without parole sentences and trial courts imposing the same, or politicians grandstanding in response to a high-profile crime, may have preferred to send a different message, but in practice many people serving life without parole were released, and the average time served under life *without* parole sentences and life *with* parole sentences was comparable.[20]

In short, a well-oiled clemency system operated not unlike parole (or as a complement to parole) for lifers. In fact, commutation at times served as a more reliable and efficient means of release, as corrections specialists recognized in Pennsylvania in the 1930s.[21] For most of the twentieth century, in sum, distinctions between life sentences with or without parole largely had to do with the manner in which states *structured the relation between executive clemency and the administrative parole board.* In effect, the statutes restricting parole for lifers were not so much intended to forsake release as to push it to a different point of discretion.[22] Life without parole, like life with parole, was a punishment that entertained the possibility of perpetual confinement but did not foreordain it.

LWOP'S PROTOTYPE

We should not oversimplify. If, in the main, life without parole sentences existed as a vestige of clemency and, despite the difference in procedure, were not substantially different in outcome than life with parole sentences, there certainly were actors who would have preferred the situation were otherwise. On occasion, legislators, governors, judges, prosecutors, and activist members of the public put life without parole sentences to a rather different use and for different effect. Sometimes a life without parole or "natural life" sentence, more than a sanction, was a political statement, responsive to the needs of a populace and crime victims, offering reassurance about public safety and the value of property or human life. In particular, life without parole could be used by legislators or governors intent on showing themselves to be tough on crime, in response to a high-profile crime or moral panic, for instance.

A notorious example of this type of lawmaking is New York's Baumes Law of the 1920s. It was not solely a crime statute or a parole statute but in fact both; declaring "natural life" as mandatory punishment for any fourth felony offense, it was an affirmative sentence *and* a restriction on parole board power.[23] In part a crackdown during Prohibition, in part a response to public concern over organized crime and a homicide rate that was eight times that of England and Wales, the Baumes Law was largely a product of private and amateur (more than state or expert) crime commissions, which funneled public sentiments and fears into a legislative proposal seeking catharsis through penal law.[24] In this respect, the law's mandatory natural life sentence was something of a last-ditch effort, resulting from the view that other forms of punishment were not up to the task of deterring "hardened criminals" and that judges could not be trusted with sentencing discretion.[25] The Baumes Law set off a national wave of similar laws, and by the late 1930s a majority of states authorized separate sentencing schemes for repeat offenses, using New York as a model. The New York law, however, had the notoriety of being the only statute to impose a (1) mandatory, (2) natural life sentence for (3) any fourth felony offense. New York soon backed off the life sentencing provision, however, and other states followed.[26]

We should recognize in events such as the Baumes Law less a divergence in the actual practice of life without parole sentencing than a particular way of using life without parole (or natural life) sentencing as a symbolic tool.[27] For even though a natural life sentence could ultimately result in release through clemency, presentations such as those related to the Baumes Law invoked the sentence as one that would keep someone in prison until death.[28] Such extreme declarations defied general practice, but the primary aim of such explicit invocations of lifetime sentences was more immediate: an announcement of reassurance in a time of crisis. The life-until-death sentence could be a political act, a promise of safety as spectacle.

The Baumes Law life sentence may be seen in addition, much like Raymond's vision of a perpetual workhouse, as a form of internal banishment that was a secondary approach for a select few, not the norm. As Senator Baumes himself wrote, the purpose of the mandatory life for a fourth strike provision was "not punishment at all, but ... protection to the public ... [from the] incurable."[29] Such an exceptionally severe sentence had to be justified, and the law's proponents did so by bifurcating criminal types: the "embryonic criminal" distinguished from the "one who has passed beyond the embryonic stage"; the "old fashioned burglar," an amateur, from the "modern type of criminal," a careerist.[30]

To recapitulate, one historical lineage of life without parole is a precursor: a form in which life without parole was differentiated principally by the structural feature of which penal actor had discretion over release. Here is another historical lineage of life without parole: an explicit appeal to life imprisonment as a claim of societal banishment. A politics of solidarity against a background of public insecurity results in calls for natural life sentences that serve as public promises, symbolic reassurances of no release from prison. In this regard, one finds historical traces of acts that resemble contemporary US practices: promises of harsher punishment for dramatic political effect. Accordingly, we might consider this second lineage as something of a *prototype* for LWOP, rather than a precursor. Prior to the 1970s, acts such as these were occasional and belied the general practice and understanding of life without parole, but they represent what would become a common form in the final decades of the century.

AT THE PRECIPICE

For much of the twentieth century, the indeterminate sentencing paradigm— favoring open-ended sentences, review for release, and parole—prevailed in the United States. The fifty-one jurisdictions did not uniformly adopt a treatment-and-release philosophy, yet this paradigm set a tone, influencing the practices and prevailing understandings of penal policy.[31] This perspective, in which the prison was principally a temporary station for reform, from which people could make a case for release, reached its apex in the late 1950s and early 1960s. Prison programming at the time was diverse (including music, education, sports) and more than ever prisoner led. Parole, time credits for good behavior, and furloughs (day trips to a workplace or shelter off prison grounds) helped usher the incarcerated toward release. Perhaps most of all, its ascendance was reflected in a series of model penal codes that proposed ever-shorter sentence lengths for criminal offenses. The Model Penal Code (1962), the Model Sentencing Act (1963), the Standard Probation and Parole Act (1964), the Standard Act for State Correctional Services (1966), the Manual of Correctional Standards (1966), and the American Bar Association Standards on Sentencing Alternatives and Procedures (1968) all recommended that people serving life sentences be considered for parole after ten years or even immediately.[32]

Yet in just a few years, at the beginning of the 1970s, American punishment would stand at something of a crossroads. On one side was the current in punishment generally favoring rehabilitation of individuals and reduction of prison terms that had stood for decades. On the other side, to come, was mass incarceration, the largest-scale imprisonment in modern history, featuring a shift in laws and practices toward longer sentences, restrictive release practices, and a turn in penal philosophy away from rehabilitation toward retribution, deterrence, and incapacitation. As far as the death penalty was concerned, the late 1960s and early 1970s saw it crawl to a halt with a nationwide moratorium on executions in 1967 and the United States Supreme Court invalidating all death penalty statutes in 1972, only to be reborn a few years later, narrower and more closely regulated, but also used more frequently than before.

TABLE 1. Forms of Life Sentences without Parole by
State, January 1972

"Life without Parole" in Criminal Statute	Limitations on Review of Life Sentences in Parole Statute	
	All Life Sentences	Select Crimes
California	Arizona	Colorado
Michigan	Arkansas	Hawaii
Mississippi	Indiana	Idaho
Nevada	Iowa	Kentucky
South Dakota	Louisiana	Maryland
West Virginia	Nebraska	Massachusetts
	Oklahoma	Michigan
	Pennsylvania	Mississippi
	South Dakota	Ohio
	Vermont	West Virginia
	Wyoming	

Sources: Author's research; Edwin Powers, *Parole Eligibility of Prisoners Serving a Life Sentence,* 2nd ed. (Boston: Massachusetts Correctional Association, 1972).

A report prepared by Edwin Powers for the Massachusetts Department of Corrections in the early 1970s offers a unique glimpse of the laws, practices, and general sensibilities concerning release for lifers at this moment on the eve of the mass incarceration era. Whereas several states authorized natural life sentences in their criminal codes, according to Powers's study, based on a national survey of corrections departments, more than twenty had parole-code provisions restricting parole for all or a subset of lifers, requiring the governor to commute before a lifer could be paroled or use good time credits (table 1).[33] The latter type of law followed a variety of arrangements according to which a governor and an advisory executive agency (usually a board of pardons) reviewed applications, sometimes on recommendation from prison administrators, with varying degrees of formality.[34] A majority of the states precluding parole reported that life sentences were commuted in practice, and that release happened on average, depending on the state, after between seven and twenty years. Even in the historically punitive southern region, the great majority of life sentences, with or without parole, carried a reasonable possibility of release, generally after a decade of imprisonment.[35]

In this context, legal and penal practitioners well understood that a life sentence was likely to result in release. That meaning had been ingrained over decades of practice and was in line with the times. To fully appreciate how little life without parole registered on the radar of legal and penal practitioners, one must also consider then-emerging concerns with prison finances and overcrowding, which favored shorter terms.[36] Those concerns were acute in southern states with relatively underdeveloped, nascent, and decentralized corrections administrations that were facing federal court interventions over the conditions of confinement.[37]

The upshot is that, in the early 1970s, the notion of keeping people imprisoned forever was out of step—not inconceivable, but certainly not the norm. For those serving a life sentence it was reasonable to assume, if not expect, that release was a real possibility, by whichever mechanism, at some point. As French jurist Jean Bouhier wrote of imprisonment in the mid-eighteenth century, "Ordinary justice makes no use of this kind of sentence."[38] The same could have been said of perpetual imprisonment in the United States in 1970. Where life without parole sentences were authorized, this did not extinguish the sentiment of rehabilitation. The zeitgeist still favored review and release.

3. The Phenomenon to Be Explained

As the preceding chapter sets out, at the beginning of the 1970s life without parole sentences were relatively rare, most statutes authorizing life without parole (also rare) were in parole codes (not crime codes), and life without parole sentences offered a reasonable chance for release (via executive clemency). Things looked much different by the end of the century. By then, life without parole sentencing had become a common practice with a distinctly different meaning than it carried in earlier periods. Still today, it is understood as a sentence until death. Subsequent chapters embark on granular investigations of this transformation. This chapter sets a foundation by presenting a preliminary picture of life without parole in the contemporary United States—that is, of LWOP, a punishment understood to be perpetual confinement, which is widespread, prevalent, and routine.

The chapter presents a profile of LWOP in two ways. First, a case study witnesses LWOP in action, providing an opportunity to observe the nature of its practices and how key actors understand it. I take a well-known case, *Graham v. Florida*, upon which the United States Supreme Court ruled in 2010, determining that the Eighth Amendment prohibits LWOP sentences for persons less than eighteen years of age at the time of the crime.[1] For present purposes, however, it is not *Graham*'s holding that is most important. Rather, it is what the proceedings in *Graham* convey about the practice of LWOP in the first decade of the twenty-first century, when Graham was sentenced and the appeals from that judgment were litigated. The *Graham* litigation also offers vantage points from which we can see the competing meanings that different parties later attached to the context in which LWOP laws were introduced in the mid- to late 1990s. Both aspects—the acts of the 2000s and the memories of the 1990s—are helpful in grasping a picture of the practice and meaning of LWOP in the contemporary United States.

Whereas the first part of the chapter theorizes the inner workings of LWOP, the second charts its external marks. To obtain a bird's-eye view of how LWOP is used across the United States, I complement existing statistics on the number of people serving LWOP by jurisdiction over time with original research on LWOP's use in state and federal laws.[2] Together, these data provide an empirical map of the timing, scope, and prevalence of LWOP since the 1970s. The survey evinces variety across states and regions that are often found similar with respect to penal policy, prompting one to reconsider prevailing ideas about LWOP and highlighting the need for research into the proximate causes and conditions of LWOP's rise.

Each of these profiles sets a foundation for the remaining chapters by defining the contours of the phenomenon those chapters explain. The profiles also provide a basis for reconsidering everyday impressions about LWOP sentencing, prompting us to dispel preconceptions and take a closer look at the substance as well as the limits of what we know.[3]

AN EXEMPLARY CASE

The US Supreme Court has held that children should be treated differently for purposes of the Eighth Amendment. In *Roper v. Simmons* (2005), *Graham v. Florida* (2010), *Miller v. Alabama* (2012), and *Montgomery v. Louisiana* (2016), the Court recognized that children are less culpable, are more prone to impulsivity and persuasion, and possess a greater capacity for maturity and personal development than adults. Children cannot, accordingly, be sentenced to LWOP for nonhomicide crimes (*Graham*) and only in the rarest instances for homicide offenses (*Miller*).

The *Graham-Miller* mandate is now widely known. The story of Terrance Graham's sentencing, like the stories of the litigants who accompanied him and those that followed, is less so. Graham's sentencing proceeding and the ensuing litigation bear revisiting, however, for they show much about life without parole in the early twenty-first century. By the time Graham's case reached the US Supreme Court, it concerned more than a sixteen-year-old's crimes and foreshortened future; it was a referendum on a sentencing practice that crystallized years before.

The Sentencing Proceeding: LWOP in Action

In the summer of 2006, Judge Lance Day of Florida's Fourth Judicial Circuit adjudicated punishment for (then) seventeen-year-old Terrance Graham. Graham had pled guilty on a previous indictment to burglary with assault, and the sentencing court had withheld judgment, ordering Graham to serve three years of probation and twelve months in pretrial detention. Graham was released from detention after six months. Several months later, however, he violated probation, committing an armed home invasion robbery with two accomplices, followed by a high-speed chase as Graham and his companions attempted to evade police. Charged as an adult for attempted robbery with a weapon, Graham, now before Judge Day, again admitted wrongdoing. Having pled guilty to two felonies, he faced a discretionary sentence within a surprisingly broad range: a minimum of five years to a maximum of life without parole.[4]

Judge Day heard testimony from multiple witnesses concerning the young Graham's crimes. The court received a letter from Terrance Graham's mother asserting that she could provide a supportive living situation for her son.[5] Graham wrote a statement of his own emphasizing how much his mother and family members needed him. After reading his statement to the court, Graham concluded, "Your Honor, I do ask for a second chance."[6]

The presentence report recommended the minimum sentence, five years. The prosecution asked for substantially more: thirty years on the first crime and fifteen on the second, for a total of forty-five years. Judge Day, however, had something else in mind:

> Mr. Graham, as I look back on your case, yours is really candidly a sad situation. You had, as far as I can tell you have quite a family structure. You had a lot of people who wanted to try and help you get your life turned around including the court system, and you had a judge [on the first case] who took the step to try and give you direction through his probation order to give you a chance to get back onto track. And at the time you seemed through your letters that that is exactly what you wanted to do. And I don't know why it is that you threw your life away. I don't know why.
>
> But you did, and that is what is so sad about this today is that you have actually been given a chance to get through this, the original charge[s], which were very serious charges to begin with. The burglary with assault charge is an extremely serious charge. The attempted robbery with a weapon was a very serious charge. . . .
>
> And in less than two years . . . here you are . . . standing before me, literally the—facing a life sentence as to—up to life as to count 1 and up to 15 years as to count 2. And I don't understand why you would be given such a great opportunity to do something with your life and why you would throw it away. The only thing that I can rationalize is that you decided that this is how you were going to lead your life and that there is nothing that we can do for you. And as the state pointed out, that this is an escalating pattern of criminal conduct on your part and that we

can't help you any further. We can't do anything to deter you. This is the way you are going to lead your life, and I don't know why you are going to. You've made that decision. I have no idea. But, evidently, that is what you decided to do.

So then it becomes a focus, if I can't do anything to help you, if I can't do anything to get you back on the right path, then I have to start focusing on the community and trying to protect the community from your actions. And, unfortunately, that is where we are today is I don't see where I can do anything to help you any further. You've evidently decided this is the direction you're going to take in life, and it's unfortunate that you made that choice.

I have reviewed the statute. I don't see where any further juvenile sanctions would be appropriate. I don't see where any youthful offender sanctions would be appropriate. Given your escalating pattern of criminal conduct, it is apparent to the Court that you have decided that this is the way you are going to live your life and that the only thing I can do now is to try and protect the community from your actions.[7]

With those words, the judge imposed the maximum: life without parole.

Graham appealed, claiming the sentence was cruel and unusual punishment because he was not an adult when he committed the crimes. As Graham's legal challenges worked their way through the courts, the case took on broad interest. Human rights organizations mobilized in support of Graham. Some states backed Florida. Eventually, following a series of decisions in the state and lower federal courts, Graham's appeal was accepted on certiorari to the Supreme Court of the United States.

The arguments presented in the briefs before the US Supreme Court provide not only statements about the practice and meaning of LWOP in 2006 (when Judge Day sentenced Graham) and 2010 (when the Supreme Court litigation took place), but also representations of the context in which LWOP laws had been forged decades before. In the arguments of the parties and amici, one finds competing views of LWOP's history, divergent collective memories of the history of juvenile life without parole. As the litigants situated the case in the context of larger social and penal processes, they characterized LWOP's function in very different ways.

Memory 1: Essential Artillery in a Successful Crime Fight

The state of Florida's brief to the US Supreme Court begins not with an account of the crime, which is common in appellate briefs, but instead by presenting the historical backdrop for the law. The brief situates the law under which Graham was convicted in the context of a broader penal strategy. A rash of youth criminal activity was sweeping the United States in the early 1990s. It was a time of "escalating and violent crime," and reform of juvenile justice toward harsher punishment was called for widely. Florida's governor, finding juvenile violent crime "threatening the state's bedrock tourism industry," and intent on being a national leader in juvenile justice, called for a special legislative session.[8] The result was a juvenile justice reform in 1994 that established a scheme for juvenile transfers to adult court and guidelines for sentencing children in certain cases, including "violent" nonhomicide felonies, as adults.[9]

Florida acted vigorously on the new laws. As the state proudly reported to the US Supreme Court, "ninety-four percent of Florida's 301 juvenile offenders currently serving life without parole were sentenced for crimes committed in the 1990s or later."[10] The 1994 juvenile justice reforms were, further, part of a general effort to deter serious crime that culminated in a revised penal code and "a massive and accelerated prison construction program, resulting in more corrections institutions opening in the 1990s than in any other decades before or since."[11] In sum, LWOP for children was an essential part of a deliberate strategy to deter violent crime. Florida saw itself as uniquely plagued by youth crime and simultaneously part of a national consensus. Moreover, the state declared, the strategy had worked: "violent crime rates plummeted from their 1990s highs."[12]

Before the US Supreme Court in 2010, Florida presented a massive list of felony crimes for which LWOP could be imposed:

Fla. Stat. §§ 499.0051(10) (knowing sale of contraband prescription drugs resulting in death); 775.0823, 782.04, & 782.051(1) (degrees of murder & attempted murder); 775.0823(8), 787.01, & 787.02 (kidnapping and false imprisonment); 775.084(4)(a) (habitual felony offender convicted of life or first-degree felony); 775.085(1) (committing first-degree felony while evidencing prejudice); 775.0861 (committing first degree felony involving physical force or violence on religious property or during victim's participation in religious service); 775.087 (various offenses for possessing or discharging a firearm or destructive device); 775.0875(2) (taking an officer's firearm during first-degree felony); 775.31(1)(e) (facilitating terrorism); 790.16(1) (discharging machine gun in public with intent to do harm); 790.161 (destructive device causing death); 790.166(2) (using or making available weapon of mass destruction); 790.23(4) (if repeat offender, carrying a weapon while committing gang-related crime); 794.011 & 794.023 (various sexual battery); 810.02(2) (burglary with assault or battery, armed burglary, variety of burglaries causing damage to building); 812.13(2)(a) (armed robbery); 812.133(2)(a) (armed carjacking); 812.135(2)(a) (armed home invasion); 817.487 (first-degree felony committed in conjunction with tampering with caller identification system in order to deceive call recipient); 817.568(10) (first-degree felony offense committed while unlawfully using personal identification information while misrepresenting self as law enforcement officer); 843.167(3)(e) (interception of police communication to aid escape from first-degree felony); 874.04(2)(c) (criminal street gang activity); 874.10 (leading a gang); 876.38 (intentional interference with defense or prosecution of war); 893.135 (various offenses for trafficking, importing, or manufacturing illegal drugs); 914.22 (tampering with a witness in a first-degree felony case/investigation).[13]

From this list alone, it is palpable why Florida today leads the nation in LWOP sentences. The scope of crimes for which LWOP is punishment is vast, the number of laws authorizing LWOP voluminous. The breadth of LWOP in Florida is amplified even more when one considers, as the state's brief goes on to emphasize, that "about half, 150 of 301, of the juvenile offenders serving life sentences in Florida [are doing so] for a *non-homicide* offense."[14] As such, the state's answer to Graham's challenge under the cruel and unusual punishment clause of the Eighth Amendment was that a juvenile LWOP sentence for armed robbery was not unusual at all.

Briefs filed in litigation are arguments crafted for success, in which litigants frame issues strategically to best bring that about. As legal briefs go about telling stories as persuasively as possible, sometimes about events decades in the past, they present institutionalized memories that serve as a foundation for contemporary legal reasoning.[15] The state's brief in *Graham* offers one such memory, representing how the state in the twenty-first century understood its penal policy of the 1990s and, more specifically, how it placed juvenile LWOP sentencing in that frame. The state's brief was, equally, a monument of where LWOP sentencing in Florida ended up years later at the time of Graham's sentencing and in the first decades of the new millennium.

Memory 2: Moral Panic and Racialized Social Control

The narrative Florida presented in *Graham* would be reiterated two years later by Alabama in a case considering LWOP sentences for children convicted of homicide.[16] The litigation in *Miller v. Alabama* (2012), however, also supplied a counternarrative. Whereas the states continued to tell a story of violent juvenile crime and youth gangs sweeping the country, to which they had responded in the mid-1990s by hardening juvenile prosecution and sentencing laws, the separate amicus briefs of the NAACP Legal Defense and Educational Fund et al. (NAACP) and, collectively, forty-six criminal justice scholars, presented an account of stereotyping and racial fear. Dispelling the states' narrative as fantasy, the NAACP and scholars' briefs dismissed the validity of the very phenomenon that Florida and Alabama pointed to as a basis for enacting juvenile LWOP. John DiIulio, a political scientist and scholar responsible for much of the academic contribution to the moral panic around youth crime in the 1990s, was now a signatory on the scholars' brief, dismissing his earlier prediction of an inevitable juvenile crime wave as scientifically unfounded racist mythology.[17]

The scholars' brief acknowledged high levels of gun violence by youth in the late 1980s and early 1990s. The scholars also recognized a national wave of legislation between 1992 and 1999 in which nearly every state and the federal jurisdiction moved to sentence more juveniles as adults and in doing so exposed many youths to sentences of life without parole.[18] The scholars explained, however, that the panic and ensuing legislation were anchored in an imaginary figure, the "superpredator":

> radically impulsive, brutally remorseless youngsters, including ever more preteenage boys, who murder, assault, rape, rob, burglarize, deal deadly drugs, join gun-toting gangs, and create serious communal disorders. They do not fear the stigma of arrest, the pains of imprisonment, or the pangs of conscience. They perceive hardly any relationship between doing right (or wrong) now and being rewarded (or punished) for it later. To these mean-street youngsters, the words "right" and "wrong" have no fixed moral meaning.[19]

Insofar as the superpredator narrative saw deterrence as impossible, it carried with it a future prediction of great violence, to which the only perceived available response was permanent incapacitation. However, the feared "demographic time bomb"[20] of criminal activity was vastly overstated and based on inconsistent projection techniques and faulty calculations. In fact, just as the superpredator rhetoric reached a crescendo, youth homicide rates began their largest drop in modern history.[21] It should be no surprise that the prediction turned out to be myth, the scholars urged, because science shows that children have a great capacity for change and maturation. The generation of purported superpredators aged out of crime, just as their predecessors had done.[22]

Although the predicted generation of violent youth failed to materialize, it nevertheless captured the popular imagination and created a heated political climate that altered prevailing public attitudes about youth convicted of crimes.[23] The NAACP brief in *Miller* highlights how central race was to the superpredator narrative and ensuing laws: "Throughout the late 1980s and early to mid-1990s, the media, academics and politicians consistently characterized teen crime in racially coded terms."[24] Racial stereotyping fueled the hysteria and shaped the mythology. When the media reported juvenile crime, it often did so by showing youth of color, and when it reported on youth of color it did so preponderantly with respect to crime.[25] In the public consciousness, the term "superpredator" became code for young Black men, evoking race-based sentiments without explicitly mentioning race. Accordingly, the resulting disproportionality in juvenile sentencing—with Black youth comprising 60 percent of those serving life without parole—could have been expected.[26]

The briefs from the juvenile LWOP cases, in sum, present two very different memories of what generated LWOP laws—specifically, a surge of juvenile LWOP laws—in the mid-1990s. On the one hand was a racialized moral panic, which should be recognized as an immoral mistake and undone; on the other hand was a necessarily punitive and ultimately successful solution to a crime problem, an accomplishment that states regarded with pride. The following section works from the examples of the *Graham* sentencing courtroom and the US Supreme Court litigation to distill defining characteristics of LWOP in the early twenty-first century.

ANATOMY OF LWOP

When I say the *Graham* case is exemplary, the point is not that it perfectly represents every case in which LWOP is administered in the United States. To name one obvious way in which it cannot do so, the case is limited to youth, while the vast majority of people serving LWOP sentences committed crimes when they were older than eighteen. The point rather is that by looking at the sentencing proceeding, as well as the litigation narratives that subsequently built up around it, one can begin to delineate the practices, meanings, and social processes that define LWOP in the twenty-first century. The following sections work from that material to begin to theorize what LWOP sentencing is. By "theorizing LWOP," I mean abstracting elements and relations from the empirical data that help define LWOP, how it is used, and how its practice differs from the style of life without parole sentencing that came before. Theorizing LWOP also involves considering how perpetual confinement, in the form of LWOP (and more), is situated in contemporary American punishment. This book is principally concerned with the emergence of what we know as LWOP and, along with it, perpetual confinement as it is practiced in the United States. To engage in this project, we need to have a preliminary understanding of the object at the end point.

A Perpetual Sentence

Whereas in the earlier twentieth century the life without parole sentence reflected an interest in placing release decisions about some of the most serious criminals in the hands of the governor, and commutation served alongside parole as a way of managing prison overcrowding and acknowledging individual rehabilitation and reform, in the twenty-first century LWOP is far from a punishment denoting executive responsibility for penal administration.

As the sentencing proceedings and briefs in *Graham* make clear, there was little question about how many years Graham would serve and little debate about the opportunities he would have for review for release. If the sentencing had taken place decades earlier, one might have thought the judge was merely being performative, offering the victims a stronger sense of justice and closure even while the sentence had a reasonable chance of being commuted at a later date. But in 2010 that was surely not the case, as commutation of a life sentence had not happened recently in Florida. So the imposition of sentence was in a sense a goodbye, the exclusion of Graham from free society. The intent was that he would stay in prison until death, that he would have no official opportunities for review or release.

This understanding of LWOP, which pervades the proceedings in Graham's case, was also the understanding of state actors in Florida and elsewhere throughout the United States in the mid-1990s when they enacted laws authorizing LWOP for children convicted of violent crimes. LWOP is permanent incapacitation.

A Widespread Practice

Life without parole sentencing did not exist in Florida until 1983, and not for juveniles in Florida until the mid-1990s. By the time Judge Day sentenced Terrance Graham in 2006, however, LWOP sentencing in Florida had burgeoned: dozens of laws had been passed authorizing it, sometimes as mandatory punishment, for an array of crimes. Florida was not alone, and it was not only legislators, governors, and judges who used LWOP. Prosecutors employed LWOP as a charging and plea-bargaining tool; crime victims and victims' advocates sought out LWOP as justice; the anti–death penalty movement saw LWOP as a viable route to abolition; and capital defense lawyers advocated for LWOP for their clients and claimed it as a victory. Between the early 1990s and the end of the first decade of the twenty-first century, the number of people serving LWOP in the United States rose by tens of thousands, and their proportion of the prison population rose as well. In other words, LWOP did not simply expand with the tide of US punishment; it obtained a larger share.[27]

Indeed, it is noteworthy that the primary focus in the *Graham* litigation is not LWOP itself but youth: juvenile culpability, juvenile responsibility, the neurobiology of youth, and the workings of the juvenile justice system, including mandatory transfers to adult courts. In fact, the crux of the state's argument in support of Graham's sentence was that use of LWOP was widespread. The states' briefs in *Graham* and *Miller* present transfers of juvenile defendants to adult court and juvenile LWOP sentencing as things nearly every state did in the mid- to late 1990s. Far from being an outlier, juvenile LWOP sentencing was a deliberate strategy that garnered consensus across the United States and even bridged political divides. The same is true of LWOP for adults. In 1991 the state of Michigan (with support from other states as amici) made a similar argument regarding the war on drugs: LWOP was essential to prevent escalating drug crime, and on this the states had reached consensus. When the US Supreme Court upheld the drug law in *Harmelin v. Michigan* it signaled approval of LWOP for an array of crimes.[28]

Graham and its progeny leave intact the broad reach of LWOP for adults. In the early twenty-first century, if the severity of the LWOP sentence is a given, so is its widespread presence.[29] *Graham* upset the application of LWOP for children, but not the significant role LWOP plays in state penal policy. Put another way, *Graham* is a case about prosecuting and punishing children as adults, not a referendum on LWOP as punishment for serious and violent (or even nonviolent) crimes.

A Routine Practice

The act of sentencing in *Graham* marked the beginning of a perpetual imprisonment, a shattering break in Terrance Graham's life course.[30] However, Judge Day's sentencing of Graham simultaneously treated the imposition of LWOP as *routine*. It was an everyday affair in a local courtroom. The court's decision was not expected to have broad political effect. This was not a performance for public consumption. Neither the crimes nor the sentencing proceedings were network news.[31] While the words the court used were indeed dramatic, if the delivery of sentence was theater, it was a private performance before an audience including the victims who testified, Graham, his family, and courtroom personnel. It was the standard responsibility of the bench to make a decision of this magnitude: just as the court could have issued a sentence as low as five years, it could have issued a sentence of perpetual imprisonment, and anything in between. The decision that a person would never be released from prison before death was carried out as a matter of course.

Reversing Graham's LWOP sentence four years later, the US Supreme Court faulted the sentencing court for ignoring the unique frailties of youth: youth are prone to impulsivity and peer persuasion and possess a great capacity for development and maturity (Judge Day patently ignored the latter, as he deemed Graham's future and future behavior fixed). But the US Supreme Court did not censure the nature of the process itself, in which permanent incapacitation was doled out after a hearing that lasted a matter of hours, in which the court exercised discretion along a scale that had at the low end a term of as little as five years. The *Graham* proceeding, in its brevity and its matter-of-factness, is simply one example of how routine LWOP sentencing has become in the United States. And by routine I do not mean that LWOP sentencing happens a lot, although it does. I mean that when it happens it does so in the same sort of proceeding in which a judge would administer a five-year sentence. LWOP sentencing, as such, stands in stark contrast to the monthlong trials and exceptional media attention that take place around the death penalty. An LWOP sentence is not a spectacle.

A Crisis Narrative

Although Graham's sentencing took place in a local forum, the act had much in common with statements about LWOP taking place on grander stages, such as legislative debates and state of the state addresses. Whether a matter of sentencing or lawmaking, "acts of LWOP" share certain characteristics. The notion of a moral panic generally, the superpredator scare, and the specific example of the sentencing court in the *Graham* case begin from a common framing. Each is a situation in which it appears that all available alternatives have failed; a political call to action is made when nothing else will work. Legislators and governors in the mid-1990s portrayed the incorrigible superpredator as an unmitigated risk for whom no punishment short of total incapacitation would do. The Baumes Law had framed the situation in a similar way: crime continued to rise and preventive strategies had failed. On a smaller stage and a century later, Judge Day was following the script: the system has given you (Graham) a chance, your family has given you (Graham) a chance; all had been tried and failed. Defining the circumstance as Graham's choice, the court simultaneously declared its own inability, the state's inability, to resolve the situation. There was nothing left to do but incapacitate.

A situation in which the state faces an apparently unresolvable problem may be characterized as a crisis—generally speaking, "a time of intense

difficulty, trouble, or danger," "a time when a difficult or important decision must be made."[32] Crime control and punishment in the last quarter of
the twentieth century in the United States was depicted as an ongoing crisis.
Responding to rising crime rates, crime fears, and substantial doubts about
the criminal legal system in the 1970s and 1980s, some penal actors refused
to acknowledge the known limits of state punishment (e.g., that severe punishments do not deter[33]) and piled on punitive sanctions. The war on drugs
is a perennial example of such "acting out" in which lawmakers, recognizing
their limited capacity to change criminal activity, were most intent on reassuring the public.[34]

A key attribute of crisis narratives, which are less accurate descriptions
of a situation than strategic framings, is to make possible a way of doing
things that otherwise would not be expected or permitted. Social theorist
and anthropologist Janet Roitman recognizes crisis labeling as inherently
involving a normative judgment that marks a new point of orientation, in
which the state of crisis itself is offered as a new normal. By wiping the
slate clean, in effect, a declaration of crisis enables and justifies a new situational framing that may be dramatically different than the immediately
preceding frame, "allow[ing] certain questions to be asked while others are
foreclosed."[35]

Prototypical uses of LWOP such as the Baumes Law possess the quality that Roitman describes: declaring a state of crisis reset the foundation
of penal norms, opening the door to perpetual confinement. The expected
wave of superpredators in the 1990s also served this rebooting quality. In
Graham we see the same crisis narrative, yet the situation is not so fraught.
The throwing up of hands is real, but the circumstance routine. The element
of crisis around violent juvenile crime that began in the 1990s continued
twenty years later, pared down to an everyday sentencing practice.[36]

A Discriminatory Process

Swift actions taken in circumstances of insecurity and uncertainty tend
to be defensive and exclusionary.[37] The history of the superpredator laws,
articulated in the *Graham* and *Miller* briefs and elsewhere, establishes that
racial fear and stereotyping drove this wave of legislation. The purported
threat posed by an entire generation of young Black men precipitated a classic moral panic.[38] So the result, a disproportionate number of Black youth
sentenced under the laws, was hardly a surprise.

The *Graham* sentencing proceeding illustrates how the racially stereo-
typed superpredator profile, which Florida animated in the 1990s to justify
its juvenile LWOP laws, is still alive in the twenty-first century. Before the

US Supreme Court, both parties in *Graham* agreed that the crime wave that spurred the mid-1990s legislation and exposed children to LWOP did not exist at the time of Graham's sentencing (although their historical interpretations differed, as discussed earlier). Yet those laws were still on the books. Graham was sentenced under one. The superpredator scare may be long gone, but the racial stereotypes and biases that drove that moral panic are not. In sum, a real increase in juvenile crime rates over a five- to seven-year period in the 1990s, paired with racialized hysteria generated by a synergy of media accounts, academic theories, and political rhetoric, led to decades of oversentencing children based on race. The specific context in which that typecasting arose has passed, but the type itself has not.

Graham, having committed crimes—crimes that could have been punished by a relatively short term of years—was, as a young Black man, especially susceptible to perpetual imprisonment. Discrimination inflects the criminal legal system at many turns. Some laws, such as the superpredator laws, are expressly products of racial bias; other sources of discrimination and prejudice are distributed throughout the system in ways that are less obvious and more easily ignored. There are many decision points at which racial assumptions, perceptions, and preferences—including those that link race to criminality[39]—affect the outcome: the development of a penal policy proposal, a legislator's argument or vote on sentencing legislation, decisions about the manner in which to police a certain neighborhood, a law enforcement officer's suspicion about whom to stop and frisk, a prosecutor's charging decision, a jury's verdict, a judge's imposition of sentence, a parole board's decision about readiness for release, and the differential impacts of pretrial detention on the poor and the impacts of a prior criminal record throughout. Consequently, those most likely to bear the brunt of punitive lawmaking are poor and non-White Americans.[40] This is beyond a matter of who commits crime; it is a matter of how a person, having committed a crime, is punished. Black-on-White crime tends to be punished more harshly, and racial disparities tend to increase with the severity of sentence and may be greatest among prisoners serving the longest terms.[41] When one sees a disproportionate percentage of Black men serving LWOP sentences for third-degree murder (as in Pennsylvania) or a large percentage of women serving LWOP sentences convicted as accomplices to felony murder (as in California), these mechanisms are at work. The vulnerability of Terrance Graham, a Black teen, finds a specific historical precedent in the prior use of perpetual imprisonment. For centuries, perpetual confinement has been used as a threat to push people to reform and accepted as a last resort when they do not, a backstop for people deemed disposable. This is a part of its legacy.

TOPOGRAPHY OF LWOP

If *Graham* offers a starting point to examine the meaning and practice of LWOP as a sentencing device in contemporary American punishment, then prison population statistics and laws present another vantage point, revealing how LWOP appears on the surface of the penal system. To date, scholars and analysts have relied primarily on prison population data to measure LWOP's striking expansion.[42] LWOP's expansion is also, however, reflected in laws authorizing life without parole sentences. Since the 1980s, hundreds of these laws have passed nationwide.[43] On both fronts, populations and laws, state- and regional-level patterns deserve closer attention, as there has been substantial variance in LWOP's use since the early 1970s.[44]

Considering the patterns of another ultimate punishment, the death penalty, one might approach LWOP with certain expectations. In the modern death penalty era—since *Gregg v. Georgia* (1976) reinstated the death penalty after *Furman v. Georgia* (1972) invalidated it—approximately two-thirds of the states have had the death penalty at any given time. Capital punishment has been used most commonly in southern and southwestern states (and in certain northern states with a punitive bent, such as Pennsylvania). Given the strong regional character of patterns of death sentences and executions, the distribution of capital punishment across states has been attributed in significant part to regional political and cultural histories, such as a southern legacy of slavery and lynching undergirding a singular passion for the death penalty. For years the numbers on death sentences and executions painted a largely regional picture.[45]

As with capital punishment, with LWOP a few states do most of the work (figure 6). As of 2020, six jurisdictions comprised nearly 60 percent of the nearly 56,000 LWOP sentences in the United States: Florida (10,438), Pennsylvania (5,375), California (5,134), Louisiana (4,377), Michigan (3,882), and the federal system (3,536). The top dozen LWOP-sentencing jurisdictions (add Georgia, Virginia, Illinois, Mississippi, North Carolina, and Alabama) accounted for more than three-quarters of the national total. By contrast, in more than half of the states, fewer than 500 people were serving LWOP.[46]

Yet in contrast to modern capital punishment, with LWOP there is no immediately recognizable regional pattern. One might expect LWOP to thrive in the South as capital punishment has. Yet while LWOP flourishes in some southern states, including Florida, Louisiana, and Alabama, it is used far less in others. Texas did not authorize LWOP until 2005, and while the number of LWOP sentences in Texas has grown noticeably since then,

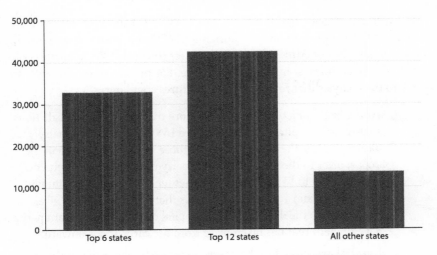

FIGURE 6.   States with largest numbers of prisoners serving LWOP, 2020.
Source: Ashley Nellis, *No End in Sight: America's Enduring Reliance on Life Imprisonment* (Washington, DC: The Sentencing Project, 2021).

the state continues to administer LWOP for a relatively narrow range of crimes.

If LWOP shares with the death penalty the quality of being an ultimate punishment, however, there are also good reasons to think that LWOP would present a different picture. For one thing, insofar as LWOP plays the role of a death penalty alternative, it may be unattractive to tough-on-crime politicians and death penalty proponents, despite its severity. Further, LWOP is not the only means of imposing perpetual confinement. As discussed previously, very long determinate terms of years may serve a similar purpose. As such, the absence of a punishment formally named "life without parole" or "natural life" does not necessarily mean that perpetual confinement is not practiced; it may well be, only under a different name or in a different form. In fact, if one adds the number of people serving LWOP sentences to the number of people serving virtual life sentences, Texas and Florida are on a par, even though Florida's use of LWOP sentences greatly outnumbers that of Texas.[47]

Another difference deserves mention: under the Eighth Amendment, the modern death penalty is strictly limited to aggravated homicide. Accordingly, the range of conduct the death penalty punishes is similar in every state. Not so with LWOP. As LWOP may be authorized for many crimes, states vary in how they use it.[48] State patterns show variance along three key vectors: (a) the *time of adoption* of LWOP; (b) the *prevalence* of the sanction (i.e., number of laws authorizing LWOP and prisoners sentenced); and (c) the *scope* of crimes and crime statuses to which LWOP applies. We should take an interest in this multivalence. For present purposes, with an eye to the analysis that follows, several features stand out:

1. At the beginning of the 1990s, no more than half of the jurisdictions that retained capital punishment used LWOP as a death penalty alternative. Further, a half dozen of those states had done so in the 1960s, prior to the modern death penalty era.[49] Comparatively few states turned to LWOP as a backup sentence to capital punishment in the 1970s and 1980s. The upshot is that the onset of LWOP as an alternative to the death penalty in capital cases is in significant part a development that has taken place from the early 1990s onward.[50]

2. LWOP laws surged in the 1990s, in part a function of tough-on-crime laws.[51] Prison population data also show large increases in LWOP from the early 1990s onward. Over the eight-year period between 1984 and 1992, the number of prisoners serving LWOP increased by approximately 9,000; between 1992 and 2002, the number of prisoners serving LWOP increased by approximately 20,000, more than twice as much.[52]

3. Despite the significant growth of LWOP from the 1990s onward, thousands of LWOP sentences were already in place by the early 1990s. The six jurisdictions that now lead the nation in LWOP population are *precisely the same jurisdictions that led the LWOP population* in 1992 (although in a different order, see figures 7 and 8).[53] This indicates that by the end of the 1980s, before widespread use of LWOP in the capital punishment arena and prior to the tough-on-crime surge of the mid-1990s, a foundation had been built in state law and policy that set a course for future patterns in LWOP sentencing. In short, significant arrangements that shape how states use LWOP today were already in place by the early 1990s.

One can see from these patterns that narratives about anti–death penalty activism and tough-on-crime laws driving LWOP say much about the 1990s onward. They say less, however, about what happened before, which is significant. Legal enactments and population patterns alone cannot tell us how that foundation was laid. The lack of clear regional features suggests, too, that the manner in which states use LWOP may have less to do with the

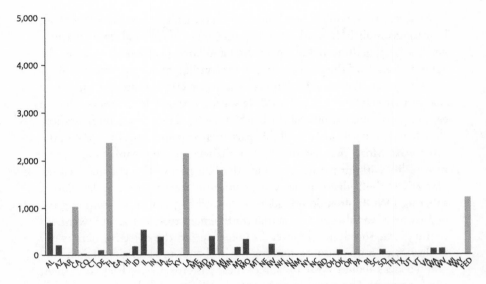

FIGURE 7. Prisoners serving LWOP by US jurisdiction, 1992. *Note:* Alaska, Indiana, and Maryland did not provide data. *Source:* Kathleen Maguire, Ann L. Pastore, and Timothy J. Flanagan, *Sourcebook of Criminal Justice Statistics* (Washington, DC: Bureau of Justice Statistics, 1992).

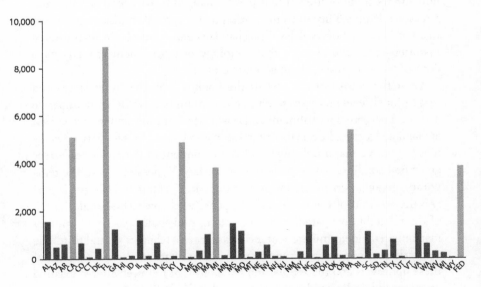

FIGURE 8. Prisoners serving LWOP by US jurisdiction, 2016. *Source:* Ashley Nellis, *Still Life: America's Increasing Use of Life and Long-Term Sentences* (Washington, DC: The Sentencing Project, 2017).

broad features that unite them than with (1) the choices of penal actors about how to accomplish the goals of state punishment given local state capacities and existing institutional arrangements and laws; (2) local ideas about the appropriateness of the punishment; or (3) contingent occurrences like high-profile crimes, federal court interventions, or criminal justice initiatives that impact laws and practices. While southern states, for instance, share a certain penal foundation and similar history leading to mass incarceration, they have not necessarily used this particular instrument—LWOP—in the same way. More, one has to consider changes in the meanings and practices of life without parole, on which the first part of this chapter focused. Narratives about death penalty opposition or tough-on-crime legislation spurring LWOP often do not address those changes, instead assuming the punishment was always a perpetual confinement that, in the late twentieth century, was simply used more. As noted earlier, the objective here is not to disparage commonsense notions but to begin to reconsider taken-for-granted ideas about LWOP in light of these patterns, to step back from them and look anew. The common sense offers, at best, a sketch.

In sum, to comprehend LWOP's rise one must go beyond patterns of sentences and laws. To understand variation in how LWOP is used, why life without parole began to develop more quickly in the 1970s and 1980s, and how the meaning of life without parole changed from a sentence allowing a reasonable possibility of commutation to a perpetual confinement, investigation is needed of local-level mechanisms and cultural and institutional histories—the type of work that sociology of punishment scholars have done of late with respect to mass incarceration.

Over the course of the rest of the book, I look closely at state- and institutional-level processes to set out an account of how life without parole become a perpetual punishment and how perpetual confinement become an at-hand concept and everyday practice in the United States. Part 2 examines how three major upheavals in US punishment in the 1970s and 1980s generated conditions that made the rise of LWOP possible: first, the temporary invalidation of capital punishment in *Furman v. Georgia* (1972) and the creation of the modern death penalty (chapter 4); second, the fall of the rehabilitative paradigm in corrections and challenges to its primary instruments, indeterminate sentencing and parole (chapter 5); and third, the retrenchment of executive clemency and commutation (chapter 6). Each of these upheavals and the actions and reactions that followed altered existing practices and understandings about punishment and laid foundations upon which perpetual confinement increasingly made sense.

PART II

Eruptions

4. The Complex Role of Death Penalty Abolition

What "everyone knows" about LWOP can be captured in two sweeping claims. First, invalidation of existing capital punishment statutes by the United States Supreme Court in *Furman v. Georgia* (1972), along with later abolition efforts by anti–death penalty activists and litigators, catalyzed LWOP as an alternative form of ultimate penalty. Second, where laws calling for LWOP arose outside the capital context, they did so in response to high crime rates and social unrest amid a flow of tough-on-crime sentencing policy that included three-strikes and truth-in-sentencing laws. In the former view, LWOP is a fixture of capital sentencing and death penalty politics. In the latter view, LWOP is representative, if not exemplary, of the policy that produced mass incarceration. This chapter and the next two question and complicate these conventional explanations, drawing on in-depth state-level histories to excavate the conditions of LWOP's emergence in greater detail. The present chapter confronts the first of these narratives by combining a national survey of state legislation following *Furman* with an extended analysis of the impact of *Furman*—one of the monumental events in late twentieth-century US punishment—in a single jurisdiction, the state of Florida.[1]

The first state to reenact capital punishment after *Furman,* Florida now holds more LWOP prisoners than any other.[2] The conditions and events that led to more than ten thousand people serving LWOP sentences in the Sunshine State therefore offer a window into understanding LWOP at its most virulent. Florida is also significant because it implicates archetypes with a powerful hold on current thinking on American punishment. Much recent penal state scholarship rests on a story of regional similarity that presents the American South (or Sunbelt) as a particular kind of "penal place" where shared experiences of slavery, decentralized government, and fiscal conservatism buttress a pro–death penalty alignment and punitive approach to corrections, offering a fertile base for harsh sentencing policy.³ In discussions of southern penalty, as in talk of the death penalty and mass incarceration, Florida is exemplary.

Given that Florida has a penal climate in which punitive practices are institutionally and culturally entrenched and mass incarceration has flourished, one might expect LWOP to have emerged there with pace-setting intensity. And because the death penalty has been especially prized in Florida, one might expect LWOP to have come on there after *Furman* with especial force. At a glance, then, Florida's leadership in LWOP sentencing seems what one would expect, an understandable result of death penalty abolition dynamics and the punitive turn working together. Yet as this chapter emphasizes, LWOP did not begin in Florida as a direct response to *Furman* and took hold there in the death penalty context more than two decades later—long after LWOP had become a regular state practice in non-capital cases. In showing how neither the standard story of backlash nor regional narratives explain the rise of LWOP in Florida, this chapter uses the example of this state to introduce a new narrative about the complex role of death penalty abolition in the rise of perpetual confinement nationally.

Rather than provoke an immediate rush to LWOP, invalidation of capital punishment had more slowly developing consequences. *Furman* broke what had been a long-standing working relationship between the death penalty and parole, under which a mainline system prioritizing rehabilitation served most prisoners, and the death penalty took care of the dangerous few (with a blurry area in between for recidivists). The temporary absence of capital punishment in *Furman's* wake upset this division, and in doing so raised some anxiety-provoking questions: Without the death penalty, what is the punishment for the worst of the worst? How many years does a life sentence really amount to? Can the worst of the worst be safely housed in the general prison population? In this inquisition, life sentences were exposed as open-ended and more lenient in practice than one might expect. After *Furman*, states were concerned with how to confine formerly death-eligible prisoners; and this in turn contributed to structural changes in law and to discursive and ideological shifts in practice. The breakdown of the death penalty–parole relationship, as such, set in play actions that impacted state criminal and penal law well after the reinstatement of capital punishment and laid foundations that would undergird not only LWOP but, more generally, key policies leading to mass incarceration. Attention to the backlash to *Furman* has overshadowed these more diffuse and longer-lasting effects.

THE POST-*FURMAN* "RUSH" RECONSIDERED

Of the many significant and field-altering developments in US criminal law in the 1970s, a major one was capital punishment's being abolished in 1972 and then restored four years later. In *Furman v. Georgia*, the US Supreme Court, in a splintered decision, invalidated the death penalty nationally, as imposed in every state and the federal system. Thousands of people on death row were resentenced to life. *Furman* stands as a watershed moment in US sentencing, after which the death penalty would never be the same. The most visible consequence, as scholars have chronicled well, was a widespread backlash in which thirty-six states quickly enacted new laws authorizing the death penalty in a narrowed and more regulated form.[4] Four years after *Furman*, the US Supreme Court approved several of the revised state statutes.[5] The modern death penalty apparatus ensued, a highly regulated system of laws and practices governed by a complex Eighth Amendment jurisprudence.[6]

With *Furman*, a NAACP Legal Defense Fund litigation strategy that began by challenging racial disproportionality in capital sentencing culminated in a challenge to the arbitrary imposition of death sentences. If submerged in the ultimate litigation, however, the role of race in death penalty prosecutions and sentences and the historical relationship between capital punishment and lynching was not lost in practice. Even as legal claims based on racial discrimination gave way before the US Supreme Court to challenges to structure and procedure, strong racial undertones remained and contributed to the backlash.[7]

Backlash dominates how *Furman* is seen historically, and this has framed perceptions of the history of LWOP. One common story about LWOP appears memorably in print in a *Harvard Law Review* note in 2006.[8] As developed and restated in subsequent literature, the claim has two parts. First, after the *Furman* decision invalidated capital punishment, states responded with a "pushback in the form of life-without-parole statutes" that was "promoted by prosecutors and enacted by law-and-order legislators who were fearful of facing a punishment scheme without a capital option."[9] Second, after capital punishment was officially reinstated, "the debate over life without parole flipped. Prosecutors who had wanted life without parole statutes in order to keep violent criminals in prison now wanted the specter of parole in order to convince juries to sentence defendants to death"; some abolitionists, meanwhile, looked to LWOP in an effort to reduce death sentences.[10] From these beginnings in the capital context, the narrative goes, LWOP spread outward.

To an extent, this narrative gels with what we know of LWOP today. LWOP is indeed the alternative to the death penalty in every state. Yet in the absence of in-depth study, there has been little basis for carefully evaluating the account. It consists of an aggregation of impressions, including those of knowledgeable scholars and legal professionals, but impressions nevertheless.

Exhibit A

To begin, it is useful to revisit what state legislatures actually did in the capital sphere after *Furman*. Alabama is often offered as a case in point, and it tracks the conventional narrative well. Life without parole did not exist in Alabama before *Furman*. Parole for lifers was available at any time given a unanimous vote by the Board of Pardons and Paroles, otherwise after ten years, and after fifteen years for commuted death sentences.[11] Following *Furman*, Alabama was the first state to introduce LWOP as a death penalty alternative, with the Death Penalty and Life Imprisonment without Parole Act of 1975. Accounts of LWOP's sudden appearance in Alabama emphasize that support was widespread among the public and anchored by prosecutors, who preferred the sentence for its efficiency and its ability to avoid ongoing appeals and obtain pleas. The most vocal opponents were the Department of Corrections and prisoners, parties concerned about safety and conditions inside the prison.[12] Alabama soon authorized LWOP in more laws: as a discretionary penalty for certain second serious felony offenses in 1977, as a discretionary sanction for certain drug offenses in 1978, and in 1979 as a mandatory sentence for certain repeat felonies.[13] Between 1980 and 1982 Alabama's LWOP population rose from less than a dozen to nearly eighty.[14] An early 1980s journalistic account suggested that these developments heralded a new wave in punishment, dubbing Alabama "the criminal justice laboratory in which the impact of life without parole sentences will be studied."[15]

If Alabama's story is in line with the conventional narrative, however, the alleged widespread rush to LWOP in capital statutes after *Furman* never really happened. Of the roughly two-thirds of US states that reacted to *Furman* by turning back to capital punishment, most sought to circumvent arbitrariness with a *mandatory death penalty*, requiring the death penalty after a conviction; other states proposed life *with* parole as the alternative sentence; a few states that had used life without parole as the alternative to the death penalty before *Furman* simply reenacted what they had before (figure 9).[16] Across the nation, only Alabama can be said to have turned directly to LWOP in response to *Furman*.[17] In fact, many

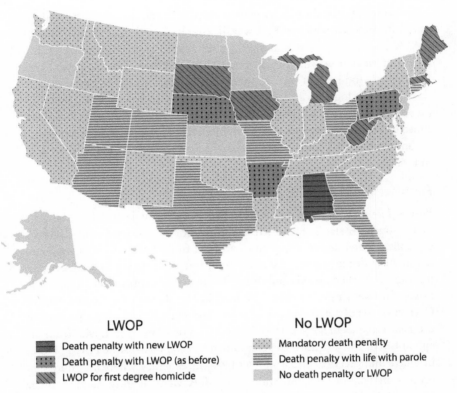

LWOP
- Death penalty with new LWOP
- Death penalty with LWOP (as before)
- LWOP for first degree homicide

No LWOP
- Mandatory death penalty
- Death penalty with life with parole
- No death penalty or LWOP

FIGURE 9. Initial legislative responses to *Furman v. Georgia. Source:* Author's research.

southern states did not authorize LWOP for more than a decade afterward; some did not apply LWOP to capital cases until the early 1990s, and then did so alongside truth-in-sentencing or three-strikes legislation, exhibiting a confluence with the punitive policies that generated mass incarceration. The conventional narrative of a post-*Furman* rush to LWOP breaks down empirically.

It is worth recalling that in practice a distinction between life with parole and life without parole was not pronounced at the time; both could result in release from prison after a dozen or so years (chapter 2). Moreover, the notion of life without parole as a sentence without release went against the prevailing approach to punishment in jurisdictions that favored treatment and rehabilitation. It also bears emphasis that in the early 1970s life without parole's place in American criminal justice was limited. It was

not a common punishment. It played no part in the litigation that culminated in *Furman* (chapter 8). Overall, there was a lack of knowledge of
LWOP as a punishment that would hold people in prison forever or as a
punishment that was distinct from any other life sentence. And yet there
were people (one might refer to them as penal entrepreneurs) who, despite
the prevailing logic about life without parole, preferred to regard and promote LWOP as a punishment without release. In the early 1970s, however,
those interests rarely prevailed. One important reason was the fierce opposition of prison administrators and staff, a phenomenon that can be seen
in Florida.

Florida after Furman

Before *Furman*, life without parole had never been law in Florida. Like
many southern states, for much of the twentieth century Florida lacked a
centralized penal bureaucracy and a store of funds with which to build and
maintain multiple prisons. There was a central prison (Raiford State Prison),
but the state relied heavily on convict leasing, road camps, chain gangs, and
prison farms.[18] Imprisonment took hold in Florida with the Department of
Corrections (FLDOC), created in 1957. The FLDOC came into its own in
the 1960s thanks in large part to Secretary Louis Wainwright, who from his
appointment in 1962 until stepping down in 1986 transformed the FLDOC,
in image and practice, into a standardized bureaucracy where an interest in
professionalization, rehabilitation, and safety went hand in hand.[19] Under
Wainwright, the state's rehabilitative moment peaked in the 1970s, even
as the indeterminate sentencing model and the idea of rehabilitation were
nationally under siege.

A number of factors, however, threatened designs for a limited and
orderly prison focused on treatment and reintegration. The FLDOC's aim
to professionalize and modernize conflicted with preexisting interests in
decentralized work camps. Prison capacity remained limited, and political
conflicts slowed resource allocation.[20] Further, Florida's increasing crime
rate led the South, fueling prison admissions.[21] Consequently, despite the
FLDOC's aims, overcrowded and dangerous prison conditions persisted.
In 1971 racial uprisings flared at Raiford.[22] In 1972, a life-sentenced prisoner filed a prison conditions lawsuit that resulted in a two-decade federal
oversight of Florida prisons.[23] In this context, prison overcrowding and the
FLDOC's relatively nascent rehabilitative orientation converged to keep
time served to a minimum. People serving life sentences in Florida—more
than a thousand admitted to prison between 1957 and 1972—served fewer
than ten years on average and were immediately eligible for parole.[24]

Yet life without parole held a prominent place on Florida's post-*Furman* agenda for several reasons. First, Democratic governor Reubin Askew, a strong critic of how capital punishment was applied, recognized LWOP's value as a capital sentencing alternative. Upon taking office in 1971, with *Furman* pending, Askew declared he would sign no death warrants, effectively joining a national moratorium on executions.[25] After *Furman*, Askew quickly appointed a commission to study capital punishment.[26] Both branches of the state legislature followed suit. In July 1972 the House Select Committee on the Death Penalty announced a schedule of meetings and public hearings, listing three "significant questions which must be answered":

1. By what constitutional procedure may the death penalty be imposed?

2. To what crimes should the death penalty be applicable?

3. Is life imprisonment without parole desirable from the viewpoint of the burden and danger placed upon correctional personnel?[27]

A second reason was that the state's attorney general, Robert Shevin, lobbied for life without parole. In 1967, as a state senator, Shevin had unsuccessfully introduced a bill calling for a twenty-year mandatory minimum on life sentences. Before the legislature in 1972, he earned lawmakers' attention with similar talk, proposing life without parole not as a capital alternative but as part of a general strategy promoting mandatory minimum sentences.[28] Shevin advocated reinstating capital punishment as a mandatory penalty limited to seven forms of aggravated, premeditated homicide. Aware that this would exclude certain crimes that were death eligible prior to *Furman*, including some homicides and rape, he urged that they receive mandatory *"life imprisonment without parole."*[29] Shevin was one who, even before *Furman*, cast life without parole as perpetual confinement.

Shevin's position was countered, however, by another element of Florida's penal state: the FLDOC. FLDOC's organizing against life without parole began before *Furman*, in 1971, when Askew introduced and the legislature passed a law stating that in the event of abolition, death-sentenced prisoners would be resentenced to life without parole.[30] That law never went into effect because the Florida Supreme Court, influenced by the FLDOC's stance, moved first to resentence the state's death row prisoners to life *with* parole.[31] After *Furman*, FLDOC opposition to LWOP persisted, coming to a head in a message from Secretary Wainwright to the House Select Committee. Nominally supportive of capital punishment, Wainwright emphasized that the FLDOC "unanimous[ly] oppos[ed]" life without parole for the very reasons that historically limited its use: space was precious and carrots for reform necessary for prison order.[32] If capital punishment were not reinstated, Wainwright urged, legislators must ensure that lifers remained eligible for parole:

> If you will mentally place yourself in the place of one of these offenders, I think you can visualize their feelings of despair. When the law allows a judge to sentence a human being to life imprisonment without parole, he actually loads the gun and cocks it, the discharge will come sooner or later. This discharge or adjustment to their situation and environment could be massive escapes, assaulting or killing personnel or other inmates, taking hostages, or general chaos in our prison system.[33]

Corrections ideology also played a role. Per Wainwright, it was a "fact [] recognized by each and every agent of this system" that "all the offenders need help in order to develop different values, personalities and attitudes toward their environment."[34] "It would be wrong," he argued, "to enact a law that would make self-motivation for lifers impossible, and would exclude them from institutional programs of rehabilitation," in effect "subject[ing] [them] to wholesale 'warehousing' of human beings."[35] The "ultimate end of the no-parole law," Wainwright portended, would be "the end of Death Row and the establishment of 'LIFE ROW.'"[36]

In the summer of 1972, the matter took on a human face in legislative hearings at Raiford, at which testimony from prison officers and prisoners proved especially influential:

REPRESENTATIVE SAVAGE: Can you give me any kind of personal projection as to what is going to be the attitude of hiring and keeping correctional officers if we abolish the death penalty? Second, if we institute life without parole? Can you tell me what your problem is going to be with your officers, not your inmates just your officers?

CAPTAIN COMBS: It's my personal feeling that we will have great difficulty in acquiring personnel to operate the institution.

REP. SAVAGE: Now as an alternative, if we go along with the Supreme Court and don't recommend the reinstatement of the death penalty under certain circumstances and say that capital crimes shall be punished by life *with* hope of parole, will you have a very serious problem then?

CAPT. COMBS: Well, I think we would have a problem but not near so much as we would if we had the situation where an individual had no hope whatsoever.

REP. SAVAGE: Well, would it be a true statement for me to believe then that if I believe in abolishing the death penalty I also ought to consider the correctional officer and say that all lifers will be eligible for parole if I want to keep proper management?

CAPT. COMBS: I would certainly hope so, yes sir. . . . If we abolish capital punishment, certainly, I think anyone who is committed to our care should have the hope of making parole some day.[37]

One guard reported that if life without parole replaced the death penalty, "I think I would have to give up [my job]. . . . I'm afraid my life would be in danger."[38] Some prisoners interviewed felt the same way.[39] FLDOC Deputy Secretary David Bachman put an exclamation point on the matter: "What you're doing is creating an impossible situation where a man has no hope. . . . I'll tell you the truth. . . . I'm afraid if this thing goes through [life without parole], we're going to have some people killed as a result of it. . . . I do really believe there shouldn't be any of these 'no parole' provisions enacted."[40]

In Florida after *Furman*, the most influential arguments against life without parole came from prison administrators, prisoners, and prison staff, who, rather than pitch life without parole as an alternative to the death penalty, marshalled it as a principal reason the death penalty should be maintained.[41] Convinced by their testimony, most legislators voted against including life without parole in the death penalty replacement bill.[42]

Beyond Backlash

Florida's failure to implement life without parole as a capital alternative after *Furman* was not exceptional. In most states, LWOP did not come into play as a death penalty alternative until years later: in some, following the reaffirmation of capital punishment in *Gregg*; for others, decades afterward; and for many in the first instance for uses other than capital punishment (table 2). The turn to LWOP as a death penalty alternative was a post-*Gregg* effect and one spread out over time.[43]

Recognizing Alabama as a counterexample rather than an exemplar of how LWOP played out in the majority of states after *Furman* is significant

TABLE 2. First and Second LWOP Enactments in Southern States after *Furman*

State	1970s	Later	Target
Alabama	1975		Death penalty alternative
	1977–1979		Habitual offenses
Arkansas	1973*		Death penalty alternative
	1975		Habitual offenses
Florida		1989	Murder (law officer)/some drug offenses
		1990	Some drug offenses
Georgia		1993	Death penalty alternative
		1993	Habitual offenses
Louisiana	1976*		Death penalty alternative
	1977		Some sex/drug offenses
Mississippi	1976		Habitual offenses
		1994	Death penalty alternative
North Carolina		1994	Death penalty alternative
		1994	Habitual offenses
South Carolina		1986	Homicide with prior violent felony
		1995	Death penalty alternative/habitual offenses
Texas		2005	Death penalty alternative
		2007	Some sex offenses

*Applied life without parole as death penalty alternative prior to *Furman*.
Source: Author's research.

as a matter of historical timeline, but more, it matters for how one perceives *Furman*'s impact on the development of life without parole sentencing. Focusing on life without parole as a backlash response in capital statutes after *Furman* distracts from the other ways in which invalidation of the death penalty set the stage for LWOP, overlooking the more dynamic and complex interactions between capital and noncapital arenas and the general influence that invalidation of the death penalty had on sentencing policies and practices.

Indeed, the *Harvard Law Review* article often cited for the idea that *Furman* spurred pushback in the form of LWOP laws also offered another theory, one that has largely been overlooked. This theory presents the death penalty and parole as complementary institutions, each helping make the other possible. Historically, the article notes, "the two movements have seesawed back and forth, playing off each other, with the possibility of parole often used as a scare tactic to push for stronger capital statutes."[44] It also worked the other way: people might more readily support parole for most prisoners knowing the most dangerous would receive the death penalty. Capital punishment and parole, in short, stabilized one another. Tensions one raised the other relieved, and the two developed together over the course of US penal history.

By this logic, when *Furman* invalidated capital punishment, it destabilized a longtime arrangement and opened it up for reconsideration, casting doubt on how the penal system would deal with prisoners just off death row, a favorable parole decision away from release.[45] While certain scholars have emphasized *Furman*'s role in animating public fears about dangerous criminals, the significance of the death penalty–parole balance remains underplayed in literature on US penal policy in the late twentieth century.[46] It is well known that *Furman* provoked a backlash of new capital statutes and then a long and ongoing series of US Supreme Court decisions that have come to define the modern death penalty. But rarely spoken of is *Furman*'s impact outside the death penalty arena.

FURMAN'S OTHER EFFECTS

Dismantling the death penalty opened a sphere of public and professional inquiry fraught with tensions about the release of prisoners and the reliability of life sentences. In the penal system, *Furman* destabilized—structurally, discursively, and ideologically—more than death penalty terrain. It provoked reassignment and restructuring of punishments and challenged prevailing ideas about parole and indeterminate sentences, inviting discussions that gave renewed and deeper consideration to mandatory minimum sentencing, truth-in-sentencing, and determinate sentencing. Further, ripple effects shot throughout the system as the ideological wall separating capital punishment from the rest of sentencing in the United States was, at least for a brief period, broken. On multiple levels—from the material necessity of restructuring penal codes to the ideological ramifications of recognizing that the death penalty–parole balance was no longer—*Furman* laid groundwork that would be a foundation for LWOP and influence perspectives on life sentences and the people serving them.

Structural Effects: Displaced Death Penalties

After *Furman*, as states crafted replacement statutes, be they mandatory or discretionary, with unitary or bifurcated sentencing proceedings, the scope of death-eligible offenses was narrowed in order to meet constitutional muster. In many states, revision of death penalty statutes coincided with a general overhaul of penal codes and dovetailed with a transfer of previously death-eligible crimes—including kidnapping, rape, and second-degree murder—to noncapital felony categories. These structural shifts, which took place outside the capital realm, posed a question *Furman* had already provoked: if the death penalty was not available, under what sentence would people convicted of the most serious and violent crimes be confined?

Florida's answer, rather than introduce LWOP as punishment for formerly death-eligible crimes, was to introduce long mandatory terms. As lawmakers interpreted *Furman* to require narrowed application of the death penalty, crimes displaced from the capital context (kidnapping, rape, war and terrorism crimes) landed in a new legal category: the "life felony," less serious than a capital felony but more serious than a felony of the first degree.[47] Before *Furman*, a "life" sentence in Florida amounted on average to parole release after ten years; the punishment for a "life felony," however, was a mandatory minimum of thirty years—twenty years stiffer.[48] This is an example of how downgrading the punishment for some serious offenses from death resulted in longer-term sentences, establishing a foundation for an upward trajectory in severity in the coming years, as long mandatory minimums got longer. Within a decade, life itself would become a mandatory minimum as life without parole became the punishment for life felonies. Over time the scope of life felonies gradually expanded, and people convicted of once-capital crimes comprised a substantial share of Florida's LWOP population.

Similar processes unfolded in Louisiana and Pennsylvania. Louisiana responded to *Furman* by redefining murder into first- and second-degree categories. The penalty for the former remained death or life imprisonment; the penalty for the latter was initially life with a twenty-year mandatory minimum.[49] The minimum was raised to forty years in 1975, and then to mandatory life without parole in 1979. Similarly, after moving aggravated kidnapping and rape out of the capital statute, the state imposed mandatory penalties for those crimes, which gradually increased, reaching life without parole in 1978 and 1980, respectively.[50] Pennsylvania responded to *Furman* by redefining murder into first, second, and third degrees.[51] The penalty for the new second-degree murder, redefined to include only felony murder, formerly a capital crime, was mandatory life without parole.[52] Between 1980 and 2015, approximately one-fifth of all people sentenced to life in Pennsylvania were convicted of murder in the second degree.[53]

In 2016 Florida had the highest LWOP population in the country; Pennsylvania was second, and Louisiana third.[54] Structural changes to noncapital sentencing after *Furman* set the base upon which LWOP and other perpetual imprisonments in those states were built in coming years. I have focused on the Florida case, and noted Louisiana and Pennsylvania, but similar effects were likely felt to some degree in all states that retained capital punishment after *Furman*.

Discursive and Ideological Effects

If discourse marks the boundary of ways in which ideas can be put into language, then to say that death penalty abolition changed discourse means that it changed the boundaries of what could be said, the ways in which it could be said, and by extension the effects statements would have. One witnesses *Furman*'s effects on ways of speaking and thinking about punishment in Florida's post-*Furman* legislative hearings, where a space was opened to talk about parole board discretion, truth in sentencing, and mandatory minimum sentences, themes less common under a rehabilitative paradigm that eventually took hold as pillars of US penal policy.

Resentencing death row prisoners to life after *Furman* shone a spotlight on life sentences. It was a shocking realization for many that a life sentence amounted in actuality to a term of years, and often a relatively short one at that. Invalidation of the old death penalty schemes thus illuminated a disconnect between what the public thought was going on and what *was* going on with sentencing, precisely the sort of phenomenon that legal scholar William Stuntz deemed critical to criminal justice pendulum swings.[55] *Furman*, then, by cutting the line that once held between the death penalty and parole, not only posed a crisis of management for penal institutions but also contributed to already growing public worries over which prisoners were dangerous and whether or not penology could tell.

In this context, the FLDOC's opposition to LWOP had implications for the ensuing debate. Because the FLDOC strenuously opposed life without parole, the conversation turned to alternative ways of restricting release for people convicted of serious noncapital crimes. Those alternatives included mandatory minimum sentences and limits on judicial and administrative discretion, as well as the issue of a sentence meaning what it says. These were not new ideas. But to that time they had little momentum. The light that death penalty abolition shone on indeterminate sentencing and parole rejuvenated the status of these ideas, giving them a prime-time forum and new leverage.[56]

The hearing testimony of Attorney General Shevin offers an example. He recalled that the life without parole bill he had proposed years earlier as a state senator "never got out of committee because all the prison officials and all the parole officials came down and argued very strenuously against the legislation." "However," Shevin argued, "in subsequent years the value of that legislation has been shown."[57] By "value," Shevin alluded to parolees who had committed violent crimes after being released from prison, a concern amplified in the context of death penalty abolition. This time, with the possibility of a legal system without capital punishment squarely before the legislators, Shevin's argument met with success. A mandatory minimum was placed on the life sentence alternative in the replacement capital statute, and interest was piqued about mandatory minimums generally. In a meeting after Shevin's presentation, a congressman asked, "Would it serve the ends of criminal justice if we made sentences mandatory then in every other case?"[58]

Arguments for mandatory minimums dovetailed with arguments against discretion. A Palm Beach prosecutor urged the legislature to limit parole on life sentences for second-degree murder, finding parole review unreliable.[59] Other witnesses voiced similar concerns about judges, leading a House Committee member to state: "I am changing very quickly my attitude toward the discretion that we grant the judiciary. If we allow a number of years up to life we're going to be subject to a great deal of criticism when they start giving these guys two years, five years. I think we'd better think about those minimum amounts of time the judge is gonna have to give because judges have too many other ways of circumventing sentencing anyway. . . . So I would say seven years to life, 10 years to life, whatever number you want to take."[60] The legislator's statement reflects in turn a third concern: whether sentences should mean what they say. On this point, Shevin had an answer: "Our society has traditionally expected the retribution effect of the death penalty . . . and now in certain cases no longer has it available. Society ought to be able to expect that a life term means substantially life."[61] Sentences meaning what they say, mandatory minimums, limits on discretion—with each concern, a debate that began over whether to revive capital punishment extended to penal policy generally.

These discussions in the Florida legislature exemplify ongoing struggles, nested in local political and institutional contexts, punctuated by particular events, in which actors with preexisting interests take advantage of changed terrain.[62] But they also illustrate something more; they show how, through discussions about life and death sentences, lawmakers began to reconsider how they thought about punishment and to critically examine the indeterminate sentencing paradigm. The archives, as such, reveal the roots of shifts in ways of thinking about punishment that foreshadow some of the very positions now recognized as staples of the punitive turn.[63] Disproportionate focus on whether *Furman* spurred a rush to LWOP, therefore, overlooks what is arguably a more significant effect: namely, the opening *Furman* provided for competing penal paradigms. On a more specific level, one should consider the implications for ways of thinking about life sentences and the people serving them.

The Life Sentence. Under indeterminate sentencing, the life sentence was exemplary, an open-ended punishment providing an opportunity for release from prison upon evaluation by a parole board. *Furman* changed the frame, casting the life sentence as a backup for the death penalty, a role in which it would be expected to mean no release from prison. Shevin's claim to this effect, echoed by legislators, illustrates how the debate over reinstatement of capital punishment was linked to a crisis in the meaning of the life sentence. Life imprisonment *without release* was always the dark underbelly and last resort of indeterminate sentencing, but death penalty abolition invited looking at the life sentence in a new way. Open-ended sentencing with release was never the intended result for those condemned to death. In the post-*Furman* context, therefore, the life sentence faced an identity crisis. Rather than an open-ended sentence that might last a lifetime, a fixed penalty certain to do so was needed. What *Furman* did, precisely with respect to life sentencing, was to force such a reconsideration of meaning.

The Lifer. When *Furman* destabilized the death penalty–parole balance, there were material effects: narrowing of the death penalty pushed former death-eligible crimes into the noncapital sphere, and abolition moreover pushed people sentenced to death row into the general population. There were also ideological effects: temporary abolition threatened the imagined distance, which undergirded the early- to mid-twentieth-century relationship between capital punishment and prison sentences, between the few people who must be executed and the rest, who could be redeemed.

The predicament is vividly displayed in legislative hearings that took place in the visitors area of the Old East Wing at the Florida State Prison at Raiford in August 1972, where legislators interviewed people serving life sentences, divided into two types, on their feelings about the death penalty. First were those formerly sentenced to death whose sentences had been commuted (or were in the process of being commuted) after *Furman*: one, for example, had been in the general population almost three weeks, another two weeks and a day, while another was waiting to be reclassified. Second were those in the general population sentenced to life for violent offenses in which no one had been injured. Two questions were asked. First, do capitally sentenced prisoners pose a danger to the general population?[64] Second, does the death penalty deter? The answer delivered by the non-capitally sentenced prisoners was that death-sentenced prisoners were a particularly dangerous type, unlikely to be deterred. As the committee chair, Representative Jeff Gautier, remarked after the hearings:

> I think the most convincing statement that I heard during the entire thing was when a lifer in Raiford in maximum security at that time stated that unless the death penalty—he thought that after the prevailing calm disappeared that there were going to be wholesale murders of inmates and prison personnel. He went on to say that if the death penalty were not reinstated, he didn't think it would be safe for his mother to go to Sunday school. That was one of the most telling arguments. He still had an FBI record that wouldn't wait.[65]

The Raiford interviews present a unique moment of overlay between two types of lifers, old and new. The redeemable prisoner with a chance overlaid with the former death-row prisoner with a commuted sentence, whom the state had previously condemned. Scholars have remarked on how the policy turns that produced mass incarceration reflect a change of perspective on the nature of criminal subjects.[66] One sees like changes brewing in the post-*Furman* conversations of southern legislators as they decided on whether or not to resuscitate the death penalty.

FURMAN'S LESSONS

Furman brought into play multiple processes relevant to LWOP and mass incarceration: (1) structural changes in which displaced death penalties became new crime categories that would soon be punishable by LWOP; (2) discursive changes as a space opened, in part through those displacements, to talk about parole limits, judicial and administrative discretion, truth in sentencing, and mandatory sentences; and (3) ideological changes, as penal actors reconsidered penal aims, penal instruments, and perspectives on life sentences and the people serving life sentences.[67]

The notion of a "rush" to LWOP after *Furman*, accordingly, presents a limited picture that captures neither the scope nor the dominant character of the relationship between *Furman* and LWOP. More salient is that the possibility and short-lived reality of abolition presented circumstances in which alternatives to the death penalty were reconsidered and alternative ways of thinking about and sentencing non-death-eligible prisoners were discussed and implemented. This is not to say that indeterminate sentencing was pushed to the brink because of processes set in motion by death penalty abolition. But a more modest point is no less important: *Furman* unsettled the penal field in ways that benefited certain interests and disadvantaged others, and as it did it encouraged and made possible a rethinking about the nature and meaning of the life sentence and life-sentenced prisoners. This is a markedly different account than one in which LWOP simply appears as a ready-made backup option for capital statutes after *Furman*.

Life without parole is in part a "death penalty thing," but never only that.[68] LWOP is now deeply intertwined with capital punishment; most people serving LWOP in the United States have been convicted of first-degree murder. Yet much of LWOP's development transpired outside the capital context and in fact paved the way for later use in the capital arena. Florida's history highlights this. In 1994, more than twenty years after *Furman*, Florida eventually turned to LWOP as the alternative sanction for capital murder.[69] In the interim, as events outside the capital arena built LWOP, most people life sentenced for capital crimes (other than those subject to an exception for murder of a law enforcement or judicial officer) continued to have parole eligibility after twenty-five years. As the scope of noncapital LWOP sentencing widened in Florida, it accentuated an illogical situation in which people serving capital life sentences were parole eligible while lifers convicted of noncapital crimes were not.[70] There was, consequently, an "inequity" in the law to such an extent that, as one state senator wrote emphasizing the law's perverse effect, "our courts are facing a number of situations in which defendants are actually 'pleading up' in order to gain parole."[71] When the state eventually adopted LWOP as the alternative for all death penalty offenses in the 1990s, legislators were responding to this inequity and the accelerating growth of LWOP in noncapital law. The lack of LWOP in capital cases was an increasingly inexplicable anomaly that eventually had to fall.

5. The Collapse of a Penal Paradigm

The United States has a comfort level with perpetual confinement today that from a historical perspective demands some explanation. Given the peripheral status of perpetual confinement in prior decades, one might expect such a severe punishment would have to undergo some sort of clearance, a vetting or quality check, before achieving prevalent use. Yet that was not the case. LWOP arose for years in the United States without much attention. The US Supreme Court did not entertain a per se challenge to LWOP (or any form of perpetual confinement) under the Eighth Amendment until 2010, and that review and the resulting mandate were restricted in scope to people who were youths when they committed the crime.[1] Scholars have pointed to one reason that life without parole long evaded such scrutiny: the death penalty provided cover.[2] While the forcible taking of life by execution has been a point of active debate and an object of careful inspection by courts for centuries, perpetual imprisonment has not.

Certainly capital punishment has provided a distraction. Yet there are other reasons for the lack of vetting, which have to do with the US history with indeterminate sentencing. A rehabilitative penal philosophy long framed life sentences as open-ended punishments defined by the opportunity for parole review. Accordingly, if a life-sentenced individual stayed in prison until their death, the outcome had to do with how the sentence played out in a particular case, and therein arguably with respect to the individual's own behavior in prison, rather than with the inherent cruelty of the sentence. In short, one reason life sentences were not addressed head on as cruel and unusual was that their actual boundaries were blurry, and in practice the time to be served under the sentence was not clearly defined.

A second, related reason concerns the manner in which life sentencing developed near the twentieth century's end. During the 1970s and 1980s,

American penal policy embarked on something of a journey. That journey resulted in a harsher penality defined by long, fixed sentences, but it did not always start there. In many jurisdictions the punitive turn was preceded by a period of reform in which the principal policy goals were "consistency, transparency, proportionality, accountability, and regularity."[3] Some of the reforms begetting LWOP aimed for fair and efficient sentencing, not harsher punishment. Others produced LWOP as a consequence of awkward incongruities, as legislators and judges attempted to translate a sentence without a set duration (the life sentence) into a fixed sentencing model reliant on quantitative measures such as administrative credits or gain time. As penal ideology shifted, the way in which actors understood life without parole was likewise in flux. In the archives, one finds some state actors assuming that a life without parole sentence anticipates release but simply puts matters in the governor's hands, well into the 1980s and early 1990s. Although the life without parole sentence is now utilized quite deliberately as a punitive tool, especially since the mid-1990s, its development in the preceding decades was complex. In sum, the diverse and growing use of LWOP was not contested more often in part because the punishment's meaning was varied and not always clear. It could be said that LWOP as it is understood today—that is, as perpetual confinement—did not make a formal entrance.

To understand LWOP's emergence, therefore, and to understand the way in which this punishment now uniformly recognized as a perpetual prison term rose to prominence with fewer obstacles and challenges than one might expect, one must examine the turn away from the "rehabilitative ideal" that had guided American penal policy from the early twentieth century onward.[4]

The first part of the chapter briefly recalls the unique stature of the life sentence under indeterminate sentencing and situates life sentencing in the context of a major shift in practice and official ideology of American punishment at the end of the twentieth century. The second part of the chapter illustrates less intentional and not so intentionally punitive ways in which life without parole was generated, given the unique history of the life sentence in the United States, demonstrating how key early laws that brought LWOP into being were not necessarily crafted with incapacitation as the goal. A far cry from the intentionally punitive character that characterizes LWOP today, indirect processes of growth and accumulation were more consequential than is often recognized. The third part of the chapter, finally, illustrates a quite different process that happened when states cut back on parole. Looking to LWOP, actors started to exercise perpetual confinement in other ways. One of this book's arguments is that, as life without parole came to be thought of as a punishment precluding release, it carried with it a general idea of perpetual confinement, forging a prominent place for permanent imprisonment in the nation's penal imaginary. To illustrate how the growth and transformation of life without parole inspired other practices of imprisonment until death, I focus here on rogue yet widespread efforts by sentencing courts to apply perpetual imprisonment in cases where LWOP was not authorized.

Overall, the 1970s and 1980s mark a period of experimentation in the penal field, particularly so with respect to lifetime sentencing. One finds life with parole becoming life without parole, life without parole becoming perpetual confinement (LWOP), and LWOP acting as a model that provokes perpetual confinement in other forms.

PARADIGM CRISIS

As Michele Pifferi explains in a comparative study of US and European criminology, paths that were relatively the same for much of the nineteenth century diverged at century's end.[5] In the United States a penal philosophy focused on treatment and review for release held sway. The life sentence, a uniquely open-ended punishment, epitomized the new penal strategy, allowing prisoners an opportunity to change and the newly celebrated expertise of parole commissioners to assess their rehabilitation. In contrast, most Western European jurisdictions adopted a fixed sentencing approach. That model also valued reform in prison but allowed little back-end change in sentences, relying instead on prison terms of limited length—to be followed, if necessary, by post-punishment detention.

Those divergent choices had path-defining consequences for thinking and practice concerning life sentencing. In European states the life sentence has occupied a limited space and has been received with great caution. There it is seen not as an opportunity but as a hold on the entire life of an individual and, to that effect, as an abuse of state power. The perspective is reflected in European treatises that take issue with the very notion of a life sentence. Some commentators go so far as to view life imprisonment as characteristic of an absolutist state.[6] By contrast, the United States lacks a tradition of critical discussion about perpetual imprisonment and, more specifically, the form and function of a lifetime prison sentence under a determinate sentencing model.[7] Put another way, in the United States the turn to indeterminate sentencing and parole in the early twentieth century shelved questions about perpetual imprisonment that European nations delved into deeply a century ago.

One should not overstate the reach of rehabilitation in US practice. Indeterminate sentencing was likely never adopted in a pure form (even jurisdictions that turned strongly to a treatment approach did not impose entirely open-ended sentences and instead identified minimum terms after which review for release could occur).[8] Further, law on the books aside, Progressive Era penal policies often served more as rhetoric than as reality during the interwar years.[9] And when rehabilitation gained traction midcentury, certain states turned to rehabilitative ideas and practices more aggressively than others.[10] It is important, in sum, to take into account the variation in implementation at the state level, where the fortune of rehabilitative policy and practice was shaped by local penal histories and cultures and was an ongoing affair, subject to struggle, featuring periodic victories for competing interests.[11] Yet however uneven in practice, for most of the twentieth century and especially from the 1950s to the 1970s, the rehabilitative ideal served as a sort of common sense among penal elites, making up part of the sentencing and corrections toolkit even in jurisdictions that favored a meaner and tougher approach. One can appreciate the variation with which states adopted rehabilitation, in rhetoric and in practice, while simultaneously acknowledging the rehabilitative model's standing as an official ideology that was identity defining for US punishment.[12]

The dismantling of that official ideology in the 1970s and 1980s, and the period of transition that states entered afterward, has generated an industry of scholarly work. Prevailing theories, with different emphases, point to a variety of broad social, political, economic, and cultural changes: a rightward political shift, a discrediting of welfare, a backlash against civil rights, law and order politics, neoliberal economics, and increased mobility and suburbanization.[13] Those broad developments spurred increasing crime rates, greater public insecurities about crime, more hostile perspectives toward criminals, and greater public identification with crime victims.[14] In response, new political approaches arose by which state actors increasingly used penal policy to address public insecurities once managed by social welfare programs.[15] In this milieu, the rehabilitative ideal was criticized across the political spectrum and the penal field. In the words of criminologist Joan Petersilia, the "pillars of the American corrections systems—indeterminate sentencing coupled with parole release, for the purposes of offender rehabilitation—came under severe attack and basically collapsed."[16]

Ways of thinking about punishment destabilized to such an extent, David Garland suggests, that what was needed was not only reconsideration of penal justifications or more effective ways of carrying out already identified aims, but new descriptive theories of punishment; in other words, the penal field needed to go back to the drawing board and rethink what it had taken for granted.[17] As such, rehabilitation's collapse left a gap with nothing immediately ready to fill it.[18] States navigated the crisis differently, channeling broader forces through local institutional arrangements, histories, and cultures en route to local laws, policies, and practices. Parole and open-ended sentencing practices were curtailed and, in some states, eviscerated. Sentencing guidelines held sway for a time but gave way to determinate sentencing systems, which in turn succumbed to punitive popular currents.[19] Rehabilitation did not totally disappear but was recast in line with new penal regimes.[20]

As practices and ways of thinking about punishment shifted, the life sentence—a punishment measured by "life" rather than a number of years—was placed in a unique and awkward position. How to use an open-ended sentence in a fixed framework? How to apply a "life" sentence to be "true"? One may look back to the path taken in US punishment a century earlier, which bypassed hard discussions about perpetual punishments while adopting indeterminate sentencing. Consequently, when the indeterminate model collapsed in the late twentieth century, US jurisdictions lacked (1) a well-developed strategy of nonretributive civil commitment as a follow-up to a penal term and (2) an established dialogue to consult on limiting the lengths of prison terms. As a result, moves that began to reshape life sentences into perpetual confinements met with little resistance or challenge.

PAROLE RESIDUE

The period from 1975 to 1984 was a sentencing reform period, characterized by the adoption of sentencing guidelines and determinate sentencing schemes. As Michael Tonry explains: "A primarily but not only liberal reform movement sought to make procedures fairer and sentences more predictable and consistent. Conservatives wanted greater certainty for political and crime control reasons, and liberals in order to increase consistency and fairness, but their conceptions of the problem and its solution were similar."[21] LWOP emerged in many states when back-end release practices such as parole were limited or removed. As Tonry notes, some surprising, even shocking, elements of mass incarceration policy are fairly characterized as "residue of the movement away from indeterminate sentencing."[22] These are elements that emerged during the shift to determinate sentencing, often without receiving much if any direct attention. Here again, Florida is exemplary. Life without parole entered Florida as a by-product of such reform initiatives of the early 1980s, when abolition of parole generated widespread

LWOP; these were reforms prioritizing fairness, consistency, and efficiency in sentencing, not severity and incapacitation.

Fairness and Efficiency Reform

In the early 1980s people sentenced to life in Florida had several levels of criminal justice mechanisms by which they might obtain review and release. First, they were entitled to parole review after a minimum portion of time served. Second, by statute they were entitled to mandatory clemency review after ten years if their disciplinary record was clean. Third, there was the "gain time" system, by which a prisoner accrued a certain amount of time off their sentence for every month without a disciplinary incident. All told, life-sentenced prisoners in Florida served on average less than a dozen years before release. During the late 1970s nearly three hundred life-sentenced prisoners were released annually on parole or to some form of community supervision; over the same period, roughly an equal number were admitted annually into the system.[23] This confluence of admission and release comported with the reigning philosophy of the FLDOC at the time, which stressed an "opportunity" for all people imprisoned, including those serving life sentences, to demonstrate an ability to live in society.

As the 1970s turned into the 1980s, "distaste for [the] fundamental thesis of the indeterminate philosophy, that postconviction officials should have power over time served," grew in Florida, as elsewhere in the United States, among both liberal and conservative critics.[24] The public perception of determinate sentencing reform was that it would "bring truth to prison sentences."[25] But criminal justice actors were also concerned with arbitrariness and outlier effects of discretion. Whereas the public perceived parole as too soft, some state officials worried the parole agency was not releasing prisoners expeditiously enough to withstand increasing prison admissions.[26] Florida courts appointed a task force to study sentencing reform. The task force recommended alternatives to incarceration and restrictions on discretion, over statutory increases in sentence lengths or spending on new penal facilities.[27] Among the task force's most substantial proposals were to implement sentencing guidelines and abolish the Parole and Probation Commission, which had long been under scrutiny.[28] The legislature adopted both: the resulting law gave the Parole Commission a sunset date and eliminated parole for all noncapital crimes as of October 1, 1983.[29]

Interest in curbing the discretion of judges was also brewing. As a former chief justice of the Florida Supreme Court pointed out, "Where people show up at Raiford [State Prison] for life crimes, they are similarly situated in terms of past criminal history, [but] one's doing five and one's doing

twenty. . . . That's what guidelines are aimed at."[30] To remedy such disparities, legislators took direct aim at life felony cases, for which judges were
authorized to impose either a life sentence or a sentence with a mandatory
minimum of at least thirty years. By the latter route, sentencing judges
retained power over release for up to one-third of the sentence imposed;
some were in the practice of "imposing 700 or 800 years sentences so the
judge can in effect . . . act as a parole board."[31] The consequences were
potentially fatal: as one legislator exclaimed, referring to the fate of a prisoner with a seven-hundred-year sentence, "he won't ever make it."[32] In an
effort to curb this practice, legislators replaced the thirty-year minimum
with a forty-year maximum.[33]

As with parole, the concern with judicial discretion, in both public and professional spheres, was not in the first instance that sentences were not harsh
enough. Rather, it was that sentences were arbitrary and release practices
inconsistent. Restricting discretion and abolishing parole, it was thought,
could solve those problems. And in the process, reform would "mak[e] the
system less complex so the person on the street can understand."[34]

Cutting Off Lifers

If one guiding principle of Florida's 1983 sentencing reform was to even out
sentencing and make it more consistent, another was to address the ongoing
prison overcrowding crisis. Like many states at the time, Florida was under
court order to reduce its prison population.[35] Legislators understood that
abolishing parole could aggravate overcrowding.[36] Accordingly, abolishing
parole was viable only if another release mechanism compensated.[37] Built
into the reform therefore was a plan to offset any sentence-length increases
resulting from the move to fixed sentencing by expanding gain time.[38] As
one commentator noted, "A model prisoner would be able to work off up
to forty-five percent of the sentence through good behavior" and "without
such incentives, officials say, it would be impossible to keep order in the
prisons."[39]

The law's effects, however, were not the same for all prisoners. A separate regulation precluded prisoners not sentenced to terms of years—that is,
death-sentenced or life-sentenced prisoners—from accruing gain time unless
the governor first commuted the sentence.[40] During legislative hearings, the
Parole Commission voiced doubts about placing the responsibility for life-
sentenced prisoners solely with the governor, noting that the commission
had been created precisely because the executive was overwhelmed with
clemency applications. The governor's task force, too, recommended allowing people serving life sentences to earn gain time without commutation.

But the matter received little discussion, and no such provision surfaced in the resulting law.[41]

In the following years the synergy between parole abolition and the gain time restriction worked a significant split in the treatment of life-sentenced and long-term prisoners, a division that had not existed before. On the one hand, gain time provisions led to an overall shortening of sentence lengths, which more than offset the impact of parole abolition for people serving long terms.[42] On the other hand, people sentenced to life could not put gain time to use. Moreover, life-sentenced prisoners' opportunities for release declined as clemency disappeared as a meaningful route of review (a phenomenon discussed in the next chapter). A long-standing statutory mechanism requiring the governor to annually review lifers who had served ten years on good behavior was not in regular operation.[43] Further, the new burden on the executive was significant. In the summer of 1983, 9.9 percent of the Florida prison population was sentenced to life (2,736 prisoners), with an intake averaging over 300 new lifer admissions per year.[44] The governor's office ultimately did not struggle with this new burden so much as neglect it. The statutory mechanism was soon dissolved: a 1986 amendment excluded people serving capital life sentences, and in 1988 the legislature repealed the statutory mechanism altogether.[45] As clemency withered for noncapital lifers, so did any reasonable possibility of release.

Did the Florida legislature see the unique bind into which it had placed people serving noncapital life sentences? The legislative record suggests not. To be sure, many legislators supported strong punishment for violent crime as well as reserving prison space for people who committed serious and violent crimes.[46] But the principal aim of the 1983 reform was not to increase existing punishments or preclude releases. Rather, expanded gain time provisions were meant to offset the sentence-lengthening impact of parole abolition, and limits on the sentences imposed for life felonies were to preserve some possibility of release.[47] Some lawmakers certainly recognized the risks that came with placing lifers' fates in the governor's hands. But the better explanation is that the legislature, in the midst of a vast system overhaul, did not carefully contemplate the logistics of clemency or the impact this could have on people serving life sentences. In 1983 clemency retrenchment was by no means a sure thing; indeed, a statutory mechanism in place called for executive review. This is not to say the outcome of parole abolition was entirely unintentional or unforeseen. But little thought was given to the quite severe consequences of the shift. The hearings record single legislators voicing concern, while the attention of the majority of legislators was firmly elsewhere.

Sentencing guidelines, parole abolition, and gain time tend to dominate talk about the 1983 reforms. Less discussed is the uniquely severe treatment that resulted for people sentenced to life. From the mid-1990s onward, LWOP statutes have been used frequently by legislators as declarations to show toughness on crime, but the now expansive use of life without parole in Florida began with, and in effect was made possible by, a fairness-and-efficiency reform. The 1983 reform was Florida's most understated move toward LWOP and, in a single stroke, its most substantial.[48] It set in place a broad foundation of sentences that would become perpetual confinement as the meaning and practice of life without parole shifted from a sentence in which a governor would consider commutation to a sentence without a reasonable possibility of release.[49] As the Florida history shows, at times the introduction of LWOP was less an intentional act than a residual accretion.

PROMISES OF PERPETUAL CONFINEMENT

From the mid-1970s onward, US crime and punishment policy needed credibility repair, and as the previous section illustrates, one way in which states sought to attain it was by reducing the discretion of key actors, judges and parole administrators most of all. Over time, however, failed reform efforts fed the sort of political circumstances that Mona Lynch characterizes as "competing toughness," environments that rewarded what Jonathan Simon refers to as "governing through crime."[50] Every state has a different history of the punitive turn, but among many one finds a common pattern: in circumstances of doubt about criminal justice and in the midst of policy tug-of-war, competing toughness coupled with governing through crime generated a cycle of reforms in which sentencing laws ratcheted up in severity with successive legislative enactments.[51]

In addition to sustaining a rising tide of punishment, concerns about crime and crime policy nourished a terrain of public distrust in which promises of perpetual confinement could flourish as instruments of public reassurance. As the dismantling of indeterminate sentencing and parole generated life without parole as residue (described earlier), the shift also generated circumstances that were fertile ground for what had been a long-standing but relatively infrequent way of using life without parole: a promise of no release.

A classic example is New York governor Nelson Rockefeller's 1973 state of the state address. Rockefeller proposed punishing drug crimes with life without parole, a sentence quite unknown to the New York penal system at the time. Legislators promptly rejected the proposal, interpreting Rockefeller's move as a political ploy to ante up his drug-law scheme and indirectly impose executive demands on sentence lengths, which was a legislative prerogative.[52] The war on drugs, an enterprise in which different offensives were posed in different states at different times, punctuates LWOP history, and some have seen in Rockefeller's declaration a stirring of change in criminal justice practice, a first shot in the racially coded politics of the drug war.[53] But Rockefeller's declaration was also a signature event with respect to perpetual confinement. In Rockefeller's act—a throwing up of hands in response to a crisis, admitting an inability to rectify the situation by any other means—exasperation with crime control met public insecurity, resulting in LWOP as a pledge of reassurance. What seemed arrogant and out of place in 1970s New York, however, was far from unusual by century's end. LWOP became a go-to sentence for serious drug crimes and other serious offenses, pronounced even in situations where it was superfluous.[54]

Promises of LWOP did more than reassure an anxious public. They brought the *idea* of putting a person in prison for life and the *practice* of imposing a lifetime prison term into the toolkit of penal professionals. LWOP as a promise of perpetual confinement served as a model for actors, such as sentencing judges, to replicate. In a time when legislatures were taking back control of sentencing from courts and parole, some courts "acted out" by imposing extreme sentences. The following history from Michigan illustrates a particular case in which sentencing courts, inspired by the state legislature's partial but incomplete use of LWOP, bent the law to impose death-in-prison sentences by other means where LWOP was not technically available. Through such practices, perpetual confinement was becoming a more common idea among actors in the penal field. In this regard, virtual life sentences too were artifacts of transition.

Law and Order Reform

Michigan has a long history with life sentencing. It was the first US state after the colonial era to eliminate capital punishment, instituting life imprisonment as its ultimate penalty in 1846.[55] Traditionally a leader in progressive prison reform, Michigan pioneered the rehabilitative prison model in 1869, parole in 1885, and indeterminate sentencing at the turn of the century.[56] Throughout most of the twentieth century in Michigan, as in many states, life without parole sentences could end in release just as life with parole sentences could.[57]

Michigan penal policy took a punitive turn in the late twentieth century, however, and changes relating to life sentencing and parole played a part. The 650-lifer law, passed in spring 1978, made life without parole the mandatory sentence for trafficking or possessing 650 grams or more of certain controlled substances.[58] Another key moment was a public ballot initiative known as "Proposal B." Winning a strong majority of the popular vote, and made official by constitutional amendment later the same year, Proposal B was a referendum on parole review, eliminating good time credits and parole eligibility for more than eighty crimes, ranging from violent to personal injury to property offenses.[59] While Proposal B converted sentences for a few offenses to mandatory life without parole (life without parole was otherwise authorized in Michigan for first-degree murder and for certain drug offenses via the 650-lifer law), its most significant effect had to do with these dozens of other crimes to which it applied. Under prior law all sentences for "life or a term of years" were eligible for parole after ten years.[60] Proposal B, however, authorized judges, if not imposing life sentences, to set minimum terms longer than ten years, much longer if they wished.[61] This was quite different from reforms, such as the 1983 Florida law discussed previously, that eliminated parole *and* restricted judicial power.

The expansive discretion awarded to sentencing judges for Proposal B crimes generated an uneven effect. In the late 1980s and into the 1990s Michigan lifers and long-termers encountered a circumstance in which (1) a life sentence (with parole eligibility arising after ten years) could be far less than life, and (2) a term of years (under the broad discretion authorized by Proposal B) could be far more than life. Judges who regarded this disparity as an artifact of legislative oversight took to imposing extremely long mandatory terms in order to replicate life without parole in areas where the legislature had not authorized it. Such knowing imposition of sentences that would outlast prisoners' life spans, a novel consequence of the increasing notoriety in Michigan of LWOP as a death-in-prison term, generated a brief but tenacious struggle among Michigan appellate courts.[62]

An Old Doctrine against Sentences Exceeding Life Spans

A key device in this struggle was a century old. In 1888, a twenty-three-year-old facing a fifty-year sentence argued that his sentence was "a life sentence, in effect" and disproportionate to his crime. Resolving the case on another issue, the court nevertheless announced the following: "[T]he Constitution has not left the liberty of the citizen of any state entirely to the indiscretion or caprice of its judiciary, but enjoins upon all that unusual punishments shall not be inflicted. Where the punishment for an offense is for a term of years, to be fixed by the judge, it should never be made to extend beyond the average period of persons in prison life, which seldom exceeds 25 years."[63] The emphasis placed on the "average period" of "prison life" indicates the basis for the decision was not only disproportionality between crime and punishment, but also the indignity of death in prison. This doctrine lay dormant for nearly a century before being revived by Michigan appellate courts in the late 1980s to combat the aggressive sentencing practices that developed under Proposal B.[64]

The first appellate decision to invoke the doctrine in the contemporary context concerned a conviction for two Proposal B crimes, armed robbery and first-degree criminal sexual assault, for which the sentencing judge had imposed a mandatory minimum sentence of one hundred years. Looking to the century-old case (*Murray*), the appellate court wrote:

> *Murray*'s value lies not in the absolute numbers it offers. Its recommendation of a twenty-five-year cap on the prison sentence of a twenty-three-year-old defendant reflects the harshness of life when the opinion was written. More important is *Murray*'s recognition that a sentence for a term of years should consider a defendant's life expectancy. An indeterminate sentence "for any term of years" must be . . . fashioned with consideration of a defendant's life expectancy at the time of sentencing as determined by the trial judge.[65]

A footnote, reprimanding the sentencing court, offered an additional justification: "A sentence of one or more centuries in prison violates the spirit and intent of the indeterminate sentencing statutes. . . . Any changes in the parole provisions of the 'lifer law' should be made by the Legislature, not the judiciary."

Many legal challenges followed, raised by people sentenced to minimum terms well beyond their life spans. In *People v. Legree*, for example, a prosecutor had foregone a first-degree murder prosecution, which if successful would have returned a mandatory LWOP sentence, and obtained instead convictions for second-degree murder and first-degree criminal sexual conduct (Proposal B crimes), for which the court imposed a sentence of 150–500 years.[66] The appeals court appreciated that serious crimes demanded serious punishments but found the sentence illegal, echoing *Murray*:

> With the exception of first-degree murder and certain major drug offenses, where life imprisonment without parole is required, the Legislature has authorized and approved a sentencing scheme of indeterminate sentences. . . . [A]s a result, some trial judges, as evidenced by this case, avoid imposing a life sentence which has the potential of parole after ten years in an effort to impose an even greater sentence. . . . We see no reason to exalt form over substance. In form this is an indeterminate sentence; in substance it is just as determinate as a life sentence without the possibility of parole.[67]

The state's highest appellate court soon weighed in, in a case (*Moore*) in which the sentencing court, imposing a minimum of one hundred years, had been explicit about its intention: "Because the appellate courts of our state have said that in point of fact a life sentence for this sort of crime allows him to be reviewed in ten years, I intend to utilize numbers with the belief that the law requires that the numbers be served before you become eligible for review."[68] Reversing, the Michigan Supreme Court held that a sentence to a term of years must be a sentence that the prisoner "has a reasonable prospect of actually serving."[69] Yet the court's holding adhered to a norm of review for release that, in the late 1980s, was fading fast. The *Moore* decision, as such, set an unstable precedent that would be debated for years.

The Old Doctrine's Demise

Following *Moore*, dozens of cases in which courts imposed de facto LWOP sentences for Proposal B crimes were remanded for resentencing. And in many cases where sentencing courts imposed death-in-prison terms, lower courts reversed. Some court panels, however, adopted a different strategy. Working within but also around the *Murray-Moore* rule, these courts took an optimistic view of prisoners' life expectancy, estimating it to be in the eighties if not the nineties.[70] As the *Moore* rule became increasingly distorted, even judges who once supported the doctrine lost confidence in it.

In 1994 the Michigan Supreme Court justice who penned the dissent in *Moore* wrote for the majority of the court in a 4–3 decision that overruled *Moore* and rescripted the legislative narrative of Proposal B.[71] Upholding a 60- to 120-year prison term for criminal sexual conduct, the decision criticized appellate courts for abstracting from the gruesome horror of crimes in attempts to reduce sentence lengths. Public initiative Proposal B, it emphasized, was expressly intended to eliminate prisoners' opportunities for review and release. As such, it was a mistake to interpret the law as precluding terms of years that pushed parole eligibility beyond an incarcerated person's life expectancy. In dissent, the court's chief justice attempted to mitigate views that would equate parole review with release, emphasizing that "being subject to the jurisdiction of the Parole Board and actually being paroled are two distinctly different prospects," a position mirrored in policy efforts at the time.[72] The decision, however, effectively marked the end of *Moore* and life expectancy as a sentencing limit.

On one level the *Murray-Moore* debate, which occupied the Michigan Supreme Court for more than half a decade, concerned a changing culture of sentencing, reflected in the judges' different interpretations of the intent behind Proposal B. On another level, the debate involved a struggle over the power to punish—that is, over which branch of the penal state would have authority to decide whether those who commit serious, violent, sometimes high-profile crimes have a realistic opportunity for review and release during their lifetimes. Was the purpose of the statutory "life or any term of years" language to prevent life-span-exceeding punishments? Was the intent of Proposal B to end such restrictions? Those were questions judges answered differently. To see the fracas over *Moore* simply as a struggle between the legislature, judiciary, and parole board oversimplifies, as does casting it merely as a cultural tug-of-war between judges with different positions on sentencing. The two levels ran together.

Virtual Life Sentences as Artifacts of Transition

We might return here to Michael Tonry's idea of residue and the notion of growing pains associated with the indeterminate-to-determinate sentencing paradigm shift, as old practices took on new meanings. "Under indeterminate sentencing," Tonry recognizes, "every prisoner in some systems was eligible for parole release after serving one year, no matter how long the maximum sentence announced by the judge."[73] Judges might impose very large numbers of years in cases where they were horrified by the facts and wanted to make a statement. Yet, Tonry notes, these high maximum sentences were symbolic, imposed in circumstances where parole eligibility would attach anyway. The practice, Tonry points out, ingrained in judges a habit of imposing long sentences, often for rhetorical or symbolic effect, which remained when states shifted away from indeterminate sentencing and parole, contributing to a rather uncritical acceptance of long prison sentences that *actually* resulted in long times served.[74]

The extremely long minimum sentences imposed by Michigan courts following Proposal B could be seen as such residue of transition. But the preceding discussion shows more was going on. Judges were not imposing extreme maximum sentences assuming parole would pick up the slack or unreflectively engaging in anachronistic practices. They were intentionally imposing exorbitant minimum sentences to prevent parole review and impose de facto LWOP sentences beyond where the legislature authorized. Some sentencing judges explicitly stated as much. In sum, Proposal B did more than leave old practices meaning something new. It shifted the distribution of the power to punish toward sentencing courts, which were inspired by new LWOP laws to generate perpetual imprisonment in other ways. Rather than residue, we might call this type of judicial activism— itself an artifact of the shift away from indeterminate sentencing and parole in American punishment—*runoff*.

PRECIPITATE FROM A PERIOD OF EXPERIMENTATION

As indeterminate sentencing and parole were dismantled, one could imagine the life sentence might simply have been written out of penal law, replaced with a sentence of a fixed number of years. But that is not what happened. As rehabilitation faded as a prevailing penal aim, and as parole was limited in scope or altogether removed, the character of the life sentence began to change. Some reforms altered life sentences in indirect and awkward ways, as leftover aspects from an earlier system entered in a residual manner, while other laws and initiatives expressly touted LWOP as a permanent prison term.[75] This was a gradual development, and each state has its own story. What the states share, however, is that each jurisdiction, faced with a changing penal climate in the 1970s and 1980s, yielded its own answer to the problem of how to punish serious and violent crime. LWOP is one way. Virtual life sentences are another. The manner in which each state dealt with the upheaval in penal philosophy laid the groundwork for the state's subsequent use of life without parole.[76]

A final point demands emphasis. If the Michigan history provides a vivid example of struggles over the power to punish in a period of penal transition, it also shows life without parole and other sentences of imprisonment until death evolving side by side. Formal LWOP laws and the long mandatory terms that judges imposed for Proposal B crimes were technically different punishments and differed with respect to the arm of the criminal justice apparatus (legislature, judiciary, parole board) that pulled the strings. But they shared an intent to imprison people with no reasonable possibility of release. At the crux of the judicial debate was an effort to make imprisonment until death a reality. In the Michigan cases, the commonality between formal LWOP and de facto LWOP is not only that the sentences *achieved* the same thing (imprisonment until death), but also that the actors imposing the sentences *intended*, often expressly, the same thing (again, imprisonment until death). LWOP served as a reference point for judges who wished to impose death-in-prison sentences by other means. In that regard, the cases offer an example of how life without parole enabled the general spread of perpetual confinement, of how, as an idea and as a practice, perpetual confinement came in from the margins to play a regular part in American punishment.

6. Governors and Prisoners

Throughout most of US history, executive clemency, a discretionary decision entrusted to a governor and/or a board of pardons, was utilized as an instrument of mercy. Often exercised in the form of commutation of sentence, clemency was also a practical tool to even out sentencing injustices and regulate prison populations. Over the close of the twentieth century and into the twenty-first, however, as governors sought to use crime and punishment to political advantage or became concerned that increases in prison populations and heightened scrutiny of criminal justice decisions would render executive review procedures either unacceptable or unmanageable, clemency practices were retrenched. What we know as LWOP would not exist without the retrenchment of clemency, regardless of tougher sentencing laws and execution alternatives. Understanding the emergence of life without parole as a form of perpetual confinement, therefore, demands an examination of the atrophy—and in some cases, the active restructuring—of this age-old practice.

Just as changes in clemency are a major chapter in the emergence of LWOP, it is also true that life sentencing is important in the history of clemency. For many years commuting life sentences was one of the most significant exercises of state clemency, particularly in states where life-sentenced prisoners were not eligible for parole and that relied on clemency to manage prison release. Yet most scholarly coverage of clemency's contemporary demise is directed toward the waning exercise of the US president's pardon power or the diminished use of clemency in capital cases. The literature on clemency, as such, has been missing in life sentencing a rather key entry.

To illustrate the relationship between the disappearance of executive clemency and the institutionalization of LWOP, this chapter focuses on Pennsylvania, a state in which all life sentences have been without parole since the 1940s. Relying on governors' papers from the state archives as well as historical legislative materials, case law, and news media, I focus on interactions between the state governor, the governors' cabinet, the department of corrections, and people serving life sentences during a pivotal period beginning in the early 1970s. Drawing out the changes that followed, the chapter shows how in Pennsylvania the law of life sentencing did not change so much as the practice did. Changes in practice, moreover, were accompanied by changes in the way that state actors thought about release from prison, as assumptions favoring release turned to assumptions that there would be none. This history brings into view a past way of thinking about and practicing life sentencing that is distinguishable from the present and shows the contingent happenings, arrangements, and processes by which that earlier form changed.

The history also brings into focus something else that is hard to envision from the present—namely, the deterioration of a social relationship, a discarded line of conversation that, however conflicted and tenuous, once existed between governors and prisoners. The 1970s were troubled times in Pennsylvania prisons, with racial hostility, lethal violence, reports of widespread prison rape, and a legacy of pharmaceutical and biochemical testing on prisoners. Yet within that chaos there existed, for a time, a dialogue in which lifers had some voice in their own future and governors learned from some of their most alienated subjects.

The following discussion, then, recounts two transformations. First, it shows how LWOP, more than a product of lawmaking, emerged in Pennsylvania in significant part through processes of change to executive clemency. Second, it shows how alterations to commutation laws and practices redefined how people sentenced to life envisioned themselves, their relationship to the state, and their possibilities for action. The retrenchment of commutation in Pennsylvania, completed by the mid-1990s, is by now a well-known story. Thousands have felt its impact. History illuminates the possibility of an alternative, a relationship through which state executives kept in touch with the dignity of incarcerated people and the purpose and end of punishing: a way of knowing prisoners that was, at least for a time in Pennsylvania, as key to the meaning of life sentences as it was to the meaning of governing.

CLEMENCY AND PUNISHMENT

As a tool of governance, clemency is multifaceted. On the one hand many of clemency's functions are political: a check for erratic judicial sentencing practices; a mechanism for relieving prison overcrowding; a vehicle for expressing the values and power of the state; an instrument for political deal making; or a signal of needed law reform.[1] On the other hand clemency is an exercise of mercy that is personal and cultural, "informal and idiosyncratic," guided by "widely shared understandings of excuse, mitigation, and blame-worthiness."[2] The pardon power, as such, sits on "the border of sovereignty and law," straddling "our culture's desire for rule-governed conduct and the ungovernability of mercy."[3]

Commutations were "vital features of the U.S. criminal justice system" during the nineteenth century and for much of the twentieth.[4] During the twentieth century efforts were made in the federal jurisdiction and in many states to formalize and bureaucratize clemency by attaching a board of pardons or by replacing it with parole.[5] Still, some laws remained in effect that restricted parole boards from deciding release for life sentences, holdovers from a traditional system by which the state governor (with or without an advisory body) was expected (if not legally required) to exercise discretion and release prisoners through the clemency power. By these methods, many states granted release for lifers with regularity,[6] in decisions that were by turn subjective and objective, political and administrative, demonstrative and low-key.

From the late 1970s and early 1980s onward, however, clemency practices wilted.[7] On paper, statutes precluding parole for lifers did not change much if at all. But the reality of how sentences played out in practice became distinctly different. This was especially fateful in states that relied throughout the twentieth century solely on clemency for deciding the length of life terms, where prisoners' expectations of certain commutation practices were deeply ingrained and featured significantly in decisions about whether to go to trial or accept a plea.[8]

In recent decades the resistance of governors and elected members of pardons boards to commuting life sentences has been marked by the dwindling of justifications deemed viable for clemency, most notably mercy.[9] Marie Gottschalk attributes this to a turn toward retributive punishment.[10] Jonathan Simon connects it to the transformation of executive power in the late twentieth century, as clemency is inconsistent with a style of governing that thrives on promises to lock up and throw away the key.[11] Rachel Barkow links clemency's decline to the rise of the administrative state.[12] While these are convincing explanations of clemency's downturn, each leaves out something important about the character of what has been lost: namely, clemency's role as a channel of communication, specifically between the governor and those incarcerated.

Clemency is a means of establishing a relationship with the governed. It is an institution in which criminal procedures and politics are blurred with personal interactions and communications. As Otto Kirchheimer explained, describing "clemency's unavoidable dialectics": "Clemency is deeply immersed in the substructure of politics, its campaigns and strategies, its assumptions and symbols. But at the same time it provides the possibility of transcending the configurations of the day and introducing a touch of subjectivity into the rational rule whereby we attempt to govern human relations."[13] One casualty of the retrenchment of commutation, accordingly, is this channel that put the governor and the governor's advisors in conversation with people serving life.

A PENNSYLVANIA PREHISTORY

The pardon power has a long, contentious history in Pennsylvania as a "component of the criminal justice system."[14] The power sits formally with the governor, but the governor is not the only one involved. Early on, governors worked with pardons clerks to assess clemency petitions. The Pennsylvania Constitution of 1874 formalized the process, creating an executive agency—a board of pardons consisting of the attorney general, lieutenant governor, secretary of internal affairs, and secretary of the commonwealth—to tailor the governor's authority. The governor could commute sentences only upon recommendation of the board.[15]

In the early 1900s, a board of parole overseen by the judiciary was authorized to review cases of prisoners who had served minimum terms and recommend them for release. This was a cost- and capacity-saving measure but also stemmed from a belief that rehabilitation occurs more effectively outside the prison. The board of pardons and the governor could still reduce minimum sentences and release prisoners at any time and continued to exercise this power, primarily in cases with long or life sentences. In 1929 the board of pardons' authority was extended, giving the board power to supervise people released on parole.[16]

For the first three decades of the twentieth century, then, there was a confluence in the functions of pardons and parole, despite their distinctly different backgrounds. Notwithstanding parole's purportedly "scientific" basis, in Pennsylvania executive actors were better informed and made fewer but more reliable release decisions. Roughly nine times more prisoners were released by parole than pardons, but the latter had a far lower recidivism rate. A senior parole official attributed the difference to "the material which the Board of Pardons has at hand," including background history, letters from prosecutors and judges, psychiatric and institutional histories, and post-release plans. If commutation was politically controversial, often challenged as arbitrary and subjective, there was nevertheless evidence that it was an effective means of ensuring public safety as well as the well-being and reintegration of the formerly imprisoned. It was, therefore, "a worthwhile gamble for society to use the power of clemency judiciously."[17]

In 1939 a governor's commission recommended formally separating pardons and parole. The Parole Act of 1941 (Section 17) did so, establishing an independent administrative agency with general paroling authority over all prisoners. Another part of the act (Section 21), however, precluded the new agency from deciding release for "convicts condemned to death or serving life imprisonment" (which included, at the time, people convicted of first-degree murder or repeat second-degree murder). An absence of legislative history and evidence of legislative intent regarding this discrepancy creates something of a block for historical research. On the one hand the limitation on life and death cases was consistent with a practice by which the parole board could act only after a prisoner had served a minimum sentence, which life sentences and death sentences technically lacked. On the other hand there is reason to think that more than a technicality gave rise to this distinction; the assessment finding commutation successful in deciding when people convicted of the most serious crimes were ready for release indicates that the effectiveness of clemency also played a role. Whatever the intention, the division of labor between Sections 17 and 21 formalized a difference between lifers and other prisoners by which the former were "without parole."[18]

From the 1940s through the 1970s, this difference had little practical import. Commutation for lifers was regular. The usual practice was to commute to a sentence six to twelve months out, so the prison could evaluate and prepare the person for release.[19] In this regard, the Pennsylvania commutation practice for lifers was similar to practices in other states that did not authorize parole or restricted its use. As one legislator put it in 1961: "In the year 1954, life imprisonment in Pennsylvania meant that a prisoner had to serve 19.6 years in the penitentiary. . . . [I]n 1958, it meant that he had to serve 17.2. . . . This is what life imprisonment means."[20]

Clemency for a life sentence, in sum, was a well-oiled administrative channel, but it was also informal, idiosyncratic, and even somewhat personal. Although clemency was technically available for all prisoners (however long the sentence), and pardons always could be granted (even to those already released), it was the governor's exclusive responsibility to decide release for people serving life sentences. This generated a line of communication between lifers and the executive with the potential to be mutually beneficial.

PERSONAL TALK

In the early 1970s, the prisoners' rights movement reached an apex in the United States. Nationwide, organizing inside and outside prisons brought attention to conditions of confinement and questioned the prison as an instrument of punishment. Prison uprisings punctuated the environment. The uprisings at Attica in New York and San Quentin in California became national spectacles.[21] These events polarized public opinion and pushed state actors in different directions. One path took the claims of incarcerated people seriously and saw the uprisings as protests calling for serious thought about how corrections administrations attended to the needs of the human beings housed in state custody. Another path reacted to uprisings as acts of race-based mutiny if not violent revolution, redressing prisoners as manipulative and dangerous. These were pivotal moments in US corrections, when perspectives on crime, people who committed crimes, and the role of the prison were subject to change; and turbulent ones, not only in terms of a crisis of faith in penal philosophy but with respect to the challenges that violent altercations and racial tensions presented on the ground in everyday practice.

The history of Pennsylvania prisons in the 1960s and 1970s is similarly fraught. Throughout the 1960s pharmaceutical and biochemical testing, a notorious incident of race-based exploitation and medical experimentation on incarcerated people, occurred at Holmesburg, a prison in Philadelphia that was home primarily to Black prisoners and staffed by Black officers and White administrators.[22] In 1970, Holmesburg experienced an uprising, which the Philadelphia mayor construed as a race riot, in which many people were injured and two guards killed. As pressure mounted to curtail prisoners' liberties and heighten security, incarcerated people's advocates pushed back seeking improved conditions and due process rights.

Taking office in January 1971, Pennsylvania governor Milton Shapp stepped into this crisis. His administration's response to prisoners in the wake of the Holmesburg uprising, the effects of which carried well into the following year, cannot be detached from this historical context. On October 14, 1971, Wycliffe Jangdharrie, president of the West Philadelphia chapter of the NAACP, wrote to Shapp: "We are sitting on a 'powder keg' set to go off at any moment. Revolution is in the air, and when legitimate pleas for humanitarian treatment and prison reform are ignored we must all pay the consequences."[23] In response, rather than portray prisoners as dangerous or take the opportunity to set a law-and-order tone or send a message to Black nationalists, the Shapp administration introduced legislation to improve prison programming and arranged visits to Pennsylvania's largest prisons to meet with incarcerated people, prison staff, and administrators.

Early the next year, Shapp visited Western State Penitentiary. As he put it, "I spent . . . twelve hours inside this medieval structure, not just inspecting its facilities but more importantly talking at great length to the warden, top members of his staff, to guards, and to many prisoners. It was 3AM on Friday morning before I returned to the outer world."[24] Days later, Shapp received a letter from the prison's superintendent, Joseph Brierley. The letter made clear that Shapp's questions at the facility predominantly had to do with lifers. Of specific interest was programming, including prerelease furloughs, from which lifers were excluded. As Brierley emphasized, "It concerns a matter of grave importance to us and the 119 men who are serving life sentences in our institution. For as we develop programs towards the fulfillment of economic efficiency, civic responsibility, and self-realization for the majority of our residents, the men serving life sentences are undergoing, by exclusion, increased punishment."[25] Noting that "the average lifer serves approximately 18 years before his sentence is commuted and he is paroled to the community," Brierley explained:

> A life sentence, in the State of Pennsylvania today, is tantamount to perpetuating all the forces of life in the individual without purpose; to engender in him hope, faith and possible meaning to life and then to thwart its fulfillment. As a result, they develop a feeling of impotence flowing from the nature of their sentence which nullifies all their personal accomplishments and causes them to question the efficacy of such programs. This is perhaps the ultimate in punishment and it's exactly what our men are presently suffering by being deprived of total participation in our community programs due to legislation and the length of incarceration they must face. . . . They witness daily the reintegration of other residents into the community while they must stand idly by. It's as though they are caught in a nether land where they can neither walk, fly, nor swim.[26]

Five days later, Shapp appeared before the Senate Judiciary Committee and introduced two life-sentenced prisoners "selected by their fellow inmates to be their representatives to present their views to you today." As Shapp recounted:

> I met these men last week under circumstances I shall never forget. . . .
> For five hours last Thursday I engaged in a rap session with between
> 40 and 50 of the men who are serving the longest sentences in the
> Western Penitentiary. Many were lifers. The men in that group,
> because they are the ones who are serving the longest, have become the

leaders within the prison. The system of leadership works there just about the same way it does in the General Assembly.

For five hours—from just before 5PM to just before 10PM I sat with these men as they revealed how the system of justice now in effect strips them of human dignity, of hope for the future and of about any chance to ever again participate meaningfully in society.

Introducing the two men, Hardy and Szymanski, Shapp asserted: "I do not know what they are going to say this morning or if I will agree with what they say, but I do know that if we are to reform our system of justice in Pennsylvania in any meaningful manner, we certainly must, at the very least, listen to the views of those most affected by any changes that you as lawmakers and I as Governor shall make."[27]

The Shapp administration partnered programming with a second aim: to establish a minimum term for life sentences, after which lifers would be parole-eligible regardless of commutation. In 1971 Attorney General Shane Creamer spearheaded this effort, which would have channeled release decisions away from the governor's office.[28] The focal point, again, was conversations with people serving life sentences. Relying on lifers to determine their own fate, however, was in part counterproductive. Lifer Jon Yount recalled six "Attorney General Rap Sessions," during which the attorney general invited a dozen prisoners, representatives from different state prisons, to his office and asked them to agree on a minimum term. The effort was undercut by lifers' divergent views ("Six times these elected representatives attempted to agree on a minimum term and six times they failed!"), which differed in part based on the time people had served and expected to serve.[29] The complexity of lifer views was amplified by the divergent positions of lifer organizations from different prison institutions.[30]

Discussions continued during the next legislative session. Hearings before the 1973 House Judiciary Committee highlight critical issues on which passage of a reform bill turned. Two legislators visited Graterford Prison, where lifers announced they opposed a fifteen-year minimum because "the average time right now is about eighteen years for commutation and they didn't like the idea of having a fixed period." David Terrell, who was incarcerated at Dallas Prison and appeared before the committee to share grievances about programming, corroborated this assertion:

> This here [the proposed fifteen-year minimum] we think is the intention of putting a ceiling on the time that a lifer would serve but in actuality it puts a base on it. . . . Right now a man is eligible for parole on life in one, two, three years. He can get commutation at any time and make commutation and go out on parole in one or two years. Very few do but

some go out in twelve or thirteen, right, and the bill would actually put a base on there and there are a lot of men in institutions that should never serve fifteen years.[31]

More prisoners appeared at hearings on the bill and fielded legislators' questions about minimum sentences, but that was not their focus. Rather, much in the mode of the times, they sought to discuss programming and conditions of confinement.[32]

To understand the Shapp administration's response to unrest in Pennsylvania prisons, one must see it as informed by a historical clemency practice for lifers that had been active for decades. Prior to the Shapp administration, the commutation grant rate for applications from lifers was steady at 25–30 percent, and during Shapp's tenure it increased. Memoranda to the governor, reviewing the board of pardon's recommendations for commutation during Shapp's first term, offer a sampling of how the administration approached clemency. The lieutenant governor and counsel to the governor, cabinet members in charge of clemency, urged that to improve the process there was "a vital need for prisoners to personally appear before the Board" and that "each prisoner should be represented by counsel."[33] The papers also demonstrate a practice of erring on the side of commutation, with recommendations phrased in terms such as "looks like a good bet" and "looks like this is a risk worth taking." The interoffice correspondence displays an approach that sought to even out the system and extend compassion and mercy. As with the prison reform efforts noted previously, the clemency efforts reflect a practice of listening to incarcerated people's concerns, considering their needs, and making an effort to understand residents from diverse social backgrounds.

One ought to recognize, however, the limits of this conversation. Clemency decisions are informed by executive actors' personal experiences and viewpoints. Shapp and his officials did not visit all prisons. They focused on institutions that housed male prisoners and invited representatives from those institutions to the legislature to speak. It appears officials did not visit the women's prison at Muncy, and whether the Shapp administration took into account the concerns of women serving life sentences is unclear.[34] In this light, a letter to Shapp from LaDainty Little, president of the Pennsylvania Lifer's Association at Muncy, asking to "know more about" a proposal developed by a lifers' association at another prison, must also be read as a call for inclusion in a conversation between the governor and prisoners that was predominantly gender specific.[35]

This chapter has emphasized the active approach to clemency that Shapp's administration maintained despite the racial hostilities, lethal violence, and heated debates over prison reform—the increasing politicization of penal policy—that took place during his tenure. But the Shapp administration began with more sensitivity to prisoners than it ended with. During his second term Shapp made only half as many commutation grants as in his first term, and the rate of acceptance of board recommendations declined from nearly 100 percent through 1975 to just over 50 percent in 1979, the final year of Shapp's governorship.[36]

Today, the dignity with which lifers were treated in Shapp's statements before the legislature and in Brierley's letter, as well as the process of listening to prisoners before making decisions about sentencing and release, seem foreign. This is because while the letter of the law precluding parole for lifers remained the same in ensuing decades, the law's meaning, and related perceptions of incarcerated people and the treatment they are due, changed dramatically. Within a matter of a decade, under different gubernatorial oversight, the clemency rate for lifers in Pennsylvania fell to zero, and a governor was elected on a campaign platform that placed retrenchment and even restructuring of long-standing commutation protocol at the top of the agenda.

LEGAL LIMBO

The 1973 bill that would have established a right to review for release after fifteen years never passed out of committee. The ambivalence with which prisoners responded to it left the issue, despite the Shapp administration's interest, in a legal limbo. From the present, one is tempted to look back at this open plane of conversation between lifers and the governor as a moment in which reform was possible and then lost, as a transition point in the history of Pennsylvania penal policy with a new meaning of life sentences on the horizon.

Of specific import are two pieces of legislation from 1974. Spurred by the United States Supreme Court's decision in *Furman* (chapter 4), in March 1974 Pennsylvania removed unintentional felony murder from the capital statute, redefined it as second-degree murder, reclassified all homicides previously in the second-degree category as third degree, and made the new penalty for second-degree murder a mandatory life sentence. Months later, in December 1974, the state enacted a new penal code, which reiterated a general right to parole but expressly precluded it for first-degree murder. Because Section 21 of the 1941 act had precluded parole for all people "serving life imprisonment," it was not clear whether lifers sentenced under the new second-degree murder law were eligible.[37]

With this discrepancy, confusion in Pennsylvania courtrooms and legislative discussions over lifers' eligibility for release, which existed throughout the twentieth century, rose to a new level.[38] Hearings show that lawmakers anticipated people convicted of second-degree murder would indeed have sentences commuted and be released after a period of roughly twenty years. As one state representative put it: "A sentence of life imprisonment is not necessarily a sentence of life imprisonment."[39] That seems to have been the understanding of many incarcerated people as well, for more than a decade passed before anyone convicted of second-degree murder claimed their eligibility for parole. Yount, a life prisoner who lived through this period of transition, explained: "Clearly, inmates were not inclined to fix a system they did not perceive as broken! Such a languid view may be excused for prisoners serving parole-eligible indefinite sentences inasmuch as there was no evidence—at least until the mid-Eighties—that, except for some parole violators, any non-lifer had served an entire maximum term of total confinement."[40] In light of a historically active clemency practice, the absence of parole was not yet a substantial concern.

Over the next decade, however, a number of events altered this. Taking the helm in 1979, Governor Richard Thornburgh quickly turned to crime as a political talking point. The Thornburgh administration brought prison building to Pennsylvania, not because it was immediately necessary (Pennsylvania had the seventh lowest prison population per capita of any state in 1980), but prospectively as a way to prevent overcrowding, anticipating the effects of forthcoming harsh sentencing laws. A prison hostage crisis in October 1981, although resolved peacefully, legitimated this law-and-order direction.[41] Statutes expanding the range of life sentences have been rare in Pennsylvania history, but at that moment "mandatory life imprisonment without parole" was approved as punishment should the death penalty ever again be unavailable and introduced explicitly in two bills: one for arson murder and one for a third violent felony conviction.[42] In each, the language "without parole" was superfluous, functioning to express condemnation rather than increase the actual punishment, punctuation against a backdrop soon set by clemency retrenchment.[43]

With a prison-building strategy on the horizon, clemency practice began to change. In 1980, attorney general became an elected position, lending increased political pressure to commutation decisions. More generally, Thornburgh's crime and punishment philosophy did not lend itself to mercy: Ronald Reagan's victory in the 1980 presidential election infused state-level crime politics with new energy, providing a model for political success emulated by many gubernatorial candidates across the nation, including

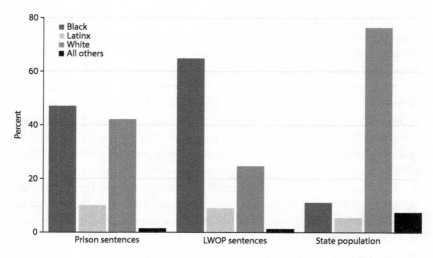

FIGURE 10.   Race and ethnicity of people serving LWOP sentences in Pennsylvania, 2016. *Source:* Quinn Cozzens and Bret Grote, *A Way Out: Abolishing Death by Incarceration in Pennsylvania* (Pittsburgh, PA: Abolition Law Center, 2018).

Thornburgh.[44] There is a diminished need for clemency in an environment where building more beds is a priority, and as economic constraints lifted, the uses for clemency changed. Thornburgh approved fewer than 10 percent of the recommendations he received, granting fewer commutations between 1979 and 1986 than Shapp ever granted in a single year.[45]

Suddenly, lifers who thought they had in clemency a channel out of prison, a reliable opportunity for review for release, realized they did not. Prisoners challenged changes in the nature of clemency practice, arguing that their right to release had been detrimentally adjusted ex post facto. In Pennsylvania and elsewhere, a disingenuousness characterized this transition: courts reinterpreting language sometimes nearly a century old applied a contemporary understanding of back-end release for life sentences that was far different from what historical documents referred to and from what incarcerated people in states such as Pennsylvania had long understood.[46]

The first legal challenge seeking clarification of the disconnect between the 1941 act and the 1974 laws came in the midst of these changes. As clemency receded, a legal right of parole was needed to take its place. Franklin Castle, sentenced to life for second-degree murder, argued he was eligible for parole under the 1974 laws.[47] This was a time, however, when legislatures and courts were thinking differently about life sentences than in prior decades. Sidestepping the disconnect between old and new laws, Pennsylvania courts held that with the 1974 law the legislature intended the life sentence itself to be a mandatory minimum. This interpretation closed the loophole, and while it did not preclude parole after commutation, the remoteness of that possibility was precisely what Castle had sought to work around.

The impact of the second-degree murder provision on the scale of life sentencing in Pennsylvania has been substantial: second-degree murder convictions account for nearly a quarter of contemporary life sentences in Pennsylvania.[48] The impact, moreover, has been racially disproportionate: Black Pennsylvanians serve life sentences at a rate eighteen times that of White Pennsylvanians (figure 10); and the disproportionality is greater for life sentences for second-degree murder than for first-degree.[49] The pardon memos from the Shapp files suggest that second-degree murder convictions—which in Pennsylvania mean homicides committed without intent—are precisely the types of cases the administration would have scrutinized and seriously considered for release.

POLITICAL TALK

The reality of life sentencing in Pennsylvania changed away from public view, but high-profile events and political debate in the 1990s brought clemency to the forefront and spurred an aggressive restructuring of the Pennsylvania Board of Pardons. No longer simply a matter of novel legal interpretations or shifts in executive discretion, by the end of the 1990s an amendment to the state constitution concerning the membership and decision-making of the board structurally altered how clemency was issued.

With rising prison admissions came some recognition that release mechanisms were still necessary. The governor who followed Thornburgh, Robert Casey (1987–1994), was known on occasion to define his own path, but more often, when Casey's advisers recommended denying a clemency application, he concurred. Victims' advocates, meanwhile, increasingly pushed for open board hearings and information on board members' individual votes.[50] During his tenure Casey granted commutation to twenty-six people serving life sentences, one of which would come back to end the gubernatorial bid of his lieutenant governor.

The changing tide of clemency and court decisions like *Castle* spotlighted a need for organized efforts at reform and resistance.[51] One such effort was 1992 HB 1382, which would have provided lifers a chance at parole without requiring commutation. A state sentencing commission member remarked that the bill had "about as much chance of getting through the Legislature in these law and order times as one of the state's 2,400 lifers has of getting a commutation."[52] Still, the bill prompted discussions among incarcerated people, their families, and activists over whether efforts were better focused on parole legislation or commutation practices and whether one effort might undercut the other.[53] As one person serving a life sentence put it, "By our acceptance of the demise of commutation and our starting in another direction, much energy is being expended on a dream of future legislation instead of working for the reality of commutation today. For the hundreds of Pennsylvania life-sentenced prisoners incarcerated twenty or more years . . . who have excellent prison records, solid and responsible community support, and are recognized by authorities as those who should have been released years ago, we must demand this process regain its stature."[54]

By 1994, the chorus of voices for and against made clemency a heated political topic. On the one hand, Casey's slim record of commutation grants was criticized by his own Commission on Corrections Planning, which compared his eleven commutations between 1990 and 1993 to nearly five hundred in Texas during the same period.[55] On the other hand, gubernatorial candidate Tom Ridge, running against Lieutenant Governor Mark Singel, characterized the number of commutations under Casey as recklessly high. Ridge's position was echoed by Mark Schweiker, a candidate for lieutenant governor, who firmly opposed even talking about commutation: "In this day and age with the concern about personal safety, we ought not to be talking about releasing violent offenders that have been given life sentences." Recalling earlier times, Shapp's lieutenant governor Ernest Kline noted this was the first election he could remember in which "the Pardons Board has been used in a political attack campaign" and called it "a bad precedent."[56] Robert Cornille, a district attorney of Allegheny County and former police chief of Pittsburgh, opposed the attack on commutation and argued Pennsylvania should "get smarter on crime, not tougher."[57] Also in favor of review for release of lifers was the Department of Corrections: at 140 percent of capacity, the department lobbied against mandatory life terms and for legislation reflecting that "the older the criminal gets, the less likely [they] will return to crime."[58]

Despite the coalition of interests opposed, Ridge zeroed in on pardon board reform, writing newspaper editorials to justify his attacks on Singel's voting record.[59] Ridge's criticisms were arguably over the top, but the public's perspective changed drastically a month before the election when Reginald McFadden, a Black man life sentenced for the murder of an elderly woman—released by Casey and Singel—was arrested in New York for rape and was considered a prime suspect for murder.[60] Singel's campaign was shaken and never recovered in the polls, leading to Ridge's victory.[61] The

McFadden incident opened a new interrogation about recidivism, and the racialized image of the dangerous prisoner that had taken hold in the early 1970s after the violent incident at Holmesburg, and another at Graterford, flared again.[62]

Adding fuel to the fire, in May 1995 Robert Simon, another former Pennsylvania prisoner, paroled after serving twelve years on a ten- to twenty-year sentence, was indicted in New Jersey for the murder of a patrol officer. Ridge, who had already ordered judiciary committee hearings on the pardons process, now ordered an investigation into parole as well.[63] During these pardon and parole inquests, prison releases came to a near standstill. Meanwhile, plans solidified for the state's first prison geriatric unit, a "prison nursing home" that opened in July 1995.[64]

The McFadden incident had a considerable impact on clemency in Pennsylvania, but one should not see it as a sharp break. Retrenchment was already under way with Thornburgh, and Ridge had used clemency as a political tool well before. The life sentence had been in transition for years, and the McFadden and Simon incidents brought this to a head. What followed, however, seared the life sentence's new meaning into the consciousness of those in Pennsylvania prisons. Amid the election melee, a constitutional amendment was proposed requiring unanimous board of pardons approval for commutation of a life or a death sentence; the amendment also proposed placing a victim advocate on the board. As one lifer, concerned with the ramifications of the amendment on the cusp of the vote, stated, "As long as that hope of freedom was there, I was willing to work hard. . . . With the door closed, I doubt very much I could keep my focus. I think there will be a lot of problems, a lot of frustration."[65] The amendment was approved by the legislature, setting the course for a public ballot. Opposition to the amendment was broad based and included the Department of Corrections, which feared that foreclosing commutation would endanger prison staff.[66] Nevertheless, the ballot initiative passed in November 1997 and was upheld after legal challenges in 2001. The energy that Pennsylvania governors and boards of pardons had once devoted to speaking with prisoners had been redirected to silencing them.

ADVERSE AWAKENING

"Awakening" is a way of referring to productive coping by people serving life and long-term prison sentences, in which they acknowledge responsibility and pledge to care for themselves and others and work toward a positive experience in the prison and toward release.[67] In Pennsylvania,

Governor Ridge's war on commutation produced an awakening of a different sort. When lifers came to in 1995 and in the years following, they found that no amount of personal transformation mattered with respect to release. The ballot initiative restructuring the board of pardons was pivotal in this regard. While the proposed initiative sparked resistance from a wide coalition of interests, once the initiative passed, clemency emerged as an entirely political conversation in which the voices of incarcerated people and their advocates were bypassed. This cast a new shadow. As one prisoner put it, the constitutional amendment restructuring the pardons board "inflict[ed] [Governor Ridge's] opinions on future governors," while fixing in place changes in the nature of commutation practice that had been developing for more than fifteen years.[68] In following years, few quality candidates were granted commutation, much less hearings before the board, and fewer lifers applied.[69]

Afterward, the possibilities for people serving life sentences in Pennsylvania, specifically with respect to their capacity to influence state actions bearing on release, were fundamentally different than they had been in the 1970s. This in turn affected their perspectives and the actions they took. The old perspective was that one had to work to get out of prison. An organized and routine process of executive review and commutation substantiated this view. The new perspective was captured by Sharon Wiggins, who was sentenced to life at the age of seventeen and served forty-five years before passing away still imprisoned in 2013, as she described how other women lifers' perceptions of her changed over time: "I had preached for so long and said if you do the right things, eventually someone will see you. Now I run across a situation where people say to me 'you've done everything and still nobody is listening.'"[70] With changes to commutation laws and practices, lifers' identities transformed alongside the sentence they served.

Life sentencing's late twentieth-century history in Pennsylvania illustrates a contemporary style of governance that Jonathan Simon called "governing through crime." More specifically, it exemplifies a way of doing things in clemency that Simon dubbed the "governor as prosecutor": a position that seeks "to identify . . . with prosecutorial fervor and loyalty to victims by rejecting any power role of neutral judgment or individualized assessment with respect to violent crime (and perhaps all crime)."[71] It is a political performance that demonizes people who have committed crimes, plays on racial fears, and turns the failure to act—denying clemency—into a statement.[72]

Being forgotten is rightly recognized as integral to the condition of serving an LWOP sentence.[73] But in states with a history such as Pennsylvania's the attribute takes on a specific meaning. Where prisoners once talked to governors and were invited by executives to speak before legislatures and visit their office suites, gubernatorial candidates now talked to each other about not talking to prisoners, and prisoners talked to themselves or to advocates at arm's reach from the political process. To highlight the Shapp administration's approach to clemency is not to overlook its critical limitations: the voices of women lifers were not part of the conversation, and release based on mercy remained susceptible to the whims of state actors. Nor is it to overlook the deplorable conditions that Pennsylvania prisoners often experienced or the violence and racial hostilities that animated Pennsylvania prisons in the 1970s. It is to emphasize how, even in the midst of that strife, people serving life sentences were responsibly reviewed for release. It is to recognize a style of punishment in which knowing about those the state punished most harshly is an essential practice; in which the governor better understands punishment, its purposes, and where and when it should end; and in which prisoners have a voice and some sense of hope.

The vernacular for natural life sentencing today is "LWOP," but for Pennsylvania's history the acronym hardly seems appropriate. The history of LWOP in Pennsylvania is predominantly a matter of change to the practices, and eventually the laws, of clemency, and a story of similar changes, the products of shifts in practice and legal culture as much as law, can be told of other states, such as Louisiana.[74] As the Pennsylvania case makes clear, needed is a word or phrase that can capture this new parole-less and clemency-less form and simultaneously mark its distinction from past practices with similar names that relied on personal interaction and allowed some degree of a chance.

The opening section of this book presented two historical inquiries. The first concerned prior modes of perpetual penal confinement, different ways of thinking about and carrying out confinement for the entire life of a prisoner. Examining five systematic schemes of punishment, I argued that for all their divergent features, each granted perpetual confinement a significant yet circumscribed role, insofar as perpetual confinement operated as a backup or alternative track of punishment. The second historical inquiry concerned the prior use of life sentences precluding parole and established that for much of the twentieth century release from prison under a life without parole sentence remained a reasonable possibility, frequently realized, even as perpetual confinement remained on deck. The next four chapters documented a remarkable change in the use and meaning of life without parole sentencing from the early 1970s onward. Chapter 3 charted general patterns, and chapters 4 through 6 have offered detailed accounts of how life without parole was transformed as a result of major upheavals in US punishment.

The third part of the book examines how the new practices and understandings of LWOP, enabled by the major upheavals in US punishment, solidified in the legal and penal fields. In doing so, the discussion expands from states to key national-level developments. Each chapter focuses on a different institutional site: the seventh chapter on the US Supreme Court and how upheavals in the legal and penal fields in turn influenced legal strategies, litigation practices, and eventually judicial decisions and constitutional law; the eighth chapter on the national anti–death penalty movement and how LWOP's position in abolition efforts was transformed at the national level between the 1960s and the mid-1990s; and the ninth chapter on prisons and prison administrators and how justifications historically offered for resisting LWOP altered in the context of changes in the penal field and no longer posed an impediment to perpetual confinement. At each of these sites, the embedding of changed practices and understandings removed prior obstacles to perpetual confinement and provided LWOP with a legitimacy that it had previously lacked.

PART III

Adaptation and Solidification

7. The US Supreme Court's Ambivalent Crafting of LWOP

As changes during the 1970s and 1980s to criminal laws and penal policies and practices shifted the meaning of life without parole, people facing death in prison and their advocates responded with new litigation and legal strategies: where criminal laws were restructured after *Furman*, people convicted under new laws opposed increased penalties; as parole-eligible sentences gave way to lengthy fixed terms, people challenged terms that would exceed their life expectancy; and where clemency withered, people reliant on mercy for release from prison took issue with the changing nature of executive practices.[1] As these new legal challenges filtered through the courts, some resulted in changes in local legal precedent, in turn implicating state laws and policies and leading to differences between states. Eventually, lines of this emerging precedent demanded the attention of the United States Supreme Court.

In such processes, the Supreme Court plays a pivotal role. The Court's statements formally interpret the Constitution of the United States, of course, but they also send less formal signals to lower courts and criminal justice actors about how to proceed and to state lawmakers about how to structure sentencing laws. The Court's decisions are important to the history of life without parole sentencing in precisely this way. This chapter examines the processes that occurred as these different currents arrived at the US Supreme Court, presenting a historical and sociological account of LWOP as it was forged in litigation during the last quarter of the twentieth century. Specifically, the chapter rereads five cases—*Schick v. Reed* (1974), *Rummel v. Estelle* (1980), *Hutto v. Davis* (1982), *Solem v. Helm* (1983), and *Harmelin v. Michigan* (1991)—in which the Court considered the constitutionality of life with parole, life without parole, and very long-term sentences between the early 1970s and the early 1990s, a period during which the practice and meaning of life without parole in the United States demonstrably changed.[2] Each of the cases is well known and has been the subject of much doctrinal interpretation.[3] The following discussion incorporates doctrinal analysis, but takes a different tack. Whereas doctrinal analysis focuses on how the Court interprets the Constitution, applies existing precedent, and changes the law, I focus on the US Supreme Court's role in crafting LWOP and, in doing so, on what this series of cases on life sentencing shows about the Court's role in processes of legal change.

Annotating a close reading of the US Supreme Court's written opinions with the briefs of the parties and amici, oral arguments, archival materials, legal scholarship, and case law, the chapter develops two primary points.[4] The first point is that over the course of these cases the Court was doing more than simply deciding the constitutionality of life sentences. It was encountering the major upheavals in American criminal justice that this book has discussed in previous chapters: (1) the temporary invalidation and then strict constitutional regulation of the death penalty, (2) the crisis of indeterminate sentencing and rehabilitation as a penal ideal, and (3) the withering of clemency as an executive practice. As the Court considered life sentencing under these circumstances, its decisions in effect wove the major upheavals into the fabric of constitutional law.

The second point is that in these cases—through the processes of briefing, oral argument, internal deliberations, and written decisions—the Court was defining what life without parole, under the changed circumstances, had come to mean. In contrast to the meaning of life without parole that prevailed for most of the twentieth century, LWOP emerged from this precedent as a sentence precluding any reasonable expectation of release—in short, as a form of perpetual confinement. Perpetual confinement, moreover, emerged as an acceptable practice. In sum, the following exposition shows how across this line of cases a new meaning of LWOP developed, and how the path to that new meaning was propelled, in each successive case, by large-scale changes in American punishment.

A strain of sociolegal literature describes the meaning-making activity of the US Supreme Court (and other appellate courts) as "the settling of legal meaning." By "settling," scholars refer to how court decisions, insofar as they define and tailor legal categories, bring about the determinacy of legal concepts.[5] Settling is involved in the processes this chapter describes, but the processes of institutionalization described here are also broader and deeper. The Court's pronouncements trace back not only to other court decisions but to major upheavals in the penal field and to the resulting material, discursive, and ideological changes that shaped the background upon which the Court adjudicated. One might name this more expansive process *solidification*, reflecting not just a decision maker's sifting through of possible options, but also the coagulation of an arrangement of practices and understandings stretching throughout the penal field.

THE CASES

The line begins with *Schick v. Reed*, a case that demonstrates the prior way of thinking about life without parole that existed for most of the twentieth century. Successive cases then show the influence of major upheavals. In *Rummel v. Estelle*, the Court was faced with efforts to expand a nascent death-is-different jurisprudence to life sentences. In *Hutto v. Davis*, a shift away from indeterminate sentencing began to register in the Court's precedent. In *Solem v. Helm*, as the Court addressed clemency retrenchment, it adopted what the state of South Dakota called a "novel idea," that life without parole sentences are distinct and more severe than other life sentences. In *Harmelin v. Michigan*, the Court took a final step: finding LWOP constitutional for a first-time drug possession offense, the Court at once accepted LWOP as a distinctly severe punishment yet *also* considered it representative of long fixed terms, which were increasingly prevalent in state and federal legislation at the time. Across the cases, the meaning of LWOP, the relationship between LWOP and other life and long-term sentences, and the bases for distinguishing between them were in flux.

Schick v. Reed *(1974): Life without Parole Is Like Life with Parole*

When legal commentary discusses life without parole's rise as a function of the courts, a starting point is often *Schick v. Reed*.[6] The case involved the presidential commutation of an American army sergeant who was serving a death sentence under a military statute for the murder of a child. While the alternative to the death penalty under military law was a life sentence *with* parole, President Dwight D. Eisenhower used the federal presidential pardon power to commute Maurice Schick's death sentence to a life term with the condition of *no parole*. Schick, who already had served twenty years in prison, argued that invalidation of capital punishment in *Furman* should void his commutation and, further, that the no-parole condition added in a jurisdiction that did not authorize life without parole exceeded the pardon power. For a majority of the US Supreme Court, a century-old case in which the president had commuted a death sentence to a sentence of natural life settled the issue, as it demonstrated that conditional commutations were constitutional and, further, that no-parole life sentences were permissible conditions.[7]

Some commentators argue that the Court, by endorsing the commutation, in effect affirmed the constitutionality of life without parole and sparked its greater use. Such claims, however, likely overstate *Schick*'s impact. The central legal arguments in the case concerned the authority of the president to commute sentences and add conditions. Challenges to the severity of the sanction itself, however, were relegated to footnotes in the parties' briefs, and the constitutionality of the life without parole sentence per se was not addressed in the Court's decision. Sentences of life without parole, moreover, had been upheld by state and federal appellate courts for years before.[8]

Schick is nevertheless important for life without parole history because it demonstrates a baseline in thinking about life without parole, which was being debated in the footnotes of the Court's opinion and the litigants' briefs. In fact, the litigation and the Court's decision evince just how unformed any notion of life without parole as a unique and distinct punishment was in the mid-1970s. Footnote 11 of Schick's brief, for example, suggested that life without parole was a cruel and unusual punishment.[9] In response, the federal government offered the following argument:

> For most of the Nation's history, premature release by way of parole was the exception, not the rule. It was not until 1910 that automatic eligibility for parole was generally made available in the federal system and for those sentenced to life imprisonment not until three years later. . . . Nor is there anything foreign to our system of jurisprudence in imposing a no-parole condition in the case of a life sentence. Indeed, current federal law permits a life sentence without possibility of parole for some narcotic offenders. . . . And there are no less than twenty states in which parole eligibility—at least without the Governor's approval—is expressly denied to all or some who are sentenced to life imprisonment. Moreover, even where there is no statutory rule, it is not unusual for a prisoner to serve out his remaining life in prison. In the federal system, that may happen more or less predictably because, when convicted, his life expectancy does not exceed fifteen years, or because it is foreseeable that parole will be denied. In many state systems, a very long sentence will assure that result. . . . The upshot is that imprisonment for life is not an uncommon occurrence in American criminal law.[10]

The government's historical summary, urging that lifetime imprisonment was not unique, alights on the fact that, in practice, a life without parole sentence resembled other life and long-term sentences: all might result in death in prison, all might result in release. Justice Harry Blackmun's oral argument notes offer some insight into why Schick's footnoted effort to distinguish a no-parole life sentence from other sentences by which a person might die in prison was ultimately not convincing. Blackmun wrote, "He still can be commuted today!!" Blackmun interpreted the no-parole condition as one that would potentially be resolved by commutation, which was an entirely reasonable expectation at the time.[11]

Contemporary interpretations of *Schick* sometimes overlook the fact that life without parole has not always been regarded as a distinctively severe punishment. Instead of seeing *Schick* as a spark for LWOP, the better interpretation is that *Schick* was a harbinger of changes to come, signaling how questions about the meaning of life sentences would ripple through legislative discussions in *Furman*'s wake.

Rummel v. Estelle (1980): The Defining Influence of the Modern Death Penalty and the Declining Importance of Local Release Practices

The line between life without parole and life with parole sentences remained indistinct well into the late 1970s. An unsuccessful petition for certiorari several years after *Schick* helps illustrate this. *Carmona v. Ward* involved two prisoners, each convicted under the 1973 New York Rockefeller drug law and sentenced to mandatory life with parole.[12] Martha Carmona was serving six years to life for possessing one ounce of cocaine; Roberta Fowler was serving four years to life for selling an ounce of cocaine to an undercover officer. Carmona and Fowler each challenged the proportionality of their punishment and argued that the Supreme Court should address the severity of their sentences at face value—namely, as sentences that could last for the remainder of their lives. Arguing that all life sentences should be considered the same regardless of whether and when they allowed parole, the petitioners followed prior New York decisions in which courts had determined that a sentence's appropriate measure was the statutory maximum, rather than the actual time one could reasonably expect to serve.[13] The Second Circuit Court of Appeals eschewed the New York approach; taking parole practice into account, the court anticipated parole would be fairly assessed and provided if and when due. Although the US Supreme Court denied certiorari, Justice Thurgood Marshall dissented in favor of Carmona's argument. Given the parole board's "nearly limitless discretion," Marshall objected, "petitioners could not claim any realistic expectation of release."[14] A life with parole sentence, Marshall emphasized, could result in death in prison too.

Two years later, William Rummel appeared before the US Supreme Court to appeal his sentence under a Texas statute that mandated life with parole upon conviction of any three felonies, violent or nonviolent. Rummel, whose felony offenses consisted of forgery, theft, and credit card fraud, in an amount totaling $229, took the same approach as the plaintiffs in *Carmona*: he characterized his sentence as a life sentence, period.[15] In response, Texas emphasized Rummel would be eligible for parole after twenty years, in as few as twelve years with good time credit, and even sooner if he gained trustee status in prison. Like *Carmona*, the case turned on the role of local release practices in defining the nature of the punishment.

A majority of the circuit court panel agreed with Rummel: life meant life. En banc, however, the circuit court reversed the panel's decision, finding that given administrative credits and expected parole practices time served under a life sentence in Texas would not be significantly longer than prison time for like criminal conduct in other states. A majority of the US Supreme Court agreed with the en banc decision, after looking to a wealth of information provided by the Texas Department of Corrections on average time credits and parole probabilities. In dissent, Justice Lewis Powell also looked to actual practice in Texas, but reached a different conclusion. Under Texas law, the governor could reject parole grants, and in fact, Powell emphasized, the sitting governor had rejected nearly 80 percent of them. Powell therefore found the possibility of release uncertain and urged that because life with parole sentences ultimately rested in the governor's discretion, they were effectively the same as life sentences without parole.

Two points about *Rummel* deserve emphasis. First, despite their differences, the majority and dissenting opinions agreed that the severity of a life sentence was to be evaluated not on its face but by looking at the local history of parole or clemency practice. The majority focused on parole; in dissent, Justice Powell focused on the fact that the governor overrode parole recommendations at a high rate. As put in a concurrence that Justice Blackmun drafted but never issued, "The punishment imposed here is not easily defined."[16]

The second point to note is how capital punishment jurisprudence after the Court's 1972 decision in *Furman* and its 1976 decision in *Gregg* influenced the *Rummel* decision. Rummel made an effort to fit his claim within then-recent death penalty jurisprudence. At the time, the line of distinction between cases that received heightened proportionality review (namely, capital cases) and cases that did not was whether the sentence permitted consideration of *rehabilitation*. Rummel hoped to extend to his case the heightened procedural protections and stricter proportionality requirements the

Court was developing for capital punishment, by arguing that under a life sentence in Texas a meaningful consideration of rehabilitation was foreclosed.[17] This line of distinction, however, would soon be challenged, for death-is-different jurisprudence intersected with a second major transformation in American punishment: the crisis of indeterminate sentencing.

Hutto v. Davis *(1982): The Crisis of Indeterminate Sentencing Strikes Proportionality Jurisprudence*

As this book has emphasized, for most of the twentieth century the life sentence was exemplary of a penal system directed toward rehabilitation; a way of thinking prevailed by which life and long-term sentences, while different in form, shared a possibility of rehabilitation and release. The *Rummel* majority followed this line of thinking, distinguishing a death sentence from Rummel's life with parole sentence because the latter allowed for some possibility of rehabilitation, "however slim."[18] The distinction between the death penalty and the case at hand was drawn at rehabilitation, something parole review would allow and execution would not.

A footnote drafted by Justice William Rehnquist late in the *Rummel* deliberations, however, introduced a different perspective. Rather than distinguish capital punishment because it eschewed rehabilitation, Rehnquist distinguished capital punishment and corporal punishment from prison sentences. "Once the death penalty and other punishments different in kind from [] imprisonment have been put to one side," he wrote, "there remains little in the way of objective standards for judging."[19] Rehnquist's move, in short, replaced rehabilitation with *imprisonment*.

The significance of the move was not lost in chambers, as distressed memos from other justices' clerks show. A clerk for Justice Blackmun described the footnote as coming "dangerously close to saying that all terms of years and life sentences—including life sentences *without the possibility of parole*—are all-but-exempt from Eighth Amendment attack." "That is bad law," the clerk continued, "and even if it is good law, it goes way farther than necessary on the facts presented here."[20]

Ultimately, Rehnquist's footnote would be highly consequential. Two years later, in *Hutto v. Davis*, the footnote rose to text, leading to a substantial change in the Court's proportionality jurisprudence and the way in which the Court viewed life sentences.[21] For two counts of possession of marijuana with intent to distribute, Virginia sentenced Roger Davis to the maximum: consecutive prison terms totaling forty years and $20,000 in fines. A federal appellate panel rejected Davis's Eighth Amendment claim, noting that the US Supreme Court "has never found a sentence for a term of years within the limits authorized by statute to be, by itself, a cruel and unusual punishment." Sitting en banc, the federal appeals court reversed. But the US Supreme Court affirmed the panel opinion, glossing Rehnquist's footnote: "In [*Rummel*], we distinguished between punishments—such as the death penalty—which by their very nature differ from all other forms of conventionally accepted punishment, and punishments which differ from others only in *duration*. . . . In short, *Rummel* stands for the proposition that federal courts should be [reluctant] to review legislatively mandated terms of imprisonment, and that successful challenges to the proportionality of particular sentences should be exceedingly rare."[22] Whether rehabilitation would be meaningfully considered was no longer the element that distinguished death sentences from other punishments for Eighth Amendment purposes.

The Rehnquist footnote in *Rummel,* and the shift in logic it represented, cemented in *Hutto,* did not occur in a vacuum. It occurred in a legal and penal environment in which indeterminate sentencing was giving way to determinate sentencing. *Hutto* reflects the Court coming to grips with the fall of rehabilitation as a primary penal aim, as it assessed the constitutionality of prison sentences that are reasonably likely to result in death in prison. The resulting ruling helped pave the way for a new perspective on life without parole—that is, as a prison term of particularly long duration.

Solem v. Helm *(1983): The Fall of Clemency and the Ascent of a "Novel Theory"*

Throughout the 1970s and early 1980s the US Supreme Court received several petitions challenging life without parole sentences, but heard none. *Solem v. Helm* is therefore a keystone: it is the first case in which the Court considered the constitutionality of a life sentence without parole under the Eighth Amendment.[23] The case came from South Dakota, a jurisdiction that had long precluded parole for all life sentences and relied on clemency to govern release. Since the mid-1970s, however, clemency practice in South Dakota had been moribund. Jerry Helm was a seven-time recidivist. His crimes, committed over a period of fifteen years, were nonviolent felonies. Several involved breaking into unoccupied buildings, one involved theft, and another driving under the influence. The crime of conviction was presenting a false check for $100, to which he pled guilty and which standing alone would have incurred a maximum punishment of five years' imprisonment and a fine. Given the prior convictions, however, Helm, thirty-six years old at the time, was sentenced to life without parole.

For decades South Dakota had used commutation to regulate release for life-sentenced prisoners in the same way that many other states used parole.[24] It therefore was not surprising when, during Helm's 1979 sentencing proceeding, the court inadvertently equated Helm's sentence to a parole-eligible one: "It will be up to you and the parole board to work out when you finally get out, but I think you certainly earned this sentence and certainly [have] proven that . . . the only prudent thing to do is to lock you up for the rest of your natural life."[25] South Dakota's subsequent petition to the US Supreme Court emphasized that Helm's sentence was one "without parole but with a right of commutation."[26] As the South Dakota attorney general noted in oral argument, distinguishing the Texas statute in *Rummel*, "In Texas they have a little different procedure. There the Board of Pardons and Paroles acts. In our state, if someone gets a life sentence there is a series of requests for commutation. . . . You have it in this case, only it's not called parole. It's called commutation." Parole, the state added, was an event no more reliable than a commutation.[27] Commutation practice in South Dakota, however, had decisively changed in recent years. Helm offered statistics showing twenty-two sentences commuted and twelve denied between 1964 and 1975, but none commuted and twenty-two denied since then. The South Dakota attorney general, in other words, was describing a historical practice that was vanishing.

By asking courts to interpret the meaning of life without parole as rooted in present practice rather than a decades-old statute, Helm invited them to recognize a distinction between life with parole and life without parole. As the South Dakota attorney general put it, Helm was arguing "there are three categories of sentences—life with parole, life without parole, and death": a "novel theory."[28] Helm's argument took what had been a question of "practice"—whether a reasonable possibility of release by parole or commutation actually existed—and transformed it into a theoretical issue of "kind."

At the US Supreme Court, Helm's argument confounded the justices. In *theory*, as a clerk in Justice Blackmun's chambers wrote, there were "significant differences between life with and life without parole":

> [Parole] includes the right, under state law, to have one's rehabilitation considered. The absence of the possibility of parole, even if there is a possibility that turns on executive discretion, is the very thing that likens Helm's sentence to the death penalty—it rejects the goal of rehabilitation as a bedrock purpose of criminal justice. . . . [T]he whole idea of parole is that the offender may become rehabilitated; pardon or commutation has no such necessary component.[29]

Yet in *practice*, the same clerk noted, distinctions between life without parole, life with parole, and very long-term sentences were murky:

> First, in practice there is little difference between a sentence of life without parole and four consecutive 99-year sentences making parole available at the earliest in 75 years. Absent commutation a middle-aged man receiving such sentences will die in prison. Second, the line between Rummel's life with parole and the life without parole here is not etched in marble. As . . . pointed out in *Rummel*, there was no right to parole in Texas, but instead the parole board merely made recommendations to the governor who could accept or reject the recommendations in his discretion.[30]

Blackmun's clerk's memo foreshadowed the Court majority's decision, which found Helm's sentence unconstitutional and ultimately rested on theoretical more than practical grounds. Drawing on a centuries-old criticism of clemency as an arbitrary method plagued by favoritism and caprice, the Court distinguished the ad hoc nature of clemency from the "scientific" nature of parole.[31] However theoretically apt, the distinction was less clear in practice. Indeed, a case decided by the Court just weeks before had turned on the fact that clemency was a real possibility.[32] Justice Warren Burger emphasized as much in dissent, writing: "The Court's opinion necessarily reduces to the proposition that a sentence of life imprisonment with the possibility of commutation, but without possibility of parole, is so much more severe than a life sentence with the possibility of parole that one is excessive while the other is not. This distinction does not withstand scrutiny."[33] One might criticize Justice Burger for clinging to an understanding of life without parole that was fading as clemency withered. But he was right to recognize that the Court in *Helm*, for the very first time, drew a firm distinction between the meaning of life sentences that allowed parole and life sentences that did not.

After *Helm*, lower courts tended to see LWOP as a distinctly severe sentence.[34] As courts steered away from the potential flood of litigation should *Helm* apply to all imprisonments, their decisions reinforced a split between life without parole and life with parole and very long fixed-term sentences. For example, the question in an Alabama case considered after *Helm* was "whether a sentence of 99 years for a nonviolent felony is 'cruel and unusual.'" Interpreting *Helm* to apply only to life without parole sentences, the Court denied relief.[35] An old understanding by which life without parole, life with parole, and ninety-nine-year sentences would have been assessed based on expected local release practices had given way to a new understanding in which life without parole was considered uniquely severe.

Harmelin v. Michigan *(1991)*: *LWOP in the Punitive Turn*

Much happened in American punishment between 1983, the year in which the US Supreme Court decided *Helm*, and 1991, when the Court next spoke on the proportionality of a life without parole sentence. In the penal field, determinate sentencing, which promised to eliminate disparities in sentencing and release practices, had resulted in long fixed sentences that were not necessarily proportionate or consistent. In national politics, the war on drugs had expanded. In that context, the punishment of life without parole, which courts across the country began to treat as distinctly severe after *Helm*, was rising along with a legislative trend toward greater use of long fixed terms.

The Supreme Court's decision in *Harmelin v. Michigan* must be read in this context.[36] Ronald Harmelin was convicted under Michigan's 650-lifer law.[37] Passed in 1978, the law was in effect an early shot in the war on drugs, extreme legislation imposed for maximum deterrent effect (chapter 5). As the *Harmelin* litigation would reveal, however, by 1991 the law was no longer an outlier in American criminal justice but representative of the prevailing philosophy supporting long fixed mandatory sentences.

Harmelin, a person with a history of substance use who had no prior criminal record, was convicted of possessing 672.5 grams of cocaine.[38] His brief to the Court opened with a passionate claim decrying how the lived experience of LWOP is distinctly severe:

> A prisoner serving a long sentence, even a sentence that looms into the twilight years of his life, can still keep his dreams alive. He can imagine, as he lays down in his cell at night, what he will do when he is finally paroled. He can plan what good things he can do to make up for the wrongs he has committed. He can dream of the things he can do to perhaps make this world a better place for everyone. He can dream of his loved ones, and how once he is reunited with them he will be able to spend hours with them making up for lost time. He has a reason to obey the prison laws. He has a reason to act like a human being. He has a reason for living. His soul is alive.[39]

The qualitative difference between LWOP and other prison terms, Harmelin argued, reached a moral level. "A hundred or even a thousand such judicial decisions could not make right that which is so clearly wrong," he urged. "Our descendants will look back on this peculiar period of our history with horror and shame."[40]

In contrast to prior cases, in *Harmelin* the state did not attempt to elide LWOP with life with parole sentences. Instead of downplaying LWOP's distinctive cruelty, Michigan embraced it. Instead of claiming a possibility of release by commutation, however slim, Michigan heralded LWOP as a sentence permitting no possibility of release. Briefs and arguments supporting the state lauded LWOP as a mandatory sentence that effectively removed discretion from court and parole board alike. This position was consistent with the penal environment of the early 1990s, in which mandatory minimum sentences were common and in which incapacitation, retribution, and deterrence had replaced rehabilitation as prevailing penal aims. Entering as amicus curiae to defend the use of severe determinate punishments, specifically in the war on drugs, the US government listed the many statutes in which the federal system employed LWOP, as well as the many federal and state cases in which LWOP for drug offenses had been upheld.[41]

One may recall how, in *Helm*, the state argued that life without parole was like other life and long-term sentences because it could still result in release. Denying relief, the *Harmelin* majority acknowledged this slim possibility. But the rhetoric had changed: the majority now emphasized that there was a "negligible difference between life without parole and other sentences of imprisonment" because they too could result in death.[42] Justice Antonin Scalia hammered the point during oral argument: "What about 30 years to a 50 year old or to a 60 year old? Does that amount to life imprisonment?" And again, "Life imprisonment for a 20 year old is no different from a 20 year sentence for a 70 year old. . . . Life imprisonment isn't different from a flat term of years for an elderly person, is it?"[43] The amicus brief of the Washington Legal Foundation, a victims' advocacy organization, put the point succinctly in a way that remains apt today: if an LWOP sentence were to entitle a prisoner to heightened standards of proportionality review, "then courts would also have to place de facto life sentences in that category as well. A 60-year-old drug dealer who is given a 60-year prison term, even with the possibility of parole after serving one third of that time, has been effectively given a life sentence. . . . Does that mean any term of years greater than the defendant's life expectancy is a severe sentence under the [*Helm*] analysis?"[44]

In sum, the argument was not that many sentences are extreme, but instead that sentences one can reasonably expect to exceed a prisoner's life span are rarely cause for concern. In American punishment in the early 1990s, LWOP had increased in use, but so had very long determinate and mandatory minimum sentences. To see LWOP as cruel or unusual punishment would have required dismantling a good deal of contemporary sentencing law and damming the current of American punishment.

THE CULMINATION OF AN
INSTITUTIONALIZING PROCESS

Viewed from a historical-sociological perspective, the five cases discussed in this chapter can be seen as parts of a process in which the Supreme Court was encountering and coming to terms with major upheavals in American punishment, as it fielded litigants' challenges to the changes those transformations wrought in local law. One might picture the process itself as a weaving. Making the warp is legal doctrine, existing court precedent, pertaining in the majority of these cases to Eighth Amendment standards. Cutting across the precedent, as a weft, are the major upheavals (figure 11).

Sociolegal literature on the ways in which courts perform a "settling of legal meaning" recognizes that laws' meanings are socially constructed and that "'determinacy' is a social achievement rather than an inherent quality of legal rules and concepts."[45] But in the cases from *Rummel* to *Harmelin* there is also an even more dynamic process at work: the Court was not simply choosing among options; rather, the ground from which the choices sprang was changing. Each of the major upheavals had effects on not only the Court's decision but the framing of the legal challenges and arguments: *Furman* sparked a death-is-different jurisprudence into which life sentences and long terms of years would try to fit; the fall of indeterminate sentencing and entrance of determinate sentencing changed the distinguishing feature of death sentences from not rehabilitative to not prison terms, aligning all prison sentences together under the Eighth Amendment; and with the withering of clemency, what was once largely a theoretical and structural distinction between the office allocated discretion to make the release decision (parole vs. executive) became increasingly defined as a distinction in outcome, in severity.

As those effects built on one another and a new meaning of LWOP distilled, the import of local release practices as a basis for evaluating the constitutionality of life and long-term sentences, once so key, declined, and the focus turned from back-end practices and local circumstances to a distinction between clemency and parole. In the process, two new designs were produced. First, LWOP was defined as a punishment distinctly more severe than life with parole. Second, LWOP was defined as an ordinary punishment that, while extremely severe, nevertheless has much in common with long determinate terms.[46]

Together, these designs contributed to a picture of perpetual confinement as a regular practice, a way of thinking about and practicing perpetual confinement that is, in the United States, historically unique. Across the

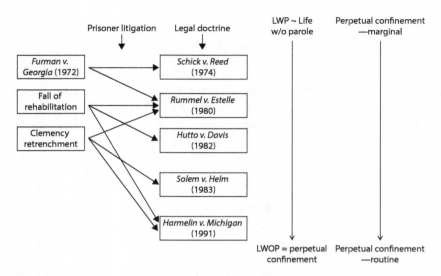

FIGURE 11. Flowchart of emergence of LWOP and perpetual confinement: US Supreme Court.

cases one can trace the movement of perpetual confinement from being classified with the death penalty (insofar as it also prohibits rehabilitation, such that it might have entailed on that basis heightened constitutional protection) to being distinguished from the death penalty (as a prison term, and hence not entitled to heightened scrutiny). Under the first basis of distinction (rehabilitation), perpetual confinement would have been of great concern; under the latter (imprisonment), its legitimacy was all but assumed. The adoption in *Hutto v. Davis* of the argument in Justice Rehnquist's *Rummel v. Estelle* footnote, therefore, should be remembered as a key moment, when death-in-prison terms were quietly shuttled from heightened Eighth Amendment standards to a noncapital proportionality framework—a moment when LWOP became defined as perpetual confinement and perpetual confinement became recognized as acceptable under the Eighth Amendment for punishing a variety of crimes and criminal statuses.

The US Supreme Court decisions, in sum, can be seen as the culmination of an institutionalizing process in which the influence of the major upheavals on law and practice was translated, solidified, and legitimated. Going forward from *Harmelin*, LWOP as a sentence of perpetual confinement would be at hand, available as punishment for a variety of crimes. It would be well known to diverse actors across the penal field—including anti–death penalty activists, victims' advocates, politicians, and other tough-on-crime entrepreneurs—and as a matter of public conversation. LWOP as perpetual confinement would also increasingly be a lived reality for tens of thousands of people aging into death in prison. One can see the plateau that this line of cases reaches in *Harmelin* as setting a foundation for the proliferation of LWOP that followed in the 1990s and, in doing so, acknowledge the journey that life without parole has taken from a punishment that once offered a reasonable possibility of release.

It is important to place this avenue of US Supreme Court jurisprudence within the context of the book's larger argument about life without parole and death-in-prison sentences, and to relate these jurisprudential developments to contemporary Eighth Amendment questions about the distinction between LWOP and punishments labeled de facto LWOP or virtual life sentences. In recent cases, the Court has extended an Eighth Amendment jurisprudence once reserved for capital cases to either prohibit or strictly limit the imposition of LWOP where an individual committed the crime before they were eighteen years old. An issue that has steadily grown in importance is why those rulings should not also apply to juveniles serving sentences that are like LWOP as a practical matter—that is, sentences that are reasonably likely to end in death in prison—but produced by slightly different processes and under different names. If LWOP is the "other death sentence," then these virtual death-in-prison sentences are the "other LWOP"—and by extension, *other* other death sentences. Yet from the perspective of constitutional law, as a result of the cases described in this chapter, LWOP holds an ambivalent position relative to other life and long-term sentences, cast as distinctly harsh but also grouped with other prison terms in distinction from the death penalty for purposes of Eighth Amendment analysis.

The historical accounts presented in this chapter and this book bear on these contemporary legal issues. For as this book shows, LWOP and other life or very long-term sentences have not always been perceived as distinct in outcome, nor have courts treated them as such. The division between LWOP and other death-in-prison sentences that currently steers the US Supreme Court jurisprudence is an artifact of the present—or more precisely, a product of the recent past. The analysis here reveals that prevailing distinctions between LWOP and virtually equivalent sentences are not natural or logical so much as a product of social, political, and historical factors, derived from struggles and contingencies in particular institutional contexts. If death is different, with LWOP it is not so clear.

8.   Abolition and the Alternative

With the United States Supreme Court's ruling in *Harmelin v. Michigan*, an Eighth Amendment jurisprudence that some may have expected to present a formidable impediment to perpetual imprisonment proved otherwise. At the same time, other actors and interests that one might have expected to stand as obstacles to LWOP also either failed to materialize or faded away. Paramount among these is the anti–death penalty movement.

Today every jurisdiction that maintains capital punishment authorizes LWOP as an alternative sanction; the LWOP option in capital cases is a matter-of-fact facet of US criminal justice.[1] In attaining this role, LWOP has been championed by individuals and by groups who oppose capital punishment, and indeed by a cause seeking abolition of the death penalty that is sensitive to violations of human dignity.[2] To be sure, not all death penalty opponents support LWOP; a number of lawyers and commentators still find LWOP morally indefensible or see it as a substantial impediment to penal reform.[3] Yet in recent decades, the national death penalty abolition movement has embraced LWOP, and LWOP in turn has contributed to the decline in death sentencing across the United States.[4] LWOP now finds widespread support among major abolitionist organizations and holds a central role in abolition strategy.

There is some paradox here. Indeed, the notion that advocates of death penalty abolition would push strongly for *another* sanction that is widely considered inhumane recalls a puzzle with deep historical roots in the criminal justice annals. More than two hundred years ago, when reformers sought to end corporal and capital punishment on grounds of disproportionate cruelty, some proposed perpetual confinement instead.[5] For centuries, this apparent disconnect has raised a question: Why would a reform inspired by principles of human dignity replace one inhumane sentence with another of different, yet comparable, severity?[6]

This chapter examines how the anti–death penalty (ADP) movement came to favor life without parole, whose role in national abolition efforts was transformed between the 1960s and the mid-1990s.[7] Throughout, it documents how death penalty opponents handled the problem of the alternative—their "agonies" over the issue, so to speak.[8] The significance of ADP activity in LWOP history is often expressed as foundational, credited with bringing about a rush to LWOP following the invalidation of capital punishment in *Furman v. Georgia* (1972), then endorsing LWOP as an alternative after capital punishment was reinstated in *Gregg v. Georgia* (1976) and companion cases several years later.[9] Close attention to the role LWOP played in debates and discussions over the alternative sentence, however, helps reveal that LWOP's rise in the abolition movement must be understood as a much more gradual change. Rather than entering with a big part in the 1970s, the ADP took its leading role in the early 1990s only after LWOP had already begun to emerge in noncapital quarters. This is important to recognize, not only as a matter of historical accuracy but because it helps show just how ingrained LWOP is in broader penal developments and trends.

The first part of the chapter addresses the issue of the alternative in the context of the NAACP Legal Defense Fund (LDF) litigation of the 1960s and continues through the movement's responses to the US Supreme Court's decisions in *Furman* and *Gregg* in the 1970s. I demonstrate that for the LDF and their cadre throughout the 1970s, the issue of the alternative was a troubling topic that strategists struggled to avoid, and life without parole was at once a marginal legal consideration and a significant moral concern. As such, life without parole is scarcely to be found in abolition arguments preceding *Furman,* suppressed during the litigation that immediately followed and kept quiet after the death penalty's reinstatement.

The second part of the chapter investigates the combination of developments in penal and legal fields, power struggles, and contingent events that propelled a majority of the movement, after much resistance and ambivalence, to embrace LWOP in the late 1980s and 1990s. I emphasize how the growing use of LWOP in non–death penalty quarters provided a key backdrop for the movement's acceptance of the punishment. At that point, roughly two decades after *Furman,* LWOP was already an emergent penal form. Long divided over LWOP, the movement may not have convincingly justified the turn, within its own ranks or outside them, without the existing buildup of LWOP in drug laws, habitual offender laws, and laws abolishing parole.

In the chronology of LWOP history, then, the national anti–death penalty movement's support of LWOP arrives relatively late. Yet in the historiography of life without parole, arguably no interest group has been framed as more important. As such, it bears listening to what abolitionists say and do not say about life sentencing and to how what they say about life sentencing has changed.

LIFE WITHOUT PAROLE AND THE NAACP LEGAL DEFENSE FUND STRATEGY

Historically, Stuart Banner writes, "One could not credibly argue against the death penalty without proposing something else to take its place." In the late eighteenth century, Banner explains, the alternative that anchored abolition efforts was the prison, a then-new technology: "The prison and the anti–death penalty movement went hand in hand."[10] At the end of the twentieth century, abolition movements found a salve for capital punishment in a tool that promised the prison's enduring, uncompromising, and permanent use: LWOP. That was not so, however, when the contemporary, "third wave" ADP movement developed in the 1950s, 1960s, and 1970s.

Literature on this "third wave" has been quick to point to a key difference from those prior: it was driven by lawyers rather than political activists. Defense attorneys with a nucleus at the LDF drove a turn that, in a very real way and not without criticism, "bypassed" the public.[11] Identifying courts as the forum for attacking the death penalty framed the issues of debate in a certain way.[12] The LDF litigation strategy began with the argument that the death penalty was racially discriminatory and imposed in a manner that was arbitrary, cruel, and unusual, in violation of the Eighth Amendment.[13] As the constitutional attack developed, it focused increasingly on procedure (challenging the death qualification of juries and unified, rather than bifurcated, sentencing proceedings).[14] In this agenda, the issue of the alternative sentence had no direct legal significance. If the topic came up it was interstitial.

A Footnote at Best

The marginality of LWOP in the LDF litigation complemented common sense about life sentencing at the time. In the late 1960s, life sentencing remained firmly entrenched in the doctrine of indeterminate sentencing and the philosophy of treatment and rehabilitation that had prevailed in American corrections in most jurisdictions since the first decades of the twentieth century. Indeed, the third wave of the ADP movement arose during what, in hindsight, appears as the apex of that penal paradigm. Activists and legal practitioners of the 1950s and 1960s well understood that the great majority of life sentences were parole eligible and could result in release. It was reasonable to assume that release was a real possibility for most people serving life sentences, by some mechanism, at some point. For the strategists of the movement, and in general at the time, the reference to a "life" sentence meant "without parole" *only* when someone said "life without parole," and even then commutation might be on the horizon.

With this in mind, it is no surprise to comb the briefs, oral arguments, and archival materials of the third wave prior to *Furman* and find no mention of life without parole. Discussion of the alternative is also absent from the histories of LDF litigation that were written shortly after *Furman*, and which can rightly be read as part of the abolitionist discourse of the time.[15] As LDF attorney and strategist Michael Meltsner stated in retrospect: "The legal abolitionists of the sixties and seventies did not worry about Life Without Parole (LWOP); quite understandably too because we saw our business saving lives of clients in jeopardy of execution, overwhelmingly due to race and poverty."[16]

An example from the 1976 litigation that culminated in the US Supreme Court decisions in *Gregg v. Georgia* and its four companion cases (*Jurek v. Texas, Proffitt v. Florida, Roberts v. Louisiana, Woodson v. North Carolina*) is telling.[17] The petitioners filed a joint brief with the Court, arguing that a death sentence would deter violent crime no better than a non-death sentence.[18] The state's brief (in *Proffitt*) answered, "Naturally, Respondent assumes Petitioner is speaking of some form of life imprisonment without parole. Respondent submits that the Legislature could validly conclude life imprisonment without parole would not be adequate to deter some individuals from committing homicide in the future."[19] But the petitioners' joint brief was nowhere so explicit, nor were any of the other briefs filed on their behalf. Rather, the closest an LDF brief came to addressing the alternative sanction was a footnote (no. 9) in the reply brief. The footnote, offered to support the argument that meaningful alternatives to the death penalty can punish and deter, pointed to an accompanying appendix that presented a fifty-two-jurisdiction list of 408 statutes authorizing "life imprisonment or [a] term of imprisonment of fifty years or more." Most of these laws authorized indeterminate life sentences, with a smattering of statutes authorizing 99-year or 100-year sentences for aggravated crimes. And contrary to the state's assumption, the petitioners did not distinguish or even mention life without parole sentences. While discussions of an alternative to capital punishment percolated in the public sphere after *Furman*,[20] in the LDF strategy the issue was dropped to a footnote that grouped life and very long-term sentences together en masse.

First Sightings

The issue of the alternative arose at last, if only briefly, in the oral argument of *Woodson v. North Carolina*, the case in which the US Supreme Court rejected mandatory death sentencing statutes and demanded individualized sentencing proceedings in capital cases. Justice Lewis Powell confronted petitioner's counsel, Anthony Amsterdam, asking whether a life without parole sentence served in solitary confinement might be a proper sentence for someone who set off a hydrogen bomb. Amsterdam responded:

> The question of life without parole is [] not before the Court. I think that under certain limited circumstances, it may be permissible to incarcerate somebody [under such a sentence]. . . . [I]t seems to me [we have the] constitutional and normative question mixed up. I see no constitutional objection at all for life imprisonment without parole. As far as a normative provision goes, I do not think it is a wise thing, but I am not sure that this Court is called upon to make those kinds of judgments.[21]

A second justice pursued the issue: You must have an alternative in mind, he asked Amsterdam, what do you think it should be?[22] As Amsterdam started, the justice pushed back: "I am asking you, Professor Amsterdam, what do you think is constitutional and valid, would you think the type of a punishment that I have just suggested would be constitutionally valid?"[23] Amsterdam answered simply, "Yes."[24] Justice Warren Burger inserted that the Court had received pleadings arguing that life without parole in solitary confinement itself was a cruel and unusual punishment.[25] Amsterdam answered: "It is neither . . . and everybody on death row appreciates the difference. I think there is a difference between death and imprisonment."[26] This forced response stands as the only direct statement the LDF ever made about life without parole to the US Supreme Court.

Even after the Supreme Court revived the death penalty in 1976, the issue of the alternative was not on the agenda at the 1977 NAACP planning and strategy session at Howard University, organized to form a law and social science research agenda,[27] which focused extraordinary effort on holding the line. As Marie Gottschalk notes, the post-*Furman* ADP strategy was three-pronged: (a) ACLU lobbying, (b) LDF litigation challenging the new death penalty statutes, and (c) a social science agenda that involved dozens of research assignments meted out to willing scholars nationwide.[28] Reviewing the planning documents of this elaborate strategy for social and psychological research—on race discrimination, the death penalty's deterrent effect, its cost, and public opinion on capital punishment—which are so impressive in scope and specificity, it is hard not to notice the absence of any discussion of the alternative sanction.[29] In this light, it is fair to say that the third wave's position on life without parole was, throughout the 1970s and well into the 1980s, both internally restrained and publicly silent.

Bedau versus Barzun

Not all abolitionists shared the LDF's approach to the alternative. In large part, the LDF's legal strategy bracketed a source of tension within the movement. One way to understand this is to look at how the issue of the alternative played more generally in ADP activism before and during the LDF litigation. Here, the writings of Hugo A. Bedau—a professor of philosophy involved in abolitionist organizing in New Jersey and Massachusetts from the 1950s and later pivotal in the LDF social science research agenda—are particularly valuable. To posit Bedau as a spokesman for the abolition efforts of the mid- to late twentieth century would not tell the whole story, for Bedau held views that not all others shared. Bedau, however, was integrally involved with the movement and was perhaps the most systematic thinker about the death penalty, both philosophically and morally, among the third wave. His public statements, which grew out of work on these issues from 1958 through 2000 and appear in forums ranging from scholarly journals to legislative hearings, largely reflect the arguments that the abolition effort perceived as most important. Amid the sea of abolition literature produced in the United States since the 1970s, Bedau provides an intelligent and well-informed barometer.

Another philosopher writing on capital punishment was Jacques Barzun. When quizzing Amsterdam during the *Woodson* oral argument about the severity of life without parole, Justice Burger was referring to an opinion piece by a former director of the Minnesota Department of Corrections that argued that life imprisonment was the cruelest punishment.[30] Amsterdam was not aware of the piece, but he was familiar with related questions posed a decade earlier by Barzun: If the death penalty is objectionable because it violates the sacredness of human life, why do abolitionists not also raise the same argument against war or against the use of self-defense?[31] Why do they not also oppose lethal violence against animals, or against those stationed in relatively remote places? In short, "Where does the sanctity of life begin?"[32] Barzun directed his point more specifically to "the happy advocates of the life sentence."[33] "The enemies of capital punishment—and liberals generally," he stated, "seem to be satisfied with any legal outcome so long as they themselves avoid the vicarious guilt of shedding blood. They speak of the sanctity of life, but have no concern with its quality."[34] Liberal abolitionists, he continued, seemed to disregard reports about the difficulties if not horrors of confinement: "They do not see and suffer the cell, the drill, the clothes, the stench, the food: they do not feel the sexual racking of young and old bodies, the hateful promiscuity, the insane monotony, the mass degradation, the impotent hatred."[35] Why, as the abolitionist movement sought to end the death penalty, claiming execution violates the right to life, would not the same or similar arguments apply to a life sentence? "In my view," he concluded, "to profess respect for human life and be willing to see it spent in a penitentiary is to entertain liberal feelings frivolously."[36]

While today Barzun's challenge has been deleted from Bedau's compendium, in 1964 Bedau attempted a response—which remains, so far as the history of LWOP is concerned, a significant moment. Bedau did little to defend the apparent contradiction in abolitionist thinking, as he acknowledged: "The formulation of an optimum alternative to the death penalty is a subject that few abolitionists ever thoroughly discuss. No doubt they would if they thought there was some hope of enacting such ideal legislation in the near future. As it is, however, abolitionists in America during the past decade [the late 1950s and early 1960s] have found themselves at one time or another defending almost every conceivable alternative."[37] Bedau further reasoned in a separate essay in the same volume that "if the only alternative to capital punishment were life imprisonment without possibility of parole, indeed, without the strong likelihood of release from prison after some years, except in a few cases, it is far from clear that abolition of the death penalty should be greeted as much of an improvement."[38] Bedau preferred an alternative inspired by former Sing Sing warden Lewis Lawes: life with a mandatory minimum sentence of twenty years, which Bedau would have reduced "by half."[39]

In certain respects, Barzun's challenge was—to recall Banner's comment about the necessity of an alternative to abolition—an obvious one.[40] The alternative sanction was something to which, Bedau agreed, abolitionists should give serious thought and about which they should have an answer at hand.[41] Yet having distinguished his own view, Bedau conceded that for most American abolitionists life sentencing was of little concern.[42]

Am I the Only One to Whom It Seems to Matter?

Following *Furman*, in October 1972 the LDF held a strategy meeting at which its ambitious social science research strategy was born. Bedau brought up life without parole. He emphasized the "need to be on guard not to supply ammunition for those who want to impose life imprisonment without possibility of parole."[43] No other statements regarding life without parole, in response to Bedau or otherwise, were recorded. Subsequent meetings followed a similar trajectory: if the issue of the alternative was on the agenda at all, it was marginal and, as evinced by the empirical projects actually carried out, nominal.[44]

An apropos signature of abolitionist ambivalence is Bedau's casual letter to Amsterdam in early July 1973, entitled "Absurdly Long 'Life' Terms for Murder."[45] Provoked by a newspaper clipping reporting on a Texas man sentenced to ten thousand years for murdering a police officer—in which the judge remarked that only one penalty was appropriate, but "unfortunately, the Supreme Court of the United States has made that punishment unavailable to us"[46]—Bedau wrote:

> The attached clipping has been kicking around on my desk for nearly two months, and I suddenly realized why. I am disturbed that one of the several adverse side effects of our success to date has been an enormous increase in such absurdly long prison sentences. That is, since the jury cannot sentence to death, they will sentence to life plus life plus . . . the comment of Judge Brown in the enclosed encourages such speculation.
>
> John Austin, late philosopher of Oxford, once cracked, "Any frying pan in a fire." Perhaps that is the attitude we should take, too. However, we would be in a bit better position if we could argue: (a) these artificially long sentences do not really affect eligibility for parole; (b) they do not affect eligibility for gubernatorial commutation of sentence; (c) they do not affect the rights and privileges of the prisoner while in prison; and (d) other things I cannot think of. Other considerations: (i) since *Furman* such artificially long sentences really have not been on the increase; (ii) Texas plus one or two other states has a long tradition of such silly sentencing; and (iii) other things I cannot think of.
>
> Apart from (d) and (iii), are any of the above true? Am I the only one to whom it seems to matter?[47]

The letter's specific concern—substitute sentences for the death penalty during abolition—was short-lived because capital punishment was back in play three years later. Nevertheless, Bedau's letter is important as at once an indirect plea for empirical research on alternative sentences and an expression of bona fide concern over the lack of attention in the LDF campaign to the issue of the alternative.

A Question of Individual and Collective Conscience

Despite Bedau's perceived isolation, it would overstate things to say that after *Furman* the ADP movement was altogether uninterested in the alternative.

Amsterdam's correspondence with ADP activists not involved in the legal campaign sheds additional light on the matter. Two letters, a decade apart, show both the persistence of the issue and the lack of resolution.

In 1973, a reformer wrote to inform Amsterdam of a bill proposing as the death penalty alternative life with eligibility for parole at one-half of life expectancy, which failed by one vote in the Connecticut senate. "Your 'special life sentence' proposal sounds very interesting," Amsterdam responded. "I would indeed be grateful to know more about it; perhaps I can promote the idea in other States notwithstanding its heartbreakingly narrow defeat in Connecticut."[48] Despite this, it is not clear that a special life sentence proposal was ever considered in the sprawling LDF agenda.

In 1986, a decade after *Gregg*, as executions were beginning to register in the public sphere, a member of the corrections task force of the Missouri Catholic Conference, an ADP organization, wrote to Amsterdam seeking empirical research supporting the effectiveness of LWOP as an alternative. Amsterdam pointed to no empirical studies but speculated about five "decision points" at which criminal justice decision makers would consider LWOP: legislatures enacting laws, prosecutorial charging decisions, jury decisions, appellate court review, and executive commutation decisions. "In theory," he wrote, "I guess that empirical studies might be made of the impact of the no-parole alternative at the latter four decision points at least, but I'd be very leery of the results of such studies, because the identification and analysis of control variables would be so difficult as to near impossibility, particularly since comparisons would necessarily have to be made cross-jurisdictionally or cross-temporally." He added that "no studies of the sort have yet been conducted, and I know of no one who has either plans or money to conduct any."[49]

Amsterdam allowed that, based on conversations with practitioners, "the no-parole alternative *does* cause some substantial number of decisions to be made against the death bent option at each of the decision points." But, he added:

> Whether that should lead you to accept the no-parole alternative as a lesser evil is a terribly difficult judgment call, as to which nobody's insights but your own are worth much. On the one hand, long-term imprisonment without the possibility of parole *is* a distinct evil. (It's almost impossible to justify penologically, except on the theory that parole authorities are likely to err in favor of premature release—a theory that flies in the face of the innate and inevitable conservatism of all parole authorities. So the long-term no-parole sentence is a pure political sop, indefensible as anything else.) On the other hand,

long-term-imprisonment–without-the-possibility-of-parole ain't death;
and it is not always even what it sounds like, since it *can* be ameliorated, in rare cases, by commutation. . . . How anyone comes out in this
tug of evils has got to be a question of individual conscience—or, in the
case of a group, collective conscience.

Amsterdam closed the letter with the following: "The usual means of avoiding the difficult ultimate polar judgments by creative conception of intermediate options is not available here, precisely *because* the issue is entirely one
of political symbolism, where resourceful and practical intermediate options
cut no ice."[50]

Perhaps here, in a letter to a searching disciple, lies an answer for why
LDF strategies always posed matters in terms of (1) capital punishment versus abolition instead of (2) capital punishment and specific alternatives, and
consistently back-burnered the issue of the alternative despite its pressing
importance before and after *Furman*. Lawyers make contextual arguments
scraping the fringe of legal relevance all the time, when those arguments
serve a clear purpose. But here, there was no easily identifiable practical and
morally satisfying solution.

Amsterdam's response to Bedau's 1973 letter reflects the same, and hints
at the response that Amsterdam provided, when forced, during the *Woodson* argument:

> I received your July 6 memo titled "Absurdly Long 'Life' Terms for
> Murder" yesterday. . . . Such crazy sentences were notoriously (but
> how frequently I do not know) handed down in Texas and elsewhere
> for non-capital crimes prior to *Furman*. Since *Furman*, I have read of
> one or two in cases of crimes carrying a death penalty invalidated by
> *Furman*. I doubt, although I cannot be sure, that *Furman* increased the
> use of this type of sentence in any case other than those where, prior to
> *Furman*, the defendant would clearly have been sentenced to die.
>
> In such cases, I suppose that Barzun [] would raise the question which
> was the frying pan and which was the fire. My experience with men on
> death row leads me to believe that they have little trouble answering
> the [] question, at least in terms of personal preference. In dealing with
> several hundred condemned men, I have encountered only three—and
> I know of only one other—who preferred death to confinement in prison
> for life (or 10,000 years). Among these four, two changed their minds as
> execution day approached and the other two were demonstrably [living
> with a mental illness].
>
> I find some comfort in all of this. I find still more in [Professor]
> Charl[es] Black's observation that abolition of the death sentence will
> probably have a long-term tendency to make society less tolerant of
> brutally long prison sentences generally. Charlie makes the valid point

that the elimination of death as a possible penalty changes the extreme benchmark against which all other sentences are judged and found tolerable by comparison. It forecloses the reasoning that goes, "If we could kill the son of a bitch, we surely are not cruel in imprisoning him for a thousand years instead."

Neither comfort is the comfort of certainty. . . . Still, I conclude—not without disquietude, but without substantial doubts—that we do better to fly to ills we know not of than to bear the ones we have.[51]

Decades after the debate with Barzun, after *Furman*, and after this correspondence with Amsterdam, Bedau returned to the issue of the alternative. In 2004, facing LWOP firmly entrenched and prevalent in capital statutes, Bedau wrote: "LWOP is probably completely unnecessary as an alternative to the death penalty. Its current popularity is owing not to rational judgment of its necessity to protect the public or to mete out deserved retribution, but to public anxiety over premature or irrational release of still-dangerous felons and by those opponents of the death penalty who are willing to clutch at any straw, any frying pan in a fire."[52]

LIFE WITHOUT PAROLE MOVES TO THE CENTER

Although LDF strategists had largely avoided the issue of the alternative, by the late 1980s LWOP's role in the abolition movement was beginning to change, and by the millennium LWOP would claim a central role in abolition strategy. In the early 1990s at most half of death penalty states used LWOP as an alternative capital sentence; but by 2000, nearly all.[53] This statistic itself invites us to see LWOP's relationship with the death penalty, now vigorous, less as something that blossomed from *Furman* than as something that developed in subsequent decades. The aggressive use of LWOP as a death penalty alternative from the 1990s onward evidences a departure from the ambiguous, opaque, and ambivalent way in which abolitionists in prior decades presented life as an alternative to death, publicly and privately.

Histories of the death penalty often offer little about the penal field more broadly. Yet there were significant developments in sentencing that impacted capital punishment. Life without parole sentencing was growing, and often not as a death penalty phenomenon; the use of LWOP was expanding for a variety of crimes. Understanding the nature of LWOP's presence in US states in the late 1980s into the early 1990s, discussed in prior chapters, is critical for understanding how the abolition movement engaged with LWOP as the crisis of death sentences and executions ripened.

Only with attention to these adjacent circumstances—LWOP's increasing use in the noncapital sphere and still-limited use in many states for capital cases—can one understand why the anti–death penalty movement, increasingly desperate to stem the tide of executions and death sentences as the 1980s and 1990s progressed, unified behind LWOP how and when it did.

Backlog and Blood

By the mid-1980s, new elements defined the landscape of capital punishment. The US Supreme Court was backtracking on its nascent Eighth Amendment law for capital cases, and a series of decisions in the October 1983 term, authored by conservative members of the Court, retreated from what had theretofore been an expanding jurisprudence of mitigation. This "deregulation" of death-sentencing procedure[54] was eye opening for death penalty opponents, as it indicated that the modern death penalty was here to stay.

Meanwhile, death sentences were increasing, and slowly too were executions. The first execution under the modern death penalty was the electrocution of John Spenkelink in Florida in 1979.[55] Then in 1983 five electrocutions took place nationwide, and in 1984 there were twenty-one.[56] On a political level, for abolitionists the uptick in executions signaled defeat and was a source of despair. On a moral level, it was a source of disgust, even horror.[57] On both counts, it was a wake-up call. Accompanying death sentences and executions was a backlog of prisoners on death row. It soon became clear that executions, slowed by Eighth Amendment challenges on appeal, would not happen expeditiously.[58] Public demonstrations against capital punishment, rare throughout the 1970s and the early 1980s, resumed.[59] No one could say how long executions would continue, but given the tenor of the Rehnquist Court, capital punishment was not something that litigation, this time around, seemed likely to stop.

Voices For and Against

From the early 1980s onward, a less generous Eighth Amendment jurisprudence, coupled with increasingly active state capital punishment systems, demanded strategic reconsideration. As Henry Schwarzschild, director of the American Civil Liberties Union Capital Punishment Project, identified in a memorandum to Ira Glasser, executive director of the ACLU: "It is widely agreed that we are now passing from a period in which the prevention of all executions was a valid (though imperfectly achieved) objective into one where executions are going to become relatively more routine and will occur in increasing numbers, with no foreseeable lessening of judicial, legislative, political, and public support for the death penalty."[60]

"The question is therefore properly asked," Schwarzschild urged: "Should not our program response change in the context of a radically different situation?"[61]

For some, reconsidering strategy included reconsidering *the role of the alternative* in the strategy. Rather than avoid the topic, some prominent abolitionist thinkers—litigators, activists, and scholars—now sought to highlight LWOP and to justify it on legal, moral, and practical grounds.[62] One early proponent was David Bruck, a Harvard-trained South Carolina capital defense lawyer and regular contributor to *The New Republic*, who would become one of the nation's most respected death penalty defense advocates. Bruck's experience as a trial and post-conviction litigator informed his position on LWOP. While the LDF appellate strategy had avoided the issue, in the practical world of courtrooms and juries the alternative was a daily problem. As Bruck argued to the US Supreme Court a decade later, LWOP was a necessary alternative because capital jurors wanting to avoid a death sentence but ensure incapacitation faced a stifling uncertainty about the meaning of a life sentence since discussion of parole was off limits.[63] Jurors who asked about parole and received no meaningful answer from the Court soon returned with a death sentence. The "myth of early release," Bruck believed, was precisely why the death penalty retained support.[64]

Robert Johnson, a scholar and ethnographer of corrections practices on American death rows, presented another important argument. Without marginalizing LWOP's cruelty or endorsing it, Johnson recognized that "true life sentences are only rarely meted out in our courts, and never with explicit recognition that this sentence—in which the offender is slated to spend his entire remaining life in prison—is in fact a kind of death penalty."[65] Johnson painted the prison as an acceptable and cost-effective cemetery of sorts for individuals convicted of the most serious homicide offenses, positing LWOP as something of a fair trade: "In effect, they give their civil lives in return for the natural lives they have taken. A true life sentence, then, can and should be used as a practical moral alternative to the death penalty, a civilized and potentially even civilizing application of the golden rule in the extreme case of a cold-blooded and unmitigated murder."[66]

Bruck and Johnson shared an additional point, which referenced a talking point that was becoming one of the movement's most promising: miscarriages of justice.[67] As Johnson put it, "A life sentence is a painful punishment, but it can be borne with dignity. It can also be changed."[68] In contrast to execution, LWOP posed problems that, while serious, could be deflected downstream. In that light, LWOP offered an immediate promise of certainty that could be especially influential to capital jurors, but it also promised some future possibility. Abolitionists could hold out the former message for the public, while reserving the latter for themselves.

If certain abolitionists had made peace with LWOP, however, a majority of the movement had not. Schwarzschild, well known for advocating a path of moral opposition to the death penalty that extended to LWOP, wrote to Johnson in March 1985 that LWOP was "mindless," "humanly and economically wasteful," and "morally repellant in its very assumptions," adding that if he did not object to LWOP it would only be as "a reluctant gesture of legislative realism."[69] As Herbert Haines explains, the anti-LWOP position "was clearly the dominant one among movement leaders during the decade following the revival of the death penalty. People who attempted to initiate a discussion at . . . conferences or in the movement's newsletters of suitable terms of incarceration for convicted murderers during those years were often greeted by stony silence."[70]

A range of responses to LWOP thus existed within the movement that rarely confronted each other in conversation. Two developments, however, would break the deadlock between abolitionists who approved of LWOP and those who did not: public opinion polls and a new and improved media platform.

Opinion Polls and a New Media Platform

Opinion polls were long an integral part of the LDF social science research strategy, but they provided a surprising spark for the movement's turn on LWOP when they took to asking about alternative sentences. A poll commissioned by Amnesty International in Florida in 1986 showed that public support for the death penalty fell significantly when life without parole was offered as an alternative, and even more when the alternative sentence was life without parole with restitution.[71] At the time, the poll's questions on LWOP represented, in effect, a putting out of feelers, but the responses turned out to be substantial for the future direction of the abolition movement. With the US Supreme Court backtracking on its regulations of capital case procedure and with social tensions over the death penalty mounting, the opinion polls showing support for LWOP offered empirical evidence of a path forward, a "positive" aspect that could be partnered with the many criticisms of cost, miscarriages of justice, and so on.

Journalist David von Drehle captured the situation well in a 1988 *Miami Herald* editorial series ("The Death Penalty: A Failure of Execution"), written as Florida was coming to grips with the reality of the new mode of capital punishment. Interviewing judges, prosecutors, defense lawyers, and death penalty proponents and opponents, von Drehle found that all opposed the death penalty *as applied*.[72] Since the revival of the death penalty, Florida had been a leader—in passing new death penalty legislation, in sentencing the most to death, and in holding the first modern electrocution in 1979. By 1988, however, it was clear that the system was bogged down, clogged with death row prisoners waiting for execution. Another problem was cost: approximately $3.2 million per prisoner, roughly six times more than for prisoners sentenced to life without parole.[73] A primary reason was the complex legal procedure and appellate architecture that must accompany modern capital punishment and need not accompany any other sentence.[74] After noting that "more and more people are asking whether something so costly, slow and inefficient as the death penalty is worth the trouble," von Drehle turned to life without parole. "[Life without parole] sentences are rare in America," he wrote. "Opponents argue it would be more cruel than execution. Some prison officials worry that these lifers would wreak havoc because they would have no incentive for good behavior." Yet, he recognized, "the idea of an ironclad life sentence instead of death is popular among Americans, according to several recent polls."[75]

As post-*Furman* and post-*Gregg* strategies gradually shifted toward bringing the message to the public, the movement went a significant step further when, in May 1990, the National Coalition to Abolish the Death Penalty (NCADP) received a grant from the MacArthur Foundation to establish the Death Penalty Information Center.[76] The DPIC's primary purpose would be to "develop proactive media strategies against capital punishment and to collect and provide information about the death penalty to the press."[77] Ostensibly, the DPIC was to be a neutral and objective news organization, yet its board was staffed with ADP activists and litigators, and its first offices were within the NCADP.[78] Issues were to include race, innocence, and cost and to reflect a new breadth of death penalty opposition, including victims, prosecutors, and conservative lawmakers. Most of all, the intention was to change the picture—the public would link the death penalty first and foremost with, rather than serial killers, the dysfunction of the criminal justice system.

The DPIC's first months were inauspicious. Only one major report was issued (on race in death sentencing); contributions to TV coverage were underwhelming; the MacArthur Foundation, disappointed with the output, threatened to withdraw funding; and the DPIC director resigned.[79] A first order of business for the new director, Richard Dieter, was to consolidate and centralize LWOP's growing role in the national movement.[80] In the early months of 1993, Dieter circulated a draft of a report that would ultimately be titled "Sentencing for Life: Americans Embrace Alternatives to the Death

Penalty."[81] The paper emphasized that across US states the lengths of prison sentences were increasing, "a significant change from twenty years ago when the death penalty was temporarily suspended by the Supreme Court's ruling in *Furman v. Georgia*."[82] Specifically, "Forty-five states (plus the District of Columbia) presently employ a life sentence in which there is no possibility of parole for at least 25 years. Thirty-three of those jurisdictions use a life sentence in which parole is *never* possible. Yet parole information is often withheld from jurors in capital cases and the use of these severe sentences is unknown to most of the public."[83] In short, LWOP was more present than most people knew, even as it was quite popular:

> Death penalty support shrinks to less than 50% when the public is presented with a variety of alternative sentences. Most Americans, however, are unaware that the length of imprisonment embodied in these alternatives is now the norm almost everywhere in the country. . . . One of society's best kept secrets is that the length of sentences which people would apply for first-degree murder are already in place and functioning in most of the United States.[84]

Clemency for capitally sentenced prisoners serving LWOP, the paper also emphasized, would be "very remote."[85]

While the paper accurately stated LWOP's growing presence, there was something of a sleight of hand at work. The statistics reflected the number of states that authorized LWOP—but not necessarily as a capital alternative. Using "states authorizing LWOP" (for any purpose) as a key variable glossed over the fact that less than two-thirds of the states with capital punishment employed LWOP (as a mandatory or discretionary alternative) in all capital murder cases.[86] Further, of the states that did *not* use LWOP as a full capital alternative, many were in the South (including Florida, Georgia, North Carolina, South Carolina, Texas, and Virginia)—the very region where most death sentences were issued and in which LWOP as an alternative would be of the most use. Some of those southern states (including Georgia, North Carolina, and Texas) did not use LWOP at all at the time.

An unspoken aim of the DPIC piece, one might surmise, was to generate LWOP as a capital alternative in those key states—South Carolina, North Carolina, Mississippi, Georgia, Florida, and Texas—where, at that time, it existed in the *capital context* in only a very limited way (Florida and South Carolina) or not at all (the rest).[87] In doing so, the DPIC had identified a phenomenon that scholars of punishment are only now beginning to recognize: practices amounting to life without parole were increasingly prevalent, to a point that, by the late 1980s and early 1990s, they could be considered normal, not extraordinary. Significantly, the normalized presence of LWOP to which the DPIC pointed was largely the result of a *general* increase in use of life without parole sentences, couched in a general trend toward determinate and long sentencing.

Ten Reasons to Oppose LWOP, and Thirty-Nine Other Possibilities

One of the people to whom Dieter sent a draft of the DPIC report was Jonathan Gradess, executive director of the New York State Defenders Association.[88] In the late 1980s, New York governor Mario Cuomo made headlines by proposing life without parole in solitary confinement, with restitution and without clemency, as a replacement for the death penalty.[89] Cuomo dubbed this distinctly harsh twist on life sentencing "death by incarceration."[90] Cuomo's championing of LWOP likely helped emblazon LWOP in the minds of death penalty opponents in the New York region, including Gradess. But while many in the ADP movement refrained from addressing LWOP head-on, Gradess was more vocal, presenting papers on LWOP at law and legal training conferences throughout the early 1990s.[91]

Gradess generally took the position that one did not need an alternative to capital punishment at hand to credibly oppose it, but the issue was far more nuanced than identifying a single replacement sanction. In a widely circulated memo, he offered thirty-nine alternatives, which focused not on sanctions but on more general actions toward criminal justice reform. These included targeting the root causes of crime; promoting changes to housing, education, and health care; attending to mental illness and intellectual disability, domestic violence, and abuse; and training in nonviolence, alternative dispute resolution, and policing. For Gradess, in short, capital crime stemmed from the same circumstances as crime more broadly. "Life imprisonment without parole," he emphasized, "should not be on the list. It is too easy, too cruel, too impractical, too anti-client, too inhuman and too immoral to permit a credible campaign." To his memo proposing thirty-nine alternatives, Gradess attached a document offering "Ten Reasons to Oppose Life Imprisonment without Parole."[92]

The impending DPIC report, therefore, was a source of concern for Gradess and like-minded death penalty opponents. In January 1993, Gradess mailed a packet of materials to Dieter, which included the memo and the attachment. The packet also included a brief statement by a formerly incarcerated person, recently released, named Charles Culhane, who compellingly explained his transformation while serving a life (with parole) sentence.[93] And it included a memorandum interpreting the results of a study by Northeastern University researchers that found Governor Cuomo's

Ten Reasons to Oppose Life Imprisonment without Parole (LWOP)

1. There are alternatives to the death penalty which address the real problems of crime. LWOP is not one of them.
2. LWOP is immoral. There is something profoundly ironic on the one hand asserting the sacred nature of life, the life worthiness of [people with intellectual disability] and the existence of mitigating factors in the lives of people sentenced to death and on the other hand suggesting a heartlessly cruel, throwaway sanction for the same people.
3. 25 years as a penal (apolitical) sanction is quite sufficient for: (a) holding the truly dangerous; (b) allowing for the legitimate exercise of criminal justice discretion; and (c) reducing the likelihood of recurring criminality.
4. The public does not demand LWOP. Public opinion supports lesser sanctions. Our job and the job of politicians is first to ask and then to lead.
5. LWOP will inevitably fail, returning the call for the death penalty when we are not here to fight it. Let's bury the death penalty on the merits of its own evil. Many who support LWOP do so in the belief that some 20 years from now the political fervor will have died down and the State will release those people sentenced to LWOP or repeal the LWOP statute. We cannot rely on this generosity of human spirit; we must exhibit that generosity. AJ Muste said, "the means are the end in the making."
6. The Furman release data are as supportive of release under LWOP as under the death penalty, i.e., this class of offenders is unlikely to recidivate. Moreover, Furman releases represent the same exercise of discretion now available under our parole system, i.e., only about 238 are out.
7. We have LWOP in practice.
8. LWOP undermines the cost argument against the death penalty and contains its own. It also raises other problems that the criminal justice community has not thought through (i.e., geriatrics in prison).
9. LWOP goes too far. It alters the role of defense, prosecution, the judiciary and corrections, dramatically increases the stakes of a criminal case, jeopardizes the alternatives movement and threatens to replace the current sentence for most if not all homicides.
10. LWOP is not supported by many opponents of the death penalty and, therefore, we will lose constituents. It is for this reason that the abolitionist movement has opposed taking a position on LWOP as policy even while we all use it as an important ingredient in debating and defeating the death penalty.

Source: Letter from Jonathan Gradess to Richard Dieter, January 7, 1993, Capital Jury Project Papers, Series 4, box 1, folder 32, National Death Penalty Archive, M. E. Grenander Department of Special Collections and Archives, University Libraries, University at Albany, State University of New York.

proposed "death by incarceration" was no more palatable to New Yorkers than execution.[94]

On receiving a revised draft of the DPIC report from Dieter in early February 1993, Gradess wrote the leaders of several major abolition organizations that also opposed LWOP outright: the NCADP, the LDF, and the ACLU. The letter evinced an effort to narrow the argument for LWOP, suggesting more emphasis on LWOP's costs and on the possibility of clemency and parole.[95] It also revealed a coalition of allies, some at the top of powerful national organizations, with a shared distaste for LWOP.

Despite such protests, four years after the DPIC report, Texas was the only southern state without LWOP as a death penalty alternative. As states continued to adopt LWOP as the capital alternative, gradually bringing the number of death penalty states using LWOP to near unanimity, the logic fueling the DPIC position grew stronger. More, as abolitionists fueled LWOP's adoption and use, embracing LWOP also served to rejuvenate the movement's cause. As Herbert Haines establishes in his study of the movement in the mid-1990s, for abolitionists, turning to LWOP served to reaffirm their shared commitment to abolishing capital punishment and helped put back together their fraying band.[96] As LWOP stabilized as *the* death penalty alternative over the course of the 1990s, and the possibility of other options grew dimmer, more and more the difficult question of the alternative seemed to have found an answer.

LWOP EMBEDDED

Herbert Haines's study of the ADP movement in the mid-1990s ends with a proposal that reflects the movement's perceptive reading of contemporary US punishment and LWOP's resulting newfound centrality to the movement's strategy. With LWOP *already present*, Haines argued in 1996, a pro-LWOP view "would undermine the death penalty without first requiring ordinary people to change their fundamental feelings about crime and justice."[97] Haines called for an "abolition dividend"—a policy bartering increased use of LWOP (and other long-term sentencing for serious and violent crimes) in exchange for death penalty abolition—urging that a "pragmatic critique of the death penalty that portrays it as wasteful government spending and actively supports *specific alternative means* to prevent and control crime provides the best hope for undermining support for capital punishment, even among more conservative groups and its staunchest advocates."[98] Haines's proposal, which spoke to political realities and to the internal dilemmas that abolitionists confronted, as well as the ongoing tension between utility and morality that abolitionism entailed, is significant as a monument of a transition that, while far from complete, had in large part already taken place by the time his book was published.

The ADP's turn to LWOP did not happen in full until two decades after *Furman,* and rather than introduce a new form of punishment onto the scene, the ADP highlighted a penal form that was already emergent. This has implications for how one understands LWOP's place in the movement and the movement's role in LWOP history. Rather than seeing LWOP as a punishment initially generated by abolition and abolition efforts, LWOP is better seen as an emerging feature of a changing penal landscape with which the ADP movement long wrestled and ultimately settled on only after LWOP had grown substantially outside the capital arena.[99] Yet the movement would indeed play a pivotal role in accelerating LWOP's use and solidifying its place in US punishment going forward. It was through the movement's use of LWOP, among other factors, that LWOP's standing as a prominent feature of US punishment was secured in ensuing years.[100]

9.   Life Prisoners, Lifetime Prisons

If the United States Supreme Court might have applied constitutional proportionality principles to curtail LWOP sentencing (chapter 7), and the
anti–death penalty movement could have combated LWOP (chapter 8),
there was another obstacle that, with history as a guide, one would have
expected to find in LWOP's way but ultimately was not: the opposition of
prison administrators and staff to punishments without hope. Throughout
the twentieth century and before, conventional wisdom in penal practice
held that prisoners with no reasonable opportunity for release were dangerous. There was also a corollary: the worse the conditions of confinement, the less the hope, and therefore the more dangerous the perpetual
prisoner. Given departments of corrections' concerns about the day-to-
day safety and effective management of penal institutions, practices such
as parole and clemency and administrative tools such as good time were
essential. They offered a basis of hope *and* a means of release, sustaining
prisoner morale while *also* helping to keep prison populations at levels
that facilities could physically absorb. Perpetual prison sentences worked
against each of those functions, thwarting hope and straining capacity. The
penal philosophy of rehabilitation, moreover, as much as it influenced any
given jurisdiction's policies and practices, provided an additional obstruc-
tion, as perpetual confinement ran contrary to the principle that prisoners
should be given a chance to prove themselves reformed and worthy of
release.

It is no surprise then that in the 1970s penal administrators and corrections officers stood among LWOP's staunchest critics. As we have seen
(chapter 4), in some jurisdictions state departments of corrections were a
significant force in blocking LWOP and played a notable role in directing
the punishment's historical course. By the mid-1990s, however, the vocal

and practical opposition that departments of corrections once presented to LWOP sentencing had largely subsided.

This chapter examines how the justifications that state actors historically offered for resisting LWOP receded during the 1980s and 1990s in a context of hardening penal policy, prison overcrowding, and ultimately prison expansion. It simultaneously considers the related issue of how and why state legislators who initially opposed large-scale spending on prisons and corrections altered their position, and how this corresponded with LWOP's ascent. Building prisons and managing prison beds requires transfers of resources that could have been used elsewhere, in education or welfare programs, for instance. In hindsight, one appreciates that the scale at which certain US states use LWOP has been made possible only as a consequence of the prison-building enterprises of the late twentieth century. When it comes to the question of what became of corrections' resistance to LWOP, one must also inquire into the related decisions of legislators to support prison construction.[1]

A number of scholars have provided detailed state-level histories of mass incarceration, chronicling the circumstances in which states turned to prison building.[2] I cover a similar space and time, but do so with a particular emphasis, focusing on how the shifts in department of corrections and legislative perspectives leading to prison building generated conditions of possibility for LWOP as perpetual confinement. Specifically, the discussion in this chapter recognizes how prison expansion removed certain obstacles— namely, concerns about safety and space—that had long shaped professionals' opposition to life without parole.

Again, Florida offers an important case because, as shown in earlier chapters, the Florida Department of Corrections (FLDOC) posed a formidable barrier to life without parole sentencing in the immediate wake of *Furman*. All states have their idiosyncrasies, but as I have emphasized throughout, the major upheavals in criminal justice were felt by all states and trickled down. The political and administrative challenges that Florida's penal elites faced in the 1970s and 1980s had much in common with those confronted elsewhere. I emphasize two shifts in particular, both of which intersected with a burgeoning state commitment to prison expansion.

First is a shift in thinking about prisoners and prison safety. Under the rehabilitative model that reigned in the FLDOC in the 1970s, the average prisoner was perceived as an individual who had done wrong but would respond to treatment and programming and reenter the community. By the late 1980s, however, prisoners convicted of serious and violent crimes were increasingly perceived as a dangerous bloc, and as LWOP became more prevalent, concerns once trained on LWOP were dispersed across the general prison population.

Second is a shift in thinking about resource constraints associated with long-term and lifetime punishments and how much future costs should be considered while crafting penal policy in the present. As Heather Schoenfeld has shown, overcrowding in Florida prisons was transformed from a problem to be solved by incarcerating fewer people into a problem to be solved by building more prisons.[3] As prison building alleviated concerns about overcrowded conditions and prison *safety*, it simultaneously alleviated concerns about the *space* needed to hold large numbers of people for life or long terms. Here, too, long-standing concerns—about making large investments in a state penal apparatus and funding an enterprise that would do so for decades to come—did not entirely go away but instead were rerouted years down the road to future lawmakers. On both fronts, prison safety and prison space, obstacles that had stood in the path of perpetual confinement for centuries, fell away.

GAME WARDENS AND OLD AGE HOMES

Social science research appropriately focuses much attention on the pains of imprisonment experienced by people serving life sentences. Yet the experiences and concerns of prison administrators and staff warrant attention as well.[4] Prison administrators and corrections officers approach life sentences with an eye to the risks and demands of prison management. Among those risks is that a person without a reasonable possibility of release from prison may be particularly dangerous and undeterred. Following invalidation of the death penalty in *Furman* in the early 1970s, and on through the 1980s, just what to expect from the rising number of prisoners serving life without parole sentences was a recurring discussion among criminal justice professionals.

In Alabama, for example, the "controversy" over life without parole centered on a split not along political lines but rather within the usual coalitions.[5] The division had much to do with the issue of safety—specifically, the question of which posed a bigger risk: releasing life-sentenced prisoners with the possibility they would recidivate or removing parole and leaving prisoners to ponder whether they had anything to lose by committing violence inside prison walls. The latter concern was paramount for those living and working inside the prison. One Alabama prisoner called LWOP "a dangerous trap for us to live in and more so for the officials that have to work here."[6] Alabama corrections administrators and officers, in accord with the American Correctional Association, also warned against LWOP.[7] Prosecutors, however, while often politically aligned with corrections officials, diverged here. Some rejected the argument about corrections officer safety as overblown; given a choice, those prosecutors insisted, they would take safe streets over safe prisons. Some favored LWOP because it did not come with the procedural and appellate baggage one could expect following a death sentence; in the words of an Alabama assistant attorney general, "Courts don't mind affirming life without parole sentences."[8]

Aside from safety, also a concern for prison administrators were resources. Keeping large numbers of people imprisoned until death would necessitate either releasing more people incarcerated for lower-level crimes or expanding prison capacity. Further, it would entail paying for food and shelter over many years as lifers aged. As Stewart and Lieberman observed in their interviews with penal stakeholders in Alabama and Georgia in the early 1980s, LWOP opponents ranging from corrections officials to human rights lawyers argued, on the one hand, that turning to LWOP would "create a new breed of superinmates, prone to violence and uncontrollable" *and*, on the other hand, that prisons would "be filled to overflowing and, years down the road, [] those states will be burdened with thousands of aging inmates."[9] Some criminologists anticipated that LWOP's greatest impact on corrections would come from imprisoning people into old age and the associated challenges of providing geriatric and palliative care. "Someone in correctional departments with large populations," criminologist Derral Cheatwood urged, "has to begin to think in terms of maximum security convalescent homes."[10] A spokesman for the Alabama Department of Corrections argued similarly, with reference to an automobile advertisement popular at the time: "Are we supposed to open up old age homes for these people? It's kind of like that oil filter—you can pay me now or pay me later."[11] On another note, as Morris Dees, then director of the Southern Poverty Law Center, put it, "Someday people will come to their senses and realize it's the young men who commit crimes. When you get toothless and bedridden, you're not a danger to anyone."[12]

The two arguments, about safety and about resources, rely on different views of individuals serving life sentences. One envisions an uncontrollable threat of violence, the other a passive and deteriorating invalid. LWOP was a worry from the former perspective because it could render the prison a powder keg, and from the latter because it could render the prison a geriatric holding space. Prison administrators and staff faced being "game wardens" as well as presiding over "old age homes."[13] These were not either-or options. Rather, the two concerns reflect what administrators and staff expected from a prisoner at the different poles of a life or long-term prison sentence: the game warden and the old age home were joined by the passage of decades in prison, over the course of which the once dangerous young lifer would become the aged veteran.[14]

What happened to the concerns about LWOP that so many prison administrators and staff held, to such an extent that an agency could shut down a bid to place life without parole in a replacement capital statute (as in Florida in 1972) or push a governor to veto a proposed death penalty law because it included life without parole as an alternative sanction (which happened in Georgia in 1982)?[15] The specific answer varies by jurisdiction, but there are some recurring features.

Knowing what we know in the present, one might surmise that as more people serving LWOP sentences were admitted to state and federal systems, prison administrators and staff came to recognize many lifers as model prisoners. Drawing on interviews in Washington State, Steve Herbert explains that prison staff refer to people serving life without parole as "easy keepers" because they stay out of trouble, are productive with their time, model positive behavior, and serve as mentors for younger prisoners.[16] Herbert's findings corroborate what research has consistently reported for decades: people serving life sentences tend to be a positive influence, a constructive presence in the prison.[17] Safety-related concerns about LWOP may not entirely go away, but are tempered over time by experience, as administrators and staff come to realize that people sentenced to life, as they age, are likely to become important contributors to prison morale.[18] Lifers, rather than generate safety concerns, more likely ameliorate them.[19]

Yet if concerns about the risks posed by prisoners without hope have been tempered over time as perpetual confinement has grown, this is a phenomenon evinced primarily in recent years. In the 1980s and 1990s there were more immediate factors. One such factor, related to but distinct from concerns about the dangerousness of LWOP-sentenced prisoners, was a general concern about the dangerousness of prisoners convicted of serious and violent crimes. To the question of "Do Inmates with Natural Life Terms Pose Discipline Problems?," Macdonald and Morgenbesser found that "state corrections agencies did not believe that these inmates represented a *particular* discipline problem."[20] Officials in Nevada (which made life "with or without the possibility of parole" the first-degree murder alternative in 1957) and Illinois (which turned to life without parole after *Gregg*, in 1977), for example, stated they did not believe a life without parole sentence rendered an individual a markedly higher risk than a long-term sentence.[21] As concerns about prisoners convicted of serious and violent offenses broadened, in other words, LWOP appeared less of a unique problem.

Another factor shaping departments of corrections' opposition to LWOP was the will of other parties. In some circumstances, corrections' opposition to LWOP was simply overridden by competing political interests. This was the case in Alabama, for example, where prosecutors prevailed as life without parole was introduced in the mid-1970s as an alternative punishment in the state's new death penalty statute and in the state's habitual offense laws.[22] Studies more than a decade after the enactment of the 1975 habitual offense law show that Alabama Department of Corrections representatives continued to see LWOP sentences as causing overcrowding, jeopardizing safety, demanding treatment for the aged, and simply wasting resources.[23] One finds similar resistance to life and long-term sentences in the statements of Louisiana prison wardens well into the 1980s, lamenting the disappearance of the former ten-year, six-month commutation protocol, as they urged that parole or commutation could ease the burdens of a system bursting at the seams.[24]

Losing the struggle was eventually the outcome for the FLDOC, too. After Florida abolished parole in 1983, rendering all life sentences without parole, the FLDOC grew accustomed to LWOP—because it had to. As Mona Lynch remarks in documenting the efforts of Arizona penal administrators to deal with the state's "cheap and mean" approach to sentencing and corrections: "For the most part, prison institutions are mere recipients of their population."[25] Schoenfeld's report from an interview with former FLDOC secretary Louis Wainwright supports the point: "Realizing that they had no ability to stem the flow of prisoners, but would be held responsible anyway, Department of Corrections administrators became the biggest advocates for increasing capacity by building new institutions."[26]

THE CONSTANT GAME WARDEN: DISPERSING SAFETY CONCERNS

A computer-generated list recommended Charles Street's name for release. Two weeks later, on November 18, 1988, Street killed two Dade County law enforcement officers in what was reported as a drug-related episode.[27] As it featured a recidivist released through administrative gain time procedures who murdered two police officers in a drug incident, the event touched on three of the state's most critical criminal justice issues: habitual offending, drugs, and failed prison release reforms. The Street case soon became the prism through which criminal justice gripes in Florida were seen.

Those gripes were rehashed for public consumption in a four-part editorial series in the *St. Petersburg Times* in January 1989. The legislature, the editorial argued, was fouling up because people convicted of violent crimes were being released under the gain time system to make room for new admittees, many of whom had been convicted of nonviolent offenses. The result was more crime, even murder: "When Charlie Henry Street got loose on Nov. 18, it was no mistake. The state pushed him out of Martin Correctional Institution only eight years into a 15-year sentence for attempted murder because it wanted his bed for another convict. Now two cops are dead."[28] The paper outlined what it saw as an intricate mess: prosecutors want leverage, lawmakers want certainty, and mandatory sentences result, which increases prison crowding, demanding releases, which are then determined by an automatic mechanism that eschews a review. Street was exemplary: "Those releases are no secret anymore. Charlie Henry Street, the man who benefitted from early release and now stands accused of killing two police officers, has made certain of that. What his case illustrates is the idiocy of stuffing prisons and then blindly releasing those who won't fit."[29] The editorial ended with a pointed message: prison is not for everyone; make it for those who commit violent offenses, and make sure they stay there.[30]

In introductory remarks at the 1989 Florida legislative session, the chair of the House Criminal Justice Committee, Representative Ron Silver, a Democrat, noted that the Street case "demonstrates a lot of the problems that are wrong with the criminal justice system."[31] At the first committee meeting, new FLDOC secretary Richard Dugger was invited to speak about the Street incident. "I would like to stand up here and tell you that Charlie Street was a very rare exception," Dugger began. "Truth is, he really isn't."[32] Street had dozens of disciplinary infractions, but that was not uncommon. He had received some gain time, and he had forfeited some. He had served about 55 percent of his sentence, a higher percentage than most prisoners. Street was "like hundreds of others," Dugger explained, a person on the margins who is "sometimes good, sometimes bad, sometimes in between."[33] He was the kind of person the system generally would release when it reached 97 percent capacity. "I'm sorry to say," Dugger concluded, "he is not unusual."[34]

Characterizing Charles Street as a "not unusual" prisoner meant there were a lot of people in Florida prisons who had committed serious but not the most serious crimes (such as Street's initial offenses), with ambivalent prison disciplinary records (like Street), who might (if Street was any indication) be expected to ramp up to more serious crime upon release. As the newspaper editorials made clear, public concern over dangerous prisoners intersected with disillusionment over recent reforms; parole and gain time started to look like holes in the wall. If gain time and parole—the solutions favored by Dugger and the FLDOC—were no longer viable, the department's message to legislators was to build.[35] In order to hold without early release all prisoners like Street, Dugger exclaimed, "We would need about ten more prisons than we have now."[36]

Schoenfeld emphasizes how elected officials in Florida ultimately reinterpreted a federal court injunction on prison overcrowding as a call for more prison beds rather than fewer prisoners; in short, a prisoners' rights movement ultimately begot a prison building enterprise.[37] The Street incident galvanized this, and Dugger's testimony before the legislative committee illustrates the logic behind the turn: if not better policy, then additional resources. Dugger's testimony also illustrates the department's new perspective on prisoners as safety risks. Under the rehabilitative mind-set that reigned in the FLDOC in the 1970s, the average prisoner was seen as an individual who had done wrong but could respond to treatment and programming and reenter society. Dugger's testimony indicates just how much that picture had faded by the late 1980s.

The legislative referendum on release policy that centered on Street coincided with a noticeable demographic shift in the Florida prison population. From the inception of the FLDOC in 1957 through the mid-1980s, African Americans, although constituting far less than 50 percent of Florida's population, made up nearly half of the state prison population—that number rose even higher, to 60 percent, in the late 1980s and early 1990s.[38] This demographic shift, which partly reflects the racially disproportionate impact of Florida sentencing policy in the 1980s, should be taken into account as context for Secretary Dugger's remarks. Racialized framings were amplified in the late 1980s and early 1990s in Florida as a victims' rights movement stressed a dichotomy between White victims and Black criminal defendants.[39] When Dugger characterized Street as a prisoner who was "not unusual," the norm Dugger spoke of corresponded with a racial distribution in the prison, still relatively new, in which most prisoners, like Street, were Black.

The legislative discussion following the Street incident did not open directly into a conversation about LWOP sentences, but I have focused on it because it illustrates something important about the context in which lawmakers and corrections officials and staff encountered perpetual confinement. The "game warden" position that corrections balked at, an increasingly racialized construct, now applied to all people serving long terms. As an incapacitative logic prevailed, with lengthening sentences and hardening perspectives on prisoners, LWOP receded as a specific concern.

OLD FOLKS' HOMES OF THE FUTURE: DEFLECTING CONCERNS ABOUT RESOURCES

The prison expansion that followed in Florida reduced safety concerns related to overcrowding and understaffing. But prison building and added spending on corrections also ameliorated another constraint: the shortage of space and resources needed to confine large numbers of prisoners for a lifetime. If states once lacked the penal capacity to hold people for very long periods, the prison-building enterprises of the 1980s and 1990s changed that.

Scholars offer a number of explanations for why US states committed to prison building in the 1980s and 1990s.[40] Prison building became a memento of a successful political tenure for governors.[41] Warehouse prisons served as a core element of a neoliberal social control strategy.[42] For states keen to spend as little as possible on prisoners, prison building was an unwelcome but necessary response to skyrocketing admissions.[43] In economic crisis, California found that building prisons provided investment and employment opportunities in rural areas and was a strategic way of managing surpluses in finance capital, land, labor, and state capacity.[44] Beyond a practical matter of dealing with material realities, building was a means of reassuring a restive public after cycles of policy failure.[45]

Yet there was resistance to prison expansion, from both liberal legislators who preferred to spend on education and welfare and socially conservative politicians who balked at spending money on prisoners, an unpopular demographic. A survey of case studies of prison overcrowding litigation finds that "time and again, governors and legislatures paid lip service to prison reforms but were recalcitrant when it came to funding those changes, instead preferring ad hoc measures for as long as possible."[46] Discussing Arizona in the early 1980s, Lynch notes: "Although there was little sympathy for criminals in the state throughout its history, there was a coexisting pressure not to create a huge bureaucracy to deal with that population."[47] On Florida, Schoenfeld describes how in 1982 the bipartisan Overcrowding Task Force recommended modest prison expansion, but only as a stopgap, preferring policies other than building over the long term to reduce prison admissions and manage prison releases.[48]

Florida sentencing policies of the 1980s, however, generated ever-increasing admissions, to which LWOP contributed a share: more than two thousand new prisoners between 1984 and 1992.[49] The impact of LWOP sentencing on prison capacity was accentuated, moreover, because one could expect the beds occupied by people serving LWOP to be filled until those occupants died. As one reform effort after another failed, as Democrats lost their hold on the state legislature, the pressure to capitulate to punitive penal policy grew,[50] and legislators who once had opposed broad sentencing legislation gradually agreed to "open the gate a little wider."[51] In this manner, as the 1990s wore on, conservative lawmakers found in liberals begrudging but reconciled allies.

Large-scale prison building finally broke through in Florida in 1995. Legislators from across the political spectrum (Republicans, conservative North Florida Democrats, and liberal Democrats) found common ground in a four-bill crime package that included a truth-in-sentencing law, expanded habitual offense legislation, and a profligate allocation of money for prison building to accommodate the expected increase in admissions the new laws would produce.[52] Years earlier, in the House of Representatives, Democrat Ron Silver, now a senator, had opposed similar legislation. Now, Republican legislators sponsoring the bill package found him an ally. Referring to the late 1980s, when he had chaired the House Criminal Justice Committee in the wake of the Street case, Silver explained his change of perspective:

> It seems to me that when we talk about these out [future] years . . . that what happened in the past was it wasn't properly presented. What we did was we reduced the time that these people [convicted of serious and violent crimes] served and I don't think that people recognized that's what was happening. . . . [D]o you wanna let these other people out in order to put these people in? Or do you want to spend more money to build the more prison beds that are needed? . . . In the past what we've said is we can't afford to do it because of all these tremendous expenses in the out years and we wind up doing nothing. . . . [W]e can't do it that way anymore.[53]

A former prison warden explained at a colloquium on prison crowding in the early 1980s: "Unlike many social problems, prison crowding is really very simple to define. . . . When the population has grown beyond the capacity of the prison to hold it, only three things can be done. Either reduce the number coming in; reduce the time they stay; or expand the capacity of the system."[54] When Florida decided to build, it alleviated space constraints that otherwise weighed against large numbers of long-term and LWOP sentences. In doing so, it removed an obstacle that had stood in the way of lifetime sentences from the colonies onward. More beds would allow longer holding in greater numbers. In the process of shifting policy on prison building, as such, positions were taken and ways of thinking were adopted that resonated with perpetual confinement. Decisions were made that enabled LWOP by removing, dispersing, and deflecting what had been long-standing concerns.

A resonance between the decision to build and the political promise of an LWOP sentence bears emphasis. Prison building was, as Senator Silver stressed, meant to deal with the "now." It served as an immediate fix to the problem of overcrowding and errant releases by eliminating the necessity for releases. It also left costs and administrative complications related to managing aging prisoners for legislators and prison managers in decades to come. In such efforts, the prison-building enterprise exhibits a character of disregard: disregard of responsible fiscal management, disregard of social programs on which the funds could otherwise have been spent, and disregard of the life prisoners who, despite whatever transformation they might achieve over decades in prison, could be denied a meaningful opportunity for release. Like LWOP sentencing, prison investment went forth with an express lack of care for the future, via conscious decisions to not know how legislators and penal administrators would manage down the road. We might think of arguments for prison building as a crisis narrative that reframed the problem and upset existing standards, enabling a new norm—allowing large-scale expansion to be thinkable and helping lead legislators who had once opposed prison expansion to approve it.[55]

The "out years"—as Senator Silver referred to decades yet to come— have now arrived. The aging crisis posed by life sentences, first recognized years ago, has come to fruition. The number of prisoners aged fifty-five or older has grown dramatically, as has the number of elders dying in US prisons.[56] Thousands of people sentenced to life in the late twentieth century have become senior citizens in confinement. Many sources contribute to the number of people aging into dying in US prisons,[57] but life sentencing is a significant factor. As with the shift in perspective on dangerous prisoners, the shift in perspective on building positioned LWOP to thrive, free of constraints that had limited it in the past.

Conclusion

This book has investigated the history of life without parole and perpetual confinement in the United States. It has engaged in an examination with a broad historical scope as well as a lens focused on specific states and institutions. Doing so has (1) exposed life without parole as a punishment that was, until recently, not without some reasonable possibility of release, and (2) revealed perpetual confinement as a type of punishment that, while always having a role in penal policy, has rarely if ever been so routine and so central to the daily operations of the criminal justice system. In closing, I would like to accentuate certain messages with which the book leaves us concerning LWOP, institutionalization, the study of punishment, and the predicament of perpetual confinement in the contemporary United States. The first point has to do with understanding the processes by which punishments develop and change. The second point concerns the social ramifications of LWOP and other forms of perpetual confinement. The final point situates this book's historical account in the context of contemporary penal policy and reform.

REMEMBERING: ON EMERGENCE AND INSTITUTIONALIZATION

In a century marked by human rights treaties and civil rights victories, one might expect that perpetual confinement would be considered a shockingly cruel practice, on a level with the death penalty. In times of economic constraints, such as the United States has experienced more than once in the early twenty-first century, one might think that holding tens of thousands of people in confinement for their entire lives, and paying for it, would be deemed a rather questionable strategy—a strategy that, if one were to pursue it, would demand heightened scrutiny. Framed in these terms, the scale of perpetual confinement and its active role in contemporary US punishment is sobering. Justice needs to be served, but this is a peculiar way to go about it. To understand the unique attachment to LWOP in the United States, this book has argued, one must look not only to its increased use and the variance in its application, but also past the proximate causes at play in specific locales to the frameworks of practices and understandings in the background.

LWOP Remembered: From Proximate Causes to Backgrounds

Recent work in the sociology of punishment emphasizes the importance of local-level study and a focus on ongoing struggle. Social changes do not happen suddenly out of the blue. What appear as large-scale shifts or breaks at a distance, upon more local inspection reflect incremental changes and gradual developments. When social terrain shifts, new opportunities arise, and fortunes change.[1] Relatedly, ideas percolate: what seems a sudden innovation may be better explained as a series of amendments to ideas with a longer history.[2] Through state- and local-level inquiry one also finds that broad-scale social changes do not have blanket results. In other words, the shape and variety of penal change has to do with its proximate causes: broader trends influence local law, policy, and practice only as they are filtered by specific histories, structural arrangements, and culture.[3]

The state- and institutional-level inquiries in this book operate with these principles in mind and show them at work. Perpetual confinement is an idea that has been around since the beginning of the United States; if LWOP is now having its moment, the notion of putting people away forever is hardly new. Consider, for example, the cadres of moral entrepreneurs who pitched life without parole laws as perpetual confinement in the early twentieth century. Those prototypical views of LWOP found more agreeable terrain in the US penal field from the 1970s onward. The varied landscape of life without parole laws and their implementation in the contemporary United States, moreover, defies a unified national or even regional approach; it must be explained by state-level developments. Throughout, this study illustrates how local conditions and struggles translated major upheavals to determine penal outcomes; major shocks to the structure and ideology of capital punishment, to sentencing and corrections, and to clemency generated new laws, policies, and practices *only* as they "operated through"[4] specific arrangements on the ground.

The continuity between past and present, however, can be overstated. An idea or practice, despite sharing a name, should not be uncritically accepted as the same object in its new context. Historical epistemology applies this insight to the study of natural science, but it is no less applicable to the social world.[5] A similar theme runs through scholarship on institutions that emphasizes the need for material and cultural "infrastructure" for certain ways of doing and thinking to emerge.[6] One can relate the point to the history of life without parole. It would not do to say that no individuals or groups in the 1970s or 1980s advocated life without parole with its current meaning in mind; to be sure, there were some who did: Attorney General Shevin in Florida (chapter 4) and death penalty defense litigator and abolitionist David Bruck (chapter 8) are examples. But the perspectives on life without parole held by Shevin in the 1970s and Bruck in the 1980s were not *widely* held, and they were not widely held in significant part because a general understanding of life without parole as perpetual confinement had not yet gelled in the legal and penal fields or in American society.

This book has shown the *processes* by which understandings and practices of life without parole and perpetual confinement changed. Underlying this is the idea of a background and, relatedly, conditions of possibility. Gabriel Abend refers to such conditions as "enablers," which can come in many forms: concepts or ideas; technologies or physical tools; and organizations and related rules, protocols, and laws.[7] Generally speaking, there is a need, in other words, for an infrastructure that supports any given meaning or practice via some process of validation, be it recognition, corroboration, or resonance.[8] When the national anti–death penalty movement urged a turn to LWOP as an alternative in 1993, for example, it did so upon a landscape in which many states were already using LWOP and on the heels of the US Supreme Court declaring that LWOP, as perpetual confinement, was a constitutional punishment even for nonhomicide offenses.

In a series of lectures at Syracuse University in 1986, anthropologist Mary Douglas noted that in most cases what are recognized as new scientific theories are not so new; rather, they consist of ideas that were introduced earlier but did not then enjoy a fit with current thinking, what Douglas called "coherence":

> [A] theory that is going to gain a permanent place in the public repertoire of what is known will need to interlock with the procedures that guarantee other kinds of theories. . . . Most rediscovered theories turn out not to have built originally on the current cognitive infrastructure. . . . Often when a new scientific discovery has been rejected and left to lie inert until later, it is precisely an idea which lacked formulaic interlocking with normal procedures of validation.[9]

A mental representation that is more than a fleeting impression, Émile Durkheim recognized, needs to align with "the nature of things" or "it would never [be] able to acquire an extended and prolonged empire over intellects."[10] Modifying the point for contemporary society, Douglas advised, "The principle of coherence is not satisfied by purely cognitive and technological fit. . . . [I]t [also] needs to be compatible with the prevailing political values."[11]

This book has shown how major transformations in US punishment should be seen as key, if not *the* key, enabling conditions for life without parole. Each presented new ways of thinking and practicing in which LWOP as a punishment without reasonable possibility of release found validation. A death penalty that is narrowed, rather than a death penalty that can be expected to address all dangerous offenders, creates the need for other sure ways of no release. A determinate sentencing approach, rather than open-ended sentencing with parole, supports fixed sentences that mean what they say. Clemency practice that is no longer a means of regulating prison populations and is highly risk averse will necessarily generate perpetual prison stays. The notion of life without parole as a sentence from which prisoners would not be released aligned with each of these substantial changes.

With such prerequisites, penal forms, not unlike scientific theories or any form of lasting social practice, become stabilized; in effect, they are *remembered*. With LWOP, a multitude of vectors, not all punitive, served as anchors in its rise. Then prevailing punitive political values and social attitudes—the "nature of things" in the United States, at least since the 1980s and 1990s—received LWOP and helped it proliferate.

LWOP as Emblem: From Life without Parole to Perpetual Confinement

In providing an account of the transformative processes that led to LWOP's emergence and contemporary practices, this book has witnessed perpetual confinement changing its status, moving from a specter on the margins to an important player at the crux of the system. The first chapter, considering historical schemes of punishment, showed how perpetual confinement played a significant role in projects with divergent aims, such as banishment or incapacitation, as in Daniel Raymond's perpetual workhouse, but also treatment and rehabilitation, as in Frederick Wines's Progressive Era model. Perpetual confinement was a product of various intentions, produced in many ways, and took different shapes and served different uses depending on its context. What those divergent projects shared, however, was that in each, across varying logics, perpetual confinement served significant *yet circumscribed* purposes.

Since the late 1970s, US states have adopted sentencing schemes in which prison sentences are imposed for fixed terms of years, which are often mandatory and often very long. The best reflection of LWOP's role in this system is the US Supreme Court decision in *Harmelin*, which, in upholding a mandatory LWOP sentence for a first-time drug possession offense, signaled that LWOP was a justifiable punishment for a wide variety of crimes and endorsed the widespread use of perpetual confinement. But LWOP is not alone.

In states that use parole today, the possibility of release exists on paper in much the way it did in Progressive designs, but practices have hardened. Most life sentences with parole have a mandatory minimum of around twenty-five years, and parole grants have withered.[12] Parole boards may deny release with little regard for a prisoner's efforts at rehabilitation, focusing instead on circumstances of the offense that will never change.[13] Rules or protocols extending the number of years or months that prisoners must wait between parole reviews diminish opportunities for release.[14] In other words, the backstop of the indeterminate sentencing model has expanded: many parole-eligible prisoners are held perpetually despite being technically eligible for release.[15] California is an example. The state authorizes LWOP narrowly, using it primarily for first-degree homicide, yet life *with* parole is available for a broad range of crimes. In the 1990s and into the early twenty-first century, the state applied parole so cautiously that it amounted to a policy against releasing people serving life sentences, via a combination of retrenched parole grants and gubernatorial vetoes of release recommendations.[16] Zimring and Johnson compare LWOP in this environment, in which "voter-passed initiatives and politically sensitive governors make the release through parole of any first degree murderer a very rare and visible event," to "shipping coals to Newcastle."[17]

Further, some states use prison terms likely to exceed life expectancy in the way other states use LWOP. Whether one is referring to "extreme sentences" of more than two hundred years or "virtual life sentences" of more than forty years or fifty years, such sentences are prevalent in the United States, and a substantial number of prisoners are serving sentences likely to outlast their life span.[18] A study in the federal system finds that judges issuing "extreme sentences" tend to view them as equivalents of natural life sentences.[19] As with the example of Michigan in the 1980s (chapter 5), many long fixed terms are imposed with the intention of confining people until death. If, under indeterminate sentencing, courts once used extreme sentences to make a point, knowing well that parole or clemency would modify the sentence if and when appropriate,[20] sentencing courts and legislators today know that these practices once expected to mediate disproportionate sentences have atrophied. As Kazemian and Travis summarize: "Individuals sentenced to life with the possibility of parole, or not sentenced to life imprisonment at all, may spend their lives in prison. These latter two scenarios have become increasingly likely in recent years."[21]

Together, these forms of punishment comprise what is likely the largest number of persons imprisoned without release for criminal law violations in the nation's history. We should see LWOP then as the tip of a broader problem. But we may also see LWOP as something of an enabler. More than a sanction, LWOP has become a way of understanding different types of penal practices. Litigants, policy analysts, and scholars now classify punishments that are not formally LWOP, but nevertheless achieve the result of imprisonment until death, as "de facto" or "virtual" equivalents of LWOP. As policy analysts urge lawmakers to address extremely long fixed sentences, retrenched parole grants, and LWOP under the same umbrella, and as advocates urge courts to extend the legal precedent for youth serving LWOP to youth serving these other punishments, LWOP is the reference point.

When people key on particularly visible and topical punishments, such as the death penalty, they tend to overlook other, sometimes equally harsh practices.[22] The heightened scrutiny given to capital cases, as such, is a stark contrast to the routine processing of LWOP. Emphasis on LWOP, likewise, may underplay the severity of other practices resulting in imprisonment until death. But more than camouflage these practices, LWOP has validated them, as it has helped ingrain perpetual confinement as an approach to which penal professionals and the American public are accustomed and of which they are tolerant. Once a concept or practice "become[s] sedimented and routinized," it is "available to actors."[23] It is *at hand*. Put another way, once practices and understandings are institutionalized, people act on them more reflexively.[24] It is therefore not surprising that it is after the US Supreme Court decision in *Harmelin* that one sees (1) the mid-1990s surge of tough-on-crime laws using LWOP; (2) the first national dataset recording life with and life without parole sentences in every state, in 1992;[25] and (3) the national anti–death penalty movement turn to LWOP as an alternative, in 1993. As LWOP stabilized as a regular penal practice, it normalized the idea of putting people away forever.[26] Perpetual confinement is now seen, in the penal field and society alike, not simply as something that happens on occasion for expedience or along a secondary track, but as a *normative way of punishing*.

Because practices and understandings solidify to form institutions, and a resonance with our lived experience and "the nature of things" is essential for the stability of sentiments and beliefs, symbols not only represent social meanings that already exist but also serve to reinforce them. LWOP—a punishment now fixed and coherent enough to be contemplated, intended, even expected—has served as a symbol in this way.[27] When parole commissioners or governors dismiss parole for political reasons, or when legislatures authorize, prosecutors seek, and judges impose sentences that may reasonably be expected to outlast a prisoner's life span, they do so knowing perpetual confinement to be a practice that, via LWOP, is authorized and implemented quite ordinarily. Perpetual confinement is more real because LWOP is there as a reference point, to stabilize the idea and the practice.

David Garland notes that "laws and state actions do not simply 'express' [] sentiments—they also seek to transform and reshape them in accordance with a particular vision of society. Such changes are often slow and require extensive ideological work, but the moral sentiments which are internalized by individuals do change over time as new normative codes are legislated and new generations are socialized in accordance with them."[28] So it is with the rise of LWOP, which is both reflective of and responsible for a change in cultural perspective concerning the practicality, the functionality, and by extension the morality, of sentencing people to live out their natural lives in a cell.

FORGETTING: ON DISREGARD, NEGLECT, AND HARSH PUNISHMENT

A core feature of LWOP—by which I mean life without parole as perpetual confinement—is its abject cruelty. The harshness of the sentence is arguably on a par with or exceeds that of the death penalty. Another core feature of LWOP is that it is often expressly racially motivated: the disproportionate number of people of color serving the sentence is evidence, as are laws that target particular demographics. But LWOP has also been enabled by less direct, no less damaging, biases. There is a line of disregard that runs throughout the history of perpetual confinement and a character of neglect at the core of the way in which LWOP is used in contemporary American punishment as a promise of reassurance; disregard is deeply a part of the social fabric of this institution, and neglect is inherent in LWOP, its primary contemporary form. In fact, the institutionalization of LWOP as perpetual confinement can be seen as a model of how disregard factors in mechanisms of punishment.

Perpetual Confinement and Disregard

In 1995, Michael Tonry characterized the marked and persistent disparate impacts of US sentencing policy on non-White Americans, and particularly on Black Americans, as "malign neglect," brought about by "policymakers' indifference to the racial effects of their policies."[29] Tonry urged legislators to "think about the foreseeable effects of crime control policies" on non-White groups and communities and, "when policies are likely to burden members of [those] groups disproportionately and, through them, their families and communities, [to] reconsider the policies."[30] He pointed to the war on drugs as an example, concluding that its disparate impacts on Black Americans "make it clear that many policymakers do not much worry about the racial ramifications of their decision."[31] LWOP played a significant role in the war on drugs (the Federal Sentencing Act of 1984 and the Michigan 650-Lifer Law of 1978 are prominent examples), and malign neglect as such resounds in the history of LWOP. However, the history of perpetual confinement in the United States also reveals other, if less flagrant, no less discriminatory forms of ignoring.

To appreciate the role of disregard in contemporary life sentencing, it pays to recall the nature of life imprisonment in the early United States and perpetual confinement's role in early penal theories. In early US experiments with prisons, and in the Progressive Era reforms, perpetual confinement was not the target outcome for most cases, but it was a possible outcome that penal systems inherently accepted for prisoners, a class consisting primarily of people who were poor, immigrant, or not White. In other words, a reason that people were able to be imprisoned and then held forever without any strong objections had something to do with the prejudice, underlying the penal enterprise, toward the types of people that would be imprisoned and, in some circumstances, be exploited as penal laborers.

More recently, as we have seen, perpetual confinement was not the target outcome for some of the early laws that brought LWOP into being. The Florida legislature abolished parole with no clear intention to make all life sentences into LWOP, but existing administrative provisions rendered them so. In Pennsylvania, there was no express legislative decision to turn life without parole into perpetual confinement, but changed executive practices made it so. Key reforms in the states that now use LWOP the most were not necessarily crafted with "total incapacitation"[32] as a primary goal, yet those reforms generated an infrastructure that enabled prolific use of LWOP. In an insightful prehistory of mass incarceration, *The Prison and the Gallows*, Marie Gottschalk examines "how institutional capacity, especially state capacity to pursue mass imprisonment as public policy, was built up well before."[33] A similar trope works with the US turn to LWOP: before many recognized LWOP as a perpetual sentence, it was generated through decisions with other principal concerns. The rise of LWOP as perpetual confinement has as much to do with indirect and incidental developments as with intentional ones.

This is not simply a point about indirect consequences; it is about the tacit acceptance of extreme punishments. The prior buildup of LWOP influenced later action, allowing actors who wished to promote LWOP to invest it with the kind of legitimacy that comes from already being there. In 1991, states supporting LWOP before the US Supreme Court pointed to its widespread use; in 1993, death penalty abolitionists drew support for LWOP by showing, in a vital DPIC report, that states were already sentencing people to LWOP outside the capital context; departments of corrections resisted for years, but once LWOP was authorized by law, they lived with it and in turn advocated for more prisons to alleviate overcrowding, which contributed to dismantling another key historical obstacle, prison space. As much as each of these developments involved actions that produced LWOP, they also involved unstated acceptance of the increasing use of perpetual confinement, to which they responded.

While challenged on occasion, LWOP as perpetual confinement in the United States has largely emerged, and been accepted, without critical attention. To interpret this failure, one must look back to the ambivalence toward perpetual confinement that characterized earlier practices and to how assumptions about the lessened dignity of the people imprisoned fostered acceptance of imprisonment without release (chapter 1). One must also look back to the divergent paths taken by the United States and European states in the early twentieth century (chapter 5): embracing indeterminate sentencing, the United States did not develop the sort of critical dialogue about lifetime confinement that has limited its use elsewhere, and when the nature of life sentences in the United States shifted at century's end, the lack of such a critical tradition allowed perpetual confinement to develop relatively unchecked. If actors in earlier centuries accepted perpetual confinement as an ever-present possibility, most likely to be applied to disempowered individuals and marginalized social groups, actors of the 1990s accepted it as a natural reality.

Tonry, recognizing the racially disparate impacts of US sentencing laws and policies, remarked, "Americans have a remarkable ability to endure suffering by others."[34] Extending the argument to a continuum of forms of disregard, the late twentieth-century history of LWOP and perpetual confinement could adopt the statement as a refrain. Racial discrimination and other biases are neither absent nor overt in tacit acceptance, but are embedded deeper down—reflected, as in perpetual confinement's earlier history, in a disregard for suffering that cannot be easily extracted from a judgment about the dignity of the people who will suffer.

LWOP and Neglect

Taking what this book has shown, and building on prior theorizations of LWOP,[35] one can draw an additional point, which has less to do with the nature of perpetual confinement historically than with the essence of the prevailing way in which LWOP manifests today—namely, as a promise of reassurance. As a promise of reassurance, LWOP finds its purchase in two related ways: first, in the *immediacy* of the responsive act, which offers a quick fix or reward, and second, in the absolute quality of the proclaimed sentence, which offers *removal* of the problem. At root, however, LWOP's claims to immediacy and to removal are not necessarily true. For even if a prisoner has no meaningful review for release, that person's life has yet to be lived, and it will be lived out in prison under state supervision. The duality between these symbolic functions and LWOP's actual implementation lends it a third inherent quality, which is at the crux of LWOP's singular character as a punishment: *neglect*.

Immediacy: LWOP as Death Penalty   In the mode of governance Garland calls "acting out," the "most pressing concern is to do something decisive, to respond with immediate effect to public outrage, to demonstrate that the state is in control and is willing to use its powers . . . to reassure a distrustful public that the system will not betray them once the case goes out of view."[36] The LWOP sentence is particularly well suited for such demonstrations, because, as Sharon Dolovich observed, "In one move . . . [i]n one stroke, the target is permanently exiled, foreclosed from ever making a case for release."[37] One might suggest that the death penalty, a corporal punishment, accomplishes much the same. The death penalty is an unqualified condemnation, a sentence for which rehabilitation is irrelevant: with execution, the prisoner's life is ended and the punishment complete. Yet in the United States, given complex constitutional procedural requirements and the exacting scrutiny the Sixth and Eighth Amendments demand, death penalties end up mired in years of appeals and reversed sentences. Closure, as such, is elusive for the victims of capital crimes. Not so with LWOP, for which there is no right to counsel after direct appeal and no heightened constitutional standards. As Evi Girling recognizes, with this LWOP may claim a finality that the death penalty, with its multitude of appeals and frequent reversals, cannot: "The [LWOP] sentence is immediate with no delay, no 'second lifetime' on death row. It appears not to overpromise and under-deliver death, like the death penalty with its many exits, delays and judicial and political uncertainty. It does what it says on the tin – you die in prison, little possibility of review of the case, review of sentence, mercy."[38]

The value of such immediacy comes not simply in reassuring the general public, but more specifically in assuaging crime victims. The imposition of a LWOP sentence, per Girling, is "a covenant with victims that can be kept, not at the moment of death, but in the finality of an unconditionality of the sentence."[39] Jonathan Simon and Zimring and Johnson, respectively, theorize the logic of contemporary US punishment as a zero-sum game, heralding victims' interests while denigrating the dignity of people who have committed crimes.[40] The victims' rights movement in the United States took flight in the 1980s, fueled by the recognition of victim testimony in capital sentencing trials, and began to peak in the early 1990s, with widespread criminal justice reforms giving victims a greater voice in sentencing and release decisions. The image of the victim that has animated US penality ever since puts pressure on penal state actors to be unforgiving and risk averse; any leniency shown a criminal defendant may slight the dignity of the victim. This combination results in a modus operandi that punishes for as long as possible and with as little risk as possible. LWOP, Simon suggests, best exemplifies this imbalance, "defin[ing] the logic of contemporary penality" as it "embrace[s] the totalizing promise of prison incapacitation extended to the very limits of life."[41]

One sees this extreme dichotomy at work in the *Graham* sentencing proceedings (chapter 3). The court's choice of LWOP from within a range of five years to life exemplified a total trade-off between the victim and the person who committed the crime. The sentence's terminal nature provided a sense of both immediacy and closure.

Removal: LWOP as Banishment   If LWOP can be likened to a death sentence, it can also be likened to another historical punishment that was equally experienced as final by the state and the public: transportation. Transportation is a classic form of banishment in which a person is placed on a boat and taken to another continent, not to return, with little concern lingering on the mainland about how things will turn out for the person upon arriving on a distant shore. One might think of the remote island workhouse envisioned by Daniel Raymond (chapter 1), where the prisoners were to carry on unsupervised. Transportation involves a removal from a land or territory, LWOP a displacement from public life, but both share a sense of a community being done with an individual. Another way to put it is that the person has been removed.

Dolovich notes that LWOP involves an "emotional driver" beyond the "hatred and rage often expressed against criminal offenders": a "denial of a shared social membership, and of a common humanity that lies at the heart of the impulse to exclude."[42] The contemporary United States, Dolovich argues, is characterized by a social hostility that deems certain populations not merely "wicked" but "contamina[nts]."[43] Along with the immediacy of the act, therefore, the notion of removal gives LWOP an absolute quality, an aspect of unconditionality, that may be reassuring.[44]

But in significant respects both the immediacy and the absolute removal that an LWOP sentence promises are myths. The sentence is not immediately complete. Instead, it is served over years and decades. Nor is it absolutely certain that a person will never leave prison. Commutation may be an unreasonable expectation, but it is not impossible.[45] If not exactly true to reality, the LWOP sentence nevertheless performs closure for some victims and communities, even as it sets off a chain of new harms in other communities. In that regard, LWOP is less an ultimate resolution than a ritual that allows letting go of what happens elsewhere and later.

Neglect: LWOP, Neither Execution nor Transportation In sum, an LWOP sentence promises to cut things off in ways that the sentence does not and cannot, in actuality, achieve. LWOP is promised to be a punishment that provides immediacy in the sense of corporal punishment and provides closure of the sort that comes with expelling someone to another shore. On both counts, one might observe, LWOP seeks to lose its nature as a punishment effectuated through a process of imprisonment. On both counts, LWOP also comes up short. *LWOP is a death penalty. LWOP is banishment. But LWOP is not an execution or a transportation.*

The contrast between the punishment's symbolic functions and its actual implementation—this duality between (1) the immediate removal that LWOP claims to achieve and (2) the residual imprisonment that will last for years if not decades—is a core feature of the punishment and has figured in the processes of its emergence. Moreover, the duality has consequences. There are human consequences, which directly affect the experience of the people serving the sentence. There are political and administrative consequences, which concern how jurisdictions attend to the responsibilities of holding a person in confinement, including in-prison treatment and programming and the structural capacity to keep hundreds if not thousands of people imprisoned for years until death. The consequences also extend outward, beyond the prisoner to the family and communities and beyond the state to the public sphere.

Human consequences. One cruelty of the LWOP sentence, insofar as it provides no opportunity for review for release, is that it gives no institutional reed to grasp for hope. Another cruelty is that whatever positive accomplishments people achieve in prison will not be known. Knowing that a person serving LWOP will not leave prison, there is less incentive to make programming available for them. Further, putting a person in prison forever is a punishment whose collateral consequences reach all those who will be affected by the perpetual absence of the person who is a loved one, a family member, a friend, a neighbor. As do all imprisonments, the sentence creates a physical hold on the person confined, but also a tie to the institution on all those who care deeply about the incarcerated person. "Doing time together" applies to the plight of all people who have loved ones and friends in prison.[46] The permanent impact, however, of a perpetual confinement permits little hope—for family and friends as for the imprisoned—unless it grows out of utter despair.

Law and policy consequences. On a political level, the proclamation of LWOP is meant to have immediate effect in the present, yet how it actually plays out down the road is less of a concern. The ramifications manifest in multiple ways. The expenses of feeding and housing prisoners through old age and death are left to a later generation of administrators and politicians. Adults serving LWOP are not entitled under the US Constitution to life history presentations, to attorneys throughout their appeals, or to other heightened procedural protections that death-sentenced prisoners receive (as in *Graham*, the process may be the same for a sentence of LWOP or a sentence of five years). Outside the death penalty arena, the punishment of serious and violent crimes, barely regulated by the Constitution, is also relatively unsupervised by many state governments that allow perpetual confinement for a broad range of conduct. Indeed, a presumption of nonscrutiny seems to apply to the implementation of punishment at the "hard end."[47] This is evident in the bifurcated penal policy of recent reform initiatives, which specify low-end reforms in detail but are often silent on the punishment for serious and violent offenses and may even promise to increase it.[48]

Just as prisoners serving LWOP will no longer be known, the law and policy governing perpetual confinement has been less scrutinized. Just as human consequences extend beyond the sentenced individual to families and communities, uncritical approaches to hard-end sentencing have broader effects. Extreme prison terms and practices of perpetual imprisonment alter ways of thinking about punishment, potentially transforming penality, shaping institutional practices and individual beliefs. Just as the death penalty has corrosive social effects, perpetual confinement does too.

"LWOP memorializes our rage."[49] Yet even as this memorial stands, as long as prisoners remain imprisoned and alive, the promise remains uniquely unfinished. LWOP acts like an end but in fact is not. Consequently, LWOP is fundamentally a process of neglect, symptomatic of a willingness if not eagerness to forget what happens after sentence and in prisons, to forget the responsibility of imprisonment and the people who are the prisoners. This is not simply incapacitation in the sense of warehousing or throwing away the key for public safety; it is also a clearing or closure of the public mind, and perhaps of the public interest. Rather than anger, there is "unconcern."[50] Rather than a public catharsis and working through, LWOP presents a different public urge or need with respect to crime: to file it away. If the death penalty in the contemporary United States can be characterized as a matter of discourse more than death,[51] LWOP is a punishment that is principally about forgetting and silencing, rather than talking.

CODA: PERPETUAL CONFINEMENT AND AMERICAN PENAL POLICY

The history in this book has an eye to the present and in conclusion must return to it. What does the history of LWOP's emergence offer for thinking about the complicated relationship between the death penalty, LWOP, and de facto death in prison sentences, and for those inclined to consider reform of American punishment, what does it suggest about how to proceed?

As use of the death penalty diminishes and long-term penalties amounting to death in prison increase, the time is ripe to rethink where the lines are drawn in American punishment between the most severe sentences.[52] From the standpoint of LWOP, pressing questions about ultimate penalties stand on either side. Looking in one direction, LWOP has been widely accepted as an alternative capital sanction, responsible in no small part for decreasing use of the death penalty. Looking in the other direction, LWOP has significant commonalities with other prison sentences. Very long terms of years that are sure to outlast a prisoner's life span also result in death in prison. On the one hand, its arguably unique harshness makes LWOP an effective tool for death penalty abolition and a punishment for which a limited extension of Eighth Amendment "death is different" jurisprudence is justified. On the other hand, the undeniable similarity of the lived experiences of people serving LWOP and those serving de facto LWOP sentences supports an argument that the procedural protections granted to juvenile LWOP sentences should apply more broadly. Questions from both directions confront the US Supreme Court's Eighth Amendment jurisprudence. The former path seems unlikely to offer relief for virtually equivalent punishments that logically demand similar constitutional protection. The latter path seems to dilute the argument that "LWOP is different too," which was successful in heightening the constitutional protections for youth in the cases of *Graham* and *Miller*.

The complicated relationship between these ultimate penalties is amplified by the context of reform. On the one hand lies the death penalty's decline and possible demise. Every death penalty state currently uses LWOP as an alternative capital sanction, and LWOP is one important reason that a strong consensus has evolved in support of abolition. So, replacing the death penalty with LWOP seems a natural next step should the death penalty end: at some point in the not too distant future LWOP may become the next ultimate penalty in retentionist states. But with the possibility of abolition also comes an opportunity, if not a responsibility, to reconsider the role of penal policy and practice more broadly.

As Michel Foucault pointed out while France considered abolishing the death penalty in 1981, rather than ask which punishment should replace the death penalty, the critical question ought to be whether or not society will adhere to a mode of punishment that distinguishes a class of individuals for permanent penal exclusion, be it by death or by imprisonment. "The real dividing line among penal systems," Foucault wrote, "does not pass between those which include the death penalty and others; it passes between those which allow definitive [absolute] penalties and those which exclude them." "The abolition of the death penalty will probably be easily approved," he remarked, "but will there be a radical departure from a penal practice that . . . maintains that certain individuals cannot be corrected, ever[?]"[53] In Foucault's view, the biggest danger was not the risks former death row prisoners would pose, but another he worried the legislature would fail to address—that "of a society that will not be constantly concerned about its code and its laws, its penal institutions and its punitive practices": "By maintaining in one form or another the category of individuals to be definitively eliminated (through death or imprisonment), one easily gives oneself the illusion of solving the most difficult problems: correct if one can; if not no need to worry, no need to ask oneself whether it might be necessary to reconsider all the ways of punishing: the trap door through which the 'incorrigible' will disappear is ready."[54] Foucault's point was that the death penalty was symptomatic of a deeper malady. Abolishing capital punishment presented an opportunity to do more than simply replace the death penalty with something else; it offered an opportunity to cure that malady by reconsidering and reorienting the penal system and society.

How might the spirit of Foucault's concern over the penal classification of individuals for "definitive elimination" apply in the contemporary United States? This book has offered multiple answers. To begin, one must be vigilant to question taken for granted ways of thinking. Narratives have consequences, insofar as they incline actors to see things in certain ways and follow certain paths, and insofar as they privilege certain tracks of constitutional interpretation, legal argument, and policy reform while obscuring others. Perceiving LWOP as a product of the death penalty context (a prominent narrative about LWOP's rise) has encouraged litigants and courts to examine challenges to LWOP sentences by seeking to extend the US Supreme Court's death penalty jurisprudence. The court's cases prohibiting LWOP sentences for juveniles proceed in that mode.[55] Yet a reform approach that portrays LWOP as a punishment so uniquely cruel that it could qualify for another "different" sort of jurisprudence, along the lines of the death penalty model, has the effect of differentiating LWOP from other punishments that generate like results. This book has shown how life without parole came to be distinguished from other lifetime sentences only in recent decades; LWOP's history reminds us how sentences amounting to death in prison, by any measure, were once dealt with in comparable ways.

The historical genealogy presented in this book, accordingly, may realign the way one thinks of LWOP and distinguishes it from other penalties, and provide an empirical foundation for reorienting the approach to LWOP in constitutional litigation. Is there anything inherently cruel about a life without parole sentence if clemency is a structured and regular mode of release? Is life with parole a constitutionally acceptable punishment when parole boards fail to meaningfully consider a prisoner's individual background and efforts in prison? Relying on abstract distinctions between life *without* parole and life *with* parole, or between LWOP and de facto LWOP sentences, obscures the nature of the problem. Showing the history and processes of transformation in LWOP and perpetual penal confinement reframes the issues in ways that demand looking beyond a death penalty framework and offers a guide for recalibrating proportionality jurisprudence to focus on whether the expected back-end outcome of the sentence is, to borrow Foucault's term, "definitive," much as jurists did decades ago.

The other conventional narrative about LWOP—that it arose as part and parcel of the tough-on-crime policy that created mass incarceration—also has limits for reform. Over the past decade, widespread state-level reform efforts have sought to undo the excesses of penal policies of the 1990s and early 2000s that produced mass incarceration.[56] The blueprint for most of these efforts consisted of bipartisan groups of state legislators, administrators, and stakeholders collaborating with policy analysts and advisers to generate plans for reducing the size of state prison populations. The focus of the programs, implemented in a majority of the states, was on reducing sentence lengths, improving treatment programs in prison, and using alternatives to imprisonment for prisoners convicted of low-level crimes. But it was common to emphasize how prison space would be reserved for people who commit serious and violent offenses; contemporaneous with low-level reforms, one finds rhetoric and legislation calling for increased penalties for the hard end, including LWOP. At the root of the reform program, then, was a bifurcation according to which low-end and high-end offenses were distinguished and allocated to different sentencing regimes. The reforms aim at mass incarceration but tend to leave out a sizeable portion of incarcerated people—namely, those convicted of serious and violent crimes who are serving long-term and life sentences.[57] Just as LWOP's history shows how severe punishments can be generated by reforms generally intent on reducing prison capacity and sentence lengths, one sees the same possibility with contemporary bifurcated reform efforts.

While these two contemporary reform projects—one directed at low-level crimes and the other at death penalty abolition—focus on different ends of the criminal justice spectrum, it is hard to overlook that their proposed alternatives point to the same result: more perpetual prison terms. The dual reform efforts therefore illustrate the extent to which American punishment and society have reached a comfort level with perpetual penal confinement. But more, the reform efforts emphasize how perpetual confinement is a phenomenon that stands independent of both the death penalty and mass incarceration. If both reform projects were to achieve their aims, the United States (the fifty states and the federal system) could (1) abolish the death penalty, (2) pursue a more cost-effective and reduced use of the prison, and yet (3) maintain perpetual confinement, almost certainly at higher levels. More perpetual confinement, in short, is the promise of contemporary reform.

The question Foucault raised in France in 1981, accordingly, has traction in the contemporary United States. Shall states simply replace the death penalty and nevertheless maintain a logic of punishment by which some are destined to be permanently excluded? Or will we allow that all people have a capacity for redemption and "that every penalty whatsoever will have a term"?[58] In the limits of current Eighth Amendment jurisprudence and the united aims of disparate reform efforts appears a social issue that the United States has yet to confront: perpetual confinement is commonplace. Sentences to death in prison, once a concern, are now routine.

In his essay, Foucault acknowledged that granting all prisoners some opportunity for release could be "a path of anxiety." But by taking that path, he urged, society would remain vigilant to its responsibility in punishing and observant of the dignity of the people imprisoned. Rejecting punishments of "definitive elimination," he observed, "is to make penal practice a locus of constant reflection, research, and experience, of transformation."[59] The choice at hand, then as now, is not between the death penalty and no death penalty. It is between a system that fools itself with the illusion it has solved the problem of punishment by declaring divisions and casting some out, and a system that remains reflective, alert to how it carries out punishment and vigilant about when and how it needs to change. "It is good for ethical and political reasons," Foucault concluded, "that the authority that exercises the right to punish should always be uneasy about that strange power and never feel too sure of itself."[60] LWOP and perpetual confinement emerged as routine punishment in the United States from just such a lack of critical reflection.

Acknowledgments

Gratitude for a many-year project requires a long look back to all those who inspired and helped direct one's thoughts and research paths. This project's beginnings spring from the Sociology Department at New York University, and my thanks there begin with David Garland. In an early meeting, David once mentioned that he had read certain books many times for many different reasons, on each occasion gleaning something new. I can honestly say that over the course of years this has been the case for me with David's own work, and the opportunity to discuss the sociology of punishment with him and receive his comments on my attempts to make sense of it was invaluable. At NYU, I also benefited from the guidance of Lynne Haney, Ann Morning, and Steven Lukes. I owe a great deal to each of them, for they helped shape my understanding of social science.

Work on this book continued at the Department of Criminology, Law & Society at the University of California, Irvine, which has been a source of great support and inspiration, replete with professional and caring colleagues. With respect to the book in particular, Simon Cole, Michael Gottfredson, Mona Lynch, Keramet Reiter, and Carroll Seron provided sage advice and support at many key turns. I am grateful to Valerie Jenness, who took an active interest in this book precisely because it had important things to say about society beyond life without parole. The department was gracious to sponsor a book workshop and invite tremendous participants, and I thank department chairs Mona Lynch and Simon Cole for helping make it possible. UCI graduate students provided valuable contributions: thank you, Ekaterina Moiseeva for exceptional research assistance; Ginny Oshiro for perceptively reading and commenting on the manuscript; and Joanne DeCaro, Ernest Chavez, Diego Rochow, and Delaney Mosca for being valuable interlocutors. I am also grateful to Katie Tinto and the participants in the UCI Life Sentencing Practicum for the opportunity to work through these ideas in a creative and dynamic forum.

At the University of California Press, gracious thanks to editor Maura Roessner, whose interest in this book early on gave me confidence that UC Press was the place to publish. That confidence was only reinforced along the way. Thanks to editorial assistant Madison Wetzell for guidance throughout; Lia Tjandra and the design team for helping craft a striking cover; project editor Cindy Fulton, Jon Dertien, Sharon Langworthy, and the entire production team for their careful work; and Teresa Iafolla and the marketing and publicity team for their superb help with promotion. A very sincere thanks as well to Juliana Froggatt and Shanon Fitzpatrick for teaching me something about writing, including my own.

I am grateful to colleagues and friends who took time to read and comment on all or part of this book. David Garland, Dirk van Zyl Smit, Catherine Appleton, and Marc Mauer provided extremely helpful comments on the entire manuscript. For insight on particular chapters, I thank Gabriel Abend, Simon Cole, Valerie Jenness, Mona Lynch, Michael Meltsner, and Carroll Seron. Philip Goodman, Armando Lara Millán, and Heather Schoenfeld carefully read a late version of the manuscript and provided me with more sage advice than I likely put to use. Along the way, many shared knowledge and insights, offered comments, collaborated on conference panels and presentations, and generally helped me to generate a knowledge of the laws and practices of imprisonment until death, including Michael Campbell, Alessandro Corda, Offer Egozy, Francisco Javier de León Villalba, Burk Foster, Nazgol Ghandnoosh, William Goldsby, Marie Gottschalk, Mary Katzenstein, Laura Kelly, Issa Kohler-Hausmann, Julilly Kohler-Hausmann, Jessica Henry, Margaret Leigey, Odette Lieneau, Beatriz López Lorca, Joe Marguiles, Ellen Melchiondo, Michael Meltsner, Ashley Nellis, Josh Page, Michelle Phelps, Joan Porter, Aziz Rana, Ashley Rubin, Jonathan Simon, Tobias Smith, Robert Werth, and Marion Vannier. A note of heartfelt gratitude to the communities of sociology, law, law and society, and criminology scholars who have inspired and continue to inspire me, many of whose works are cited herein.

There are also mentors and friends from my days as a capital defense lawyer to whom I am ever grateful. Foremost among these are John Blume, Sheri Johnson, Russell Stetler, and Drucy Glass—their influence on me has been greater than likely anyone, at this point, may perceive.

I owe thanks to the National Science Foundation, Mellon/ACLS, and New York University for grants and fellowships that supported the work. Parts of the book draw from articles already published or selected for publication: I thank *Law & Society Review*, *Law & Social Inquiry*, and *Social Justice* for permitting me to rewrite, adapt, and substantially revise that material here, and to the anonymous reviewers and editors of those journals for their valuable feedback. I owe thanks to the research and reference staff at each of the archival sites: the Florida State Library and Archive; the National Death Penalty Archive in the M. E. Grenander Department of Special Collections and Archives, University at Albany, State University of New York; the New York State Library and Archive; the Pennsylvania State Library and Archive; the Texas State Library and Archive; and the Library of Congress. I spent many days poring over statutes and session laws from the early United States to the present in the Cornell University Law Library Earl J. Bennett Statutory Collection. Much of that material does not appear in the text, but the research was vital, and I am grateful to the Cornell Law Library staff for their generosity.

Special thanks are due to Stanley "Spoon" Jackson for the cover drawing, which conveys his enormous spirit, talent, and creativity, but also expresses a deep despair. Serving an LWOP sentence since 1978, Spoon has lived through the transformation this book is about. May you receive the chance for freedom that is so, so long overdue.

The point of calling out and into question the history of life without parole is never to discount the gravity of crimes committed or the suffering, pain, and destruction that crimes have caused. It is to recognize that people grow and that growth deserves to be seen and recognized. This is for Kamell Evans, Dempsey Hawkins, Spoon Jackson, the Phoenix Players at Auburn Prison, and for all those who have lived, and are living, life sentences, and who prove every day and every year that they are more than the worst thing they have ever done.

I am thankful for the lifelong encouragement of my parents, Carol and Nick, and my sister, Nicole. I am deeply grateful for the friendships that provided rejuvenation and inspiration as I carried out this project in various locales. I thank most of all my family, Lindsay Gilmour and Rhi Gilmour Seeds, who surrounded me with support, joy, more joy, and space.

Notes

INTRODUCTION

1. Kathleen Maguire, Ann L. Pastore, and Timothy J. Flanagan, *Sourcebook of Criminal Justice Statistics* (Washington, DC: Bureau of Justice Statistics, 1992); and Ashley Nellis, *No End in Sight: America's Enduring Reliance on Life Imprisonment* (Washington, DC: The Sentencing Project, 2021).

2. Susan E. Martin, "Commutation of Prison Sentences: Practice, Promise and Limitation," *Crime & Delinquency* 29, no. 4 (1983): 593–612; and Derral Cheatwood, "The Life-without-Parole Sanction: Its Current Status and a Research Agenda," *Crime & Delinquency* 34, no. 1 (1988): 43–59.

3. Consider that articles in US national newspapers citing "life without parole" numbered fewer than five per year between 1977 and 1980. Between 2006 and 2016, more than fifty thousand American newspaper stories (approximately five thousand per year) cited "life without parole." Prior to the late 1980s, *all* mentions of "LWOP" in US newspapers referred to the noncriminal matter of employment "leave without pay." In ensuing decades, the acronym, once foreign to American vernacular and criminal law practice, has become courtroom shorthand, if not a household term, for lifetime imprisonment.

4. Charles J. Ogletree and Austin Sarat, eds., *Life without Parole: America's New Death Penalty?* (New York: New York University Press, 2012) ("America's new death penalty"); and Jonathan Simon, "Dignity and Risk: The Long Road from *Graham v. Florida* to Abolition of Life without Parole," in *Life without Parole*, ed. Ogletree and Sarat, 282–310 ("define[] the logic").

5. "Penality" refers to the complex of "sanctions, institutions, discourses and representations" that contribute to punishment as a social institution. David Garland, *Punishment and Welfare: A History of Penal Strategies* (Aldershot, UK: Gower, 1985), x. "Penality" is distinguishable from "penal system" (or "criminal justice system"), which usually focuses on institutional practices and tends to assume rather than show systematicity, and from "punishment," which may refer simply to a sanction and in any case offers a rather

narrow view of a social phenomenon with a variety of purposes and meanings. See David Garland and Peter Young, *The Power to Punish* (London: Heinemann, 1983), 21–23.

6. Dirk van Zyl Smit and Catherine Appleton, *Life Imprisonment: A Global Human Rights Analysis* (Cambridge, MA: Harvard University Press, 2019).

7. Dirk van Zyl Smit, *Taking Life Imprisonment Seriously: In National and International Law* (Norwell, MA: Kluwer Law International, 2002); see, e.g., *Vinter and Others v. The United Kingdom*, ECtHR July 9, 2013.

8. *Graham v. Florida*, 560 U.S. 48 (2010); *Miller v. Alabama*, 567 U.S. 460 (2012); *Montgomery v. Louisiana*, 577 U.S. __, 136 S. Ct. 718 (2016); and *Jones v. Mississippi*, 593 U.S. __, 141 S. Ct 1307 (2021).

9. Dirk van Zyl Smit, "Punishment and Human Rights," in *The SAGE Handbook of Punishment and Society*, ed. Jonathan Simon and Richard Sparks (London: SAGE, 2013), 395–415.

10. Christopher Seeds, "Bifurcation Nation: American Penal Policy in Late Mass Incarceration," *Punishment and Society* 19, no. 5 (2017): 590–610; and Marion Vannier, "Normalizing Extreme Imprisonment: The Case of Life without Parole in California," *Theoretical Criminology* 25, no. 4 (2019): 529–39.

11. Rachel E. Barkow, "The Court of Life and Death: The Two Tracks of Constitutional Sentencing Law and the Case for Uniformity," *Michigan Law Review* 107, no. 7 (2009): 1145–205.

12. Introducing the first book of essays dedicated to LWOP, Ogletree and Sarat assert: "While a substantial body of scholarship focuses on efforts to explain the late 20th century incarceration boom in the United States, little attention has been focused specifically on LWOP. When it is talked about, LWOP is folded into broad theories seeking to explain America's penchant for incarceration." *Life without Parole*, 10.

13. Michael Tonry, *Sentencing Fragments: Penal Reform in America, 1975–2025* (New York: Oxford University Press, 2016).

14. Carol Steiker and Jordan Steiker, "The Death Penalty and Mass Incarceration: Convergences and Divergences," *American Journal of Criminal Law* 41, no. 2 (2014): 189–207.

15. See Carol Steiker and Jordan Steiker, *Courting Death: The Supreme Court and Capital Punishment* (Cambridge, MA: Belknap Press, 2016), 297.

16. Enoch Wines and Theodore Dwight, *Report on the Prisons and Reformatories of the United States and Canada* (Albany, NY: Van Benthuysen & Sons, 1867), 276.

17. Jessica Henry, Christopher Salvatore, and Bai-Eyse Pugh, "Virtual Life Sentences: An Exploratory Study," *Prison Journal* 98, no. 3 (2018): 294–313; and Nellis, *No End in Sight* (sentences that outlast life spans); and Kevin R. Reitz and Edward E. Rhine, "Parole Release and Supervision: Critical Drivers of American Prison Policy," *Annual Review of Criminology* 3 (2020): 281–98 (consistently denied parole release).

18. E. Ann Carson and William J. Sabol, *Aging of the State Prison Population, 1993–2013* (Washington, DC: Bureau of Justice Statistics, 2016); and

E. Ann Carson, *Mortality in State and Federal Prisons, 2001–2018* (Washington, DC: Bureau of Justice Statistics, 2021).

19. Per Stanley Cohen, criminal justice can be divided into a "hard end," which consists of incarceration, reserved for "career criminals, dangerous offenders, recidivists, psychopaths, incorrigibles or whatever," and a "soft end" for those convicted of lower-level offenses, which operates "by a sort of 'inclusive' control, the techniques of which are therapeutic strategies and technologies." The two ends, Cohen theorized, are engaged in an age-old political maneuver in which severe sentencing at the hard end brokers more lenient treatment at the soft end. *Visions of Social Control: Crime, Punishment and Classification* (Cambridge, UK: Polity Press, 1985), 234. On such a distinction in contemporary US punishment, see Marie Gottschalk, *Caught: The Prison State and the Lockdown of American Politics* (Princeton, NJ: Princeton University Press, 2016), 165–95; Seeds, "Bifurcation Nation"; and Katherine Beckett, "The Politics, Promise, and Peril of Criminal Justice Reform in the Context of Mass Incarceration," *Annual Review of Criminology* 1 (2018): 235–59.

20. See, for example, Mary Douglas's reader *Rules and Meanings* (New York: Penguin, 1973), a collection of key contributions on the matter that are, as Douglas emphasizes, also rather repetitive and situated decades apart. That astute thinkers have been making a similar point off and on for centuries accents at once its importance and how easy it is to overlook.

21. On US punishment, see Michelle Alexander, *The New Jim Crow: Mass Incarceration in the Age of Colorblindness* (New York: New York Press, 2012), 225–29; David Garland, *The Culture of Control: Crime and Social Order in Contemporary Society* (Chicago: University of Chicago Press, 2001), 131–33, 181–82; Jonathan Simon, *Mass Incarceration on Trial: A Remarkable Court Decision and the Future of Prisons in America* (New York: The New Press 2014), 5–10; and James Q. Whitman, *Harsh Justice: Criminal Punishment and the Widening Divide between America and Europe* (New York: Oxford University Press, 2003); see also Liam Kennedy, "'Today They Kill with the Chair Instead of the Tree': Forgetting and Remembering Slavery at a Plantation Prison," *Theoretical Criminology* 21, no. 2 (2017): 133–50. On life sentencing, see especially Sharon Dolovich, "Creating the Permanent Prisoner," in *Life without Parole: America's New Death Penalty?*, ed. Charles Ogletree and Austin Sarat (New York: New York University Press, 2012), 96–137; Simon, "Dignity and Risk."

22. On the "politics of disregard," see Ann Stoler, *Along the Archival Grain: Epistemic Anxieties and Colonial Commonsense* (Princeton, NJ: Princeton University Press, 2009). Stoler presents the politics of disregard as an "epistemic habit" of not paying attention to facilitate participating in a socially oppressive enterprise (there, colonialism and empire).

23. Garland, *Culture of Control*, vii.

24. See especially the reports published by The Sentencing Project, of which the most recent is Nellis, *No End in Sight* (2021).

25. van Zyl Smit, *Taking Life Imprisonment Seriously*. For another pioneering work on life without parole in the United States, see Cheatwood, "Life-without-Parole Sanction."

26. van Zyl Smit and Appleton, *Life Imprisonment*; Steve Herbert, *Too Easy to Keep: Life-Sentenced Prisoners and the Future of Mass Incarceration* (Oakland: University of California Press, 2018); Margaret Leigey, *The Forgotten Men: Serving a Life without Parole Sentence* (New Brunswick, NJ: Rutgers University Press, 2015); Marc Mauer and Ashley Nellis, *The Meaning of Life: The Case for Abolishing Life Sentences* (New York: The New Press, 2018); Ogletree and Sarat, *Life without Parole*; and Steiker and Steiker, *Courting Death*.

27. For additional scholarship in social science and in law, see Catherine Appleton and Bent Grøver, "The Pros and Cons of Life without Parole," *The British Journal of Criminology* 47, no. 4 (2007): 597–615; Hadar Aviram, *Yesterday's Monsters* (Oakland: University of California Press, 2020); Gottschalk, *Caught*; and Dirk van Zyl Smit and Catherine Appleton, *Life Imprisonment and Human Rights* (Oxford: Hart Publishing, 2016). For theoretical analyses of LWOP, see Sharon Dolovich, "Creating the Permanent Prisoner," in *Life without Parole*, ed. Ogletree and Sarat; Simon, "Dignity and Risk"; Andrew Dilts, "Death Penalty 'Abolition' in Neoliberal Times," in *Death and Other Penalties: Philosophy in a Time of Mass Incarceration*, ed. Geoffrey Adelsberg, Lisa Guenther, and Scott Zeman (New York: Fordham University Press, 2015), 106–29; and Evi Girling, "Sites of Crossing and Death in Punishment," *Howard Journal of Crime and Justice* 55, no. 3 (2016): 345–61. For accounts authored or coauthored by individuals serving life sentences, see, among other works cited in the following pages, Ron Wikberg, "A Graphic and Illustrative History, 1879 to 1979: Life Sentences in Louisiana" (mimeographed document, 1979); and Jon Yount, "Pennsylvania: Parole and Life Imprisonment" (Prison Policy Initiative, February 2004).

28. An exception, published as the present book went to press, is Marion Vannier, *Normalizing Extreme Imprisonment: The Case of Life without Parole in California* (Oxford: Oxford University Press, 2021).

29. See Jim Stewart and Paul Lieberman, "What Is This New Sentence That Takes Away Parole?," *Student Lawyer* 11, no. 2 (1982): 14–39; Julian Wright, "Life-without-Parole: An Alternative to Death or Not Much of a Life at All?," *Vanderbilt Law Review* 43, no. 2 (1990): 529–68; and Harvard Law Review Association, "A Matter of Life and Death: The Effect of Life-without-Parole Statutes on Capital Punishment," *Harvard Law Review* 119, no. 6 (2006): 1838–54.

30. For example, Nellis, *No End in Sight*.

31. See the essays collected in van Zyl Smit and Appleton, *Life Imprisonment and Human Rights*.

32. Mona Lynch, "Mass Incarceration, Legal Change, and Locale," *Criminology & Public Policy* 10 no. 3 (2011): 673–98; and Michael C. Campbell, "Varieties of Mass Incarceration: What We Learn from State Histories," *Annual Review of Criminology* 1 (2018): 219–34.

33. David Garland, "Penality and the Penal State," *Criminology* 51, no. 3 (2013): 475–517.

34. Katherine Beckett, *Making Crime Pay: Law and Order in Contemporary American Politics* (New York: Oxford University Press, 1997); Mona Lynch, *Sunbelt Justice: Arizona and the Transformation of American Punishment* (Palo Alto, CA: Stanford Law Books, 2010); Heather Schoenfeld, *Building the Prison State: Race and the Politics of Mass Incarceration* (Chicago: University of Chicago Press, 2018); and Michael C. Campbell, "The Emergence of Penal Extremism in California: A Dynamic View of Institutional Structures and Political Processes," *Law & Society Review* 48, no. 2 (2014): 377–409.

35. Valerie Jenness and Ryken Grattet, *Making Hate a Crime: From Social Movement to Law Enforcement* (New York: Russell Sage, 2001); Marie Gottschalk, *The Prison and the Gallows: The Politics of Mass Incarceration in America* (New York: Cambridge University Press, 2006); and Joshua Page, *The "Toughest Beat": Politics, Punishment, and the Prison Officers Union in California* (New York: Oxford University Press, 2011).

36. Lisa Miller, *The Perils of Federalism* (New York: Oxford University Press, 2008); Vanessa Barker, *The Politics of Imprisonment* (New York: Oxford University Press, 2009); Michael C. Campbell and Heather Schoenfeld, "The Transformation of America's Penal Order: A Historicized Political Sociology of Punishment," *American Journal of Sociology* 118, no. 5 (2013): 1375–1423.

37. For historical literature on the policies that undergirded mass incarceration see, for example, Heather Ann Thompson, *Blood in the Water: The Attica Uprising of 1971 and Its Legacy* (New York: Pantheon Books, 2016); Elizabeth Hinton, *From the War on Poverty to the War on Crime* (Cambridge, MA: Harvard University Press, 2017); and Julilly Kohler-Hausmann, *Getting Tough: Welfare and Imprisonment in 1970s America* (Princeton, NJ: Princeton University Press, 2017).

38. On the penal field, see Joshua Page, "Punishment and the Penal Field," in *SAGE Handbook of Punishment and Society*, ed. Jonathan Simon and Richard Sparks (London: Sage, 2013), 154–55; see also Pierre Bourdieu, *Outline of a Theory of Practice* (Cambridge: Cambridge University Press, 1972).

39. Andreas Glaeser, *Political Epistemics: The Secret Police, the Opposition, and the End of East German Socialism* (Chicago: University of Chicago Press, 2011), 33; see also Avner Grief, *Institutions and the Path to the Modern Economy: Lessons from Medieval Trade* (Cambridge: Cambridge University Press, 2006), 151; see generally Peter Berger and Thomas Luckman, *The Social Construction of Reality* (New York: Anchor, 1966).

40. A broad view of institutions may be contrasted with a narrower one, by which an "institution" is simply akin to an organization. In the penal field, institution in this narrower sense refers to courts, legislatures, or prisons, for example. Perhaps the most inspired statement of a broad view of institutions is Glaeser's: "Almost all aspects of social life can become institutionalized: behavior can congeal into habits, thoughts can crystallize into logics of mentalities; contacts can solidify into ongoing social relations; feelings can develop into emotive schemata or transferences; moods can extend into character; injunctions and goals can form into norms and values; dialogues can sediment as

selves; and momentary expectations can gel as hopes or even develop into eschatologies" (*Political Epistemics*, 33).

41. Glaeser refers to the ways in which specific actions, beliefs, and concepts make sense against a background of accepted ways of doing and thinking about things as "validation" (*Political Epistemics*, 24–26). The idea of a correspondence between concepts and backgrounds has roots in social theory from Émile Durkheim, *The Elementary Forms of Religious Life* (1915; New York: The Free Press, 1965), to Mary Douglas, *How Institutions Think* (Syracuse, NY: Syracuse University Press, 1986), to, more recently, Gabriel Abend's theorization of grounding, *The Moral Background* (Princeton, NJ: Princeton University Press, 2014).

42. David Garland, *Peculiar Institution: America's Death Penalty in an Age of Abolition* (Cambridge, MA: Belknap Press, 2010), 14.

43. Garland and Young, *Power to Punish*, 21–23. Studies of institutional change in the penal field, as such, have something to offer research on institutional development more generally. Ashley Rubin has done much to adapt theoretical frames from neoinstitutionalist literature to the study of punishment. See, for example, "A Neo-Institutional Account of Prison Diffusion," *Law and Society Review* 49, no. 2 (2015): 365–400.

44. Hans-Jorg Rhineberger, *An Epistemology of the Concrete: Twentieth Century Histories of Life* (Durham, NC: Duke University Press, 2010); see also Gaston Bachelard, *The New Scientific Spirit* (1938; Boston: Beacon Press, 1986); and Georges Canguilhem, "The Object of the History of Sciences," in *Continental Philosophy of Science*, ed. Gary Gutting (1968; Malden, MA: Wiley-Blackwell, 2005), 195–208.

45. Ian Hacking, *Historical Ontology* (Cambridge, MA: Harvard University Press, 2002).

46. Nikolas Rose, "Life, Reason and History: Reading Georges Canguilhem Today," *Economy and Society* 27, nos. 2–3 (1998): 160.

47. Michel Foucault, "Nietzsche, Genealogy, History," in *Language, Counter-Memory, Practice: Select Essays and Interviews* (Ithaca, NY: Cornell University Press, 1980); and Michel Foucault, *Discipline and Punish: The Birth of the Prison*, trans. Alan Sheridan (New York: Vintage, 1977), 31.

48. A "critical" historical project in this sense is one that challenges official knowledge, conventional positions, and taken-for-granted claims, upsetting the apparent naturalness or neutrality of a particular idea, practice, or policy. An "effective" history dismisses the notion of an identifiable origin or teleological end point and in doing so unsettles traditional historical perspectives. Mitchell Dean, *Critical and Effective Histories: Foucault's Methods and Historical Sociology* (London: Routledge, 1996), 4, 20. In sum, a critical and effective approach to history is distinct in both its exercise and its focus, as it prioritizes unpacking apparently natural elements of the social world.

49. Foucault, "Nietzsche, Genealogy, History," 146; see also David Garland, "What Is a 'History of the Present'? On Foucault's Genealogies and Their Critical Preconditions," *Punishment & Society* 16, no. 4 (2014): 365–84.

50. Foucault, "Nietzsche, Genealogy, History," 149–50.

51. Garland, "What Is a History of the Present," 365, 367, 376. Garland illuminates the advantages of genealogy through his own histories of the present (*Punishment and Welfare*, *The Culture of Control*, and *Peculiar Institution*). One might also consult the classic genealogies of the penal field by Foucault, *Discipline and Punish*; Robert Castel, *The Regulation of Madness: The Origins of Incarceration in France* (1976; Berkeley: University of California Press, 1988); Jacques Donzelot, *Policing the Family* (New York: Pantheon, 1979); and, more recently, Bernard E. Harcourt, *Illusion of Free Markets: Punishment and the Myth of Natural Order* (Cambridge, MA: Harvard University Press, 2011).

52. Rather than list here all the excellent scholarship on mass incarceration, I direct readers to the surveys of the literature in Jonathan Simon and Richard Sparks, "Punishment and Society: The Emergence of an Academic Field," in *SAGE Handbook of Punishment and Society*, ed. Simon and Sparks, 1–20; and David Garland, "Theoretical Advances and Problems in the Sociology of Punishment," *Punishment & Society* 20, no. 1 (2018): 8–33.

53. On the notion of "operating through" punishment, see Garland and Young, *Power to Punish*, 21.

54. For uses of periodization to delineate phases of development in contemporary American punishment, see, for example, Tonry, *Sentencing Fragments*; and Campbell and Schoenfeld, "Transformation of America's Penal Order."

55. The nine chapters, between the introduction and the conclusion, can be read as a single overarching argument or, if the reader prefers, approached as nine discrete investigations and analyses.

56. On the notion of "labeling from above," see Hacking, *Historical Ontology*, 111.

57. On the lived experience of life and very long-term sentences, see generally Stanley Cohen and Laurie Taylor, *Psychological Survival* (New York: Pantheon, 1972); and Ben Crewe, Susie Hulley, and Serena Wright, *Life Imprisonment from Young Adulthood* (London: Palgrave Macmillan UK, 2020). For social science research on the lived experience of life without parole sentencing in the United States, to begin, see the sources discussed in Christopher Seeds, "Life Sentences and Perpetual Confinement," *Annual Review of Criminology* 4 (2021): 287–309. For autobiographical accounts of serving a life without parole sentence, see, among other important work, Kenneth E. Hartman, *Mother California: A Story of Redemption Behind Bars* (New York: Atlas and Company, 2010); Judith Tannenbaum and Spoon Jackson, *By Heart: Poetry, Prison, and Two Lives* (New York: New Village Press, 2010); and the anthology *Too Cruel, Not Unusual Enough*, ed. Kenneth E. Hartman (Lancaster, CA: Steering Committee Press, 2013).

58. This text is mindful about using the term "prisoner." Throughout, I refer to "people" in state confinement, but also employ "prisoner" to describe and recognize the exercise of state power that holds people in prison.

59. See, for example, Alexander, *New Jim Crow*, 184, drawing the metaphor from Iris Marion Young.

60. Gottschalk, *Caught*; and Mauer and Nellis, *Meaning of Life*.

61. Michael Tonry uses the term "malign neglect" to "characterize poli-cymakers' indifference to the racial effects of their policies." *Malign Neglect: Race, Crime, and Punishment in America* (New York: Oxford University Press, 1995), 209.

62. Benjamin Rush, *An Enquiry into the Effects of Public Punishments upon Criminals and upon Society* (Philadelphia: Society for Social Inquiry, 1787).

63. Dolovich, "Creating the Permanent Prisoner," 125.

CHAPTER 1. PERPETUAL PENAL CONFINEMENT

1. Leon Sheleff, *Ultimate Penalties: Capital Punishment, Life Imprisonment, Physical Torture* (Columbus: Ohio State University Press, 1987).

2. See Jacques Derrida, *The Death Penalty*, vol. 1, *Seminar of 1999–2000* (Chicago: University of Chicago Press, 2013), March 1/8, 2000, lecture, dis-cussing how the death penalty is unique, and uniquely problematic, because it takes the mystery of time out of the process of dying. On the relationship between a formal death sentence and a death-in-prison sentence, see Sheleff, *Ultimate Penalties*; Andrew Dilts, "Death Penalty 'Abolition' in Neoliberal Times," in *Death and Other Penalties*, ed. Geoffrey Adelsberg, Lisa Guenther, and Scott Zeman (New York: Fordham University Press, 2015), 106–29; and Evi Girling, "Sites of Crossing and Death in Punishment: The Parallel Trade-Offs and Equivalencies of the Death Penalty and Life without Parole in the US," *Howard Journal of Crime and Justice* 55, no. 3 (2016): 345–61. Which type of "death sentence" is crueler is a debate that likely cannot be solved, just as it may not be possible for a person to objectively judge one heinous crime more morally condemnable than another.

3. Alfred Villaume, " 'Life without Parole' and 'Virtual Life Sentences': Death Sentences by Any Other Name," *Contemporary Justice Review* 8, no. 3 (2005): 265–77; Jessica Henry, "Death in Prison Sentences: Overutilized and Underscrutinized," in *Life without Parole: America's New Death Penalty?*, ed. Charles Ogletree and Austin Sarat (New York: New York University Press, 2012), 282–310. For Dirk van Zyl Smit and Catherine Appleton in *Life Imprisonment: A Global Human Rights Analysis* (Cambridge, MA: Harvard University Press, 2019), life imprisonment includes sentences formally designated as life but also (a) fixed terms of years that outlast life spans and (b) postconvic-tion indefinite detention, sometimes in the form of a civil commitment, which authorizes confinement beyond the imposed prison sentence, which may be lifelong.

4. See Dirk van Zyl Smit, *Taking Life Imprisonment Seriously: In National and International Law* (Norwell, MA: Kluwer Law International, 2002); Tapio Lappi-Seppälä, "Life Imprisonment and Related Institutions in the Nordic Countries," in *Life Imprisonment and Human Rights*, ed. Dirk van Zyl Smit and Catherine Appleton (Oxford: Hart Publishing, 2016), 461–506; and Filip

Vojta, "Life and Long-Term Imprisonment in the Countries of the Former Yugoslavia," in *Life Imprisonment and Human Rights*, ed. Dirk van Zyl Smit and Catherine Appleton (Oxford: Hart Publishing, 2016), 351–72.

5. Quentin Skinner, "Meaning and Understanding in the History of Ideas," *History and Theory* 8, no. 1 (1969): 3–53.

6. Émile Durkheim, *Rules of Sociological Method* (1895; New York: The Free Press, 1982), used the term "prenotion" to refer to "summary [working] representations . . . that we employ in [everyday] life." On how common sense presents "epistemological obstacles," see Gaston Bachelard, *The New Scientific Spirit* (1938; Boston: Beacon Press, 1986). Following Bachelard, Pierre Bourdieu, Jean-Claude Chamboredon, and Jean Claude Passeron, in *The Craft of Sociology: Epistemological Preliminaries* (1968; Berlin: Walter de Gruyter, 1991), refer to the sociological practice of being keen to not let prenotions direct research as "epistemological vigilance."

7. Systematic theories or commentaries, those that approach crime and punishment from a comprehensive perspective are, in effect, manuals of sorts: each exhibits a logic—an underlying system or set of principles—that fastens multiple layers of social context together. See Gabriel Abend, *The Moral Background: An Inquiry into the History of Business Ethics* (Princeton, NJ: Princeton University Press, 2014), using manuals of business practice as materials from which to interpret "the moral background"; and Luc Boltanski and Laurent Thévenot, *On Justification* (Princeton, NJ: Princeton University Press, 2006), using manuals of business practice as locations for identifying "orders of justification," rooted in what speakers value or deem good or right.

8. Charles Bright, *The Powers That Punish: Prison and Politics in the Era of the "Big House," 1920–1955* (Ann Arbor: University of Michigan Press, 1996), 293–95. On the relationship between the prison and society, see Philip Smith, *Punishment and Culture* (Chicago: University of Chicago Press, 2008), 179–80.

9. David Garland, *Peculiar Institution: America's Death Penalty in an Age of Abolition* (Cambridge, MA: Belknap Press, 2010) (the death penalty); and Georg Rusche and Otto Kirchheimer, *Punishment and Social Structure* (1939; New Brunswick, NJ: Transaction Publishers, 2003); and Michel Foucault, *The Punitive Society: Lectures at the Collège de France, 1972–1973*, trans. Graham Burchell (1972–1973; New York: Palgrave Macmillan, 2015), 8–10 (the fine).

10. Cesare Beccaria, "On Crimes and Punishments," in *On Crimes and Punishments and Other Writings*, ed. Aaron Thomas (1764; Toronto: University of Toronto Press, 2008); and John D. Bessler, "Revisiting Beccaria's Vision: The Enlightenment, the Death Penalty, and the Abolition," *Northwestern Journal of Law and Social Policy* 4, no. 2 (2009): 206–15.

11. Bernard E. Harcourt, *Illusion of Free Markets: Punishment and the Myth of Natural Order* (Cambridge, MA: Harvard University Press, 2011), 73–76.

12. Beccaria, "On Crimes and Punishments," 53.

13. On the death penalty as spectacle, see David Garland, "Modes of Capital Punishment: The Death Penalty in Perspective," in *America's Death Penalty:*

Between Past and Present, ed. David Garland, Randall McGowen, and Michael Meranze (New York: New York University Press, 2011), 48.

14. Beccaria, "On Crimes and Punishments"; and Graeme Newman and Pietro Morongui, Introduction to *On Crimes and Punishments*, by Cesare Beccaria, ed. Graeme Newman and Pietro Morongui (Somerset, NJ: Transaction Publishers, 2009), xl–xli.

15. Michel Foucault, *Discipline and Punish: The Birth of the Prison*, trans. Alan Sheridan (New York: Vintage, 1977), 129–30.

16. Jeremy Bentham, "Principles of Morals and Legislation," in *The Works of Jeremy Bentham*, vol. 1 (Edinburgh: William Tait, 1843), 82, 85, argued similarly that only if "particularly well calculated to answer the purpose of a moral lesson" could "the application of so severe a punishment as the infamy of a public exhibition" be justified.

17. Michael Meranze, *Laboratories of Virtue: Punishment, Revolution, and Authority in Philadelphia, 1760–1835* (Chapel Hill: University of North Carolina Press, 1996), 32–33. As Meranze emphasizes, the wheelbarrow law, which aimed to deter through public example, "embrace[d] Beccaria's dream of punishment as a well-ordered system of signs" (78, 109–13); see Rebecca McLennan, *The Crisis of Imprisonment: Protest, Politics, and the Making of the American Penal State, 1776–1941* (New York: Cambridge University Press, 2008).

18. Adam J. Hirsch, *The Rise of the Penitentiary: Prisons and Punishment in Early America* (New Haven, CT: Yale University Press, 1992); see generally David J. Rothman, "Perfecting the Prison," in *The Oxford History of the Prison.*, ed. Norval Morris and David Rothman (New York: Oxford University Press, 1995).

19. Meranze, *Laboratories of Virtue*, 120–27; and Negley Teeters, *The Cradle of the Penitentiary: The Walnut Street Jail, 1773–1835* (Philadelphia: Pennsylvania Prison Society, 1955), 30–31, 39.

20. Benjamin Rush, *An Enquiry into the Effects of Public Punishments upon Criminals and upon Society* (Philadelphia: Society for Social Inquiry, 1787).

21. Michael Meranze, Introduction to *Benjamin Rush, Essays: Literary, Moral and Philosophical*, ed. Michael Meranze (Schenectady, NY: Union College Press, 1988), v–vi.

22. To be clear, the idea of the prison did not originate with Rush, nor was Rush the first in the United States to advocate it. See Pieter Spierenberg, *The Prison Experience* (New Brunswick, NJ: Rutgers University Press, 1991); and Ashley Rubin, "The Prehistory of Innovation: A Longer View of Penal Change," *Punishment & Society* 20, no. 2 (2018): 204.

23. Rush, *Enquiry into the Effects*, 19–20, 33.

24. Rush, *Enquiry into the Effects*, 20.

25. Rush, *Enquiry into the Effects*, 21.

26. William Tallack, *Penological and Preventive Principles* (London: Wertheimer, Lea, 1889), 155; see also Colin Dayan, *The Law Is a White Dog: How*

Legal Rituals Make and Unmake Persons (Princeton, NJ: Princeton University Press, 2011), 70.

27. Rush, *Enquiry into the Effects*; see generally David Rothman, *Discovery of the Asylum: Social Order and Disorder in the New Republic* (Boston: Little Brown, 1971), 78; Foucault, *The Punitive Society*, 88.

28. Rush, *Enquiry into the Effects*, 32.

29. Donald Clemmer, *The Prison Community* (New York: Holt, Rinehart, Winston, 1940).

30. See Gustave de Beaumont and Alexis de Toqueville, *On the Penitentiary System in the United States*, trans. Francis Lieber (Philadelphia: Carey, Lea & Blanchard, 1833); Enoch Wines and Theodore Dwight, *Report on the Prisons and Reformatories of the United States and Canada* (Albany, NY: Van Benthuysen & Sons, 1867); and National Commission on Law Observance and Enforcement (Wickersham Commission), *Report on Penal Institutions, Probation, and Parole* (Washington, DC: US Government Printing Office, 1931).

31. Daniel Raymond, *Report on the Penitentiary System in the United States* (New York: Mahlan Day, 1822).

32. Raymond, *Report on the Penitentiary System*, appendix, 41.

33. Raymond, *Report on the Penitentiary System*, appendix, 42–43.

34. Raymond, *Report on the Penitentiary System*, appendix, 48–49.

35. See, for example, Stephen Allen, Samuel Hopkins, and George Tibbits, "Report," in *Journal of the State of New York* (Albany, NY: New York Legislature, 1825), 125, advocating a perpetual "criminal colony" for "incorrigibles."

36. Michel Foucault, "About the Concept of the 'Dangerous Individual' in 19th-Century Legal Psychiatry," *International Journal of Law and Psychiatry* 1 (1978): 1–18; see also Cesare Lombroso, *Criminal Man*, trans. Mary Gibson and Nicole Hahn Rafter (1896; Durham, NC: Duke University Press, 2006).

37. Norval Morris, *The Habitual Criminal* (Cambridge, UK: Longmans Green, 1951); and Ronald C. Kramer, "From 'Habitual Offenders' to 'Career Criminals': The Historical Construction and Development of Criminal Categories," *Law and Human Behavior* 6, nos. 3–4 (1982): 73–93.

38. Philip Jenkins, *Moral Panic: Changing Concepts of the Child Molester in Modern America* (New Haven, CT: Yale University Press, 2004), 26–28.

39. See also N. S. Timashefe, "The Treatment of Persistent Offenders outside of the United States," *Journal of Criminal Law and Criminology* 30, no. 4 (1939): 455–69.

40. J. A. Royce McQuaig, "Modern Tendencies in Habitual Criminal Legislation," *Cornell Law Quarterly* 15, no. 1 (1929): 62–83; and Edwin Sutherland, "The Sexual Psychopath Laws," *Journal of Criminal Law, Criminology and Police Science* 40, no. 5 (1949): 543–54.

41. Paul Tappan, "Habitual Offender Laws in the United States," *Federal Probation* 13 (1949): 28–31; and Eric Janus and Robert Prentky, "Sexual Predator Laws: A Two-Decade Retrospective," *Federal Sentencing Reporter* 21, no. 2 (2008): 90–97.

42. Meranze, *Laboratories of Virtue.*

43. Herbert William Keith Fitzroy, "The Punishment of Crime in Provincial Pennsylvania," *Pennsylvania Magazine of History and Biography* 60, no. 3 (1936): 242–69.

44. On the history of competing nineteenth-century prison models and interventions in the struggle by outside interests including labor, see Rothman, *Discovery of the Asylum*; Meranze, *Laboratories of Virtue*; McLennan, *Crisis of Imprisonment*; and Rubin, "Prehistory of Innovation."

45. William Tallack, "Long Imprisonments," *The Times* (London), September 2, 1896, 9.

46. On Progressive Era penal reform, see, for example, McLennan, *Crisis of Imprisonment*; and the brief but illuminating discussion in Philip Goodman, Joshua Page, and Michelle Phelps, *Breaking the Pendulum: The Long Struggle Over Criminal Justice* (New York: Oxford University Press, 2017), 50–69.

47. Enoch Wines, *Transactions of the National Congress on Penitentiary and Reformatory Discipline* (Albany, NY: The Argus Company, 1870), 95.

48. Frederick Wines, *The New Criminology* (New York: Kempster Print, 1904), 11–12. An analogy is drawn in the Progressive ideology between the prison and the hospital. Persons who are physically ill are committed to hospitals, from which they are released when cured; in the same way, the "socially ill" are released from prison when they have regained their social health. Physicians cannot name the day upon which the patient will be healed. No more can judges intelligently set the date of release at the time of a trial. National Commission on Law Observance and Enforcement, *Report on Penal Institutions, Probation, and Parole,* 142.

49. Frederick Wines, *Punishment and Reformation: An Historical Sketch of the Rise of the Penitentiary* (London: Swan Sonnenschein, 1895), 213.

50. W. D. Lewis, *From Newgate to Dannemora: The Rise of the Penitentiary in New York, 1746–1848* (Ithaca, NY: Cornell University Press, 1965), 42.

51. Wines and Dwight, *Report on the Prisons and Reformatories,* 298.

52. Wines, *New Criminology,* 14.

53. Zebulon Brockway, "The Ideal of a True Prison System for a State" (paper presented to the National Congress on Penitentiary and Reformatory Discipline, Cincinnati, October 12, 1870).

54. Frederick Wines, *Monograph on Sentences for Crime* (Springfield, IL: H. W. Rocker, 1885). Wines's views were rather common among, and in many ways representative of, other Progressive Era prison reformers in the United States and abroad. But more than others, Wines, who was not a practitioner, systematically developed his views, creating arguably the "prison system devised by the philosopher" that Brockway distinguished from his own blueprint "drawn from experience" (Brockway, "Ideal of a True Prison System"). It may be that no penologist in the nineteenth or early twentieth centuries devoted greater effort to theorizing or collecting empirical data on life sentencing than Wines.

55. Wines, *Monograph on Sentences for Crime*, 22; and Wines, *New Criminology*.

56. Compare Harry Elmer Barnes and Negley Teeters, *New Horizons in Criminology* (New York: Prentice Hall, 1952), 21.

57. Wines and Dwight, *Report on the Prisons and Reformatories*, 276.

58. Wines, *New Criminology*, 16.

59. Wines, *Monograph on Sentences for Crime*, 10.

60. Tallack, *Penological and Preventive Principles*, 180–81.

61. "Criminal Treatment of Criminals," *The Spectator* (London), October 18, 1855.

62. Michele Pifferi, *Reinventing Punishment: A Comparative History of Criminology and Penology in the Nineteenth and Twentieth Centuries* (Oxford: Oxford University Press, 2016).

63. Kevin R. Reitz put it this way: "There has always been a puzzle about the true personality of the process. . . . As a means of setting prison terms, the rehabilitative premise is unavoidably paired with a less compassionate incapacitative program. . . . From its origins, there has been a deep tension in underlying policies, and the potential for 'soft' and 'hard' treatment, within the indeterminate framework" ("The 'Traditional' Indeterminate Sentencing Model" in *The Oxford Handbook of Sentencing and Corrections*, ed. Joan Petersilia and Kevin R. Reitz (New York: Oxford University Press, 2012), 277.

64. On racial and social control elements of Progressive reforms, see Anthony M. Platt, *The Child Savers: The Invention of Delinquency* (Chicago: University of Chicago Press, 1977); Marie Gottschalk, *The Prison and the Gallows: The Politics of Mass Incarceration in America* (New York: Cambridge University Press, 2006); Geoff Ward, *The Black Child-Savers: Racial Democracy and Juvenile Justice* (Chicago: University of Chicago Press, 2012); and Goodman, Page, and Phelps, *Breaking the Pendulum*. On repression in practice under Progressive schemes, see Alexander W. Pisciotta, *Benevolent Repression: Social Control and the American Reformatory-Prison Movement* (New York: New York University Press, 1994). See also David Rothman, *Conscience and Convenience: The Asylum and Its Alternatives in Progressive America* (Berlin: De Gruyter, 1980), discussing how parole was accompanied at the outset by a widening net and longer sentences.

65. Highlighting the extreme power differential between state and prisoner in this manner helps one better understand European distaste for the indeterminate model (see generally Pifferi, *Reinventing Punishment*) and the left critiques of rehabilitation that arose in the late twentieth-century United States (see American Friends Service Committee, *Struggle for Justice: A Report on Crime and Punishment in America* [New York: Hill & Wang, 1971]).

66. William Edward Burghardt DuBois, "The Spawn of Slavery: The Convict-Lease System in the South," in *African American Classics in Criminology and Criminal Justice*, ed. Shaun L. Gabbidon, Helen T. Greene, and Vernetta D. Young (1901; Thousand Oaks, CA: Sage, 2002), 110–16. In the contemporary United States, it is often assumed that conditions of

confinement will meet acceptable standards. Yet one is reminded by recent examples—including litigation over California prisons leading to *Brown v. Plata*, 563 U.S. 493 (2011), as well as the many crises faced by prisons during the COVID-19 pandemic—not to take conditions for granted. On conditions, see also Bright, *Powers That Punish*; and Ethan Blue, *Doing Time in the Depression: Everyday Life in Texas and California Prisons* (New York: New York University Press, 2014).

67. Thorsten Sellin, *Slavery and the Penal System* (New York: Elsevier, 1976).

68. John Howard, *An Account of the Principal Lazarettos in Europe* (Warrington, UK: Eyres, 1789); and John H. Langbein, "The Historical Origins of the Sanction of Imprisonment for Serious Crime," *Journal of Legal Studies* 5, no. 1 (1976): 35–60.

69. DuBois, "Spawn of Slavery"; Sellin, *Slavery and the Penal System*, chs. 11 and 12. On the Thirteenth Amendment as a link between slavery and incarceration, see, for example, Dennis Childs, *Slaves of the State: Black Incarceration from the Chain Gang to the Penitentiary* (Minneapolis: University of Minnesota Press, 2020).

70. McLennan, *Crisis of Imprisonment*.

71. See Dayan, *Law Is a White Dog*; see also Rebecca McLennan, "The Convict's Two Lives: Civil and Natural Death in the American Prison," in *America's Death Penalty: Between Past and Present*, ed. David Garland, Randall McGowen, and Michael Meranze (New York: New York University Press, 2011), 191–220.

72. Dayan, *Law Is a White Dog*, 64.

73. Penal servitude in American punishment was both a northern and a southern phenomenon. As McLennan shows in *Crisis of Imprisonment*, civil death laws first paired with contractual labor practices in northern prisons, then spread to the South during the antebellum period.

74. Matthew Mancini, *One Dies, Get Another: Convict Leasing in the American South, 1866–1928* (Columbia: University of South Carolina Press, 1996), 1. On lack of a centralized bureaucracy, see William Banks Taylor, *Brokered Justice: Race, Politics, and Mississippi Prisons, 1798–1992* (Columbus: Ohio State University Press, 1993); and David Oshinsky, *Worse Than Slavery: Parchman Farm and the Jim Crow Justice System* (New York: The Free Press, 1996).

75. As DuBois wrote in "Spawn of Slavery," "The convict-lease system is the slavery in private hands of persons convicted of crimes and misdemeanors in the courts." See Douglas A. Blackmon, *Slavery by Another Name: The Re-Enslavement of Black Americans from the Civil War to World War II* (New York: Random House, 2008). On the racialized prison economies of southern states in the nineteenth century, see, among others, Edward Ayers, *Vengeance and Justice: Crime and Punishment in the 19th-Century American South* (New York: Oxford University Press, 1984); Alex Lichtenstein, *Twice the Work of Free Labor: The Political Economy of Convict Labor in the New South* (New York: Verso, 1996); and Talitha L. LeFlouria, *Chained in Silence: Black Women*

and Convict Labor in the New South (Chapel Hill: University of North Carolina Press, 2015).

76. As George Washington Cable, "The Convict Lease System in the Southern States," in *The Silent South, Together with The Freedman's Case in Equity and the Convict Lease System in the Southern States* (New York: Charles Scribner's Sons, 1889), 124, explained the rationale: "The system springs primarily from the idea that the possession of a convict's person is an opportunity for the State to make money; that the amount to be made is whatever can be wrung from him . . . and that, without regard to moral or mortal consequences, the penitentiary whose annual report shows the largest cash balance paid into the State's treasury is the best penitentiary." See also Taylor, *Brokered Justice.*

77. DuBois, "Spawn of Slavery."

78. Cable, "Convict Lease System," 129.

79. Cable, "Convict Lease System," 152.

80. Cable, "Convict Lease System," 168; see also Mary Ellen Curtin, *Black Prisoners and Their World, Alabama, 1865–1900* (New Brunswick, NJ: Rutgers University Press, 2000).

81. Cable, "Convict Lease System," 125.

CHAPTER 2. PRECURSOR AND PROTOTYPE

1. Georges Canguilhem, "The Object of the History of Sciences," in *Continental Philosophy of Science*, ed. Gary Gutting (1968; Oxford: Wiley-Blackwell, 2005).

2. Edwin Powers, *Crime and Punishment in Early Massachusetts* (Boston: Beacon Press, 1966); and Edwin Powers, *Parole Eligibility of Prisoners Serving a Life Sentence*, 1st ed. (Boston: Massachusetts Correctional Association, 1969).

3. Enoch Wines and Theodore Dwight, *Report on the Prisons and Reformatories of the United States and Canada* (Albany, NY: Van Benthuysen & Sons, 1867); and Enoch Wines, *Transactions of the National Congress on Penitentiary and Reformatory Discipline* (Albany, NY: The Argus Company, 1870). Conditions of confinement under life sentences, when used, however, could be dreadful. See, for example, Willis Dunbar and George May, *Michigan: A History of the Wolverine State* (Grand Rapids: Eerdmans, 1995), 455, discussing conditions of life imprisonment after Michigan abolished capital punishment in 1846.

4. Dirk van Zyl Smit and Alessandro Corda, "American Exceptionalism in Parole Release and Supervision," in *American Exceptionalism in Crime and Punishment*, ed. Kevin R. Reitz (Oxford: Oxford University Press, 2017), 426; see also Kevin R. Reitz, "The 'Traditional' Indeterminate Sentencing Model," in *The Oxford Handbook of Sentencing and Corrections*, ed. Joan Petersilia and Kevin R. Reitz (New York: Oxford University Press, 2012), 270–98. On the varied adoption of rehabilitation as rhetoric and in practice during the twentieth century, see chapter 5.

5. Specific examples include California imposing "life without possibility of parole" for a nonhomicide offense, aggravated kidnapping, in the 1930s (Cal. Penal Code § 209 (1933)), and Mississippi imposing life without parole for fourth-time felons, at least as far back as 1942 (Miss. Code § 4004-03 (1942)). See later in this chapter for New York's Baumes Law.

6. Edwin Powers, *Parole Eligibility of Prisoners Serving a Life Sentence*, 2nd ed. (Boston: Massachusetts Correctional Association, 1972). For example, Michigan precluded parole for lifers convicted of first-degree murder (Act 232 of 1953, § 791.234), as did Massachusetts (Mass. Gen. Laws ch. 127, § 133A; ch. 265, § 2 (eff. 1955); see Haas and Fillion, *Life without Parole: A Reconsideration* [Boston: Criminal Justice Policy Coalition, 2016]).

7. Per Justice Lewis Powell Jr. in *Solem v. Helm*, 463 U.S. 277, 303 (1983): "As a matter of law, parole and commutation are different concepts, despite some surface similarities. Parole is a regular part of the rehabilitative process. . . . The law generally specifies when a prisoner will be eligible to be considered for parole, and details the standards and procedures applicable at that time. . . . Commutation, on the other hand, is an ad hoc exercise of executive clemency. A Governor may commute a sentence at any time for any reason without reference to any standards."

8. Marie Gottschalk, *Caught: The Prison State and the Lockdown of American Politics* (Princeton, NJ: Princeton University Press, 2015), 186. See Sheldon Messinger et al., "The Foundations of Parole in California," *Law & Society Review* 19, no. 1 (1985): 69–106.

9. See, for example, Messinger et al., "Foundations of Parole."

10. Margaret Colgate Love, "The Twilight of the Pardon Power," *Journal of Criminal Law and Criminology* 100, no. 3 (2010): 1169–212.

11. Rachel E. Barkow, "The Ascent of the Administrative State and the Demise of Mercy," *Harvard Law Review* 121, no. 5 (2008): 1336, 1339.

12. According to the National Commission on Law Observance and Enforcement (Wickersham Commission), *Report on Penal Institutions, Probation, and Parole* (Washington, DC: US Government Printing Office, 1931), 133, twenty states treated parole merely as a form of clemency to be granted by the governor or a board of pardons. In twelve other states release was granted by general administrative boards. Only fourteen states had created agencies dealing specifically with parole.

13. S.D. Code § 22-6-1. See 1913 S.D. Sess. Laws ch. 287, § 1.

14. Pennsylvania Parole Act of 1941 (P.L. 861, No. 323).

15. See Ron Wikberg, "A Graphic and Illustrative History, 1879 to 1797: Life Sentences in Louisiana" (mimeographed document, 1979); and Gottschalk, *Caught*, 171.

16. Douglas C. Rigg, in "The Penalty Worse Than Death," *Saturday Evening Post*, August 31, 1957, 13–15, 50–53, offers a detailed picture of life *with* parole sentences amounting to perpetual confinement (due to infinite parole denial) in Minnesota, a state generally considered to be one of the most lenient sentencing jurisdictions in the United States. On contemporary parole practices

under which people, including those imprisoned as youth, are routinely denied parole, see, for example, Sarah Mehta, *False Hope: How Parole Systems Fail Youth Serving Extreme Sentences* (Washington, DC: American Civil Liberties Union, 2016); and Nazgol Ghandnoosh, *Delaying a Second Chance: The Declining Prospects for Parole on Life Sentences* (Washington, DC: The Sentencing Project, 2017).

17. Michael Glover, "Opening the 10-6 Floodgate," *Angolite* 15, no. 4 (1990): 59–64; and Lane Nelson, "A History of Penal Reform in Angola, Part I: The Immovable Object," *Angolite* (September/October 2009): 16–23.

18. Powers, Parole *Eligibility*, 2nd ed., 35; see also Pennsylvania Prison Society, *The Need for Parole Options for Life-Sentenced Prisoners* (Philadelphia, 1993); and Phillip Renninger, *A Study of Recidivism among Individuals Granted Executive Clemency in Pennsylvania, 1968–1981* (Harrisburg: Pennsylvania Commission on Crime and Delinquency, 1982).

19. Commutation rates of life without parole sentenced prisoners in Michigan between 1940 and 1960 were approximately 70 percent. Citizens Alliance on Prisons and Public Spending (CAPPS), *When "Life" Did Not Mean Life: A Historical Analysis of Life Sentences Imposed in Michigan Since 1900* (2006), 12. For additional points of comparison, see, for example, Giovanni I. Giardini and Richard G. Farrow, "The Paroling of Capital Offenders," *Annals of the American Academy of Political and Social Science* 284, no. 1 (1952): 85–94.

20. For a state-specific study, see Louis W. Kolakoski, "Comparative Study of Commutation and Regular Parole Cases for the State of Pennsylvania," *Prison Journal* 17, no. 2 (1937): 322–27; see generally Powers, *Parole Eligibility*, 2nd ed.

21. Kolakoski, "Comparative Study of Commutation and Regular Parole."

22. It may be useful to think of parole and clemency existing in practice along a continuum, one pole scientific and one mercy based. Closer to the center, however, the distinction between standards-based and standardless decision-making starts to blur: governors may make commutation decisions after a process of prepared deliberation in conjunction with parole or pardon boards, and parole boards may evade standards and written procedures. The relation between parole and clemency became a centerpiece in US Supreme Court decisions adjudicating the constitutionality of life sentences under the Eighth Amendment, as I discuss in chapter 7.

23. The Baumes Law(s) consisted of twenty laws named after the laws' sponsor, a New York State senator, and included provisions that allowed retrospective application of the sentencing enhancement for repeat offenses and required prosecutors and corrections officials to inform courts any time they discovered that a prisoner was a recidivist. Julia E. Johnsen, ed., *The Baumes Law* (New York: H.W. Wilson, 1929), 53–54, 66.

24. Johnsen, *Baumes Law*, 57.

25. Johnsen, *Baumes Law*, 16, 110. The Baumes Law faced much opposition, before and after it was passed, from penologists, lawyers, and judges (19–28). Many judges responded to the law by continuing to sentence

fourth-time recidivists to short prison terms (114–15). In addition, some prosecutors declined to charge eligible defendants, and juries nullified verdicts, refusing to convict (142–43, 164).

26. See, studying this retreat, Note, "Court Treatment of General Recidivist Statutes," *Columbia Law Review* 48, no. 2 (1948): 238–53.

27. See generally Joseph R. Gusfield, *Symbolic Crusade: Status Politics and the American Temperance Movement* (Urbana: University of Illinois Press, 1963).

28. Johnsen, *Baumes Law*, 59, shows this argument being made with respect to the Baumes Law.

29. Caleb H. Baumes, "The Baumes Laws and the Legislative Program in New York," 52 *A.B.A. Reporter* 52 (1927): 511, 521.

30. Johnsen, *Baumes Law*, 56, 64-65, 102–3.

31. See chapter 5 for more on the role of the rehabilitative paradigm in American punishment during the first two-thirds of the twentieth century.

32. Dirk van Zyl Smit, *Taking Life Imprisonment Seriously* (Norwell, MA: Kluwer Law International, 2002), 42; and Powers, *Parole Eligibility*, 1st ed., 12–18. Despite this, it bears keeping in mind that prison conditions often remained dreadful during this period and began to change only through aggressive litigation in the 1970s. See note 37.

33. Powers, *Parole Eligibility*, 2nd ed. The two types of laws were not mutually exclusive (Michigan and South Dakota, for instance, had both).

34. Powers, *Parole Eligibility*, 2nd ed.; see Burk Foster, "Pardons and Politics: How It All Went Wrong," *Angolite* 13, no. 1 (1988): 33–50.

35. Powers, *Parole Eligibility*, 2nd ed.

36. The extent to which life without parole as a formal sanction was all but out of mind deserves emphasis. I discuss this with respect to anti–death penalty litigation in chapters 4 and 8.

37. Many southern states have a story of a landmark federal lawsuit and related court oversight of their corrections systems. See, for example, *Holt v. Sarver*, 309 F. Supp. 362 (E.D. Ark. 1970); *Gates v. Collier*, 349 F. Supp. 881 (N.D. Miss. 1972); *Costello v. Wainwright*, 397 F. Supp. 20 (M.D. Fla. 1975); and *Ruiz v. Estelle*, 503 F. Supp. 1265 (S.D. Tex. 1980).

38. Michel Foucault, *Discipline and Punish: The Birth of the Prison*, trans. Alan Sheridan (New York: Vintage, 1977), 119; and Bernard E. Harcourt, "Course Context," in Michel Foucault, *The Punitive Society: Lectures at the College de France, 1972–1973* (New York: Palgrave Macmillan, 2015), 75n8.

CHAPTER 3. THE PHENOMENON TO BE EXPLAINED

1. 560 U.S. 48 (2010).

2. Data on statutes and session laws in this chapter and in the chapters that follow were obtained by (1) searching the laws of all fifty states and the federal system, in two legal databases, and (2) researching session laws of the states

and the federal system from the early United States to the present, for which I relied significantly on the Earl J. Bennett Statutory Collection at the Cornell University Law Library.

3. Robert K. Merton, "Three Fragments from a Sociologist's Notebooks: Establishing the Phenomenon, Specified Ignorance, and Strategic Research Materials," *Annual Review of Sociology* 13, no. 1 (1987): 1–29; see also David Garland, "Theoretical Advances and Problems in the Sociology of Punishment," *Punishment & Society* 20, no. 1 (2018): 8–33, discussing "establishing the phenomenon." For more on the use of preliminary descriptions to reframe the object of inquiry and how one studies it, see Marcel Mauss, "La Prière," in Pierre Bourdieu, Jean-Claude Chamboredon, and Jean Claude Passeron, *The Craft of Sociology: Epistemological Preliminaries* (1968; Berlin: Walter de Gruyter, 1991), 97. This sort of "epistemological vigilance" was begun in the preceding chapters by extending the historical frame in which perpetual confinement and life without parole are examined.

4. Joint Appendix, *Graham v. Florida*, 2009 WL 2163260 (No. 08-7412), 299 (U.S., 2009).

5. Letter of Mary Graham to Judge Lance Day, May 17, 2006, Joint Appendix, *Graham v. Florida*, 286.

6. Statement of Terrance Graham, May 25, 2006, Joint Appendix, *Graham v. Florida*, 288; and Testimony of Terrance Graham, May 25, 2006, Joint Appendix, *Graham v. Florida*, 375.

7. Joint Appendix, *Graham v. Florida*, 388–89, 392–95.

8. Brief of Respondent (State of Florida), *Graham v. Florida*, 560 U.S. 48 (2010) (No. 08-7412), 1–3; and 1994 Fla. Laws xviii (statement of Governor Lawton Chiles). Not all stakeholders agreed *tourist* crime was the problem. State law enforcement dismissed the focus as a ploy for national attention, seeing crime against tourists as a "symptom" of a more serious problem: increasing recidivist crime by juveniles. Florida Department of Law Enforcement, *Making Florida Safer for Floridians and Tourists: Recommendations for Short-Term Actions and Long-Term Solutions*, February 26, 1993, Florida State Library and Archive.

9. See Fla. Laws Ch. 94-209. Legislation passed the following year further increased the exposure of juveniles who commit violent crime to adult prosecution.

10. Brief of Florida, *Graham*, 55.

11. Brief of Florida, *Graham*, 4, 55–56.

12. Brief of Florida, *Graham*, 4.

13. Brief of Florida, *Graham*, 32n15.

14. Brief of Florida, 34, *Graham*, emphasis added.

15. Anthony Amsterdam and Jerome Bruner, *Minding the Law* (Cambridge, MA: Harvard University Press, 2000).

16. *Miller v. Alabama*, 567 U.S. 460 (2012). Alabama in *Miller*, as Florida in *Graham*, was supported by an amicus brief signed by nineteen states. Again,

the argument was anchored in historical references to a "steep rise in violent youth crime in the mid-1980s [which] triggered a move toward harsher penalties and made adult sentences available to juveniles." Brief of Michigan et al. (States' Amicus Brief), *Miller v. Alabama*, 567 U.S. 460 (2012) (Nos. 10-9646 & 10-9647), 17.

17. John J. DiIulio, "The Coming of the Superpredators," *Weekly Standard*, November 27, 1995, 23–28; and Brief of Jeffrey Fagan et al. (Scholars' Brief), *Miller v. Alabama*, 567 U.S. 460 (2012) (Nos. 10-9646 & 10-9647).

18. Scholars' Brief, *Miller*, 15–16. See Franklin E. Zimring, "American Youth Violence: A Cautionary Tale," *Crime and Justice* 42, no. 1 (2013): 265–98.

19. William Bennett, John J. DiIulio, and John P. Walters, *Body Count* (New York: Simon & Schuster, 1996), 27.

20. DiIulio, *Coming of the Superpredators*.

21. Scholars' Brief, *Miller*; see Zimring, "American Youth Violence."

22. Scholars' Brief, *Miller*, 28.

23. On how ideas about dangerousness motivated politicized criminological discourse and penal policy in the late twentieth century in the United States and United Kingdom, see David Garland, *The Culture of Control: Crime and Social Order in Contemporary Society* (Chicago: University of Chicago Press, 2001), 135–37. See also Katherine Beckett, *Making Crime Pay: Law and Order in Contemporary American Politics* (New York: Oxford University Press, 1997).

24. Brief of NAACP Legal Defense & Educational Fund et al. (NAACP Brief), *Miller v. Alabama*, 567 U.S. 460 (2012) (Nos. 10-9646 & 10-9647), 10.

25. NAACP Brief, *Miller*, 12–14.

26. NAACP Brief, *Miller*, 27.

27. Compare Kathleen Maguire, Ann L. Pastore, and Timothy J. Flanagan, *Sourcebook of Criminal Justice Statistics* (Washington, DC: Bureau of Justice Statistics, 1992), 633, with Ashley Nellis, *Life Goes On: The Historic Rise of Life Sentences in America* (Washington, DC: The Sentencing Project, 2013).

28. 501 U.S. 957 (1991). Michigan later softened this law and allowed parole eligibility after seventeen to twenty years, evincing how states may, if they choose, offer less punishment than the US Constitution permits. See Mich. Comp. Laws § 333.7403(2)(a)(i) (2004).

29. As Marie Gottschalk emphasizes, the scope of offenses for which LWOP may be authorized is extensive: homicide offenses, drug offenses, sex offenses, violent nonhomicide offenses, nonviolent offenses, repeat offenses. "No Way Out? Life Sentences and the Politics of Penal Reform," in *Life without Parole: America's New Death Penalty?*, ed. Charles Ogletree and Austin Sarat (New York: New York University Press, 2012), 227–81.

30. On the pains that youth experience entering prison on a life sentence, see especially Ben Crewe, Susie Hulley, and Serena Wright, *Life Imprisonment from Young Adulthood* (London: Palgrave Macmillan UK, 2020).

31. The local newspaper in Jacksonville, which had published a short article on Graham's home invasion robbery (Tia Mitchell, "Police Arrest 3 Robbery

Suspects," *Florida Times-Union*, December 4, 2004, B-1), provided no coverage of his sentencing proceeding.

32. Lexico, Oxford English and Spanish Dictionary, www.lexico.com/en /definition/crisis.

33. See Daniel S. Nagin, "Deterrence in the Twenty-First Century," *Crime and Justice* 42, no. 1 (2013): 199–263.

34. As David Garland explains about "acting out" laws: "Their capacity to control future crime . . . is less important than their immediate ability to enact public sentiment, to provide an instant response, to function as a retaliatory measure that can stand as an achievement in itself" (*Culture of Control*, 133). In a classic example, responding to a chronic drug epidemic in early 1973, New York governor Nelson Rockefeller proposed life without parole for drug crimes, emphasizing that none of his many policy efforts to resolve drug addiction had worked. Julilly Kohler-Hausmann, *Getting Tough: Welfare and Imprisonment in 1970s America* (Princeton, NJ: Princeton University Press, 2017). Rockefeller's principal aim was the policy's immediate effect, not its expected efficacy. As one legislator put it during debates on the bill, LWOP for drugs was "a panacea for 1973" (New York Senate hearing, April 27, 1973, 399).

35. Janet Roitman, *Anti-Crisis* (Durham, NC: Duke University Press, 2014), 4–5, 94.

36. On ritual and symbolism in routine penal practices, see David Garland, "Frameworks of Inquiry in the Sociology of Punishment," *British Journal of Sociology* 41, no. 1 (1990): 1–15. On the routinization of charismatic authority and related symbolisms, see generally Edward Shils, "Charisma, Order, and Status," *American Sociological Review* 30 (1965): 199–213.

37. Zygmunt Bauman, "Social Uses of Law and Order," in *Criminology and Social Theory*, ed. David Garland and Richard Sparks (Oxford: Oxford University Press, 2000), 35; see also Hans Boutellier, *The Safety Utopia: Contemporary Discontent and Desire as to Crime and Punishment* (Dordrecht, The Netherlands: Springer, 2005).

38. See generally Stanley Cohen, *Folk Devils and Moral Panics* (London: Routledge, 1972).

39. See Khalil Gibran Muhammad, *The Condemnation of Blackness* (Cambridge, MA: Harvard University Press, 2010).

40. On how race affects decision-making at different points of the penal process, see, for example, Michelle Alexander, *The New Jim Crow: Mass Incarceration in the Age of Colorblindness* (New York: The New Press, 2010); Marc Mauer, *Race to Incarcerate* (New York: The New Press, 1999); and Vesla M. Weaver, "Frontlash: Race and the Development of Punitive Crime Policy," *Studies in American Political Development* 21, no. 2 (2007): 230–65; see also Bruce Western, *Punishment and Inequality in America* (New York: Russell Sage Foundation, 2006); and Michael Tonry, *Punishing Race: A Continuing American Dilemma* (New York: Oxford University Press, 2011). On the impact of racial assumptions and preferences on life sentencing in the United

States, see Marc Mauer and Ashley Nellis, *The Meaning of Life: The Case for Abolishing Life Sentences* (New York: The New Press, 2018).

41. See, for example, David C. Baldus et al., "Racial Discrimination and the Death Penalty in the Post-*Furman* Era," *Cornell Law Review* 83, no. 6 (1997): 1638–770; and Leigh Courtney et al., *A Matter of Time* (Washington, DC: Urban Institute, 2017).

42. In all, there are six years (1992, 2003, 2008, 2012, 2016, 2020) in which the number of people serving LWOP have been counted in each state and the federal jurisdiction.

43. See Christopher Seeds, "Bifurcation Nation: American Penal Policy in Late Mass Incarceration," *Punishment and Society* 19, no. 5 (2017): 590–610.

44. Aside from several early efforts to canvas LWOP laws—for example, Julian Wright, "Life-without-Parole: An Alternative to Death or Not Much of a Life at All?," *Vanderbilt Law Review* 43, no. 2 (1990): 529–68; and Derral Cheatwood, "The Life-without-Parole Sanction: Its Current Status and a Research Agenda," *Crime & Delinquency* 34, no. 1 (1988): 43–59—and recent jurisdiction-specific surveys—for example, Dakota Blagg et al., *Life without Parole Sentences in Washington State* (Seattle: University of Washington, Law, Societies & Justice Program, 2015); and Glenn R. Schmitt and Hyun J. Konfrst, *Life Sentences in the Federal System* (Washington, DC: United States Sentencing Commission, 2015)—there are few inventories of LWOP legislation and how it has developed since the 1970s. Assessing developments in any given state requires a detailed knowledge of local laws and practices and vigilant attention to changes in the meanings and practices of life without parole over time.

45. Franklin E. Zimring, *The Contradictions of American Capital Punishment* (New York: Oxford University Press, 2003); and David Garland, *Peculiar Institution: America's Death Penalty in an Age of Abolition* (Cambridge, MA: Belknap Press, 2010). In recent years the county level has become a telling measure of use of capital punishment. See Brandon Garrett, "The Decline of the Virginia (and American) Death Penalty," *Georgetown Law Journal* 105, no. 3 (2017): 661–730; and Richard Dieter, *The 2% Death Penalty: How a Minority of Counties Produce Most Death Cases at Enormous Costs to All* (Washington, DC: Death Penalty Information Center, 2013).

46. Ashley Nellis, *No End in Sight: America's Enduring Reliance on Life Imprisonment* (Washington, DC: The Sentencing Project, 2021), 10.

47. See the population figures reported in Nellis, *No End in Sight*, 10.

48. Some states authorize LWOP for a broad range of crimes, including habitual offenses, sex offenses, drug offenses, and aggravated felonies. Many allow LWOP for first-degree murder and infraction of *either* a habitual offender statute or a sex offender statute *or* another aggravated offense. A few states allow LWOP only for capital or first-degree murder. The thousands of prisoners serving LWOP for nonviolent offenses tend to be clustered in particular states. On the latter, Jennifer Turner, *A Living Death: Life without Parole for Nonviolent Offenses* (New York: American Civil Liberties Union, 2015).

49. Those states were Arkansas, Louisiana, Nebraska, Nevada, Pennsylvania, and South Dakota. On the use of life without parole as a death penalty alternative in states retaining capital punishment, see chapter 4. As for non–death penalty states, a few had LWOP as ultimate punishment before the 1970s (Michigan, Massachusetts, West Virginia), and six turned to LWOP in the 1970s and 1980s (Iowa and Maine in 1976, Vermont in 1981, Rhode Island in 1984, Hawaii in 1986, and Minnesota in 1989).

50. As I discuss in chapter 4, contrary to what scholarly accounts have long posited, the timing of many state laws indicates that noncapital laws and policies, not the invalidation of the death penalty, buttressed LWOP's entrance as a death penalty alternative. As I discuss in chapter 8, at a national level it is more accurate to see the anti–death penalty movement's embrace of LWOP as an early 1990s development enabled by the preexisting use of LWOP in noncapital areas.

51. Michael Tonry, *Sentencing Fragments: Penal Reform in America, 1975–2025* (New York: Oxford University Press, 2016), 83–85.

52. Macdonald, Donald, and Leonard Morgenbesser, *Life without Parole Statutes in the United States* (Albany: New York State Department of Correctional Services, Division of Program Planning Research and Evaluation, 1984); and Maguire et al., *Sourcebook of Criminal Justice Statistics*; and Mauer, Marc, Ryan King, and Malcolm Young, *The Meaning of Life: Long Prison Sentences in Context* (Washington, DC: The Sentencing Project, 2004).

53. The jurisdictions leading in LWOP population in 1992 were Pennsylvania (2,417), Florida (2,376), Louisiana (2,154), Michigan (1,295), the federal system (1,177), and California (1,037). Maguire et al., *Sourcebook of Criminal Justice Statistics*, 633. No other states held more than 1,000 prisoners serving LWOP sentences in 1993. See also Burk Foster, "What Is the Meaning of Life: The Evolution of Natural Life Sentences in Louisiana, 1973–1994" (paper presented at the Academy of Criminal Justice Sciences, Annual Meeting, Boston, Massachusetts, 1995).

CHAPTER 4. THE COMPLEX ROLE OF DEATH
PENALTY ABOLITION

1. This chapter draws on a broad range of sources, including laws, judicial case decisions, criminal justice statistics, and newspaper articles, but the principal data consist of archival materials from the Florida State Library and Archive in Tallahassee. I approached the research along two lines. First, I reviewed criminal justice–related materials in subject files, legal files, bill files, legislative affairs files, press files, issue correspondence files, and files on legislative committees and task forces for governors in office between 1971 and 1998 to obtain a general frame of reference and to identify areas of concern to the various administrations (death penalty abolition and prison overcrowding, for example), including important features and concepts (such as federal court decisions or prisoner dangerousness). I triangulated these materials with reports

from two of Florida's largest newspapers, the *St. Petersburg Times* (now the *Tampa Bay Times*) and the *Miami Herald*, and publications of the Florida Department of Corrections, including annual reports and the newsletter *Correctional Compass*.

The second line of research focused on the specific laws that altered life sentencing in Florida. For pertinent laws, I studied bill summaries, staff analyses, and legislative journal entries and committee files. For the most critical bills, I looked beyond the paper trail and listened to audio recordings. Fortunately, Florida has audio-recorded legislative committee meetings and floor debates since 1969 and preserves them at the State Archive. For some proceedings, such as those of the House Select Committee on the Death Penalty of 1972, the recordings cover many days. As I proceeded chronologically, I was able to consider the development of state penal policy while researching LWOP's role therein. I followed a similar procedure with the archival collections and materials that support the following chapters.

2. Ashley Nellis, *No End in Sight: America's Enduring Reliance on Life Imprisonment* (Washington, DC: The Sentencing Project, 2021).

3. Michael C. Campbell, "Politics, Prisons, and Law Enforcement: An Examination of the Emergence of 'Law and Order' Politics in Texas," *Law & Society Review* 45, no. 3 (2011): 631–65; Michael C. Campbell, "Ornery Alligators and Soap on a Rope: Texas Prosecutors and Punishment Reform in the Lone Star State," *Theoretical Criminology* 16, no. 3 (2012): 289–311; Mona Lynch, *Sunbelt Justice: Arizona and the Transformation of American Punishment* (Stanford, CA: Stanford University Press, 2010); Robert Perkinson, *Texas Tough: The Rise of a Prison Empire* (New York: Metropolitan Books, 2010); and Heather Schoenfeld, "The Delayed Emergence of Penal Modernism in Florida," *Punishment & Society* 16, no. 3 (2014): 258–84.

4. See especially Burton H. Wolfe, *Pileup on Death Row* (New York: Doubleday, 1973); Michael Meltsner, *Cruel and Unusual: The Supreme Court and Capital Punishment* (New York: Morrow, 1974); and Evan J. Manderey, *A Wild Justice: The Death and Resurrection of Capital Punishment in America* (New York: W. W. Norton, 2013). On *Furman*'s impact on US politics and culture, see David Garland, *Peculiar Institution: America's Death Penalty in an Age of Abolition* (Cambridge, MA: Belknap Press, 2010), 254–55. Informative articles on state responses to *Furman* include Franklin E. Zimring and Gordon J. Hawkins, "Capital Punishment and the Eighth Amendment: *Furman* and *Gregg* in Retrospect," *UC Davis Law Review* 18 (1984): 927–56; and Corinna Lain, "*Furman* Fundamentals," *Washington University Law Review* 82, no. 1 (2007): 1–74.

5. *Gregg v. Georgia*, 428 U.S. 153 (1976), and accompanying cases.

6. On the byzantine nature of modern death penalty jurisprudence and its conservative turn in the early 1980s, see Robert Weisberg, "Deregulating Death," *Supreme Court Review* (1983): 305–95.

7. Many US Supreme Court justices understood *Furman* as a decision about race. Manderey, *Wild Justice*, 275–77. As it happens, post-*Furman*

legislation seems to have codified rather than ameliorated harmful racial stereotypes: death penalty statutes failed to meaningfully narrow death eligibility and did so in a manner targeting people of color. See, for example, David C. Baldus et al., "Racial Discrimination and the Death Penalty in the Post-*Furman* Era," *Cornell Law Review* 83, no. 6 (1997–1998): 1638–770; and Catherine M. Grosso et al., "Death by Stereotype: Race, Ethnicity, and California's Failure to Implement Furman's Narrowing Requirement," *UCLA Law Review* 66, no. 6 (2019): 1394–1443.

8. Harvard Law Review Association, "A Matter of Life and Death: The Effect of Life-without-Parole Statutes on Capital Punishment," *Harvard Law Review* 119, no. 6 (2006): 1838–54.

9. Harvard Law Review, "Matter of Life and Death," 1841; see also Carol Steiker and Jordan Steiker, "The Death Penalty and Mass Incarceration: Convergences and Divergences," *American Journal of Criminal Law* 41, no. 2 (2014): 205.

10. Harvard Law Review, "Matter of Life and Death," 1841. I focus on the first claim in this chapter and the second claim in chapter 8.

11. Edwin Powers, *Parole Eligibility of Prisoners Serving a Life Sentence*, 2nd ed. (Boston: Massachusetts Correctional Association, 1972).

12. Jim Stewart and Paul Lieberman, "What Is This New Sentence That Takes Away Parole?," *Student Lawyer* 11, no. 2 (1982): 14–17, 39; see also Julian Wright, "Life-without-Parole: An Alternative to Death or Not Much of a Life at All?," *Vanderbilt Law Review* 43, no. 2 (1990): 529–68.

13. Robert Sigler and Concetta Culliver, "Consequences of the Habitual Offender Act on the Costs of Operating Alabama's Prisons," *Federal Probation* 52, no. 2 (1988): 57–64; and Doris Schartmeuller, "Settling Down Behind Bars: The Extensive Use of Life Sentences in Alabama," *Prison Journal* 95, no. 4 (2015): 449–71.

14. Stewart and Lieberman, "What Is This New Sentence?," 15.

15. Stewart and Lieberman, "What Is This New Sentence?," 15.

16. As noted in chapter 3, the data on statutes and session laws were obtained by searching the laws of all fifty states and the federal system in two legal databases and by researching session laws of the states and the federal system from the early United States, working from past to present to best identify changes. See Christopher Seeds, unpublished manuscript listing statutes authorizing LWOP.

17. Illinois and Louisiana are often cited as states that, like Alabama, rushed to LWOP immediately after *Furman*, but the claims with respect to both are more accurate if stated differently. Illinois first installed a mandatory capital statute (which had no use for LWOP), and turned to LWOP only after the US Supreme Court rejected mandatory death penalty statutes in 1976. In Louisiana, all life sentences had been without parole since 1941, but a clemency protocol provided review for release after ten years and six months. The practice was discontinued after *Furman* and eventually eliminated by statute in 1979. Maine also could be seen as a state that turned to life without parole in response

to *Furman*. But it was quite a different situation: deciding *not* to enact a capital punishment statute, the state instead eliminated parole altogether and, two months before the *Gregg* decision, made LWOP the ultimate punishment.

18. Vivien Miller, *Hard Labor and Hard Time: Florida's Sunshine Prison and Chain Gangs* (Gainesville: University Press of Florida, 2012); and Schoenfeld, "Delayed Emergence."

19. Heather Schoenfeld, *Building the Prison State: Race and the Politics of Mass Incarceration* (Chicago: University of Chicago Press, 2018).

20. Schoenfeld, "Delayed Emergence"; and Schoenfeld, *Building the Prison State*.

21. Florida Department of Corrections, Annual Reports, 1970–1972, 1974–1975.

22. Howard Ohmart and Harold Bradley, *Overcrowding in the Florida Prison System: A Technical Assistance Report* (Washington, DC: American Justice Institute, 1972).

23. Heather Schoenfeld, "Mass Incarceration and the Paradox of Prison Conditions Litigation," *Law & Society Review* 44, nos. 3–4 (2010): 731–67.

24. Florida Department of Offender Rehabilitation, *An Historical Analysis of Fixed vs. Indeterminate Sentencing for Inmates Committed to the Custody of the Department of Offender Rehabilitation*, Record Group 103, Series 78, Florida State Library and Archive.

25. Martin Dyckman, "Executions Barred by Governor," *Miami Herald*, February 24, 1972, 8A.

26. Charles Ehrhardt and L. Harold Levinson, "Florida's Legislative Response to *Furman*: An Exercise in Futility?," *Journal of Criminal Law & Criminology* 64, no. 1 (1973): 10–21.

27. Letter from Jeff Gautier to Richard Pettigrew, July 27, 1972, Record Group 103, Series 19, Florida State Library and Archive.

28. Testimony of Robert Shevin, Florida House of Representatives, House Select Committee, October 12, 1972, Record Group 920, Series 414, box 59, Florida State Library and Archive. Citations to the meetings and hearings of the House Select Committee throughout this chapter refer to audio recordings, Record Group 920, Series 414, box 59, Florida State Library and Archive. See also Robert Shevin, Remarks to the Senate Criminal Justice Committee, January 10, 1975, Record Group 103, Series 78, Florida State Library and Archive.

29. Memorandum from Robert Shevin to Governor Askew et al., July 7, 1972, Record Group 920, Series 19, Florida State Library and Archive (emphasis in original).

30. Ehrhardt and Levinson, "Florida's Legislative Response," 11.

31. Gordon Harvey, *The Politics of Trust: Reubin Askew and Florida in the 1970s* (Tuscaloosa: University of Alabama Press, 2015); *Anderson v. State*, 267 So.2d 8 (Fla. 1972); and *In re Baker*, 267 So.2d 331 (Fla. 1972).

32. Louis Wainwright, Written statement to the Florida Legislature, August 17, 1972, Record Group 103, Series 19, Florida State Library and Archive.

33. Wainwright, Statement, August 17, 1972.

34. Wainwright, August 17, 1972.

35. Wainwright, August 17, 1972.

36. Wainwright, August 17, 1972 (emphasis in original).

37. House Select Committee, August 18, 1972, 146–47 (transcribed).

38. House Select Committee, August 18, 1972, 127 (transcribed).

39. Testimony of Charles Franklin Gibson, House Select Committee, August 18, 1972, 69 (transcribed).

40. House Select Committee, August 18, 1972, 162, 171 (transcribed).

41. On the role of corrections department heads and midlevel managers in initiating and defining penal policy, see Keramet Reiter and Kelsie Chesnut, "Correctional Autonomy and Authority in the Rise of Mass Incarceration," *Annual Review of Law and Social Science* 14 (2019): 49–68; see also Lynch, *Sunbelt Justice*; and Schoenfeld, *Building the Prison State.* On the influence of corrections officer organizations, see especially Joshua Page, *The "Toughest Beat": Politics, Punishment, and the Prison Officers Union in California* (New York: Oxford University Press, 2011).

42. 1972 HB 1A, Florida House Select Committee, *Report on the Florida House Select Committee on the Death Penalty* (Tallahassee: State of Florida, 1972); see also Ehrhardt and Levinson, "Florida's Legislative Response," 20–21.

43. Several states that turned to a mandatory death penalty after *Furman*, added life without parole as the alternative sentence after *Gregg*. An example is California in 1978. Hadar Aviram, *Yesterday's Monsters* (Oakland: University of California Press, 2020). Many states turned to LWOP in capital cases only much later—such as Florida, which did not add LWOP as an alternative capital sentence until 1994. Christopher Seeds, "Disaggregating LWOP: Life without Parole, Capital Punishment, and Mass Incarceration in Florida, 1972–1995," *Law & Society Review* 52, no. 1 (2018): 172–205.

44. Harvard Law Review, "Matter of Life and Death," 1840.

45. Harvard Law Review, "Matter of Life and Death," 1842.

46. For example, Jonathan Simon notes in *Mass Incarceration on Trial: A Remarkable Court Decision and the Future of Prisons in America* (New York: New Press, 2014), 35, that death penalty abolition stoked public fears of serial killers as it presented the possibility that such "monsters" might be released from prison. Those fears, Simon argues, molded public perceptions and a new "common sense" about crime prevention. The Harvard note did not pursue this claim, but rather concentrated on the subsequent effects of LWOP on death sentencing, specifically considering whether the growth of LWOP was "worth" the decrease achieved in capital sentences.

47. Fla. Laws Ch. 72-724; and Ehrhardt and Levinson, "Florida's Legislative Response," 20.

48. Charles Ehrhardt et al., "The Future of Capital Punishment in Florida: Analysis and Recommendations," *Journal of Criminal Law & Criminology* 64, no. 1 (1973): 2–10.

49. Acts 1973, No. 111, § 1 (SB 39).

50. Ron Wikberg, "A Graphic and Illustrative History, 1879 to 1797: Life Sentences in Louisiana" (mimeographed document, 1979).

51. 1974, PL 213 No. 46, 18 PaCS 2502.

52. Mark Rowan and Brian S. Kane, "Life Means Life Maybe? An Analysis of Pennsylvania's Policy Toward Lifers," *Duquesne Law Review* 30, no. 3 (1992): 661–80.

53. Data provided to author by Pennsylvania Department of Corrections, 2015; see Quinn Cozzens and Bret Grote, *A Way Out: Abolishing Death by Incarceration in Pennsylvania* (Pittsburgh, PA: Abolitionist Law Center, 2018).

54. Ashley Nellis, *Still Life: America's Increasing Use of Life and Long-Term Sentences* (Washington, DC: The Sentencing Project, 2017). In 2020, California had the third most people serving LWOP sentences, Louisiana the fourth most. Nellis, *No End in Sight*, 10.

55. William Stuntz, *The Collapse of American Criminal Justice* (Cambridge, MA: Harvard University Press, 2011).

56. See, for example, Leonard Orland, "Without Benefit of Parole," *New York Times*, July 8, 1972, 25.

57. House Select Committee, October 12, 1972.

58. House Select Committee, September 29, 1972; see also House Select Committee, October 27, 1972, discussing a noncapital bill that proposed mandatory minimums.

59. Testimony of David Bludworth, House Select Committee, September 29, 1972.

60. House Select Committee, October 27, 1972.

61. Testimony of Robert Shevin, House Select Committee, October 12, 1972.

62. See Philip Goodman, Joshua Page, and Michelle Phelps, *Breaking the Pendulum: The Long Struggle over Criminal Justice* (New York: Oxford University Press, 2017).

63. Discussions such as these can be found in other state legislative proceedings: for example, in the 1972–1973 Texas Legislature (see House Criminal Jurisprudence Committee, February 6, 1973).

64. On this matter, four correctional officers were also interviewed.

65. House Select Committee, August 31, 1972.

66. See generally David Garland, *The Culture of Control: Crime and Social Order in Contemporary Society* (Chicago: University of Chicago Press, 2001); and Simon, *Mass Incarceration on Trial*; see also Aviram, *Yesterday's Monsters*.

67. *Furman* had other significant impacts on punishment. The capital litigation that followed introduced public opinion as a key feature in criminal justice and helped forge the victims' rights movement. Marie Gottschalk, *The Prison and the Gallows: The Politics of Mass Incarceration in America* (Princeton, NJ: Princeton University Press, 2006). In addition, as reconstituted after *Furman*, capital punishment was closely regulated in a jurisprudence guided by the

notion that the death penalty, and *only* the death penalty, was different from other punishments (see chapter 7).

68. For example, California is a state where capital punishment is largely responsible for the initial move to LWOP. See Marion Vannier, "Normalizing Extreme Imprisonment: The Case of Life without Parole in California (1972–2012)," *Theoretical Criminology* 25, no. 4 (2019): 519–39. There too the introduction of LWOP as an alternative sentence cannot be isolated but must be considered along with the retrenchment of clemency and administrative review policies that changed the meaning of life sentences with parole restrictions in the 1980s and early 1990s. See Aviram, *Yesterday's Monsters*.

69. Fla. Laws Ch. 94-228. See Seeds, "Disaggregating LWOP," 196–97.

70. Florida House of Representatives, Criminal Justice Subcommittee on Prosecution and Punishment, on HB356, April 11, 1989, Record Group 920, Series 414, Florida State Library and Archive.

71. Letter from Karen Thurman to Peter Dunbar, June 16, 1989, Record Group 105, Series 1402, Florida State Library and Archive.

CHAPTER 5. THE COLLAPSE OF A PENAL PARADIGM

1. *Graham v. Florida*, 560 U.S. 48 (2010).

2. See, for example, Franklin E. Zimring and David T. Johnson, "The Dark at the Top of the Stairs: Four Destructive Influences of Capital Punishment on American Criminal Justice," in *The Oxford Handbook of Sentencing and Corrections*, ed. Joan Petersilia and Kevin Reitz (New York: Oxford University Press, 2012), 747.

3. Michael Tonry, *Sentencing Fragments: Penal Reform in America, 1975–2025* (New York: Oxford University Press, 2016), 48.

4. Frederick Allen, *The Decline of the Rehabilitative Ideal: Penal Policy and Social Purpose* (New Haven, CT: Yale University Press, 1981).

5. Michele Pifferi, *Reinventing Punishment: A Comparative History of Criminology and Penology in the Nineteenth and Twentieth Centuries* (Oxford: Oxford University Press, 2016).

6. Hartmut-Michael Weber, *The Abolition of Life Imprisonment* (Baden-Baden: Nomos, 1999).

7. Pifferi, *Reinventing Punishment*; and Dirk van Zyl Smit, "Abolishing Life Imprisonment?," *Punishment & Society* 3, no. 2 (2001): 299–306.

8. See Mabel Elliott, *Conflicting Penal Theories in Statutory Criminal Law* (Chicago: University of Chicago Press, 1931).

9. Charles Bright, *The Powers That Punish: Prison and Politics in the Era of the "Big House," 1920–1955* (Ann Arbor: University of Michigan Press, 1996); Jonathan Simon, "From the Big House to the Warehouse: Rethinking Prisons and State Government in the 20th Century," *Punishment & Society* 2, no. 2 (2000): 213–34; and Philip Goodman, Joshua Page, and Michelle Phelps, *Breaking the Pendulum: The Long Struggle over Criminal Justice* (New York: Oxford University Press, 2017).

10. Mona Lynch, *Sunbelt Justice: Arizona and the Transformation of American Punishment* (Palo Alto, CA: Stanford Law Books, 2010).

11. Mona Lynch, "Mass Incarceration, Legal Change, and Locale," *Criminology & Public Policy* 10, no. 3 (2011): 673–98; and David Garland, "Penality and the Penal State," *Criminology* 51, no. 3 (2013): 475–517; see Goodman, Page, and Phelps, *Breaking the Pendulum*.

12. David Garland defines official ideology as "the set of categories, signs, and symbols through which punishment represents itself to itself and to others." *Punishment and Modern Society* (Chicago: University of Chicago Press, 1990), 6. Garland observes that for much of the twentieth century rehabilitation was "a key element of official ideology and institutional rhetoric" in US punishment. See Dirk van Zyl Smit and Alessandro Corda, "American Exceptionalism in Parole Release and Supervision," in *American Exceptionalism in Crime and Punishment*, ed. Kevin R. Reitz (Oxford: Oxford University Press, 2017).

13. For example, Katherine Beckett, *Making Crime Pay: Law and Order in Contemporary American Politics* (New York: Oxford University Press, 1997); David Garland, *The Culture of Control: Crime and Social Order in Contemporary Society* (Chicago: University of Chicago Press, 2001); Jonathan Simon, *Governing through Crime: How the War on Crime Transformed American Democracy and Created a Culture of Fear* (New York: Oxford University Press, 2007); Loïc Wacquant, *Punishing the Poor: The Neoliberal Government of Social Insecurity* (Durham, NC: Duke University Press, 2009); and Michelle Alexander, *The New Jim Crow: Mass Incarceration in the Age of Colorblindness* (New York: The New Press, 2010).

14. Garland, *Culture of Control*; Richard Sparks, "State Punishment in Advanced Capitalist Countries," in *Punishment and Social Control*, 2nd ed., ed. Stanley Cohen and Thomas Blomberg (New York; Walter de Gruyter, 2003); and Jonathan Simon, *Mass Incarceration on Trial: A Remarkable Court Decision and the Future of Prisons in America* (New York: The New Press, 2014).

15. Zygmunt Bauman, "Social Uses of Law and Order," in *Criminology and Social Theory*, ed. David Garland and Richard Sparks (Oxford: Oxford University Press, 2000); Garland, *Culture of Control*; Simon, *Governing through Crime*; Wacquant, *Punishing the Poor*; Elizabeth Hinton, *From the War on Poverty to the War on Crime* (Cambridge MA: Harvard University Press, 2017); and Julilly Kohler-Hausmann, *Getting Tough: Welfare and Imprisonment in 1970s America* (Princeton, NJ: Princeton University Press, 2017).

16. Joan Petersilia, "Parole and Prisoner Reentry in the United States," *Crime and Justice* 26 (1999): 492.

17. Garland, *Punishment and Modern Society*, ch. 1.

18. Franklin E. Zimring and Gordon J. Hawkins, *Incapacitation* (Oxford: Oxford University Press, 1995).

19. See generally Tonry, *Sentencing Fragments*, ch. 2.

20. Gwen Robinson, "Late-Modern Rehabilitation: The Evolution of a Penal Strategy," *Punishment & Society* 10, no. 4 (2008): 429–45; Michelle Phelps, "Rehabilitation in the Punitive Era: The Gap between Rhetoric and

Reality in US Prison Programs," *Law & Society Review* 45, no. 1 (2011): 33–68; and Philip Goodman, "'Another Second Chance': Rethinking Rehabilitation through the Lens of California's Prison Fire Camps," *Social Problems* 59, no. 4 (2012): 437–58.

21. Tonry, *Sentencing Fragments*, 44.

22. Tonry, *Sentencing Fragments*, 28.

23. Florida Department of Corrections, Annual Reports, 1973–1979.

24. Pamala Griset, "Determinate Sentencing and Administrative Discretion over Time Served in Prison: A Case Study of Florida," *Crime & Delinquency* 42, no. 1 (1996): 129. Pushback against Florida's release system, which was wide open without any minimum sentences, first surfaced in the 1976 legislature in a determinate sentencing bill that Governor Reubin Askew vetoed.

25. Mike Boehm, "State's New Rules to Bring Truth to Prison Sentences," *Miami Herald*, August 21, 1983.

26. Letter from Wayland Clifton to Bob Graham, April 15, 1983, Record Group 104, Series 1215, Florida State Library and Archive.

27. Florida Corrections Overcrowding Task Force. *Final Report and Recommendations* (Tallahassee: State of Florida, 1983); see also Griset, "Determinate Sentencing," 130–31.

28. Florida House Committee on Corrections, Probation, and Parole, 1983, Final Bill Analysis HB 1012, Record Group 920, Series 19, Florida State Library and Archive.

29. Fla. Laws Ch. 83-87, Fla. Laws Ch. 83-131. Notably, the new law did not apply to capital felonies, for which the sentence remained death or life with parole eligibility after twenty-five years (chapter 4).

30. Testimony of Alan Sundberg, Florida House of Representatives, Committee on Criminal Justice, on PCB6, May 16, 1983, Record Group 920, Series 414, box 510, Florida State Library and Archive. Citations to Florida legislative meetings, hearings, and floor debates in this chapter refer to audio recordings preserved at the Florida State Library and Archive.

31. Testimony of Parker MacDonald, Florida House of Representatives, Committee on Criminal Justice, on PCB6, May 16, 1983.

32. Representative Elvin Martinez, Florida House of Representatives, Committee on Criminal Justice, on PCB6, May 16, 1983.

33. Fla. Laws Ch. 83-87.

34. Testimony of Jim Eaton, Florida House of Representatives, Committee on Criminal Justice, on PCB6, May 16, 1983.

35. Heather Schoenfeld, "The Delayed Emergence of Penal Modernism in Florida," *Punishment & Society* 16, no. 3 (2014): 258–84.

36. Stephen Doig, "Jammed Prisons to be Tackled by Legislature," *Miami Herald*, June 18, 1982.

37. Florida House of Representatives, Committee on Corrections, Probation, and Parole. *Reform Act of 1983, Questions and Answers*, Record Group 920, Series 19, Florida State Library and Archive.

38. Florida Senate, Staff Analysis and Economic Impact Statement on SB 644, May 1, 1983, Record Group 900, Series 18, Florida State Library and Archive; see also Fla. Laws Ch. 83-131.

39. Boehm, "State's New Rules to Bring Truth to Prison Sentences."

40. Fla. Admin. Code § 33-11.045(2)(f) (eff. 1980).

41. Testimony of Nancy Wilson of the Parole and Probation Commission, Florida Senate, Committee on Corrections, Probation and Parole, on SB644, April 26 and May 4, 1983, Record Group 900, Series 625, box 210; and Florida House Committee on Criminal Justice, Bill Summary of PCB6, May 13, 1983, Record Group 920, Series 19, Florida State Library and Archive.

42. See generally Griset, "Determinate Sentencing"; and Heather Schoen-feld, *Building the Prison State: Race and the Politics of Mass Incarceration* (Chicago: University of Chicago Press, 2018).

43. Fla. Stat. § 944.30; Fla. Laws Ch. 57-121. As an internal FLDOC memorandum evinced: "It has been some time since we evaluated the inmates under the provision of Florida Statute 944.30. . . . Your staff should become familiar with this statute." Memorandum from Ron Jones to Florida Department of Corrections, January 28, 1983, Record Group 104, Series 1215, Florida State Library and Archive.

44. Florida Department of Corrections, Annual Reports, 1982–1983.

45. Fla. Laws Ch. 88-122; see *Dugger v. Williams*, 593 So. 2d 180 (Fla. 1991).

46. See Florida House of Representatives, Committee on Corrections, Probation, and Parole, on HB1012, May 3, 1983, Record Group 920, Series 414, box 350, Florida State Library and Archive.

47. On the latter see also Florida House of Representatives, Staff Report on PCB6, May 16, Series 414, box 510, Florida State Library and Archive.

48. In 1984, the FLDOC estimated between ten and fifteen people were serving life without parole. Donald Macdonald and Leonard Morgenbesser, *Life without Parole Statutes in the United States* (Albany: New York State Department of Correctional Services, Division of Program Planning Research and Evaluation, 1984). By 1992, 2,376 people (2,332 men and 44 women) were sentenced to LWOP in Florida. Kathleen Maguire, Ann L. Pastore, and Timothy J. Flanagan, *Sourcebook of Criminal Justice Statistics* (Washington, DC: Bureau of Justice Statistics, 1992), 633.

49. Between 1972 and 2000, the following jurisdictions also abolished parole or passed related bills converting all life sentences to life without parole: Maine (1976), Illinois (1978), Minnesota (1982), Federal (1984), Washington (1984), Oregon (1989), Delaware (1990), Idaho (1994), North Carolina (1994), Mississippi (1995), Virginia (1995), and Ohio (1996). The factors that led these jurisdictions to curtail parole should be studied closely and not assumed to be just like those that applied in Florida.

50. Lynch, *Sunbelt Justice*, 156; and Simon, *Governing through Crime.*

51. See, for example, Burk Foster, "What Is the Meaning of Life: The Evolution of Natural Life Sentences in Louisiana, 1973–1994" (paper presented

at the Academy of Criminal Justice Sciences Annual Meeting, Boston, 1995); and Michael C. Campbell, "Agents of Change: Law Enforcement, Prisons, and Politics in Texas and California" (PhD diss., University of California, Irvine, 2009).

52. Francis X. Clines, "Legislature Open: Rockefeller Cites Need of 'Decisive' Steps to End Lawlessness," *New York Times*, January, 4, 1973; and New York Senate Record, April 27, 1973, debate on 1973 SB 6204 (bill 1065) and 1973 SB 6205 (bill 1066). Officers in the New York Department of Corrections also objected, voicing concern about the risks posed by prisoners with nothing to lose. New York State Archives, Rockefeller central subject and correspondence files, 1971–1973, 13862 72, reel 60.

53. Eric Schlosser, "The Prison Industrial Complex," *Atlantic Monthly*, December 1998, 51–77. In spring 1973 President Richard Nixon called for life without parole as a mandatory sentence for repeat drug trafficking convictions in the federal jurisdiction, noting that "the time has come for soft-headed judges and probation officers to show as much concern for the rights of innocent victims of crime as they do for the rights of convicted criminals." Richard Nixon, State of the Union Message on Law Enforcement and Drug Abuse Prevention, March 14, 1973, www.presidency.ucsb.edu/documents/state-the-union-message-the-congress-law-enforcement-and-drug-abuse-prevention. Nixon's direction was mirrored at the state level, as the Rockefeller example shows. State law developments in turn influenced national-level policy. See Michael C. Campbell and Heather Schoenfeld, "The Transformation of America's Penal Order: A Historicized Political Sociology of Punishment," *American Journal of Sociology* 118, no. 5 (2013): 1375–1423. In 1984 the federal jurisdiction removed parole, rendering all life sentences without parole, in legislation that was at once a turn away from indeterminate sentencing and the beginning of a vigorous attack on drug crime.

54. Quite a few states passed laws explicitly authorizing LWOP in circumstances where existing law already precluded parole for life sentences, as if to underscore the existing sanction. Pennsylvania did so with arson in 1982, Florida for drug offenses in 1988 and 1989. The practice can be seen more recently in South Carolina (2010) and Nebraska (2011).

55. David Garland, *Peculiar Institution: America's Death Penalty in an Age of Abolition* (Cambridge, MA: Belknap Press, 2010), 36–37.

56. Willis Frederick Dunbar, *Michigan through the Centuries* (New York: Lewis Historical Publishing Company, 1955).

57. The Citizens Alliance on Prisons and Public Spending, *When "Life" Did Not Mean Life: A Historical Analysis of Life Sentences Imposed in Michigan since 1900* (2006), 12, reports of Michigan: "Where a person sentenced to a non-parolable life term in the 1950s had nearly a seven in ten chance of gaining release in the 1970s, the chances of release for a parolable lifer sentenced in the 1970s are barely one in ten."

58. The 650-lifer law, addressed by the US Supreme Court in *Harmelin v. Michigan*, 501 U.S. 957 (1991), was aimed at the drug trade but billed equally

as a "parole law." See generally Ashley Surles, "An Unforgettable Mistake: William G. Milliken and Michigan's Mandatory Minimum Sentencing Program," *Michigan Journal of History* 5, no. 1 (2007): 1–21. At the time, it was the nation's harshest drug law.

59. Michigan Public Act 81 of 1978, 1977 HB4195, Mich. Comp. Laws § 791.233b(1) (1979). The Michigan Department of Corrections and parole board strongly opposed the bill because they expected it would overcrowd prisons, estimating they would need seven new prisons to cover it. "Foes Supporters Eye Passage of Parole Issue," *Ironwood Daily Globe*, October 17, 1978.

60. Patrick Haddad, "Effect of Proposal B on the Lifer Law," *University of Detroit Law Review* 65, no. 4 (1987–1988): 725–68.

61. Mich. Comp. Laws § 791.234(4). Proposal B did not affect life with parole sentences, because, technically, they did not have a minimum term to which such restrictions on good time and parole could apply. See *People v. Johnson*, 364 N.W.2d 654 (Mich. 1984), discussed in Haddad, "Effect of Proposal B."

62. For more on the intricacies of the Michigan legal landscape after Proposal B, see Haddad, "Effect of Proposal B"; Eric Guerin, "*People v. Moore*: The Role of Discretion in Indeterminate Sentencing," *Detroit Law Review* 3 (1989): 1275–300; and Patricia Len Staley, "Life Expectancy as a Factor in Sentencing: *People v. Moore*," *Cooley Law Review* 5, no. 3 (1988): 795–810. On trends toward punitive sentencing in Michigan generally, see Anne Yantus, "Sentence Creep: Increasing Penalties in Michigan and the Need for Sentencing Reform," *University of Michigan Journal of Law Reform* 47, no. 3 (2013): 645–96.

63. *People v. Murray*, 72 Mich. 10 (1888), 17.

64. *People v. (Oscar) Moore*, 417 N.W.2d 508 (Mich. App. 1987), *judgment modified and remanded*, 442 N.W.2d 638 (Mich. 1989); and *People v. (Timothy) Moore*, 439 N.W.2d 684 (Mich. 1989).

65. *Oscar Moore*, 417 N.W. at 514.

66. *People v. Legree*, 441 N.W.2d 433, 434–35 (Mich. App. 1989).

67. *Legree*, 441 N.W.2d at 436–37.

68. *Timothy Moore*, 439 N.W.2d at 686.

69. *Timothy Moore*, 439 N.W.2d at 693. The dissent differed in its interpretation of "the intent of the people in passing Proposal B," which, as a lower court judge put it, was "precisely" to make it "possible to put vicious criminals such as defendant in prison for life" (698; see *Legree*, 441 N.W.2d at 440).

70. *People v. Rushlow*, 468 N.W.2d 487 (Mich. 1991), upheld a sentence allowing first parole review at age eighty-seven as one a prisoner "had a reasonable prospect of actually serving." Following *Rushlow*, see, for example *People v. Weaver*, 480 N.W.2d 607 (Mich. App. 1991) (upholding 75- to 150-year sentence for assault with intent to murder where parole eligibility would occur when defendant in nineties). There are many more.

71. *People v. Merriweather*, 527 N.W.2d 460 (Mich. 1994).

72. *Merriweather*, 527 N.W.2d at 465. See Jeanice Dagher-Margosian, "Life Means Life: Parole Rarely Granted on Non-Mandatory Life Terms," *Michigan Bar Journal* 73 (1994): 1184–86.

73. Tonry, *Sentencing Fragments*, 28.

74. Tonry, *Sentencing Fragments*, 29.

75. Florida's Stop Turning Out Prisoners Act of 1995 is another product of the awkward transfer from an indeterminate to a fixed sentencing model. As legislators considered this bill requiring prisoners to serve 85 percent of their sentence, they asked: How should one calculate 85 percent of life? How does one take a percentage of an open-ended sentence? Uncertain, "they just said life means life," Representative Charlie Crist said in explaining the action. Florida Senate, floor debate on HB 687, May 4, 1995, Record Group 905, Series 1238, box 156, Florida State Library and Archive.

76. For example, Texas did not abolish parole and turned to LWOP only in 2005. The state, however, used other methods to incapacitate people convicted of serious and violent crimes. With mandatory minimum sentences of forty or fifty years or more, Texas lawmakers sent strong messages and mustered considerable political clout. Today, LWOP proliferates in Florida, Michigan has high numbers of prisoners serving LWOP and virtual life sentences, and Texas has a very high number of virtual life prisoners with a slow but growing LWOP population.

CHAPTER 6. GOVERNORS AND PRISONERS

1. Daniel Kobil, "The Quality of Mercy Strained: Wresting the Pardon Power from the King," *Texas Law Review* 69, no. 3 (1990): 569–642; and Margaret Colgate Love, "The Twilight of the Pardon Power," *Journal of Criminal Law and Criminology* 100, no. 3 (2010): 1169–212.

2. Love, "Twilight of the Pardon Power," 1176 ("informal and idiosyncratic"); and Carolyn Strange, "The Unwritten Law of Executive Justice: Pardoning Patricide in Reconstruction-Era New York," *Law and History Review* 28, no. 4 (2010): 891–930 ("blameworthiness"); see also Vivien Miller, *Crime, Sexual Violence, and Clemency: Florida's Pardon Board and Penal System in the Progressive Era* (Gainesville: University of Florida Press, 2000).

3. Austin Sarat, "At the Boundaries of Law: Executive Clemency, Sovereign Prerogative, and the Dilemma of American Legality," *American Quarterly* 57, no. 3 (2005): 611–31 ("border of sovereignty and law"); and Austin Sarat and Nasser Hussain, "The Literary Life of Clemency: Pardon Tales in the Contemporary United States," *TriQuarterly* 124 (2006): 218 ("ungovernability of mercy").

4. Marie Gottschalk, *Caught: The Prison State and the Lockdown of American Politics* (Princeton, NJ: Princeton University Press, 2015), 186.

5. Love, "Twilight of the Pardon Power"; and Sheldon Messinger et al., "The Foundations of Parole in California," *Law & Society Review* 19, no. 1 (1985): 69–106.

6. Edwin Powers, *Parole Eligibility of Prisoners Serving a Life Sentence*, 2nd ed. (Boston: Massachusetts Correctional Association, 1972). See the discussion in chapter 2.

7. Gottschalk, *Caught*, 188.

8. See Burk Foster, "Pardons and Politics: How It All Went Wrong," *Angolite* 13, no. 1 (1988): 33–50.

9. Sarat, "At the Boundaries of Law"; and Veronica Horowitz and Christopher Uggen, "Consistency and Compensation in Mercy: Commutation in the Era of Mass Incarceration," *Social Forces* 97, no. 3 (2019): 1205–30.

10. Gottschalk, *Caught*, 186–91.

11. Jonathan Simon, *Governing through Crime: How the War on Crime Transformed American Democracy and Created a Culture of Fear* (New York: Oxford University Press, 2007), 159–64.

12. Rachel E. Barkow, "The Ascent of the Administrative State and the Demise of Mercy," *Harvard Law Review* 121, no. 5 (2008): 1332–65.

13. Otto Kirchheimer, "The Quality of Mercy: On the Role of Clemency in the Apparatus of Justice," *Social Research* 28, no. 2 (1961): 170.

14. Barry Salkin, "The Pardoning Power in Antebellum Pennsylvania," *Pennsylvania Magazine of History and Biography* 100, no. 4 (1976): 510–11.

15. Louis Kolakoski and T. W. Broecker, "The Pennsylvania Parole System in Operation," *Journal of Criminal Law and Criminology* 23, no. 3 (1932): 429.

16. Louis Kolakoski, "Case Supervision of Paroled Prisoners in Pennsylvania," *Prison Journal* 13, no. 3 (1933): 9–13.

17. Louis Kolakoski, "Comparative Study of Commutation and Regular Parole Cases for the State of Pennsylvania," *Prison Journal* 17, no. 2 (1937): 325, 327; see *Com. v. Kalck*, 87 A. 61 (Pa. 1913).

18. Pennsylvania Parole Act of 1941 (P.L. 861, No. 323). See Jon Yount, "Pennsylvania: Parole and Life Imprisonment," Prison Policy Initiative, 2004, https://static.prisonpolicy.org/scans/yount/PA_parole.pdf.

19. Phillip Renninger, *A Study of Recidivism among Individuals Granted Executive Clemency in Pennsylvania, 1968–1981* (Harrisburg: Pennsylvania Commission on Crime and Delinquency, 1982).

20. Pennsylvania Legislative Journal, House, June 29, 1961, 2694.

21. Heather Ann Thompson, *Blood in the Water: The Attica Uprising of 1971 and Its Legacy* (New York: Pantheon Books, 2016); and Jonathan Simon, *Mass Incarceration on Trial: A Remarkable Court Decision and the Future of Prisons in America* (New York: The New Press, 2014); see also Eric Cummins, *The Rise and Fall of California's Radical Prison Movement* (Palo Alto, CA: Stanford University Pres, 1994).

22. Allen M. Hornblum, *Acres of Skin: Human Experiments at Holmesburg Prison* (New York: Routledge, 1998).

23. Letter from Wycliffe Jangdharrie to Milton Shapp, October 14, 1971, MG/309/14/1, box 25, Pennsylvania State Library and Archive.

24. Milton Shapp, introductory remarks to Senate Judiciary Committee on HB 680, February 15, 1972, MG/309/14/1, box 26, Pennsylvania State Library and Archive.

25. Letter from J. R. Brierley to Milton Shapp, February 14, 1972, MG/309/14/1, box 26, Pennsylvania State Library and Archive.

26. Brierley to Shapp, February 14, 1972.

27. Shapp, introductory remarks, February 15, 1972.

28. Letter from Shane Creamer to Pennsylvania General Assembly, May 24, 1972, RG/015/AA/7, Pennsylvania State Library and Archive. The move stemmed in part from criticism of pardons as a release mechanism. Views differed on whether there should be a minimum term (see transcript of testimony of Arlen Specter, House Judiciary Committee, Subcommittee on Corrections, on HB 479, April 27, 1973, RG/007/B/6, carton 25, Pennsylvania State Library and Archive).

29. Yount, "Pennsylvania," 18.

30. Letter from LaDainty Little to Milton Shapp, October 30, 1972, MG/309/14/1, box 26, Pennsylvania State Library and Archive.

31. Testimony of David Terrell, House Judiciary Committee, Subcommittee on Corrections, on HB 479, April 27, 1973.

32. Testimony of John Monroe and James Jenkins, House Judiciary Committee, Subcommittee on Corrections, on HB 479, October 5, 1973.

33. Letter from Lawrence Beaser to H. E. Kohn, June 15, 1972, MG/309/3, Group 4, carton 7, Pennsylvania State Library and Archive.

34. On the experiences of women serving life sentences, see generally Lora Bex Lempert, *Women Doing Life: Gender, Punishment and the Struggle for Identity* (New York: New York University Press, 2016); Meredith Huey Dye and Ronald H. Aday, *Women Lifers: Lives Before, Behind, and Beyond Bars* (Lanham, MD: Rowman & Littlefield, 2019); and Marion Vannier, "Women Serving Life without the Possibility of Parole," *Howard Journal of Crime and Justice* 55, no. 3 (2016): 328–44.

35. Little to Shapp, October 30, 1972.

36. Mark Rowan and Brian Kane, "Life Means Life Maybe? An Analysis of Pennsylvania's Policy toward Lifers," *Duquesne Law Review* 30, no. 3 (1991–1992): 661–80.

37. Yount, "Pennsylvania," 25–26; and Rowan and Kane, "Life Means Life Maybe?"

38. In capital cases, for example, prosecutors historically alluded to the possibility of commutation to emphasize that life sentences had "parole"; see *Com. v. Crittenton*, 326 Pa. 25 (1937); and Rowan and Kane, "Life Means Life Maybe?," 666–67.

39. Pennsylvania Legislative Journal, House, April 24–25, 1973, 775.

40. Yount, "Pennsylvania," 26.

41. Patricia Hartz, "State Prison Inmates Take Hostages: State Police Try to Enter," *Patriot News*, October 28, 1981.

42. See *Com. v. Sourbeer*, 422 A.2d 116 (Pa. 1980).

43. Legislative discussions over the 1982 arson bill evince continued confusion among lawmakers over whether life sentences for second-degree murder carried parole. One legislator, shocked to think the sentence for unpremeditated arson murder would be mandatory LWOP, was even more surprised to

find this already the law and that the arson bill, rather than installing a harsher penalty, "simply added the words 'without possibility of parole.'" Pennsylvania Legislative Journal, House, April 28, 1982, 1040–41.

44. See Michael C. Campbell, "The Emergence of Penal Extremism in California: A Dynamic View of Institutional Structures and Political Processes," *Law & Society Review* 48, no. 2 (2014): 394.

45. Rowan and Kane, "Life Means Life Maybe?," 676.

46. See, for example, on Louisiana, Foster, "Pardons and Politics"; and Ron Wikberg, "A Graphic and Illustrative History, 1879 to 1797: Life Sentences in Louisiana" (mimeographed document, 1979); on South Dakota, *Brim v. South Dakota Board of Pardons and Paroles,* 563 N.W.2d 812 (S.D. 1997).

47. *Castle v. Bd. of Probation and Parole,* 554 A.2d 625. 627–29 (Pa. Com. Ct. 1989), *appeal denied,* 567 A.2d 653 (Pa. 1989).

48. Quinn Cozzens and Bret Grote, *A Way Out: Abolishing Death by Incarceration in Pennsylvania* (Pittsburgh, PA: Abolitionist Law Center, 2018), 31; and Ashley Nellis, *Still Life: America's Increasing Use of Life and Long-Term Sentences* (Washington, DC: The Sentencing Project, 2017), 12.

49. Cozzens and Grote, *A Way Out,* 17; and data provided by Pennsylvania Department of Corrections 2015.

50. "Editorial: Pardons Unit to Consider Open Ruling," *Patriot News,* October 3, 1990, B7.

51. Pennsylvania Prison Society, *The Need for Parole Options for Life-Sentenced Prisoners* (Philadelphia: Pennsylvania Prison Society, 1993).

52. Nancy Eshelman, "Life Term Means Just That in State," *Patriot News,* August 19, 1992, B1.

53. Adam Bell, "Senate Committee Renews Calls for Reforming Pardons Process: Reginald McFadden Case Surfaces as Example of Problems," *Patriot News,* December 15, 1994, B1.

54. James Taylor, "P.O.V.—Unfettered Mercy for Lifers, Not Legislation," *Graterfriends* 10, no. 6 (1992): 8.

55. Nancy Eshelman, "In Search of Casey's Compassion," *Patriot News,* April 6, 1994, B1.

56. Sean Connolly, "Ridge Slams Singel Votes to Free Lifers: Pardon Board Actions Targeted," *Patriot News,* September 18, 1994, B1.

57. Robert Cornille, "Get Smarter on Crime, Not Tougher," *Patriot News,* May 1, 1994, B15.

58. Adam Bell, "Group Wants Parole for Some Lifers, Alternatives for Nonviolent Offenders," *Patriot News,* April 13, 1994, B3.

59. Tom Ridge, "Pardons Voting Is Appropriate Issue," *Patriot News,* September 25, 1994.

60. "Editorial: Why No Transition? Unprepared; Politics Overshadows Prime Question in Killer's Parole," *Patriot News,* October 27, 1994, A12.

61. Sean Connolly, "Crime Issue Explodes in Campaign: Arrest of Parolee Is Devastating for Singel," *Patriot News,* October 9, 1994, B1.

62. Adam Bell and Sean Connolly, "Restriction of Pardons Process Feared," *Patriot News*, October 11, 1994, A1. In 1973, violent deaths at Graterford Prison exacerbated tensions between prisoners' rights movements and correction officer unions, leading to extended discussions over prison conditions and whether to build a new high-security prison facility. See Joshua Coene, "The Contentious Prison: From Rehabilitation to Incapacitation in New South Wales and Pennsylvania, 1965–1990" (PhD diss., University of Michigan, 2016). McFadden's case has long remained a specter over clemency in Pennsylvania. See Regina Austin, "The Saga of Pennsylvania's 'Willie Horton' and the Commutation of Life Sentences in the Commonwealth" (University of Pennsylvania Law School, Public Law Research Paper, 2020).

63. Adam Bell, "Three Strike Bill Blasted," *Patriot News*, March 9, 1994, A4; and Adam Bell, "Ridge Replaces Chief of Parole: Action Follows Report Critical of Killer's Release," *Patriot News*, June 28, 1995, A1.

64. Adam Bell, "State to Provide Geriatric Wing to Aid Aging Prison Population," *Patriot News*, July 17, 1995, A1.

65. Unpublished letter submitted to *The Real News*, a Pennsylvania publication, provided to author courtesy of Joan Porter.

66. Adam Bell, "An Unlikely Team Goes to Bat for Lifers: Prison, Anti-Violence Groups Fight Stricter Commutations," *Patriot News*, October 10, 1997, B1.

67. John Irwin, *Lifers: Seeking Redemption in Prison* (New York: Routledge, 2009).

68. Richard Marra, "Did Pennsylvanians Understand?," *Graterfriends* 15, no. 9 (1997): 4.

69. Eshelman, "Life Term Means Just That in State," B1; and Pennsylvania Prison Society, *Life Sentence* (documentary, 1989, www.youtube.com/watch?v=aF5Wl19-HEs).

70. Pennsylvania Prison Society, *Life Sentence*.

71. Simon, *Governing through Crime*, 164.

72. Simon, *Governing through Crime*; and Foster, "Pardons and Politics," 49. The approach, which Ridge exemplified, also extends to other ways in which the executive wields release decisions—for example, former California Governor Gray Davis's practice of vetoing nearly all parole grants. See Hadar Aviram, *Yesterday's Monsters: The Manson Family Cases and the Illusion of Parole* (Oakland: University of California Press, 2020), 34.

73. Margaret Leigey, *The Forgotten Men: Serving a Life without Parole Sentence* (New Brunswick, NJ: Rutgers University Press, 2015).

74. The turn in Louisiana also was dramatic. Between 1972 and 1980, Governor Edwin Edwards commuted roughly two thousand sentences; during the 1970s, however, several important changes in law and policy retrenched clemency for lifers. See Foster, "Pardons and Politics"; Ron Wikberg, "The Long-termers," *Angolite* 13, no. 3 (1988): 19–58; Michael Glover, "Opening the 10-6 Floodgate," *Angolite* 15, no. 4 (1990): 59–64; Lane Nelson, "A History of Penal

Reform in Angola, Part I: The Immovable Object," *Angolite* (September/October 2009): 16–23; and Helen G. Berrigan, "Executive Clemency, First-Offender Pardons, Automatic Restoration of Rights," *Louisiana Law Review* 62, no. 1 (2001): 49–57. See also California, where the minimum time period before corrections could recommend life without parole–sentenced prisoners for commutation gradually increased from twelve to thirty years and then was effectively abandoned. Cal. Code Reg., Title 15, Section 2817, subsection (b) (amended effective September 11, 1982 and repealed January 19, 1994).

CHAPTER 7. THE US SUPREME COURT'S AMBIVALENT CRAFTING OF LWOP

1. Some of the best evidence of how the major upheavals spurred legal challenges comes from the writings of incarcerated people. Louisiana's history is among the most documented, thanks in significant part to the *Angolite*, a prisoner-edited journal published at the Louisiana State Penitentiary at Angola. See, for example, Michael Glover, "Opening the 10-6 Floodgate," *Angolite* 15, no. 4 (1990): 59–64.

2. 419 U.S. 256 (1974); 445 U.S. 263 (1980); 454 U.S. 370 (1982); 463 U.S. 277 (1983); and 501 U.S. 957 (1991).

3. The first case, *Schick*, concerns the president's commutation power. The latter four cases are known for articulating an exacting noncapital proportionality jurisprudence, a keystone of the Court's Eighth Amendment precedent. This noncapital proportionality jurisprudence—holding that prison terms, however long, will be disproportionate only in extremely rare cases—is widely criticized by legal scholars. See Richard Frase, "Excessive Prison Sentences, Punishment Goals, and the Eighth Amendment: 'Proportionality' Relative to What?," *Minnesota Law Review* 89 (2004): 572–651.

4. I refer to Papers of Justices Harry A. Blackmun, William J. Brennan, William O. Douglas, Thurgood Marshall, and Byron R. White, available at the Library of Congress, Manuscript Division, in Washington, D.C., for the cases of interest.

5. Scott Phillips and Ryken Grattet, "Judicial Rhetoric, Meaning-Making, and the Institutionalization of Hate Crime Law," *Law and Society Review* 34, no. 3 (2000): 568; and Valerie Jenness, "The Emergence, Content, and Institutionalization of Hate Crime Law: How a Diverse Policy Community Produced a Modern Legal Fact," *Annual Review of Law and Social Science* 3 (2007): 141–60.

6. 419 U.S. 256 (1974). See Julian Wright, "Life-without-Parole: An Alternative to Death or Not Much of a Life at All?," *Vanderbilt Law Review* 43, no. 2 (1990): 529–68; and Dirk van Zyl Smit, *Taking Life Imprisonment Seriously: In National and International Law* (Norwell, MA: Kluwer Law International, 2002).

7. *Ex parte Wells*, 15 L. Ed. 421 (U.S. 1856).

8. *Schick* may have had some symbolic influence, but given existing precedent at the time (see, e.g., *Green v. Teets*, 244 F. 2d 401 [9th Cir. 1957], rejecting the same legal challenge on similar facts; *State v. Taylor*, 312 P.2d 162 [Az. 1957], finding life without parole for kidnapping not cruel and unusual), *Schick*'s impact on how courts perceived life without parole sentences was likely slim. Subsequent lower court decisions attest that *Schick* was used on occasion to refute claims that life without parole was unconstitutional (see Charles J. Ogletree and Austin Sarat, eds., *Life without Parole: America's New Death Penalty?* (New York: New York University Press, 2012), 9, citing *Government of the Virgin Islands v. Gereau*, 592 F.2d 192 (3d Cir. 1979)), but the point could have been established regardless.

9. Brief for Petitioner, *Schick v. Reed*, 419 U.S. 256 (No. 73-5677), n11.

10. Brief for Respondent, *Schick v. Reed*, 419 U.S. 256 (No. 73-5677), 12, n4.

11. Oral argument notes for *Schick v. Reed*, October 23, 1974, Papers of Justice Harry Blackmun, Library of Congress. Aptly highlighting the important role executive clemency plays in the context of a life sentence, legal scholar Craig Lerner emphasizes a point that few scholars have: President Ford ultimately commuted Schick's punishment to a parole-eligible sentence in 1976. "Life without Parole as a Conflicted Punishment," *Wake Forest Law Review* 48, no. 5 (2013): 1152. Lerner, however, does not acknowledge how clemency practice and the meaning of the life without parole sanction soon changed.

12. No. 78-5531, 439 U.S. 1091 (1979).

13. Bench Memorandum, *Carmona v. Ward* (No. 78-5531), September 1979, pp. 15–16, Papers of Justice Byron White, Library of Congress.

14. 439 U.S. at 1098 (Marshall, J., dissenting).

15. *Rummel v. Estelle*, 445 U.S. 263 (1980). Rummel presented an as-applied challenge to the Texas statute. The statute itself, in place for more than one hundred years and rarely enforced, was upheld in *Spencer v. Texas*, 385 U.S. 554 (1967).

16. Draft Concurrence for *Rummel v. Estelle*, undated, Papers of Justice Blackmun, Library of Congress.

17. See *Coker v. Georgia*, 433 U.S. 584 (1977).

18. *Rummel*, 445 U.S. at 281.

19. *Rummel*, 445 U.S. at 282 n27.

20. Clerk's Memo, *Rummel v. Estelle* 445 U.S. 263 (No. 78-6386), February 24, 1980, Papers of Justice Blackmun, Library of Congress (emphasis in original).

21. 454 U.S. 370 (1982).

22. *Davis*, 454 U.S. at 373–74 (emphasis added) (quotation omitted).

23. 463 U.S. 277 (1983).

24. S.D. Codified Laws §§ 24-14-1, 24-14-5, 24-15-4; S.D. Const. Art. IV, § 3.

25. Brief of Petitioner, *Solem v. Helm*, 463 U.S. 277 (No. 82-492), A-32, quoting a dissenting state court opinion.

26. Brief of Petitioner, *Solem*, 24.

27. Brief of Petitioner, *Solem*, 21.

28. Petition for Certiorari, *Solem v. Helm*, 463 U.S. 277 (No. 82-492), 9–10.

29. Bench Memorandum, *Solem v. Helm*, 463 U.S. 277 (No. 82-492), March 23, 1983, pp. 19–20, Papers of Justice Blackmun, Library of Congress.

30. Bench Memorandum, *Solem*, March 23, 1983, p. 18, Papers of Justice Blackmun, Library of Congress.

31. *Helm*, 463 U.S. at 300–301.

32. *California v. Ramos*, 463 U.S. 992 (1983).

33. *Helm*, 463 U.S. at 316 (Burger, J., dissenting).

34. Jonathan C. Aked, "*Solem v. Helm*: The Supreme Court Extends the Proportionality Requirement to Sentences of Imprisonment," *Wisconsin Law Review* (1984): 1401–30; and anticipating lower court interpretations, see Nancy Keir, "*Solem v. Helm*: Extending Judicial Review under the Cruel and Unusual Punishments Clause to Require 'Proportionality' of Prison Sentences," *Catholic University Law Review* 33, no. 2 (1984): 479–515

35. *Ex parte Hester*, 473 So.2d 1054 (Ala. 1985).

36. 501 U.S. 957 (1991).

37. Mich. Comp. Laws § 333.7401 et seq.

38. Harmelin was arguably a "mule," a person traffickers use to make deliveries—precisely the sort of person the bill's opponents urged would take the fall for drug kingpins, the purported targets. By 1989, 123 individuals were serving mandatory LWOP sentences under the 650-lifer law, some less culpable than Harmelin. John Castine, "Mandatory Terms Fall Short: Kingpins Are Rarely Snared as Once Hoped." *Detroit Free Press*, March 10, 1990, 1A.

39. Brief of Petitioner, *Harmelin v. Michigan*, 501 U.S. 957 (No. 89-7272), 32.

40. Brief of Petitioner, *Harmelin*, 33.

41. Brief for the United States, *Harmelin v. Michigan*, 501 U.S. 957 (No. 89-7272), 1, 2, 10–13.

42. *Harmelin*, 501 U.S. at 996, citations omitted.

43. *Harmelin v. Michigan*, 501 U.S. 957 (No. 89-7272), oral argument at 13:05, 19:55.

44. Brief for Washington Legal Foundation, *Harmelin v. Michigan*, 501 U.S. 957 (No. 89-7272), 16–17.

45. Phillips and Grattet, "Judicial Rhetoric, Meaning Making," 568. Phillips and Grattet identify two elements of meaning making in judicial decisions: "construct elaboration" and "domain expansion" (578–82, 582–85). The first has to do with tailoring the definition of the concept, the latter with the reach or "the range of behaviors subsumed within a legal construct" (578). See Jenness, "Emergence, Content, and Institutionalization"; and B. Robert Owens, "Judicial Decision Making as Knowledge Work," *Law & Social Inquiry* 41, no. 2 (2016): 502–21.

46. The relation between LWOP and long fixed terms continues to trouble the Court's jurisprudence. The Court has swiveled, at times emphasizing

LWOP's similarity to long fixed terms, as in *Harmelin*, and at times emphasizing LWOP's unique severity as a means of distinguishing long fixed terms, as in *Ewing v. California*, 538 U.S. 11 (2003) and *Lockyer v. Andrade*, 538 U.S. 63 (2003), upholding twenty-five-year mandatory minimum sentences imposed under California's three strikes law.

CHAPTER 8. ABOLITION AND THE ALTERNATIVE

1. See Carol Steiker and Jordan Steiker, "The Death Penalty and Mass Incarceration: Convergences and Divergences," *American Journal of Criminal Law* 41, no. 2 (2014): 189–207; Franklin E. Zimring and David T. Johnson, "The Dark at the Top of the Stairs: Four Destructive Influences of Capital Punishment on American Criminal Justice," in *The Oxford Handbook of Sentencing and Corrections*, ed. Joan Petersilia and Kevin Reitz (New York: Oxford University Press, 2012), 737–52; and Note, "A Matter of Life and Death: The Effect of Life-without-Parole Statutes on Capital Punishment," *Harvard Law Review* 119, no. 6 (2006): 1838–54. For historical perspective on the use of LWOP in capital statutes, see Keith Harries and Derral Cheatwood, *The Geography of Execution* (Lanham, MD: Rowman & Littlefield, 1997); Julian Wright, "Life-without-Parole: An Alternative to Death or Not Much of a Life at All?," *Vanderbilt Law Review* 43, no. 2 (1990): 529–68; and Derral Cheatwood, "The Life-without-Parole Sanction: Its Current Status and a Research Agenda," *Crime & Delinquency* 34, no. 1 (1988): 43–59.

2. For a representative statement, see American Civil Liberties Union of Northern California, *The Truth about Life without Parole: Condemned to Die in Prison*, September 25, 2013, www.aclunc.org/article/truth-about -life-without-parole-condemned-die-prison: "The death penalty costs more, delivers less, and puts innocent lives at risk. Life without parole provides swift, severe, and certain punishment. It provides justice to survivors of murder victims and allows more resources to be invested into solving other murders and preventing violence. Sentencing people to die in prison is the sensible alternative for public safety and murder victims' families."

3. For example, Michael Meltsner, "The Dilemmas of Excessive Sentencing: Death May Be Different but How Different?," *Northeastern University Law Journal* 7, no. 1 (2015): 5–19.

4. As Carol Steiker and Jordan Steiker write, "At least some of the steep decline in death sentences since 2000 is a result of the availability of LWOP, though it is unclear just how much." *Courting Death: The Supreme Court and Capital Punishment* (Cambridge, MA: Belknap Press, 2016), 297. See also Michelle Miao, "Replacing Death with Life? The Rise of LWOP in the Contemporary Abolitionist Campaigns in the United States," *Northwestern Journal of Law & Social Policy*, 15, no. 2 (2020): 173–223.

5. Cesare Beccaria, "On Crimes and Punishments," in *On Crimes and Punishments and Other Writings*, ed. Aaron Thomas (1764; Toronto: University

of Toronto Press, 2008), 1–86; and Benjamin Rush, *An Enquiry into the Effects of Public Punishments upon Criminals and upon Society* (Philadelphia: Society for Social Inquiry, 1787).

6. Thorsten Sellin, "Beccaria's Substitute for the Death Penalty," in *Criminology in Perspective: Essays in Honor of Israel Drapkin*, ed. Simha Landau and Leslie Sebba (Lexington, MA: Lexington Books, 1977), 3–9; see also Hugo Bedau, "Imprisonment vs. Death: Does Avoiding Schwarzschild's Paradox Lead to Sheleff's Dilemma?," *Albany Law Review* 54, nos. 3–4 (1989): 485; and Dirk van Zyl Smit, *Taking Life Imprisonment Seriously: In National and International Law* (Norwell, MA: Kluwer Law International, 2002), 7.

7. I rely on materials from the premier archival collection of death penalty papers: the National Death Penalty Archive in the M. E. Grenander Department of Special Collections and Archives of the University Libraries at the State University of New York at Albany. Three collections were most important: the Hugo A. Bedau Papers, the Capital Jury Project Records, and the David von Drehle Papers. These materials include public papers and private correspondence; letters and memoranda; personal notes; pamphlets; conference agendas; state and regional newspapers and bar journals; and litigation documents including case decisions, oral arguments, and legal briefs. The papers of Hugo Bedau, a philosopher actively involved in abolition efforts from the 1950s onward, provide a wealth of information on movement strategy and its members' internal thought processes as well as a reservoir of official statements. The Capital Jury Project is a broad-based research program investigating jury decisions in capital cases. I focus on its correspondence, which engaged with many members of the ADP movement. Journalist David von Drehle covered the death penalty in Florida in the 1980s, a pivotal moment of change in abolition strategies. His notes from interviews with capital defense advocates and criminal justice professionals provide a rich source of information on death penalty practice and sentiments about that practice among professionals. Surprisingly, few published works on capital punishment, and none on LWOP, have relied on these resources.

8. Jeffrey Olick, *In the House of the Hangman: The Agonies of German Defeat, 1943–1949* (Chicago: University of Chicago Press, 2005).

9. A number of quality histories exist of the contemporary anti–death penalty movement. See, for example, Herbert Haines, *Against Capital Punishment: The Anti-Death Penalty Movement in America: 1972–1994* (New York: Oxford University Press, 1996); and Evan J. Manderey, *A Wild Justice* (New York: W. W. Norton, 2013). For excellent concise accounts, see Carol Steiker and Jordan Steiker, "Opening a Window or Building a Wall? The Effect of Eighth Amendment Death Penalty Law and Advocacy on Criminal Justice More Broadly," *University of Pennsylvania Journal of Constitutional Law* 11, no. 1 (2008): 155–205; Marie Gottschalk, *The Prison and the Gallows: The Politics of Mass Incarceration in America* (New York: Cambridge University Press, 2006); and Austin Sarat, "New Abolitionism and the Possibilities of Legislative Action," *Ohio State Law Journal* 63, no. 1 (2002): 343–60. On the history of the litigation leading

to *Furman*, see especially Michael Meltsner, *Cruel and Unusual: The Supreme Court and Capital Punishment* (New York: Morrow, 1974); and Burton H. Wolfe, *Pileup on Death Row* (New York: Doubleday, 1973). A selection of litigation histories written by capital defense attorneys can be found in John Blume and Jordan Steiker, *Death Penalty Stories* (St. Paul, MN: West Academic, 2009).

Most histories of modern ADP efforts have little to say about LWOP one way or another, and those that do track a narrative that this book problematizes—namely, the claim that abolition efforts in the early 1970s spurred a flood of LWOP statutes. The most engaged discussion of LWOP in prior work on the ADP movement is found in sociologist Herbert Haines's *Against Capital Punishment*. Haines, a scholar of social movements, was most concerned with how actors in the anti–death penalty movement used issue framing to achieve certain aims. Relying on interviews with activists, scholars, and lawyers involved in fighting the death penalty, he looked in detail (over a span of ten to fifteen pages) at the way actors in the ADP movement perceived and utilized LWOP. Haines's book, one of the death penalty literature's more probing works, has a different focus than mine: a social movement rather than the emergence of a punishment. Further, my account begins in the 1960s and ends in the mid-1990s, where Haines's study is situated.

10. Stuart Banner, *The Death Penalty: An American History* (Cambridge, MA: Harvard University Press, 2002), 110.

11. Haines, *Against Capital Punishment*, 44; and Manderey, *Wild Justice*, 280. See Lee Epstein and Joseph F. Kobylka, *The Supreme Court and Legal Change: Abortion and the Death Penalty* (Chapel Hill: University of North Carolina Press, 1992); and Eric Muller, "The Legal Defense Fund's Capital Punishment Campaign: The Distorting Influence of Death," *Yale Law and Policy Review* 4, no. 1 (1985): 158–67.

12. See Gottschalk, *Prison and the Gallows*, chapters 8 and 9.

13. Meltsner, *Cruel and Unusual*; and Sheldon Ekland-Olson, *Who Lives, Who Dies, Who Decides?* (New York: Routledge, 2012).

14. Meltsner, *Cruel and Unusual*.

15. Meltsner, *Cruel and Unusual*; and Wolfe, *Pileup on Death Row*.

16. Meltsner, "Dilemmas of Excessive Sentencing," 7.

17. 428 U.S. 262 (1976); 428 U.S. 242 (1976); 428 U.S. 325 (1976); and 428 U.S. 280 (1976).

18. Brief for Petitioner, *Gregg v. Georgia*, 428 U.S. 153 (1976) (No. 74-6257).

19. Brief of Respondent, *Proffitt v. Florida*, 428 U.S. 242 (1976) (No. 75-5706), 25.

20. A *New York Times* article in June 1974, for example, included an advertisement for Barbara Walters's morning show *Not for Women Only*, which asked: "Would the death penalty save lives? A 'life sentence' is usually 15 to 20 years. Would reinstating the death sentence be a deterrent to our soaring crime rate? Crime specialists and Senators debate the pros and cons." Hugo A. Bedau Papers, Series 2, box 1, folder 1.

21. *Woodson v. North Carolina*, 428 U.S. 280 (No. 75-5491), oral argument at 25:42.

22. *Woodson* argument at 26:32.

23. *Woodson* argument at 26:32.

24. *Woodson* argument at 26:32.

25. *Woodson* argument at 27:07.

26. *Woodson* argument at 27:07.

27. NAACP Legal Defense and Educational Fund, Inc., Transcript: 1977 Death Penalty Conference, Howard University, Hugo A. Bedau Papers, Series 1, box 6.

28. Gottschalk, *Prison and the Gallows*.

29. Letter from Hugo Bedau to Elliott Currie, March 14, 1973, Bedau Papers, Series 2, box 2, folder 43; see also planning memoranda, Bedau Papers, Series 3, box 4. This is especially so when one compares US strategizing to the ADP organizing going on abroad. For instance, at the Amnesty International Campaign for Abolition of the Death Penalty meeting convened in Stockholm in 1977, a working group was tasked specifically with "alternatives to the death penalty." Amnesty International, Report of Working Group B: Alternatives to the Death Penalty, Bedau Papers, Series 3, box 6, folder 19.

30. *Woodson* argument at 28:05; and Douglas C. Rigg, "The Penalty Worse Than Death," *Saturday Evening Post*, August 31, 1957.

31. *Woodson* argument at 28:05, 28:25.

32. Jacques Barzun, "In Favor of Capital Punishment," in *The Death Penalty in America*, ed. Hugo Bedau (New York: Oxford University Press, 1964), 158.

33. Barzun, "In Favor of Capital Punishment," 162.

34. Barzun, "In Favor of Capital Punishment," 161.

35. Barzun, "In Favor of Capital Punishment," 161.

36. Barzun, "In Favor of Capital Punishment," 163.

37. Hugo Bedau, *The Death Penalty in America* (New York: Oxford University Press, 1964), 231.

38. Bedau, *Death Penalty in America*, 403.

39. Bedau, *Death Penalty in America*.

40. See Banner, *Death Penalty*, 110.

41. Bedau, *Death Penalty in America*, 214.

42. Leon Sheleff pressed the point years later: "The most generally offered alternative is of life imprisonment, but very rarely is any effort made to probe the full import of such a sentence." *Ultimate Penalties: Capital Punishment, Life Imprisonment, Physical Torture* (Columbus: Ohio State University Press, 1987), 43.

43. Memorandum from Jack Himmelstein to participants in Legal Defense Fund, November 14, 1972, Minutes of October 7, 1972, Capital Punishment Meeting, Bedau Papers, Series 3, box 4, folder 3.

44. In notes from another meeting on organizing the social science research agenda, Bedau lists "alternatives to c.p." as number 9 of 10 topics for discussion. "We talked least about 7 through 10," he wrote. "Still, all ten categories

were helpful to have out in the open right at the start." Bedau to Currie, March 14, 1973.

45. Letter from Hugo Bedau to Anthony Amsterdam, July 7, 1973, Bedau Papers, Series 1, box 1, folder 1.

46. Antonio Canales, "Texan Gets 10,000 Years as Sentence for Murder," *New York Times*, May 16, 1973.

47. Bedau to Amsterdam, July 7, 1973.

48. Letter from Anthony Amsterdam to Howard Sacks, June 27, 1973, Bedau Papers, Series 2, box 1, folder 1. The bill was CB 1651. See Connecticut General Assembly, Office of Legislative Research, *Capital Punishments in Connecticut after Furman v. Georgia* (Hartford: Connecticut General Assembly, 1973).

49. Letter from Anthony Amsterdam to Stephana Landwehr, January 3, 1986, Bedau Papers, Series 4, box 3, folder 14.

50. Amsterdam to Landwehr, January 3, 1986 (emphases in original).

51. Letter from Anthony Amsterdam to Hugo Bedau, August 1, 1973, Bedau Papers, Series 2, box 2.

52. Hugo Bedau, *Killing as Punishment: Reflections on the Death Penalty in America* (Lebanon, NH: University Press of New England, 2004), 86.

53. Mark Lane, "Is There Life without Parole? A Capital Defendant's Right to a Meaningful Alternative Sentence," *Loyola of Los Angeles Law Review* 26, no. 2 (1992): 327–93; compare Death Penalty Information Center, *Year States Adopted Life without Parole (LWOP) Sentencing*, August 2, 2010, https://deathpenaltyinfo.org/year-states-adopted-life-without-parole-lwop-sentencing.

54. Robert Weisberg, "Deregulating Death," *Supreme Court Review* (1983): 305–95.

55. David von Drehle, *Among the Lowest of the Dead* (New York: Times Books, 1995).

56. Ekland-Olson, *Who Lives, Who Dies, Who Decides?*

57. See Fay Joyce, "Georgia Man Becomes Second Executed in 2 Days," *New York Times*, December 16, 1983.

58. David von Drehle, "Capital Punishment in Paralysis: Huge Caseload Bloats Lethargic, Costly System in Florida," *Miami Herald*, July 10, 1988.

59. Haines, *Against Capital Punishment*, 72.

60. Letter from Henry Schwarzschild to Ira Glasser, October 28, 1983, Bedau Papers, Series 2, box 2. The ACLU Capital Punishment Project was created in 1976 to help organize and consolidate abolition efforts nationally.

61. Schwarzschild to Glasser, October 28, 1983.

62. David Bruck, "Public Presentation of the Abolitionist Position," *Lifelines* 9 (1984): 1–3; Robert Johnson, "A Life for a Life?," *Justice Quarterly* 1, no. 4 (1986): 574–80; and Haines, *Against Capital Punishment*, 137.

63. David Bruck, "Simmons v. South Carolina and the Myth of Early Release," in *Death Penalty Stories*, ed. John H. Blume and Jordan Steiker (New York: Foundation Press, 2009).

64. Bruck, "Simmons v. South Carolina," 365.

65. Johnson, "A Life for a Life," 577.

66. Johnson, "A Life for a Life," 577–78. Other death penalty opponents were more frankly equivocal. The California Attorneys for Criminal Justice (CACJ), for example, provided in a policy statement that "because we consider the death penalty to be a greater evil than life without possibility of parole we would accept the use of life without possibility of parole at this time *if* to do so would end the use of the death penalty." "Life Without Possibility of Parole," 1990, Bedau Papers, Series 4, box 3, folder 14.

67. Johnson, "A Life for a Life"; see Bruck, "Public Presentation of the Abolitionist Position," 9.

68. Johnson, "A Life for a Life," 579.

69. Haines, *Against Capital Punishment*, 216n49.

70. Haines, *Against Capital Punishment*, 138.

71. Amnesty International USA, "Attitudes in the State of Florida on the Death Penalty: Executive Summary of a Public Opinion Survey," 1986, Capital Jury Project Records, Series 7, box 1, folder 14.

72. Von Drehle, "Capital Punishment in Paralysis." See also David von Drehle, interview notes, David von Drehle Papers, box 7, folders 4–6.

73. David von Drehle, "Life in Prison One-Sixth as Expensive," *Miami Herald*, July 10, 1988.

74. David von Drehle, "Cries for Change: Both Sides See Flaws in Capital Punishment," *Miami Herald*, July 13, 1988.

75. Von Drehle, "Cries for Change."

76. Ross Immarigeon, "Instead of Death: Alternatives to Capital Punishment," *National Prison Project Journal* (Summer 1990); and Haines, *Against Capital Punishment*. For discussion of the shift in focus from the court of law to the "court of public opinion," see Manderey, *Wild Justice*; Gottschalk, *Prison and the Gallows*; and Sarat, "New Abolitionism."

77. Immarigeon, "Instead of Death."

78. Haines, *Against Capital Punishment*, 98–99.

79. Haines, *Against Capital Punishment*, 99.

80. Mary Leary, "The LWOP Alternative: Public Favors Life in Prison," *Los Angeles Daily Journal*, April 24, 1992.

81. Richard Dieter, *Is America Ready? Alternatives to the Death Penalty* (Washington, DC: Death Penalty Information Center, January 1993), Capital Jury Project Records, Series 4, box 1, folder 17; see also Richard Dieter, *Sentencing for Life: Americans Embrace Alternatives to the Death Penalty* (Washington, DC: Death Penalty Information Center, April 1993).

82. Dieter, *Is America Ready?*, 11.

83. Dieter, *Is America Ready?*, 1–2; and Dieter, *Sentencing for Life*, 3.

84. Dieter, *Is America Ready?*, 1–2; see also Dieter, *Sentencing for Life*, 8.

85. Dieter, *Sentencing for Life*.

86. See Marie Gottschalk, "No Way Out? Life Sentences and the Politics of Penal Reform," in *Life without Parole: America's New Death Penalty?*, ed.

Charles Ogletree and Austin Sarat (New York: New York University Press, 2012), 231: "The prevalence of LWOP as an alternative sanction has increased markedly since the mid-1990s, when it was available in only sixteen death-penalty jurisdictions."

87. While most South Carolina lawmakers and law enforcement opposed LWOP because they thought it would undercut death sentencing, victims' rights advocates wanted the security LWOP provided as an alternative capital sentence. See Bruck, "Simmons v. South Carolina," 361. In 1986, the South Carolina victims' movement received a partial victory when LWOP was made available for capital defendants with a prior violent crime conviction. LWOPs first appearance in South Carolina, then, was not the result of death penalty abolition work, but of victims' advocates' efforts. Compare the adoption of LWOP in Texas in 2005. See Dave Michaels, "House Votes to End Capital Murder Parole: Move Called Victory for Victims; Death Penalty Proponents Concerned," *Dallas Morning News*, May 25, 2005.

88. See Letter from Jonathan Gradess to Richard Dieter, January 7, 1993, Capital Jury Project Records, Series 4, box 1, folder 32.

89. Mario Cuomo, "New York Shouldn't Kill People," *New York Times*, June 17, 1989.

90. Elizabeth Kolbert, "As Vote on Death Penalty Nears, Cuomo Advocates Life Sentences," *New York Times*, June 19, 1989.

91. See conference agendas in Bedau Papers, Series 2, box 3, folder 6; and in Bill Pelke Papers, 1965–2005, Series 5, box 1, folder 21.

92. Gradess to Dieter, January 7, 1993.

93. Culhane did not profess to have rehabilitated through any unique ability or effort. His point was that all prisoners have a chance to reform and the law should not foreclose this: "The variables that play a part in what happens to a life should not be stacked in favor of death (as with the death penalty) or with spiritual destruction (as can easily happen with life without parole), but in favor of life and possibility."

94. William Bowers and Margaret Vandiver, "New Yorkers Want an Alternative to the Death Penalty," April 5, 1991, Capital Jury Project Records, Series 7, box 12, folder 20.

95. Letter from Jonathan Gradess to Leigh Dingerson, Kica Matos, and Diann Rust-Tierney, February 4, 1993, Capital Jury Project Records, Series 4, Subseries 1, box 1, folder 22. See also Haines, *Against Capital Punishment*, 138, interviewing Dieter and discussing controversy over the circulated draft of the 1993 report.

96. Put another way, turning to LWOP was a "solidaristic reaction"—a means to reinforce beliefs that members of the movement held in common (e.g., capital punishment is morally wrong), which events from *Gregg* onward had disturbed. See David Garland, "Punishment and Social Solidarity," in *The SAGE Handbook of Punishment and Society*, ed. Jonathan Simon and Richard Sparks (London: Sage, 2013), 25. For more, see Haines, *Against Capital*

Punishment, whose account of the dynamics of the ADP movement in the 1990s is corroborated here with additional archival support.

97. Haines, *Against Capital Punishment,* 194.

98. Haines, *Against Capital Punishment,* 16.

99. The ADP decision to forcefully advocate LWOP was also buttressed by the *Harmelin* decision, discussed in the previous chapter. The ruling, signaling that LWOP was fair game for a wide range of crimes, surely was not lost on DPIC staff.

100. Among those other factors, the US Supreme Court in 1994 finally decided an issue—long contested in the courtroom and a focus of extensive research—about what jurors should know of the alternative to a death sentence (specifically, whether it allowed parole). See Bruck, "Simmons v. South Carolina," discussing *Simmons v South Carolina,* 512 U.S. 154 (1994); see generally John Blume, Stephen P. Garvey, and Sheri Lynn Johnson, "Future Dangerousness in Capital Cases: Always at Issue," *Cornell Law Review* 86, no. 2 (2000): 397–410.

CHAPTER 9. LIFE PRISONERS, LIFETIME PRISONS

1. The decision to build prisons is not for the legislature alone, nor is it one in which departments of corrections are the only stakeholders. The electorate also has a voice, as do local interests at the sites of new prisons. James Jacobs, "The Politics of Prison Expansion," *NYU Review of Law and Social Change* 12, no. 1 (1983–1984): 209–43; see also John Eason, *Big House on the Prairie: Rise of the Rural Ghetto and Prison Proliferation* (Chicago: University of Chicago Press, 2017).

2. Ruth W. Gilmore, *Golden Gulag: Prisons, Surplus, Crisis, and Opposition in Globalizing California* (Berkeley: University of California Press, 2007); Mona Lynch, *Sunbelt Justice: Arizona and the Transformation of American Punishment* (Stanford, CA: Stanford University Press, 2010); Robert Perkinson, *Texas Tough: The Rise of a Prison Empire* (New York: Metropolitan Books, 2010); Eason, *Big House*; and Heather Schoenfeld, *Building the Prison State: Race and the Politics of Mass Incarceration* (Chicago: University of Chicago Press, 2018).

3. Heather Schoenfeld, "Mass Incarceration and the Paradox of Prison Conditions Litigation," *Law & Society Review* 44, nos. 3/4 (2010): 731–67.

4. Joshua Page, *The "Toughest Beat": Politics, Punishment, and the Prison Officers' Union in California* (New York: Oxford University Press, 2011); and Keramet Reiter, *23/7: Pelican Bay Prison and the Rise of Long-Term Solitary Confinement* (New Haven: Yale University Press, 2016).

5. Jim Stewart and Paul Lieberman, "What Is This New Sentence That Takes Away Parole?," *Student Lawyer* 11 (1982): 15.

6. Stewart and Lieberman, "What Is This New Sentence?," 39.

7. See Stewart and Lieberman, "What Is This New Sentence?," 39.

8. Stewart and Lieberman, "What Is This New Sentence?," 17.

9. Stewart and Lieberman, "What Is This New Sentence?," 16.

10. Derral Cheatwood, "The Life-without-Parole Sanction: Its Current Status and a Research Agenda," *Crime & Delinquency* 34, no. 1 (1988): 54–55.

11. Stewart and Lieberman, "What Is This New Sentence?," 17.

12. Stewart and Lieberman, "What Is This New Sentence?," 17.

13. Stewart and Lieberman, "What Is This New Sentence?," 16, 17, reporting a member of the Georgia legislature, criticizing life without parole sentencing in 1982, warned it "would turn a prison warden into a game warden."

14. On the life course as experienced under a life sentence, see Ben Crewe, Susie Hulley, and Serena Wright, *Life Imprisonment from Young Adulthood* (London: Palgrave Macmillan UK, 2020); and Margaret Leigey, *The Forgotten Men: Serving a Life without Parole Sentence* (New Brunswick, NJ: Rutgers University Press, 2015). On the life course experiences of women serving life sentences, see, for example, the sources cited in chapter 6, note 34.

15. Stewart and Lieberman, "What Is This New Sentence?," 16.

16. Steve Herbert, *Too Easy to Keep: Life-Sentenced Prisoners and the Future of Mass Incarceration* (Oakland: University of California Press, 2018).

17. Timothy J. Flanagan, "Correctional Policy and the Long-Term Prisoner," *Crime & Delinquency* 28, no. 1 (1982): 82–95; Robert Johnson and Ann Dobrzanska, "Mature Coping among Life-Sentenced Inmates: An Exploratory Study of Adjustment Dynamics," *Corrections Compendium* 30, no. 6 (2005): 8–9; and John Irwin, *Lifers: Seeking Redemption in Prison* (New York: Routledge, 2017); see also Wilbert Rideau and Ron Wikberg, *Life Sentences: Rage and Survival Behind Bars* (New York: New York Times Books, 1992). Misconduct by people serving LWOP and virtual life sentences most often occurs early in the sentence. Crewe, Hulley, and Wright, *Life Imprisonment from Young Adulthood*; and Leigey, *Forgotten Men*.

18. See Cheatwood, "Life-without-Parole Sanction."

19. Lila Kazemian and Jeremy Travis, "Imperative for Inclusion of Long Termers and Lifers in Research and Policy," *Criminology and Public Policy* 14, no. 2 (2015): 355–95.

20. Donald MacDonald and Leonard Morgenbesser, *Life without Parole Statutes in the United States* (New York State Department of Correctional Services, Division of Program Planning Research and Evaluation, 1984), 4 (emphasis added).

21. Stewart and Lieberman, "What Is This New Sentence?," 16–17.

22. Stewart and Lieberman, "What Is This New Sentence?"; and Doris Schartmeuller, "Settling Down behind Bars: The Extensive Use of Life Sentences in Alabama," *Prison Journal* 95, no. 4 (2015): 449–71.

23. Dennis L. Peck and Ron Jones, "The High Cost of Alabama's Habitual Felony Offender Act: A Preliminary Assessment," *International Journal of Offender Therapy and Comparative Criminology* 29, no. 3 (1985): 251–64; and Robert Sigler and Concetta Culliver, "Consequences of the Habitual Offender

Act on the Costs of Operating Alabama's Prisons," *Federal Probation* 52, no. 2 (1988): 57–64.

24. See Rideau and Wikberg, *Life Sentences*, quoting Murray Henderson (warden from 1968–1975), Frank Blackburn (warden 1977–1981, 1984–1987), and R. Hilton Butler (warden 1987–1989).

25. Lynch, *Sunbelt Justice*, 144.

26. Schoenfeld, *Building the Prison State*, 82, 98. See Jacobs, "Politics of Prison Expansion," 210: "Why and when does the Department leadership decide that prison capacity must be increased?" Probably, Jacobs answered, only after lobbying unsuccessfully for "reduction of the number of prisoners through emergency release mechanisms, liberalized good time, accelerated parole, or sentencing reform" (215).

27. "Florida's 'Willie Horton,'" *Miami Herald*, November 30, 1988.

28. "A Punishing State of Affairs," *St. Petersburg Times*, January 1, 1989, 2D.

29. "Shutting the Back Door," *St. Petersburg Times*, January 3, 1989, 18A.

30. "Time to Get Tough with Violent Offenders," *St. Petersburg Times*, January 4, 1989, 2. See also the editorial series published in the *Orlando Sentinel* in August 1989 on early release policy (discussed in Schoenfeld, *Building the Prison State*, 130–31).

31. Florida House of Representatives, Committee on Criminal Justice, February 8, 1989, Series 414, box 907, Florida State Library and Archive; see also Florida House of Representatives, floor debate, May 25, 1989, Record Group 925, Series 38, box 98. Citations to Florida legislative meetings, hearings, and floor debates in this chapter refer to audio recordings preserved at the Florida State Library and Archive.

32. Committee on Criminal Justice, February 8, 1989.

33. Committee on Criminal Justice, February 8, 1989.

34. Committee on Criminal Justice, February 8, 1989.

35. Committee on Criminal Justice, February 8, 1989.

36. Committee on Criminal Justice, February 8, 1989.

37. Schoenfeld, *Building the Prison State*. In *Sunbelt Justice*, Mona Lynch chronicles similar circumstances in Arizona.

38. Florida Department of Corrections, Annual Reports. A similar shift happened nationally at the same time. See generally Bruce Western, *Punishment and Inequality in America* (New York: Russell Sage Foundation, 2006). Note, however, that scholars find much racial disparity in prison populations established prior to the 1970s as well. See Christopher Muller, "Northward Migration and the Rise of Racial Disparity in American Incarceration, 1880–1950," *American Journal of Sociology* 118, no. 2 (2012): 281–326.

39. Schoenfeld, *Building the Prison State*, 154.

40. As Jacobs recognizes, the "decision to expand prison facilities involves more than just whether to build or not to build" ("Politics of Prison Expansion," 216–17); it involves questions of what types of institutions to build and whether to renovate and adapt existing buildings or create new ones. I focus here simply on the former decision.

41. Jonathan Simon, *Governing through Crime: How the War on Crime Transformed American Democracy and Created a Culture of Fear* (New York: Oxford University Press, 2007), 155–58.

42. Loïc Wacquant, *Punishing the Poor: The Neoliberal Government of Social Insecurity* (Durham, NC: Duke University Press, 2009).

43. Lynch, *Sunbelt Justice*, 116–21, 140–43.

44. Gilmore, *Golden Gulag*.

45. See David Garland's discussion of "acting out" in *The Culture of Control: Crime and Social Order in Contemporary Society* (Chicago: University of Chicago Press, 2001), 131–35.

46. Joshua Guetzgow and Eric Schoon, "If You Built It, They Will Fill It: The Consequences of Prison Overcrowding Litigation," *Law & Society Review* 49, no. 2 (2015): 407.

47. Lynch, *Sunbelt Justice*, 112.

48. Schoenfeld, *Building the Prison State*, 98–100. See also Gilmore, *Golden Gulag*; and Eason, *Big House*, concerning the overcoming of resistance to prison building in *rural* sites.

49. Macdonald and Morgenbesser, *Life without Parole Statutes*; and Kathleen Maguire, Ann L. Pastore, and Timothy J. Flanagan, *Sourcebook of Criminal Justice Statistics* (Washington, DC: Bureau of Justice Statistics, 1992).

50. Schoenfeld, *Building the Prison State*, 120, 124–25.

51. Florida Senate, Committee on Criminal Justice, January 24, 1995, Record Group 900, Series 625, box 471.

52. Schoenfeld, *Building the Prison State*, 150–56.

53. Florida Senate, Committee on Criminal Justice, January 24, 1995, Record Group 900, Series 625, box 471.

54. Perry Johnson, "Colloquium," *NYU Review of Law and Social Change* 12 (1983–1984): 249–52.

55. See Janet Roitman, *Anti-Crisis* (Durham, NC: Duke University Press, 2014), and the related discussion in chapter 3.

56. E. Ann Carson and William Sabol, *Aging of the State Prison Population, 1993–2013* (Washington, DC: Bureau of Justice Statistics, 2016); and E. Ann Carson, *Mortality in State and Federal Prisons, 2001–2018* (Washington, DC: Bureau of Justice Statistics, 2021).

57. See Lauren Porter et al., "How the US Prison Boom Has Changed the Age Distribution of the Prison Population," *Criminology* 54, no. 1 (2016): 30–55.

CONCLUSION

1. Philip Goodman, Joshua Page, and Michelle Phelps, *Breaking the Pendulum: The Long Struggle Over Criminal Justice* (New York: Oxford University Press, 2017).

2. Ashley Rubin, "A Neo-Institutional Account of Prison Diffusion," *Law and Society Review* 49, no. 2 (2015): 365–400.

3. David Garland, "Penality and the Penal State," *Criminology* 51, no. 3 (2013): 475–517; and Mona Lynch, "Mass Incarceration, Legal Change, and Locale," *Criminology & Public Policy* 10 (2011): 673–98; see also Michael C. Campbell, "Politics, Prisons, and Law Enforcement: An Examination of the Emergence of 'Law and Order' Politics in Texas," *Law & Society Review* 45, no. 3 (2011): 631–65; and Heather Schoenfeld, *Building the Prison State: Race and the Politics of Mass Incarceration* (Chicago: University of Chicago Press, 2018).

4. David Garland and Peter Young, *The Power to Punish* (London: Heinemann, 1983), 21.

5. A classic example of how penal actors change the ways in which they think about things and, over time, their underlying assumptions about crime and punishment, is David Garland's *Punishment and Welfare: A History of Penal Strategies* (Aldershot, UK: Gower, 1985), a study of the transformation in Britain's approach to social and penal policy during the nineteenth century. The account reveals not only the development of new laws and policies, but also the emergence of new ways of conceiving of free will, criminality, and the role of state punishment, which were pragmatically organized and reorganized in relation to state practices.

6. Matthew Norton, "Classification and Coercion: The Destruction of Piracy in the English Maritime System," *American Journal of Sociology* 119, no. 6 (2014): 1537–75; and James Willis, "Transportation versus Imprisonment in Eighteenth and Nineteenth Century Britain: Penal Power, Liberty, and the State," *Law & Society Review* 39, no.1 (2005): 171–210.

7. Gabriel Abend, "Making Things Possible," *Sociological Methods & Research* 51, no. 1 (2020): 68–107; see also Gabriel Abend, *The Moral Background: An Inquiry into the History of Business Ethics* (Princeton, NJ: Princeton University Press, 2014).

8. See Andreas Glaeser, *Political Epistemics: The Secret Police, the Opposition, and the End of East German Socialism* (Chicago: University of Chicago Press, 2011).

9. Mary Douglas, *How Institutions Think* (Syracuse, NY: Syracuse University Press, 1986), 76–77, 90.

10. Émile Durkheim, *The Elementary Forms of Religious Life* (1915; New York: The Free Press, 1965), 486.

11. Douglas, *How Institutions Think*, 90.

12. Kevin Reitz and Edward Rhine, "Parole Release and Supervision: Critical Drivers of American Prison Policy," *Annual Review of Criminology* 3 (2020): 281–98; see also Marc Mauer and Ashley Nellis, *The Meaning of Life: The Case for Abolishing Life Sentences* (New York: The New Press, 2017), 33.

13. Nazgol Ghandnoosh, *Delaying a Second Chance: The Declining Prospects for Parole on Life Sentences* (Washington, DC: The Sentencing Project, 2017).

14. Ashley Nellis, *Still Life: America's Increasing Use of Life and Long-Term Sentences* (Washington, DC: The Sentencing Project, 2017), 23.

15. Kevin Reitz emphasizes that "changes in parole practices were a major contributor to US prison growth in the late-twentieth and early twenty-first centuries." "American Exceptionalism in Crime and Punishment: Broadly Defined," in *American Exceptionalism in Crime and Punishment*, ed. Kevin R. Reitz (New York: Oxford University Press, 2018), 11.

16. Jonathan Simon, "Dignity and Risk: The Long Road from *Graham v. Florida* to Abolition of Life without Parole," in *Life without Parole: America's New Death Penalty?*, ed. Charles Ogletree and Austin Sarat (New York: New York University Press, 2012), 293–94; Sharon Dolovich, "Creating the Permanent Prisoner," in *Life without Parole*, ed. Ogletree and Sarat, 110–11; and Hadar Aviram, *Yesterday's Monsters* (Oakland: University of California Press, 2020).

17. Franklin E. Zimring and David T. Johnson, "The Dark at the Top of the Stairs: Four Destructive Influences of Capital Punishment on American Criminal Justice," in *The Oxford Handbook of Sentencing and Corrections*, ed. Joan Petersilia and Kevin Reitz (New York: Oxford University Press, 2012), 747.

18. Melissa Hamilton, "Extreme Prison Sentences: Legal and Normative Consequences," *Cardozo Law Review* 38, no. 1 (2016): 59–120 (two hundred years); Glenn Schmitt and Hyun Konfrst, *Life Sentences in the Federal System* (Washington, DC: United States Sentencing Commission, 2015) (forty years); and Nellis, *Still Life* (fifty years).

19. Hamilton, "Extreme Prison Sentences."

20. See Michael Tonry, *Sentencing Fragments* (New York: Oxford University Press, 2016), 28.

21. Lila Kazemian and Jeremy Travis, "Imperative for Inclusion of Long Termers and Lifers in Research and Policy," *Criminology and Public Policy* 14, no. 2 (2015): 361.

22. See Zimring and Johnson, "Dark at the Top of the Stairs," 747.

23. Norton, "Classification and Coercion," 1548.

24. It follows from this, too, that institutions may stay on as rather empty rules, rituals, or practices, even after their original meanings have been lost or changed. One sees this, for example, with the role the myth of incorrigibility plays in the *Graham* case (chapter 3). On the influence of penal organizations and forms after they become institutionalized, see Ashley Rubin, "Punishment's Legal Templates: A Theory of Formal Penal Change," *Law & Society Review* 53, no. 2 (2019): 518–53.

25. Kathleen Maguire, Ann L. Pastore, and Timothy J. Flanagan, *Sourcebook of Criminal Justice Statistics* (Washington, DC: Bureau of Justice Statistics, 1992).

26. On the contribution of anti–death penalty activism on normalization of LWOP in California, particularly since the millennium, see Marion Vannier, "Normalizing Extreme Imprisonment: The Case of Life without Parole in California," *Theoretical Criminology* 25, no. 4 (2019): 519–39.

27. In this regard, LWOP acts in the manner of what Durkheim, in *Elementary Forms of Religious Life*, 236, referred to as an "emblem."

28. David Garland, *Punishment and Modern Society* (Chicago: University of Chicago Press, 1990), 54.

29. Michael Tonry, *Malign Neglect: Race, Crime, and Punishment in America* (New York: Oxford University Press, 1995), 209.

30. Tonry, *Malign Neglect*, 41.

31. Tonry, *Malign Neglect*, 182.

32. Simon, "Dignity and Risk"; and Jonathan Simon, *Mass Incarceration on Trial: A Remarkable Court Decision and the Future of Prisons in America* (New York: The New Press, 2014).

33. Marie Gottschalk, *The Prison and the Gallows: The Politics of Mass Incarceration in America* (Princeton, NJ: Princeton University Press, 2006), 4.

34. Tonry, *Malign Neglect*, 197.

35. See especially Simon, "Dignity and Risk"; Dolovich, "Creating the Permanent Prisoner"; Zimring and Johnson, "Dark at the Top of the Stairs"; and Evi Girling, "Sites of Crossing and Death in Punishment: The Parallel Trade-Offs and Equivalencies of the Death Penalty and Life without Parole in the US," *Howard Journal of Crime and Justice* 55, no. 3 (2016): 345–61.

36. David Garland, *The Culture of Control: Crime and Social Order in Contemporary Society* (Chicago: University of Chicago Press, 2001), 133.

37. Dolovich, "Creating the Permanent Prisoner," 96, 110.

38. Girling, "Sites of Crossing," 353.

39. Girling, "Sites of Crossing," 353.

40. Simon, "Dignity and Risk"; and Zimring and Johnson, "Dark at the Top of the Stairs."

41. Simon, "Dignity and Risk," 282.

42. Dolovich, "Creating the Permanent Prisoner," 125.

43. Dolovich, "Creating the Permanent Prisoner," 115; see also Loïc Wacquant, *Punishing the Poor: The Neoliberal Government of Social Insecurity* (Durham, NC: Duke University Press, 2009).

44. See Girling, "Sites of Crossing."

45. Before leaving office in 2018, California governor Jerry Brown commuted the sentences of 147 people serving LWOP, including 31 women. More than 5,000 people remain imprisoned under LWOP sentences in California.

46. Megan Comfort, *Doing Time Together: Love and Family in the Shadow of the Prison* (Chicago: University of Chicago Press, 2009).

47. Zimring and Johnson, "Dark at the Top of the Stairs," 741 (presumption of nonscrutiny); and Stanley Cohen, *Visions of Social Control: Crime, Punishment and Classification* (Cambridge, UK: Polity Press, 1985) (hard end).

48. See Christopher Seeds, "Bifurcation Nation: American Penal Policy in Late Mass Incarceration," *Punishment and Society* 19, no. 5 (2017): 590–610.

49. Girling, "Sites of Crossing," 355.

50. Dolovich, "Creating the Permanent Prisoner."

51. Garland argues that "the American death penalty has been transformed from a penal instrument that puts persons to death to a peculiar institution that puts death into discourse for political and cultural purposes." *Peculiar*

Institution: America's Death Penalty in an Age of Abolition (Cambridge, MA: Harvard Belknap Press, 2010), 312.

52. As Rachel Barkow notes, "How definitional questions of scope . . . are answered will be critical to the future of LWOP reform and of noncapital sentencing reform more generally." "Life without Parole and Hope for Real Sentencing Reform," in *Life without Parole: America's New Death Penalty?*, ed. Charles Ogletree and Austin Sarat (New York: New York University Press, 2012), 193.

53. Michel Foucault, "Against Replacement Penalties," in *Power: The Essential Works of Foucault, 1954–1984*, vol. 3, ed. J. D. Faubion (1981; New York: The New Press, 2000), 460.

54. Foucault, "Against Replacement Penalties," 460–61.

55. See also Marie Gottschalk, *Caught: The Prison State and the Lockdown of American Politics* (Princeton, NJ: Princeton University Press, 2015), 174.

56. Katherine Beckett, "The Politics, Promise, and Peril of Criminal Justice Reform in the Context of Mass Incarceration," *Annual Review of Criminology* 1 (2018): 235–59.

57. Gottschalk, *Caught*, 165–95; Beckett, "Politics, Promise, Peril"; and Seeds, "Bifurcation Nation."

58. Foucault, "Against Replacement Penalties," 461.

59. Foucault, "Against Replacement Penalties," 461.

60. Foucault, "Against Replacement Penalties," 461.

Bibliography

Articles from the following newspapers have been cited in the notes:
Dallas Morning News
Detroit Free Press
Florida Times-Union
Ironwood Daily Globe
Miami Herald
New York Times
Patriot News
St. Petersburg Times
The Times (London)

Abend, Gabriel. "Making Things Possible." *Sociological Methods & Research* 51, no. 1 (2020): 68–107.
———. *The Moral Background: An Inquiry into the History of Business Ethics.* Princeton, NJ: Princeton University Press, 2014.
Aked, Jonathan C. "*Solem v. Helm*: The Supreme Court Extends the Proportionality Requirement to Sentences of Imprisonment." *Wisconsin Law Review* (1984): 1401–30.
Alexander, Michelle. *The New Jim Crow: Mass Incarceration in the Age of Colorblindness.* New York: The New Press, 2010.
Allen, Frederick. *The Decline of the Rehabilitative Ideal: Penal Policy and Social Purpose.* New Haven, CT: Yale University Press, 1981.
Allen, Stephen, Samuel Hopkins, and George Tibbits. "Report." In *Journal of the State of New York.* Albany, NY: New York Legislature, 1825.
American Civil Liberties Union of Northern California. *The Truth about Life without Parole: Condemned to Die in Prison.* September 25, 2013. www.aclunc.org/article/truth-about-life-without-parole- condemned-die-prison.
American Friends Service Committee. *Struggle for Justice: A Report on Crime and Punishment in America.* New York: Hill & Wang, 1971.

Amsterdam, Anthony, and Jerome Bruner. *Minding the Law*. Cambridge, MA: Harvard University Press, 2000.

Anspach, Donald F., Peter M. Lehman, and John H. Kramer. *Maine Rejects Indeterminacy: A Case Study of Flat Sentencing and Parole Abolition*. Portland: University of Southern Maine, 1983.

Appleton, Catherine, and Bent Grøver. "The Pros and Cons of Life without Parole." *British Journal of Criminology* 47, no. 4 (2007): 597–615.

Austin, Regina. "The Saga of Pennsylvania's 'Willie Horton' and the Commutation of Life Sentences in the Commonwealth." University of Pennsylvania Law School, Public Law Research Paper, 2020.

Aviram, Hadar. *Yesterday's Monsters: The Manson Family Cases and the Illusion of Parole*. Oakland: University of California Press, 2020.

Ayers, Edward. *Vengeance and Justice: Crime and Punishment in the 19th-Century American South*. New York: Oxford University Press, 1984.

Bachelard, Gaston. *The New Scientific Spirit*. Boston: Beacon Press, 1986. First published 1938.

Baldus, David C., George Woodworth, David Zuckerman, and Neil Weiner. "Racial Discrimination and the Death Penalty in the Post-*Furman* Era." *Cornell Law Review* 83, no. 6 (1997): 1638–770.

Banner, Stuart. *The Death Penalty: An American History*. Cambridge, MA: Harvard University Press, 2002.

Barker, Vanessa. *The Politics of Imprisonment: How the Democratic Process Shapes the Way America Punishes Offenders*. New York: Oxford University Press, 2009.

Barkow, Rachel E. "The Ascent of the Administrative State and the Demise of Mercy." *Harvard Law Review* 121, no. 5 (2008): 1332–65.

———. "The Court of Life and Death: The Two Tracks of Constitutional Sentencing Law and the Case for Uniformity." *Michigan Law Review* 107, no. 7 (2009): 1145–205.

———. "Life without Parole and Hope for Real Sentencing Reform." In *Life without Parole: America's New Death Penalty?*, edited by Charles Ogletree and Austin Sarat, 190–226. New York: New York University Press, 2012.

Barnes, Harry Elmer, and Negley Teeters. *New Horizons in Criminology*. New York: Prentice Hall, 1952.

Barzun, Jacques. "In Favor of Capital Punishment." In *The Death Penalty in America*, edited by Hugo Bedau. New York: Oxford University Press, 1964.

Bauman, Zygmunt. "Social Uses of Law and Order." In *Criminology and Social Theory*, edited by David Garland and Richard Sparks, 23–46. Oxford: Oxford University Press, 2000.

Baumes, Caleb H. "The Baumes Laws and the Legislative Program in New York." 52 *A.B.A. Reporter* 52 (1927): 511–29.

Beccaria, Cesare. "On Crimes and Punishments." In *On Crimes and Punishments and Other Writings*, edited by Aaron Thomas. Toronto: University of Toronto Press, 2008. First published 1764.

Beckett, Katherine. *Making Crime Pay: Law and Order in Contemporary American Politics.* New York: Oxford University Press, 1997.

———. "The Politics, Promise, and Peril of Criminal Justice Reform in the Context of Mass Incarceration." *Annual Review of Criminology* 1 (2018): 235–59.

Bedau, Hugo A. *The Death Penalty in America.* New York: Oxford University Press, 1964.

———. "Imprisonment vs. Death: Does Avoiding Schwarzschild's Paradox Lead to Sheleff's Dilemma?" *Albany Law Review* 54, nos. 3–4 (1989): 481–95.

———. *Killing as Punishment: Reflections on the Death Penalty in America.* Lebanon, NH: University Press of New England, 2004.

Bennett, William, John J. DiIulio, and John P. Walters. *Body Count.* New York: Simon & Schuster, 1996.

Bentham, Jeremy. "Principles of Morals and Legislation." In *The Works of Jeremy Bentham,* vol. 1. Edinburgh: William Tait, 1843.

Berger, Peter, and Thomas Luckman. *The Social Construction of Reality.* New York: Anchor, 1966.

Berrigan, Helen G. "Executive Clemency, First-Offender Pardons, Automatic Restoration of Rights." *Louisiana Law Review* 62, no. 1 (2001): 49–57.

Bessler, John D. "Revisiting Beccaria's Vision: The Enlightenment, the Death Penalty, and the Abolition." *Northwestern Journal of Law and Social Policy* 4, no. 2 (2009): 195–328.

Blackmon, Douglas A. *Slavery by Another Name: The Re-Enslavement of Black Americans from the Civil War to World War II.* New York: Random House, 2008.

Blagg, Dakota, et al. *Life without Parole Sentences in Washington State.* Seattle, WA: University of Washington, Law, Societies & Justice Program, 2015.

Blue, Ethan. *Doing Time in the Depression: Everyday Life in Texas and California Prisons.* New York: New York University Press, 2014.

Blume, John H., Stephen P. Garvey, and Sheri Lynn Johnson. "Future Dangerousness in Capital Cases: Always at Issue." *Cornell Law Review* 86, no. 2 (2000): 397–410.

Blume, John H., and Jordan Steiker. *Death Penalty Stories.* New York: Foundation Press, 2009.

Boltanski, Luc, and Laurent Thévenot. *On Justification.* Princeton, NJ: Princeton University Press, 2006.

Bourdieu, Pierre. *Outline of a Theory of Practice.* Cambridge: Cambridge University Press, 1972.

Bourdieu, Pierre, Jean-Claude Chamboredon, and Jean Claude Passeron. *The Craft of Sociology: Epistemological Preliminaries.* Berlin: Walter de Gruyter, 1991. First published 1968.

Boutellier, Hans. *The Safety Utopia: Contemporary Discontent and Desire as to Crime and Punishment.* Utrecht, Netherlands: Springer, 2005.

Bright, Charles. *The Powers that Punish: Prison and Politics in the Era of the 'Big House', 1920–1955*. Ann Arbor: University of Michigan Press, 1996.

Brockway, Zebulon. "The Ideal of a True Prison System for a State." Paper presented to the National Congress on Penitentiary and Reformatory Discipline, Cincinnati, October 12, 1870.

Bruck, David. "Public Presentation of the Abolitionist Position." *Lifelines* 9 (1984): 1–3.

———. "Simmons v. South Carolina and the Myth of Early Release." In *Death Penalty Stories*, edited by John H. Blume and Jordan Steiker. New York: Foundation Press, 2009.

Cable, George Washington. "The Convict Lease System in the Southern States." In *The Silent South, Together with The Freedman's Case in Equity and The Convict Lease System in the Southern States*. New York: Charles Scribner's Sons, 1889.

Campbell, Michael C. "Agents of Change: Law Enforcement, Prisons, and Politics in Texas and California." PhD diss., University of California, Irvine, 2009.

———. "The Emergence of Penal Extremism in California: A Dynamic View of Institutional Structures and Political Processes." *Law & Society Review* 48, no. 2 (2014): 377–409.

———. "Ornery Alligators and Soap on a Rope: Texas Prosecutors and Punishment Reform in the Lone Star State." *Theoretical Criminology* 16, no. 3 (2012): 289–311.

———. "Politics, Prisons, and Law Enforcement: An Examination of the Emergence of 'Law and Order' Politics in Texas." *Law & Society Review* 45, no. 3 (2011): 631–65.

———. "Varieties of Mass Incarceration: What We Learn from State Histories." *Annual Review of Criminology* 1 (2018): 219–34.

Campbell, Michael C., and Heather Schoenfeld. "The Transformation of America's Penal Order: A Historicized Political Sociology of Punishment." *American Journal of Sociology* 118, no. 5 (2013): 1375–1423.

Canguilhem, Georges. "The Object of the History of Sciences." In *Continental Philosophy of Science*, edited by Gary Gutting, 198–208. Malden, MA: Wiley-Blackwell, 2005. First published 1968.

Capital Jury Project Papers, National Death Penalty Archive. M. E. Grenander Department of Special Collections and Archives, University Libraries, University at Albany, State University of New York.

Carson, E. Ann. *Mortality in State and Federal Prisons, 2001–2018*. Washington, DC: Bureau of Justice Statistics, 2021.

Carson, E. Ann, and William J. Sabol. *Aging of the State Prison Population, 1993–2013*. Washington, DC: Bureau of Justice Statistics, 2016.

Castel, Robert. *The Regulation of Madness: The Origins of Incarceration in France*. Berkeley: University of California Press, 1988. First published 1976.

Cheatwood, Derral. "The Life-without-Parole Sanction: Its Current Status and a Research Agenda." *Crime & Delinquency* 34, no. 1 (1988): 43–59.

Childs, Dennis. *Slaves of the State: Black Incarceration from the Chain Gang to the Penitentiary*. Minneapolis: University of Minnesota Press, 2020.

Citizens Alliance on Prisons and Public Spending. *When "Life" Did Not Mean Life: A Historical Analysis of Life Sentences Imposed in Michigan since 1900*. Lansing, MI: CAPPS, 2006.

Clemmer, Donald. *The Prison Community*. New York: Holt, Rinehart, Winston, 1940.

Coene, Joshua R. "The Contentious Prison: From Rehabilitation to Incapacitation in New South Wales and Pennsylvania, 1965–1990." PhD diss., University of Michigan, 2016.

Cohen, Stanley. *Folk Devils and Moral Panics*. London: Routledge, 1972.

———. *States of Denial: Knowing about Atrocities and Suffering*. Malden, MA: Polity, 2000.

———. *Visions of Social Control: Crime, Punishment and Classification*. Cambridge, UK: Polity Press, 1985.

Cohen, Stanley, and Laurie Taylor. *Psychological Survival: The Experience of Long-Term Imprisonment*. New York: Pantheon, 1972.

Comfort, Megan. *Doing Time Together: Love and Family in the Shadow of the Prison*. Chicago: University of Chicago Press, 2009.

Connecticut General Assembly, Office of Legislative Research. *Capital Punishments in Connecticut after Furman v. Georgia*. Hartford, CT: Connecticut General Assembly, 1973.

Courtney, Leigh, Sarah Epplier-Epstein, Ryan King, Serena Lei, and Elizabeth Pelletier. *A Matter of Time: The Causes and Consequences of Rising Time Served in America's Prisons*. Washington, DC: Urban Institute, 2017.

Cozzens, Quinn, and Bret Grote. *A Way Out: Abolishing Death by Incarceration in Pennsylvania*. Pittsburgh, PA: Abolitionist Law Center, 2018.

Crewe, Ben, Susie Hulley, and Serena Wright. *Life Imprisonment from Young Adulthood*. London: Palgrave Macmillan UK, 2020.

Cummins, Eric. *The Rise and Fall of California's Radical Prison Movement*. Palo Alto, CA: Stanford University Press, 1994.

Curtin, Mary Ellen. *Black Prisoners and Their World, Alabama, 1865–1900*. New Brunswick, NJ: Rutgers University Press, 2000.

Dagher-Margosian, Jeanice. "Life Means Life: Parole Rarely Granted on Non-Mandatory Life Terms." *Michigan Bar Journal* 73 (1994): 1184–86.

David von Drehle Papers, 1897–2003, National Death Penalty Archive. M. E. Grenander Department of Special Collections and Archives, University Libraries, University at Albany, State University of New York.

Dayan, Colin. *The Law Is a White Dog: How Legal Rituals Make and Unmake Persons*. Princeton, NJ: Princeton University Press, 2011.

de Beaumont, Gustave, and Alexis de Toqueville. *On the Penitentiary System in the United States*, trans. Francis Lieber. Philadelphia: Carey, Lea & Blanchard, 1833.

Dean, Mitchell. *Critical and Effective Histories: Foucault's Methods and Historical Sociology*. London: Routledge, 1996.

Death Penalty Information Center. *Year States Adopted Life without Parole (LWOP) Sentencing.* August 2, 2010. https://deathpenaltyinfo.org/year-states-adopted-life-without-parole-lwop-sentencing.

Derrida, Jacques. *The Death Penalty.* Vol. 1, *Seminar of 1999–2000.* Chicago: University of Chicago Press, 2013.

Dieter, Richard. *The 2% Death Penalty: How a Minority of Counties Produce Most Death Cases at Enormous Costs to All.* Washington, DC: Death Penalty Information Center, 2013.

———. *Sentencing for Life: Americans Embrace Alternatives to the Death Penalty.* Washington, DC: Death Penalty Information Center, 1993.

DiIulio, John J. "The Coming of the Superpredators." *Weekly Standard,* November 27, 1995.

Dilts, Andrew. "Death Penalty 'Abolition' in Neoliberal Times." In *Death and Other Penalties: Philosophy in a Time of Mass Incarceration,* edited by Geoffrey Adelsberg, Lisa Guenther, and Scott Zeman, 106–29. New York: Fordham University Press, 2015.

Dolovich, Sharon. "Creating the Permanent Prisoner." In *Life without Parole: America's New Death Penalty?,* edited by Charles Ogletree and Austin Sarat, 96–137. New York: New York University Press, 2012.

Donzelot, Jacques. *Policing the Family.* New York: Pantheon, 1979.

Douglas, Mary. *How Institutions Think.* Syracuse, NY: Syracuse University Press, 1986.

———, ed. *Rules and Meanings.* New York: Penguin, 1973.

Dubois, William Edward Burghardt. "The Spawn of Slavery: The Convict-Lease System in the South." In *African American Classics in Criminology and Criminal Justice,* edited by Shaun L. Gabbidon, Helen T. Greene, and Vernetta D. Young, 110–16. Thousand Oaks, CA: Sage, 2002. First published 1901.

Dunbar, Willis Frederick. *Michigan through the Centuries.* New York: Lewis Historical Publishing Company, 1955.

Dunbar, Willis, and George May. *Michigan: A History of the Wolverine State.* Grand Rapids: Eerdmans, 1995.

Durkheim, Émile. *The Elementary Forms of Religious Life.* New York: The Free Press, 1965. First published 1915.

———. *Rules of Sociological Method.* New York: The Free Press, 1982. First published 1895.

Dye, Meredith Huey, and Ronald H. Aday. *Women Lifers: Lives Before, Behind, and Beyond Bars.* Lanham, MD: Rowan & Littlefield, 2019.

Eason, John M. *Big House on the Prairie: Rise of the Rural Ghetto and Prison Proliferation.* Chicago: University of Chicago Press, 2017.

Ehrhardt, Charles, Phillip A. Hubbart, L. Harold Levinson, William M. Smiley, and Thomas A. Wills. "The Future of Capital Punishment in Florida: Analysis and Recommendations." *Journal of Criminal Law & Criminology* 64, no. 1 (1973): 2–10.

Ehrhardt, Charles, and L. Harold Levinson. "Florida's Legislative Response to *Furman*: An Exercise in Futility?" *Journal of Criminal Law & Criminology* 64, no. 1 (1973): 10–21.

Ekland-Olson, Sheldon. *Who Lives, Who Dies, Who Decides?* New York: Routledge, 2012.

Elliott, Mabel A. *Conflicting Penal Theories in Statutory Criminal Law*. Chicago: University of Chicago Press, 1931.

Epstein, Lee, and Joseph F. Kobylka. *The Supreme Court and Legal Change: Abortion and the Death Penalty*. Chapel Hill: University of North Carolina Press, 1992.

Fitzroy, Herbert William Keith. "The Punishment of Crime in Provincial Pennsylvania." *Pennsylvania Magazine of History and Biography* 60, no. 3 (1936): 242–69.

Flanagan, Timothy J. "Correctional Policy and the Long-Term Prisoner." *Crime & Delinquency* 28, no. 1 (1982): 82–95.

Florida Corrections Overcrowding Task Force. *Final Report and Recommendations*. Tallahassee: State of Florida, 1983.

Florida Department of Law Enforcement. *Making Florida Safer for Floridians and Tourists: Recommendations for Short-Term Actions and Long-Term Solutions*. February 26, 1993.

Florida House Select Committee. *Report of the Florida House Select Committee on the Death Penalty*. Tallahassee: State of Florida, 1972.

Foster, Burk. "Pardons and Politics: How It All Went Wrong." *Angolite* 13, no. 1 (1988): 33–50.

———. "What Is the Meaning of Life: The Evolution of Natural Life Sentences in Louisiana, 1973–1994." Paper presented at the Academy of Criminal Justice Sciences Annual Meeting, Boston, Massachusetts, 1995.

Foucault, Michel. "About the Concept of the 'Dangerous Individual' in 19th-Century Legal Psychiatry." *International Journal of Law and Psychiatry* 1 (1978): 1–18.

———. "Against Replacement Penalties." In *Power: The Essential Works of Foucault, 1954–1984*, vol. 3, edited by J. D. Faubion. New York: The New Press, 2000. First published 1981.

———. *Discipline and Punish: The Birth of the Prison*, trans. Alan Sheridan. New York: Vintage, 1977.

———. "Nietzsche, Genealogy, History." In *Language, Counter-Memory, Practice: Select Essays and Interviews*. Ithaca, NY: Cornell University Press, 1980.

———. *The Punitive Society: Lectures at the Collège de France, 1972–1973*, trans. Graham Burchell. New York: Palgrave Macmillan, 2015.

Frase, Richard. "Excessive Prison Sentences, Punishment Goals, and the Eighth Amendment: 'Proportionality' Relative to What?" *Minnesota Law Review* 89 (2004): 572–651.

Garland, David. *The Culture of Control: Crime and Social Order in Contemporary Society*. Chicago: University of Chicago Press, 2001.

———. "Frameworks of Inquiry in the Sociology of Punishment." *British Journal of Sociology* 41, no. 1 (1990): 1–15.

———. "Modes of Capital Punishment: The Death Penalty in Perspective." In *America's Death Penalty: Between Past and Present*, edited by David Garland, Randall McGowen, and Michael Meranze. New York: New York University Press, 2011).

———. *Peculiar Institution: America's Death Penalty in an Age of Abolition*. Cambridge, MA: Belknap Press, 2010.

———. "Penality and the Penal State." *Criminology* 51, no. 3 (2013): 475–517.

———. *Punishment and Modern Society*. Chicago: University of Chicago Press, 1990.

———. "Punishment and Social Solidarity." In *The SAGE Handbook of Punishment and Society*, edited by Jonathan Simon and Richard Sparks, 23–39. London: Sage, 2013.

———. *Punishment and Welfare: A History of Penal Strategies*. Aldershot, UK: Gower, 1985.

———. "'Symbolic' and 'Instrumental' Aspects of Capital Punishment." In *The Future of America's Death Penalty*, edited by James Acker et al., 421–51. Durham, NC: Carolina Academic Press, 2010.

———. "Theoretical Advances and Problems in the Sociology of Punishment." *Punishment & Society* 20, no. 1 (2018): 8–33.

———. "What Is a 'History of the Present'? On Foucault's Genealogies and Their Critical Preconditions." *Punishment & Society* 16, no. 4 (2014): 365–84.

Garland, David, and Richard Sparks. *Criminology and Social Theory*. Oxford: Oxford University Press, 2000.

Garland, David, and Peter Young. *The Power to Punish: Contemporary Penality and Social Analysis*. London: Heinemann, 1983.

Garrett, Brandon. "The Decline of the Virginia (and American) Death Penalty." *Georgetown Law Journal* 105, no. 3 (2017): 661–730.

Ghandnoosh, Nazgol. *Delaying a Second Chance: The Declining Prospects for Parole on Life Sentences*. Washington, DC: The Sentencing Project, 2017.

Giardini, Giovanni I., and Richard G. Farrow. "The Paroling of Capital Offenders." *ANNALS of the American Academy of Political and Social Science* 284, no. 1 (1952): 85–94.

Gilmore, Ruth Wilson. *Golden Gulag: Prisons, Surplus, Crisis, and Opposition in Globalizing California*. Oakland: University of California Press, 2007.

Girling, Evi. "Sites of Crossing and Death in Punishment: The Parallel Trade-Offs and Equivalencies of the Death Penalty and Life without Parole in the US." *Howard Journal of Crime and Justice* 55, no. 3 (2016): 345–61.

Glaeser, Andreas. *Political Epistemics: The Secret Police, the Opposition, and the End of East German Socialism*. Chicago: University of Chicago Press, 2011.

Glover, Michael. "Opening the 10-6 Floodgate." *Angolite* 15, no. 4 (1990): 59–64.

Goodman, Philip. "'Another Second Chance': Rethinking Rehabilitation through the lens of California's Prison Fire Camps." *Social Problems* 59, no. 4 (2012): 437–58.

Goodman, Philip, Joshua Page, and Michelle Phelps. *Breaking the Pendulum: The Long Struggle Over Criminal Justice.* New York: Oxford University Press, 2017.

Gottschalk, Marie. *Caught: The Prison State and the Lockdown of American Politics.* Princeton, NJ: Princeton University Press, 2015.

———. "No Way Out? Life Sentences and the Politics of Penal Reform." In *Life without Parole: America's New Death Penalty?,* edited by Charles Ogletree and Austin Sarat, 227–81. New York: New York University Press, 2012.

———. *The Prison and the Gallows: The Politics of Mass Incarceration in America.* New York: Cambridge University Press, 2006.

Grattet, Ryken, and Valerie Jenness. "The Birth and Maturation of Hate Crime Policy in the United States." *American Behavioral Scientist* 45, no. 4 (2001): 668–96.

Grief, Avner. *Institutions and the Path to the Modern Economy: Lessons from Medieval Trade.* Cambridge: Cambridge University Press, 2006.

Griset, Pamala L. "Determinate Sentencing and Administrative Discretion Over Time Served in Prison: A Case Study of Florida." *Crime & Delinquency* 42, no. 1 (1996): 127–43.

Grosso, Catherine M., Jeffrey Fagan, Michael Laurence, David Baldus, George Woodworth, and Richard Newell. "Death by Stereotype: Race, Ethnicity, and California's Failure to Implement *Furman*'s Narrowing Requirement." *UCLA Law Review* 66, no. 6 (2019): 1394–1443.

Guerin, Eric. "*People v. Moore*: The Role of Discretion in Indeterminate Sentencing." *Detroit Law Review* 3 (1989): 1275–300.

Guetzgow, Joshua, and Eric Schoon. "If You Built It, They Will Fill It: The Consequences of Prison Overcrowding Litigation." *Law & Society Review* 49, no. 2 (2015): 401–32.

Gusfield, Joseph R. *Symbolic Crusade: Status Politics and the American Temperance Movement.* Urbana: University of Illinois Press, 1963.

Haas, Gordon, and Lloyd Fillion. *Life without Parole: A Reconsideration.* Boston: Criminal Justice Policy Coalition, 2016.

Hacking, Ian. *Historical Ontology.* Cambridge, MA: Harvard University Press, 2002.

Haddad, Patrick J. "Effect of Proposal B on the Lifer Law." *University of Detroit Law Review* 65, no. 4 (1987–1988): 725–68.

Haines, Herbert. *Against Capital Punishment: The Anti-Death Penalty Movement in America, 1972–1994.* New York: Oxford University Press, 1996.

Hamilton, Melissa. "Extreme Prison Sentences: Legal and Normative Consequences." *Cardozo Law Review* 38, no. 1 (2016): 59–120.

Harcourt, Bernard E. "Course Context." In Michel Foucault, *The Punitive Society: Lectures at the College de France, 1972–1973.* London: Palgrave Macmillan, 2015.

———. *Illusion of Free Markets: Punishment and the Myth of Natural Order.* Cambridge, MA: Harvard University Press, 2011.

Harries, Keith, and Derral Cheatwood. *The Geography of Execution.* Lanham, MD: Rowman & Littlefield, 1997.

Hartman, Kenneth E. *Mother California: A Story of Redemption Behind Bars.* New York: Atlas and Company, 2010.

———, ed. *Too Cruel, Not Unusual Enough.* Lancaster, CA: Steering Committee Press, 2013.

Harvard Law Review Association. "A Matter of Life and Death: The Effect of Life-without-Parole Statutes on Capital Punishment." *Harvard Law Review* 119, no. 6 (2006): 1838–54.

Harvey, Gordon E. *The Politics of Trust: Reubin Askew and Florida in the 1970s.* Tuscaloosa: University of Alabama Press, 2015.

Henry, Jessica. "Death in Prison Sentences: Overutilized and Underscrutinized." In *Life without Parole: America's New Death Penalty?,* edited by Charles Ogletree and Austin Sarat, 66–95. New York: New York University Press, 2012.

Henry, Jessica, Christopher Salvatore, and Bai-Eyse Pugh. "Virtual Life Sentences: An Exploratory Study." *Prison Journal* 98, no. 3 (2018): 294–313.

Herbert, Steve. *Too Easy to Keep: Life-Sentenced Prisoners and the Future of Mass Incarceration.* Oakland: University of California Press, 2018.

Herrick, Emily. "Survey: Lifers, Part I." *Corrections Compendium* (April 1988): 10–11.

Hinton, Elizabeth. *From the War on Poverty to the War on Crime: The Making of Mass Incarceration in America.* Cambridge, MA: Harvard University Press, 2017.

Hirsch, Adam J. *The Rise of the Penitentiary: Prisons and Punishment in Early America.* New Haven, CT: Yale University Press, 1992.

Hornblum, Allen M. *Acres of Skin: Human Experiments at Holmesburg Prison; A Story of Abuse and Exploitation in the Name of Medical Science.* New York: Routledge, 1998.

Horowitz, Veronica, and Christopher Uggen. "Consistency and Compensation in Mercy: Commutation in the Era of Mass Incarceration." *Social Forces* 97, no. 3 (2019): 1205–30.

Howard, John. *An Account of the Principal Lazarettos in Europe.* Warrington, UK: Eyres, 1789.

Hugo A. Bedau Papers, National Death Penalty Archive. M. E. Grenander Department of Special Collections and Archives, University Libraries, University at Albany, State University of New York.

Immarigeon, Ross. "Instead of Death: Alternatives to Capital Punishment." *National Prison Project Journal* 5, no. 3 (1990): 6–9.

Irwin, John. *Lifers: Seeking Redemption in Prison.* New York: Routledge, 2009.

Jacobs, James. "The Politics of Prison Expansion." *NYU Review of Law and Social Change* 12, no. 1 (1983–1984): 209–43.

Janus, Eric, and Robert Prentky. "Sexual Predator Laws: A Two-Decade Retrospective." *Federal Sentencing Reporter* 21, no. 2 (2008): 90–97.

Jenkins, Philip. *Moral Panic: Changing Concepts of the Child Molester in Modern America.* New Haven, CT: Yale University Press, 2004.

Jenness, Valerie. "The Emergence, Content, and Institutionalization of Hate Crime Law: How a Diverse Policy Community Produced a Modern Legal Fact." *Annual Review of Law and Social Science* 3 (2007): 141–60.

Jenness, Valerie, and Ryken Grattet. *Making Hate a Crime: From Social Movement to Law Enforcement*. New York: Russell Sage, 2001.

Johnsen, Julia E., ed. *The Baumes Law*. New York: H. W. Wilson, 1929.

Johnson, Perry M. "Colloquium." *NYU Review of Law and Social Change* 12 (1983–1984): 249–52.

Johnson, Robert. "A Life for a Life?" *Justice Quarterly* 1, no. 4 (1986): 574–80.

Johnson, Robert, and Ann Dobrzanska. "Mature Coping among Life-Sentenced Inmates: An Exploratory Study of Adjustment Dynamics." *Corrections Compendium* 30, no. 6 (2005): 8–9.

Kazemian, Lila, and Jeremy Travis. "Imperative for Inclusion of Long Termers and Lifers in Research and Policy." *Criminology & Public Policy* 14, no. 2 (2015): 355–95.

Keir, Nancy. "*Solem v. Helm*: Extending Judicial Review under the Cruel and Unusual Punishments Clause to Require 'Proportionality' of Prison Sentences." *Catholic University Law Review* 33, no. 2 (1984): 479–515.

Kennedy, Liam. "'Today They Kill with the Chair Instead of the Tree': Forgetting and Remembering Slavery at a Plantation Prison." *Theoretical Criminology* 21, no. 2 (2017): 133–50.

Kirchheimer, Otto. "The Quality of Mercy: On the Role of Clemency in the Apparatus of Justice." *Social Research* 28, no. 2 (1961): 151–70.

Kobil, Daniel T. "The Quality of Mercy Strained: Wresting the Pardon Power from the King." *Texas Law Review* 69, no. 3 (1990): 569–642.

Kohler-Hausmann, Julilly. *Getting Tough: Welfare and Imprisonment in 1970s America*. Princeton, NJ: Princeton University Press, 2017.

Kolakoski, Louis W. "Case Supervision of Paroled Prisoners in Pennsylvania." *Prison Journal* 13, no. 3 (1933): 9–13.

———. "Comparative Study of Commutation and Regular Parole Cases for the State of Pennsylvania." *Prison Journal* 17, no. 2 (1937): 322–27.

Kolakoski, Louis W., and T. W. Broecker. "The Pennsylvania Parole System in Operation." *Journal of Criminal Law and Criminology* 23, no. 3 (1932): 427–48.

Kramer, Ronald C. "From 'Habitual Offenders' to 'Career Criminals': The Historical Construction and Development of Criminal Categories." *Law and Human Behavior* 6, nos. 3–4 (1982): 73–93.

Lain, Corinna Barrett. "*Furman* Fundamentals." *Washington University Law Review* 82, no. 1 (2007): 1–74.

Lane, Mark J. "Is There Life without Parole? A Capital Defendant's Right to a Meaningful Alternative Sentence." *Loyola of Los Angeles Law Review* 26, no. 2 (1992): 327–93.

Langbein, John H. "The Historical Origins of the Sanction of Imprisonment for Serious Crime." *Journal of Legal Studies* 5, no. 1 (1976): 35–60.

Lappi-Seppälä, Tapio. "Life Imprisonment and Related Institutions in the Nordic Countries." In *Life Imprisonment and Human Rights*, edited by Dirk van Zyl Smit and Catherine Appleton, 461–506. Oxford: Hart Publishing, 2016.

LeFlouria, Talitha L. *Chained in Silence: Black Women and Convict Labor in the New South*. Chapel Hill: University of North Carolina Press, 2015.

Leigey, Margaret. *The Forgotten Men: Serving a Life without Parole Sentence*. New Brunswick, NJ: Rutgers University Press, 2015.

Lempert, Lora Bex. *Women Doing Life: Gender, Punishment and the Struggle for Identity*. New York: New York University Press, 2016.

Lerner, Craig. "Life without Parole as a Conflicted Punishment." *Wake Forest Law Review* 48, no. 5 (2013): 1152.

Lewis, W. D. *From Newgate to Dannemora: The Rise of the Penitentiary in New York, 1746–1848*. Ithaca, NY: Cornell University Press, 1965.

Lichtenstein, Alex. *Twice the Work of Free Labor: The Political Economy of Convict Labor in the New South*. New York: Verso, 1996.

Lombroso, Cesare. *Criminal Man*. Translated by Mary Gibson and Nicole Hahn Rafter. Durham, NC: Duke University Press, 2006. First published 1896.

"The Longtermers: Forgotten Man Committee." *Angolite* 9, no. 3 (1984): 28–31.

Love, Margaret Colgate. "The Twilight of the Pardon Power." *Journal of Criminal Law and Criminology* 100, no. 3 (2010): 1160–1212.

Lynch, Mona. "Mass Incarceration, Legal Change, and Locale." *Criminology & Public Policy* 10, no. 3 (2011): 673–98.

———. *Sunbelt Justice: Arizona and the Transformation of American Punishment*. Palo Alto, CA: Stanford Law Books, 2010.

Macdonald, Donald, and Leonard Morgenbesser. *Life without Parole Statutes in the United States*. Albany: New York State Department of Correctional Services, Division of Program Planning Research and Evaluation, 1984.

Maguire, Kathleen, Ann L. Pastore, and Timothy J. Flanagan. *Sourcebook of Criminal Justice Statistics*. Washington, DC: Bureau of Justice Statistics, 1992.

Mancini, Matthew. *One Dies, Get Another: Convict Leasing in the American South, 1866–1928*. Columbia: University of South Carolina Press, 1996.

Manderey, Evan J. *A Wild Justice: The Death and Resurrection of Capital Punishment in America*. New York: W. W. Norton, 2013.

Marra, Richard. "Did Pennsylvanians Understand?" *Graterfriends* 15, no. 9 (1997): 4.

Martin, Susan E. "Commutation of Prison Sentences: Practice, Promise and Limitation." *Crime & Delinquency* 29, no. 4 (1983): 593–612.

Mauer, Marc. *Race to Incarcerate*. New York: The New Press, 1999.

Mauer, Marc, and Ashley Nellis. *The Meaning of Life: The Case for Abolishing Life Sentences*. New York: The New Press, 2018.

Mauer, Marc, Ryan King, and Malcolm Young. *The Meaning of Life: Long Prison Sentences in Context*. Washington, DC: The Sentencing Project, 2004.

Mauss, Marcel. "La Priere." In Pierre Bourdieu, Jean-Claude Chamboredon, and Jean Claude Passeron, *The Craft of Sociology: Epistemological Preliminaries*. Berlin: Walter de Gruyter, 1991. First published 1968.

McLennan, Rebecca. "The Convict's Two Lives: Civil and Natural Death in the American Prison." In *America's Death Penalty: Between Past and Present*, edited by David Garland, Randall McGowen, and Michael Meranze. New York: New York University Press, 2011.

———. *The Crisis of Imprisonment: Protest, Politics, and the Making of the American Penal State, 1776–1941*. New York: Cambridge University Press, 2008.

McQuaig, J. A. Royce. "Modern Tendencies in Habitual Criminal Legislation." *Cornell Law Quarterly* 15, no. 1 (1929): 62–83.

Mehta, Sarah. *False Hope: How Parole Systems Fail Youth Serving Extreme Sentences*. Washington, DC: American Civil Liberties Union, 2016.

Meltsner, Michael. *Cruel and Unusual: The Supreme Court and Capital Punishment*. New York: Morrow, 1974.

———. "The Dilemmas of Excessive Sentencing: Death May Be Different but How Different?" *Northeastern University Law Journal* 7, no. 1 (2015): 5–19.

Meranze, Michael. Introduction to *Benjamin Rush, Essays: Literary, Moral and Philosophical*, edited by Michael Meranze. Schenectady, NY: Union College Press, 1988.

———. *Laboratories of Virtue: Punishment, Revolution, and Authority in Philadelphia, 1760–1835*. Chapel Hill: University of North Carolina Press, 1996.

Merton, Robert K. "Three Fragments from a Sociologist's Notebooks: Establishing the Phenomenon, Specified Ignorance, and Strategic Research Materials." *Annual Review of Sociology* 13, no. 1 (1987): 1–29.

Messinger, Sheldon, John E. Berecochea, David Rauma, and Richard A. Berk. "The Foundations of Parole in California." *Law & Society Review* 19, no. 1 (1985): 69–106.

Miao, Michelle. "Replacing Death with Life? The Rise of LWOP in the Contemporary Abolitionist Campaigns in the United States." *Northwestern Journal of Law & Social Policy* 15, no. 2 (2020): 173–223.

Miller, Lisa L. *The Perils of Federalism*. New York: Oxford University Press, 2008.

Miller, Vivien M. *Crime, Sexual Violence, and Clemency: Florida's Pardon Board and Penal System in the Progressive Era*. Gainesville: University of Florida Press, 2000.

———. *Hard Labor and Hard Time: Florida's Sunshine Prison and Chain Gangs*. Gainesville: University Press of Florida, 2012.

Morris, Norval. *The Habitual Criminal*. Cambridge, UK: Longmans Green, 1951.

Muhammad, Khalil Gibran. *The Condemnation of Blackness: Race, Crime, and the Making of Modern Urban America*. Cambridge, MA: Harvard University Press, 2010.

Muller, Christopher. "Northward Migration and the Rise of Racial Disparity in American Incarceration, 1880–1950." *American Journal of Sociology* 118, no. 2 (2012): 281–326.

Muller, Eric. "The Legal Defense Fund's Capital Punishment Campaign: The Distorting Influence of Death." *Yale Law and Policy Review* 4, no. 1 (1985): 158–67.

Nagin, Daniel S. "Deterrence in the Twenty-First Century." *Crime and Justice* 42, no. 1 (2013): 199–263.

National Commission on Law Observance and Enforcement (Wickersham Commission). *Report on Penal Institutions, Probation, and Parole*. Washington, DC: US Government Printing Office, 1931.

National Research Council on Law and Justice. *The Growth of Incarceration in the United States: Exploring Causes and Consequences*. Edited by Jeremy Travis, Bruce Western, and Steve Redburn. Washington, DC: The National Academies Press, 2014.

Nellis, Ashley. *Life Goes On: The Historic Rise of Life Sentences in America*. Washington, DC: The Sentencing Project, 2013.

———. *No End in Sight: America's Enduring Reliance on Life Imprisonment*. Washington, DC: The Sentencing Project, 2021.

———. *Still Life: America's Increasing Use of Life and Long-Term Sentences*. Washington, DC: The Sentencing Project, 2017.

Nellis, Ashley, and Ryan S. King. *No Exit: The Expanding Use of Life Sentences in America*. Washington, DC: The Sentencing Project, 2009.

Nelson, Lane. "A History of Penal Reform in Angola, Part I: The Immovable Object." *Angolite* (September/October 2009): 16–23.

Newman, Graeme, and Pietro Morongui. Introduction to *Of Crimes and Punishments* by Cesare Beccaria, edited by Graeme Newman and Pietro Morongui. Somerset, NJ: Transaction Publishers, 2009.

Norton, Matthew. "Classification and Coercion: The Destruction of Piracy in the English Maritime System." *American Journal of Sociology* 119, no. 6 (2014): 1537–75.

Note. "Court Treatment of General Recidivist Statutes." *Columbia Law Review* 48, no. 2 (1948): 238–53.

Ogletree, Charles J., and Austin Sarat, eds. *Life without Parole: America's New Death Penalty?* New York: New York University Press, 2012.

Ohmart, Howard, and Harold Bradley. *Overcrowding in the Florida Prison System: A Technical Assistance Report*. Washington, DC: American Justice Institute, 1972.

Olick, Jeffrey K. *In the House of the Hangman: The Agonies of German Defeat, 1943–1949*. Chicago: University of Chicago Press, 2005.

Oshinsky, David. *Worse Than Slavery: Parchman Farm and the Jim Crow Justice System*. New York: Free Press, 1996.

Owens, B. Robert. "Judicial Decision Making as Knowledge Work." *Law & Social Inquiry* 41, no. 2 (2016): 502–21.

Page, Joshua. "Punishment and the Penal Field." In *SAGE Handbook of Punishment and Society*, edited by Jonathan Simon and Richard Sparks, 152–66. London: Sage, 2013.

————. *The "Toughest Beat": Politics, Punishment, and the Prison Officers' Union in California.* New York: Oxford University Press, 2011.

Peck, Dennis L., and Ron Jones. "The High Cost of Alabama's Habitual Felony Offender Act: A Preliminary Assessment." *International Journal of Offender Therapy and Comparative Criminology* 29, no. 3 (1985): 251–64.

Pennsylvania Prison Society. *Life Sentence.* Documentary, 1989. www.youtube.com/watch?v=aF5Wl19-HEs.

————. *The Need for Parole Options for Life-Sentenced Prisoners.* Philadelphia: Pennsylvania Prison Society, 1993.

Perkinson, Robert. *Texas Tough: The Rise of a Prison Empire.* New York: Metropolitan Books, 2010.

Petersilia, Joan. "Parole and Prisoner Reentry in the United States." *Crime and Justice* 26 (1999): 479–530.

Phelps, Michelle S. "Rehabilitation in the Punitive Era: The Gap between Rhetoric and Reality in US Prison Programs." *Law & Society Review* 45, no. 1 (2011): 33–68.

Phillips, Scott, and Ryken Grattet. "Judicial Rhetoric, Meaning-Making, and the Institutionalization of Hate Crime Law." *Law & Society Review* 34, no. 3 (2000): 567–606.

Pifferi, Michele. *Reinventing Punishment: A Comparative History of Criminology and Penology in the Nineteenth and Twentieth Centuries.* Oxford: Oxford University Press, 2016.

Pisciotta, Alexander W. *Benevolent Repression: Social Control and the American Reformatory-Prison Movement.* New York: New York University Press, 1994.

Platt, Anthony M. *The Child Savers: The Invention of Delinquency.* Chicago: University of Chicago Press, 1977.

Porter, Lauren C., Shawn D. Bushway, Hui-Shien Tsao, and Herbert L. Smith. "How the US Prison Boom Has Changed the Age Distribution of the Prison Population." *Criminology* 54, no. 1 (2016): 30–55.

Powers, Edwin. *Crime and Punishment in Early Massachusetts.* Boston: Beacon Press, 1966.

————. *Parole Eligibility of Prisoners Serving a Life Sentence.* 2nd ed. Boston: Massachusetts Correctional Association, 1972. First published 1969.

Raymond, Daniel. *Report on the Penitentiary System in the United States.* New York: Mahlan Day, 1822.

Reiter, Keramet. *23/7: Pelican Bay Prison and the Rise of Long-Term Solitary Confinement* (New Haven: Yale University Press, 2016).

Reiter, Keramet, and Kelsie Chesnut. "Correctional Autonomy and Authority in the Rise of Mass Incarceration." *Annual Review of Law and Social Science* 14 (2019): 49–68.

Reitz, Kevin R. "American Exceptionalism in Crime and Punishment: Broadly Defined." In *American Exceptionalism in Crime and Punishment,* edited by Kevin R. Reitz. New York: Oxford University Press, 2018.

———. "The 'Traditional' Indeterminate Sentencing Model." In *The Oxford Handbook of Sentencing and Corrections*, edited by Joan Petersilia and Kevin R. Reitz, 270–98. New York: Oxford University Press, 2012.

Reitz, Kevin R., and Edward E. Rhine. "Parole Release and Supervision: Critical Drivers of American Prison Policy." *Annual Review of Criminology* 3 (2020): 281–98.

Renninger, Phillip. *A Study of Recidivism Among Individuals Granted Executive Clemency in Pennsylvania, 1968–1981*. Harrisburg: Pennsylvania Commission on Crime and Delinquency, 1982.

Rhine, Edward E., Joan Petersilia, and Kevin R. Reitz. "The Future of Parole Release." *Crime and Justice* 46, no. 1 (2017): 279–338.

Rhineberger, Hans-Jorg. *An Epistemology of the Concrete: Twentieth Century Histories of Life*. Durham, NC: Duke University Press, 2010.

Rideau, Wilbert, and Ron Wikberg. *Life Sentences: Rage and Survival Behind Bars*. New York: New York Times Books, 1992.

Rigg, Douglas C. "The Penalty Worse Than Death." *Saturday Evening Post*, August 31, 1957.

Robinson, Gwen. "Late-Modern Rehabilitation: The Evolution of a Penal Strategy." *Punishment & Society* 10, no. 4 (2008): 429–45.

Roitman, Janet. *Anti-Crisis*. Durham, NC: Duke University Press, 2014.

Rose, Nikolas. "Life, Reason and History: Reading Georges Canguilhem Today." *Economy and Society* 27, nos. 2–3 (1998): 154–70.

———. *The Psychological Complex: Psychology, Politics and Society in England, 1869–1939*. London: Routledge Kegan & Paul, 1985.

Rothman, David J. *Conscience and Convenience: The Asylum and Its Alternatives in Progressive America*. Berlin: De Gruyter, 1980.

———. *Discovery of the Asylum: Social Order and Disorder in the New Republic*. Boston: Little Brown, 1971.

———. "Perfecting the Prison." In *The Oxford History of the Prison.*, edited by Norval Morris and David J. Rothman, 100–16. New York: Oxford University Press, 1995.

Rowan, Mark, and Brian S. Kane. "Life Means Life Maybe? An Analysis of Pennsylvania's Policy Toward Lifers." *Duquesne Law Review* 30, no. 3 (1991–1992): 661–80.

Rubin, Ashley T. "A Neo-Institutional Account of Prison Diffusion." *Law & Society Review* 49, no. 2 (2015): 365–400.

———. "The Prehistory of Innovation: A Longer View of Penal Change." *Punishment & Society* 20, no. 2 (2018): 192–216.

———. "Punishment's Legal Templates: A Theory of Formal Penal Change." *Law & Society Review* 53, no. 2 (2019): 518–53.

Rusche, Georg, and Otto Kirchheimer. *Punishment and Social Structure*. New Brunswick, NJ: Transaction Publishers, 2003. First published 1939.

Rush, Benjamin. *An Enquiry into the Effects of Public Punishments upon Criminals and upon Society*. Philadelphia: Society for Social Inquiry, 1787.

Salkin, Barry. "The Pardoning Power in Antebellum Pennsylvania." *Pennsylvania Magazine of History and Biography* 100, no. 4 (1976): 507–20.

Sarat, Austin. "At the Boundaries of Law: Executive Clemency, Sovereign Prerogative, and the Dilemma of American Legality." *American Quarterly* 57, no.3 (2005): 611–31.

———. "New Abolitionism and the Possibilities of Legislative Action." *Ohio State Law Journal* 63, no. 1 (2002): 343–60.

Sarat, Austin, and Nasser Hussain. "The Literary Life of Clemency: Pardon Tales in the Contemporary United States." *TriQuarterly* 124 (2006): 169–92.

Schartmeuller, Doris. "Settling Down Behind Bars: The Extensive Use of Life Sentences in Alabama." *Prison Journal* 95, no. 4 (2015): 449–71.

Schlosser, Eric. "The Prison Industrial Complex." *Atlantic Monthly*, December 1998, 51–77.

Schmitt, Glenn R., and Hyun J. Konfrst. *Life Sentences in the Federal System.* Washington, DC: United States Sentencing Commission, 2015.

Schoenfeld, Heather. *Building the Prison State: Race and the Politics of Mass Incarceration.* Chicago: University of Chicago Press, 2018.

———. "The Delayed Emergence of Penal Modernism in Florida." *Punishment & Society* 16, no. 3 (2014): 258–84.

———. "Mass Incarceration and the Paradox of Prison Conditions Litigation." *Law & Society Review* 44, nos. 3–4 (2010): 731–67.

Seeds, Christopher. "Bifurcation Nation: American Penal Policy in Late Mass Incarceration." *Punishment & Society* 19, no. 5 (2017): 590–610.

———. "Disaggregating LWOP: Life without Parole, Capital Punishment, and Mass Incarceration in Florida, 1972–1995." *Law & Society Review* 52, no. 1 (2018): 172–205.

———. "Governors and Prisoners: The Death of Clemency and the Making of Life Sentences Without Release in Pennsylvania." *Social Justice* 46, no. 4 (2020): 81–105.

———. "Historical Modes of Perpetual Penal Confinement: Theories and Practices Before Life without Parole." *Law & Social Inquiry* 44, no. 2 (2019): 305–32.

———. "Life Sentences and Perpetual Confinement." *Annual Review of Criminology* 4 (2021): 287–309.

Sellin, Thorsten. "Beccaria's Substitute for the Death Penalty." In *Criminology in Perspective: Essays in Honor of Israel Drapkin*, edited by Simha Landau and Leslie Sebba, 3–9. Lexington, MA: Lexington Books, 1977.

———. *Slavery and the Penal System.* New York: Elsevier, 1976.

Sheleff, Leon. *Ultimate Penalties: Capital Punishment, Life Imprisonment, Physical Torture.* Columbus: Ohio State University Press, 1987.

Shils, Edward. "Charisma, Order, and Status." *American Sociological Review* 30, no. 2 (1965): 199–213.

Sigler, Robert, and Concetta Culliver. "Consequences of the Habitual Offender Act on the Costs of Operating Alabama's Prisons." *Federal Probation* 52, no. 2 (1988): 57–64.

Simon, Jonathan. "Dignity and Risk: The Long Road from *Graham v. Florida* to Abolition of Life without Parole." In *Life without Parole: America's New Death Penalty?*, edited by Charles Ogletree and Austin Sarat, 282–310. New York: New York University Press, 2012.

———. "From the Big House to the Warehouse: Rethinking Prisons and State Government in the 20th Century." *Punishment & Society* 2, no. 2 (2000): 213–34.

———. *Governing through Crime: How the War on Crime Transformed American Democracy and Created a Culture of Fear.* New York: Oxford University Press, 2007.

———. *Mass Incarceration on Trial: A Remarkable Court Decision and the Future of Prisons in America.* New York: The New Press, 2014.

Simon, Jonathan, and Richard Sparks. "Punishment and Society: The Emergence of an Academic Field." In *SAGE Handbook of Punishment and Society*, edited by Jonathan Simon and Richard Sparks, 1–20. London: Sage, 2013.

Skinner, Quentin. "Meaning and Understanding in the History of Ideas." *History and Theory* 8, no. 1 (1969): 3–53.

Smith, Philip. *Punishment and Culture.* Chicago: University of Chicago Press, 2008.

Sparks, Richard. "State Punishment in Advanced Capitalist Countries." In *Punishment and Social Control*, 2nd ed., edited by Stanley Cohen and Thomas Blomberg. New York; Walter de Gruyter, 2003.

Spierenberg, Pieter. *The Prison Experience.* New Brunswick, NJ: Rutgers University Press, 1991.

Staley, Patricia Len. "Life Expectancy as a Factor in Sentencing: *People v. Moore.*" *Cooley Law Review* 5, no. 3 (1988): 795–810.

Steiker, Carol, and Jordan Steiker. *Courting Death: The Supreme Court and Capital Punishment.* Cambridge, MA: Belknap Press, 2016.

———. "The Death Penalty and Mass Incarceration: Convergences and Divergences." *American Journal of Criminal Law* 41, no. 2 (2014): 189–207.

———. "Opening a Window or Building a Wall? The Effect of Eighth Amendment Death Penalty Law and Advocacy on Criminal Justice More Broadly." *University of Pennsylvania Journal of Constitutional Law* 11, no. 1 (2008): 155–205.

Stewart, Jim, and Paul Lieberman. "What Is This New Sentence That Takes Away Parole?" *Student Lawyer* 11, no. 2 (1982): 14–17, 39.

Stoler, Ann. *Along the Archival Grain: Epistemic Anxieties and Colonial Commonsense.* Princeton, NJ: Princeton University Press, 2009.

Strange, Carolyn. "The Unwritten Law of Executive Justice: Pardoning Patricide in Reconstruction-Era New York." *Law and History Review* 28, no. 4 (2010): 891–930.

Stuntz, William. *The Collapse of American Criminal Justice.* Cambridge, MA: Harvard University Press, 2011.

Surles, Ashley. "An Unforgettable Mistake: William G. Milliken and Michigan's Mandatory Minimum Sentencing Program." *Michigan Journal of History* 5, no. 1 (2007): 1–21.

Sutherland, Edwin. "The Sexual Psychopath Laws." *Journal of Criminal Law, Criminology and Police Science* 40, no. 5 (1949): 543–54.

Tallack, William. *Penological and Preventive Principles*. London: Wertheimer, Lea, 1889.

Tannenbaum, Judith, and Spoon Jackson. *By Heart: Poetry, Prison, and Two Lives*. Oakland, CA: New Village Press, 2010.

Tappan, Paul. "Habitual Offender Laws in the United States." *Federal Probation* 13, no. 1 (1949): 28–31.

Taylor, James. "P.O.V.—Unfettered Mercy for Lifers, Not Legislation." *Graterfriends* 10, no. 6 (1992): 8.

Taylor, William Banks. *Brokered Justice: Race, Politics, and Mississippi Prisons, 1798–1992*. Columbus: Ohio State University Press, 1993.

Teeters, Negley. *The Cradle of the Penitentiary: The Walnut Street Jail, 1773–1835*. Philadelphia: Pennsylvania Prison Society, 1955.

Thompson, Heather Ann. *Blood in the Water: The Attica Uprising of 1971 and Its Legacy*. New York: Pantheon Books, 2016.

Timashefe, N. S. "The Treatment of Persistent Offenders outside of the United States." *Journal of Criminal Law and Criminology* 30, no. 4 (1939): 455–69.

Tonry, Michael. *Malign Neglect: Race, Crime, and Punishment in America*. New York: Oxford University Press, 1995.

———. *Punishing Race: A Continuing American Dilemma*. New York: Oxford University Press, 2011.

———. *Sentencing Fragments: Penal Reform in America, 1975–2025*. New York: Oxford University Press, 2016.

Turner, Jennifer. *A Living Death: Life without Parole for Nonviolent Offenses*. New York: American Civil Liberties Union, 2015.

van Zyl Smit, Dirk. "Abolishing Life Imprisonment?" *Punishment & Society* 3, no. 2 (2001): 299–306.

———. "Punishment and Human Rights." In *The SAGE Handbook of Punishment and Society*, edited by Jonathan Simon and Richard Sparks, 395–415. London: Sage, 2013.

———. *Taking Life Imprisonment Seriously: In National and International Law*. Norwell, MA: Kluwer Law International, 2002.

van Zyl Smit, Dirk, and Catherine Appleton. *Life Imprisonment: A Global Human Rights Analysis*. Cambridge, MA: Harvard University Press, 2019.

———. *Life Imprisonment and Human Rights*. Oñati International Series in Law and Society. Oxford: Hart Publishing, 2016.

van Zyl Smit, Dirk, and Alessandro Corda. "American Exceptionalism in Parole Release and Supervision." In *American Exceptionalism in Crime and Punishment*, edited by Kevin Reitz. Oxford: Oxford University Press, 2017.

Vannier, Marion. "Normalizing Extreme Imprisonment: The Case of Life without Parole in California (1972–2012)." *Theoretical Criminology* 25, no. 4 (2021): 519–39.

———. *Normalizing Extreme Imprisonment: The Case of Life without Parole in California.* Oxford: Oxford University Press, 2021.

———. "Women Serving Life without the Possibility of Parole." *Howard Journal of Crime and Justice* 55, no. 3 (2016): 328–44.

Villaume, Alfred. "'Life without Parole' and 'Virtual Life Sentences': Death Sentences by Any Other Name." *Contemporary Justice Review* 8, no. 3 (2005): 265–77.

Vojta, Filip. "Life and Long-Term Imprisonment in the Countries of the Former Yugoslavia." In *Life Imprisonment and Human Rights*, edited by Dirk van Zyl Smit and Catherine Appleton, 351–72. Oxford: Hart Publishing, 2016.

von Drehle, David. *Among the Lowest of the Dead.* New York: Times Books, 1995.

Wacquant, Loïc. *Punishing the Poor: The Neoliberal Government of Social Insecurity.* Durham, NC: Duke University Press, 2009.

Ward, Geoff K. *The Black Child-Savers: Racial Democracy and Juvenile Justice.* Chicago: University of Chicago Press, 2012.

Weaver, Vesla M. "Frontlash: Race and the Development of Punitive Crime Policy." *Studies in American Political Development* 21, no. 2 (2007): 230–65.

Weber, Hartmut-Michael. *The Abolition of Life Imprisonment.* Baden-Baden: Nomos, 1999.

Weisberg, Robert. "Deregulating Death." *Supreme Court Review* (1983): 305–95.

Western, Bruce. *Punishment and Inequality in America.* New York: Russell Sage Foundation, 2006.

Whitman, James Q. *Harsh Justice: Criminal Punishment and the Widening Divide between America and Europe.* New York: Oxford University Press, 2003.

Wikberg, Ron. "A Graphic and Illustrative History, 1879 to 1797: Life Sentences in Louisiana." Mimeographed document, 1979.

———. "The Longtermers." *Angolite* 13, no. 3 (1988): 19–58.

Willis, James J. "Transportation versus Imprisonment in Eighteenth and Nineteenth Century Britain: Penal Power, Liberty, and the State." *Law & Society Review* 39, no. 1 (2005): 171–210.

Wines, Enoch. *Transactions of the National Congress on Penitentiary and Reformatory Discipline.* Albany, NY: The Argus Company, 1870.

Wines, Enoch, and Theodore Dwight. *Report on the Prisons and Reformatories of the United States and Canada.* Albany, NY: Van Benthuysen & Sons, 1867.

Wines, Frederick. *Monograph on Sentences for Crime.* Springfield, IL: H.W. Rocker, 1885.

———. *The New Criminology*. New York: Kempster Print, 1904.

———. *Punishment and Reformation: An Historical Sketch of the Rise of the Penitentiary*. London: Swan Sonnenschein, 1895.

Wolfe, Burton H. *Pileup on Death Row*. New York: Doubleday, 1973.

Wright, Julian. "Life-without-Parole: An Alternative to Death or Not Much of a Life at All?" *Vanderbilt Law Review* 43, no. 2 (1990): 529–68.

Yantus, Anne. "Sentence Creep: Increasing Penalties in Michigan and the Need for Sentencing Reform." *University of Michigan Journal of Law Reform* 47, no. 3 (2013): 645–96.

Yount, Jon. "Pennsylvania: Parole and Life Imprisonment." Prison Policy Initiative, 2004. https://static.prisonpolicy.org/scans/yount/PA_parole.pdf.

Zimring, Franklin E. "American Youth Violence: A Cautionary Tale." *Crime and Justice* 42, no. 1 (2013): 265–98.

———. *The Contradictions of American Capital Punishment*. New York: Oxford University Press, 2003.

———. "Imprisonment Rates and the New Politics of Criminal Punishment." *Punishment and Society* 3, no. 1 (2001): 161–96.

Zimring, Franklin E., and Gordon J. Hawkins. "Capital Punishment and the Eighth Amendment: *Furman* and *Gregg* in Retrospect." *UC Davis Law Review* 18 (1984): 927–56.

———. *Incapacitation: Penal Confinement and the Restraint of Crime*. Oxford: Oxford University Press, 1995.

Zimring, Franklin E., and David T. Johnson. "The Dark at the Top of the Stairs: Four Destructive Influences of Capital Punishment on American Criminal Justice." In *The Oxford Handbook of Sentencing and Corrections*, edited by Joan Petersilia and Kevin R. Reitz, 737–52. New York: Oxford University Press, 2012.

Index

Founded in 1893,
UNIVERSITY OF CALIFORNIA PRESS
publishes bold, progressive books and journals
on topics in the arts, humanities, social sciences,
and natural sciences—with a focus on social
justice issues—that inspire thought and action
among readers worldwide.

The UC PRESS FOUNDATION
raises funds to uphold the press's vital role
as an independent, nonprofit publisher, and
receives philanthropic support from a wide
range of individuals and institutions—and from
committed readers like you. To learn more, visit
ucpress.edu/supportus.